JAPAN AT WAR
IN THE PACIFIC

"Two things must be stressed: the dual role of the Japanese people as accomplices and victims, and the essential continuity of the story from 1868 to 1945... So much of Japanese history has been papered over or beautified that one needs the skepticism of the criminal lawyer, the skills of the investigative journalist and the intuition of the historical novelist to explore it fully."

—Donald Calman, *The Nature and Origins of Japanese Imperialism*

"To see ordinary Japanese in World War II as simultaneously victims and victimizers offends our conventional sense of morality, but is nonetheless an important step towards recognizing that the great war in Asia was a tragedy for everyone involved."

—John Dower, *Japan in War and Peace*

"We cannot afford to be ignorant of the world in which disputes arise."
—Radhabinod Pal, *Dissentient Judgement of Justice Pal*

JAPAN AT WAR IN THE PACIFIC

The Rise and Fall of The Japanese Empire in Asia 1868–1945

JONATHAN CLEMENTS

TUTTLE Publishing

Tokyo | Rutland, Vermont | Singapore

For Angela

well, you did ask...

Contents

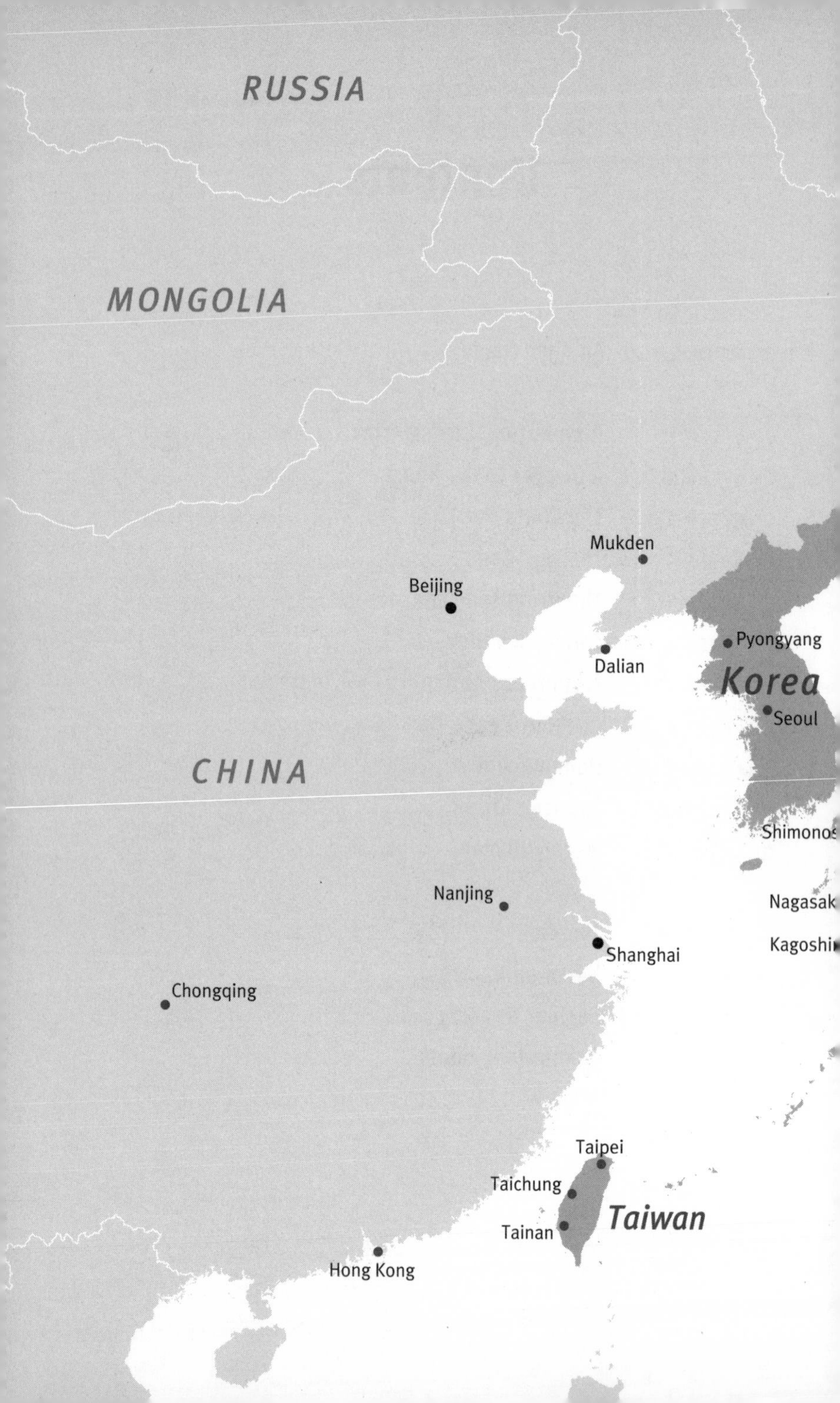
RUSSIA
MONGOLIA
Mukden
Beijing
Pyongyang
Dalian
Korea
Seoul
CHINA
Nanjing
Shanghai
Chongqing
Taipei
Taichung
Taiwan
Tainan
Hong Kong

RUSSIA

Vladivostok

Hokkaidō

Sapporo

Hakodate

Mt. Hakkōda

Honshū

Matsushiro

Tokyo

Nagoya

Kyoto

Yokohama

Mt. Fuji

Osaka

Yoshino

Hiroshima

Mt. Yoshino

Shikoku

Kyūshū

500 km

Japan in East Asia (1939)

An Alien Game

Even before U.S. Commodore Matthew Calbraith Perry set out on his historic voyage in 1852, there were mutterings in the English-language press. Six months ahead of the departure of Perry's "Black Ships" for Japan, the New York correspondent for the London *Times* observed that it was unlikely that "the most powerful maritime force we have ever sent to the East Indies" was really going there to make a hydrographic survey.

> It is very clear that after we have gone through to the Pacific, and got possession for all practical purposes, of the continent, our adventurous spirit will wish for some new field for conquest, excitement and fortune…. [T]he fact can be read now as clearly as it will be a year or ten years hence—that our aggressions on the Asiatic coast are beginning. The U.S. will shortly enact the same gunpowder drama England played in '42 with China, and we shall do it with less moderation. Already the Sandwich Islands [Hawaii], like ripe fruit, are falling into our hands. Other Pacific clusters are waiting to be gathered. And then will come Japan…[1]

For more than two centuries, the Tokugawa Shōguns had run Japan on behalf of the Emperor, shutting the country off from the outside world in order to shield it from the predations of foreign colonialists and Christian missionaries.

In that time, the world had undergone rapid transformation. While Japan slept, the United States of America had extended its power from sea to shining sea, while Britain had turned India into the jewel in its

---

[1] *Times*, April 8, 1852, p. 5. (from "our own correspondent" in New York, dated March 24).

crown. An Industrial Revolution had transformed the acquisition of raw materials and the manufacture of goods.

It had also made the world smaller. The United States of America wanted coaling ports for its whalers, and safe harbors for the China trade across the Pacific, which were two of the main, innocent-sounding reasons for Commodore Perry conveying President Fillmore's overtures.

"And, after all," continued the *Times*, "is it not inevitable that sooner or later these besotted Oriental nations must come out from their barbarous seclusion, and wheel into the ranks of civilization?" Japan had shut itself away from the outside world for 250 years, but now "civilization" was calling, and it demanded that the door be opened. Not that the *Times*'s own correspondent in New York was not aware of the likely spin-offs. Think, for example, of the fun that could be had:

> …to paint this expedition in bright colours, appealing to the pride, ambition, vanity, cupidity, and patriotism of the nation, and causing twenty-five millions of people to wait anxiously for news of "a great American naval victory off the coast of Japan &c." Nor would it be difficult to imagine what influence such a report (true or false) might have, if it happened to arrive ten days before the Presidential election. The telegraph (playing over 20,000 miles of electric wire) could be made a very valuable adjunct in this great combat.[2]

Japan was having none of it. Its policy-makers, schooled in classical Chinese, appropriated a slogan from the ancient past, when China, the center of all true civilization in their eyes, had faced foreign invasions.

"Revere the Emperor, Expel the Barbarians" (*sonnō jōi*) harked back over two thousand years, to a time when a famous duke exhorted nobles to remain faithful to their king.[3] It was dredged up in the Tokugawa period by policy advisers who likened Christian missionaries and European visitors to those barbarians of old.

---

[2] *Times*, 8th April 1852, p. 5. (from "our own correspondent" in New York, dated March 24).

[3] Strictly speaking, the original Chinese from the 7th century BCE statesman Guan Zhong was *zunwang rangyi*: "Respect the *king*, expel the barbarians." In a fudge common to Japanese appropriation of Chinese, the king character was replaced by that for the Japanese Emperor.

Perry demanded, and was given in the Treaty of Peace and Amity of 1854, a number of concessions. These included "mutual peace," the safe repatriation of shipwrecked American sailors; the sale to American ships of "wood and water" (i.e. fuel and provisions); trade transactions and the necessary currency exchange to make such things possible, the opening of the ports of Shimoda and Hakodate to American ships, and the opening of an American consulate in Shimoda. The agreement also included a "Most Favored Nation" clause, which allowed that if Japan concluded any other agreements with any foreign power, those same benefits would automatically accrue to the United States. Later agreements would append other clauses that undermined Japanese sovereignty, including caps on import-export tax, "freedom of religious expression" (which allowed the foreign visitors to practice Christianity, illegal in Japan since the 1630s), and *extraterritoriality*, which entitled foreign visitors who committed a crime to be tried by their own courts, not local law enforcement. It was, as the *Times* had predicted, a similar "gunpowder drama" to that which the British had forced on China, and would carry the same catch-all term: Unequal Treaties.

A decree was issued in the name of the Japanese Emperor, demanding that the Shōgun was to refuse these new demands, and shoo the foreigners out of his country, as befitting his job description as the "barbarian-suppressing supreme general." But such terminology was literally medieval, dating from the period when the early samurai had fought decades of frontier wars against Japan's indigenous people in the north. It had, perhaps, come to signify a responsibility for holding out unwelcome Europeans, particularly the Spanish and Portuguese whose missionaries had represented a threat to Japanese order in the 16th century, but the Shōgun's job, along with the technology at his disposal, was two centuries behind the times.

Many in Edo, the Shōgun's city, faced with visible evidence of American might, understood that some sort of reform would be necessary. For the Emperor in Kyōto, far away from the crisis, the news sounded like the Shōgun was an incompetent, no longer able to do a simple job. A similar attitude prevailed among some of the samurai clans of the far south, ever resentful of the Tokugawa's stranglehold on power, and ready to jump at the chance to suggest they might do a better job.

The experience would prove to be a disaster. With Perry's demands, and with the subsequent Unequal Treaties, the U.S. (and the European powers that piled in after it) argued that Japan has been assessed and found wanting, that it, like China and India, was a failed state that had fallen behind the times, unfit to manage its own foreign affairs. The Japanese, however, answered this challenge with an unprecedented rush to modernize (whatever that meant, and there was much argument). Doing so, it was hoped, would restore to Japan its sovereignty, and remove the Unequal Treaties it had been forced to conclude with the foreign arrivals.

Some were ahead of the game. On several occasions, promising young samurai from dissident domains sneaked out of the country to gain an advanced view of the West. One such group, the "Chōshū Five," was smuggled out to Britain for an education in 1863, even though at least two of them had been in a raiding party, part of the period's anti-foreign activism, that had attacked and set fire to the British Legation in Edo only a year earlier. One of their number, the future Prime Minister Itō Hirobumi, wrote a poem that summarized the contradictions of having to learn from his enemy how to play this new and unfamiliar game.

> Be assured—it is for the Emperor's realm
> That I embark upon this journey
> Shamed though I am in my manly pride.[4]

Itō returned to Japan in time to participate in the "Meiji Restoration" of 1868—a *coup d'état* which overturned the Tokugawa power bloc that had run Japan for the previous 250 years. The old order was replaced by an uneasy alliance among the victors, already in disagreement about the nature of Japan's response to the challenge presented by the outside world. After all, "the West" was not a single entity, but an entire gang of squabbling countries, each with their own tradition, laws and ideas.

By the 1870s, it was believed that if Japan pursued a "modern" agenda, secured its borders in a modern fashion, ran its affairs with the right amount of modern liberty and democracy, and established law and order not merely at home, but in its waters and among the struggling states on its borders, it might be admitted to the international community as an equal. Some thought that Japan could bootstrap itself into the

---

[4] Oka, *Five Political Leaders of Modern Japan*, p. 4. I put "Chōshū Five" in quotes because its usage in modern historiography does not seem to have been widespread before the release of a movie with the same title in 2006. Older Japanese sources tend to say *Chōshū goketsu*—the "five masters of Chōshū."

modern world, implementing the recommendations of the fact-finding Iwakura Mission—a bit of French law, a bit of Prussian schooling, a bit of British naval technology, until Japan could magically throw off the shackles imposed on its by extraterritoriality and tariff control.

But Japan did not have a whole continent at its disposal, like the United States, or an overseas empire like Britain's. Nor did its policy-makers necessarily believe that the world order established by the Western powers was going to endure for very long. Instead, some in Japan embraced the idea that Japan had a civilizing mission, to save not only itself, but the rest of Asia from the predations of the white race and lift it into the modern world. For many who adopted this "Pan-Asian" creed, Japan had the potential to be a savior and exemplar in the creation of a new and better world.

For centuries, China had been the dominant power in East Asia, a central hub to which all neighboring nations at least pretended to pay homage. China's collapse, at the hands of European imperialists but also domestic pressures, led to a power vacuum that was filled by two new-comers—Japan and the United States. As the decades wore on, Japan came to present itself not as an imperialist rival to the foreign powers, but as an ally of the Chinese, there to save it from the white race. Japa-nese reportage of the China situation in the late 19th century was hence very careful in its wording. Japan, argued its apologists, would go to war with the Qing—the Manchu aristocracy that had invaded in China in 1644—in order to *liberate* the Chinese from their Manchu oppressors. There was, indeed, an opportunity for Japan to become the leader of a unified, internationalist East Asia. The enduring tragedy of the period from 1868 to 1945 was how spectacularly Japan blew that chance, loot-ing its Asian neighbors, enslaving their peoples, and delivering a cure that was ultimately worse than the disease.

However, while Pan-Asianism was a popular movement, attracting millions of adherents of one kind of another, a sentiment expressed long before the events of the opening chapter of this book, and returned to by the right-wing long after the events that close it, at no point in the period did any Japanese government subscribe to the ideals of Pan-Asianism, or even use the term openly in its statements.[5] To do so would have been diplomatic suicide—a suggestion to U.S. and European allies that Japan

---

[5] Saaler, "Pan-Asianism, the 'Yellow Peril,' and Suematsu Kenchō, 1905," p. 140.

did not see itself as a fellow participant in the exploitation (or possibly shoring up) of a troubled China. Pan-Asianism remained a fringe belief, discussed by earnest students and thinkers, embraced by reformist factions in Korea, unelected political candidates and organizations such as the Black Dragon Society, occasionally couched in peaceful terms, occasionally as an ideology sure to lead to subterfuge, espionage and open race war. It did not exert much of an influence on American or European policymakers, except as a seemingly dangerous precedent for an unwanted "equality" in matters of immigration and commerce. One might even suggest that "Yellow Lives," millions of which were sacrificed in the first four decades of the twentieth century, only started to matter to the Allies when they themselves began to suffer at the hands of the Japanese.

Japan faced the temptation to involve itself in the failing Chinese regime, both to maintain commercial interests on the mainland, and protect its doorstep from foreign interference. Strategic thinking in 1870s Japan included the notion that, while U.S. ships were already crossing the Pacific, by the turn of the century, Europe would also soon be scratching at Japan's borders from the landward side, thanks to the likelihood of a railway link—this turned out to be true.[6]

The Japanese had plenty of clues that they would not be welcome on the international stage—starting in 1895 when spoils in a war against China were slapped down by an international intervention, and again in 1905, where similar gains against Russia were trimmed away. They clung on, through the first two decades of the 20th century, until the Paris Peace Conference and the League of Nations made it clear that mere modernization was not enough in a world that refused to let them into the exclusive club of the white races. Thereafter, Japan's military worked on the assumption that there would be another war, far larger than anything the world had ever seen, greater even than the Great War that was supposed to "end all wars." And then, maybe then, Japan would be left in peace.

In 1907, shortly after the Russo-Japanese War, Russia remained the most likely future adversary for the Japanese Army, while a Japanese Navy strategy report merely listed the United States as a "hypothetical enemy."[7] Five years later, as construction neared completion on the

---

[6] Calman, *The Nature and Origins of Japanese Imperialism*, p. 286.
[7] Kimura, "Securing the Maritime Trade," p. 124.

game-changing Panama Canal, the U.S. was regarded in Japan as the likely opponent in any coming war in the Pacific, even though such a conflict would not openly break out for another 29 years. The intervening standoff was concealed at first by the two nations' cooperation in the First World War, souring a little with the Paris Peace Conference, but kept under wraps for another decade under cover of the international peacemaking of the League of Nations. Even then, it was a further eight years from Japan's dramatic walkout at the League until the attack on Pearl Harbor in 1941.

As Iida Yumiko writes:

> Modernization for the Japanese was much more than the adoption of Western institutions and technologies; it involved the voluntary participation in an alien game, played by the "logic of civilization," in which the Japanese adopted the struggle to overcome their inferiority in the hope of sustaining the political and cultural autonomy of their nation.[8]

Japan hoped to beat the Western powers at their own game, which we might describe before the First World War as one of imperialism and colonialism, and from the 1920s as international trade and commerce, played within the "dark valley" of diminishing democratic authority. In both cases, the game was rigged, players arrived with different sets of pieces and different boards to play them on, while racial exclusion policies kept the Japanese out of entire rounds of play, and a global recession in the 1920s effectively stopped play altogether. By the 1930s there was a faction within the Japanese Army actively proposing a return to the isolationist attitudes of the samurai era, but with Japan's imperial borders extended to encompass the new territories required for self-sufficiency. Like their forerunners who put Emperor Meiji on the throne, they proposed a coup, a "Shōwa Restoration." That, too, failed in 1936, but even as Meiji's grandson, the Shōwa Emperor, Hirohito, shut down his rebellious officers, he risked becoming their pawn.

---

[8] Iida, "Fleeing the West," p. 409.

This book charts the factors that dragged Japan into the Second World War, a tale of national modernization and political experiments, the suppression of dissent, and the rise of a military-industrial complex that would dominate an entire nation.

The sociologist Michael Mann defines militarism as "a set of attitudes and social practices which regards war and the preparation for war as a normal and desirable social activity."[9] This would certainly describe the performance put on by Japan's samurai aristocracy in 1868, although for many of them, after two and a half centuries of peace, their state of battle-readiness was a matter of opinion. There were, however, enough of them crammed into the new Army and Navy, and enough loopholes in protocol and government rules, to ensure that military matters came to dominate budget discussions, cabinet meetings, and ultimately the Japanese government. But the military did not take over without resistance—there were politicians and pacifists who refused to believe that Japan needed to arm itself against threats real and imagined. A history of militarism hence needs to acknowledge not only those paragons of soldierly virtue, celebrated in songs and statues, but also the draft-dodgers and slackers, deserters and dissidents.

Militarism was not a foregone conclusion. It was an ideology forged in the rush to lift Japan out of its unequal treaties, and to secure a "cordon of interest" beyond its historical borders. It might have been diluted, or dispelled, had certain events not happened when they did—early, confidence-bringing victories against ill-matched opponents, dismissive foreign powers refusing to let Japan play by the rules of their own game, and a worldwide economic depression: desperate times that inspired desperate measures. Constitutionally, there was a flaw in the Meiji state apparatus that went unrecognized until it was too late—the Army and Navy (there was no separate "air force") answered directly to the Emperor, who was supposed to be tactfully silent. They therefore *imagined* what his commands might have been, and were able to impose them on successive Cabinets, over which militarily appointed Army and Navy ministers had an effective power of veto.

They were also fatally uncooperative towards one another—there are times when communications between the Army and Navy are so at-odds that they were effectively fighting different wars. They fought

---

[9] Mann, *States, War and Capitalism*, p. 166.

over different funding for competing strategies, gazumped and blocked each other's schemes, with an antagonism that reached such ludicrous proportions that the two forces could literally receive the same set of aircraft engine blueprints from Germany, and then each turn out mutually incompatible designs, even down to pipe openings and screw-threads. This could lead to what historian Asada Sadao has termed "tortuous interservice compromises," and to the authorship of strategy and policy documents in ambiguous, plausibly deniable language ill-suited for operational planning.[10]

As with my earlier *A Brief History of Japan* (Tuttle, 2017), I use popular culture in this book to examine the degree to which militarism influenced fashions, songs and stories. This allows us to look in on the home life and recreational pursuits of the everyday Japanese, but also to hear marginalized voices—of mothers worrying for the safety of their sons, and writers daring to doubt the manifest destiny of a martial Japan. I have taken a particular interest in popular songs, especially after the inclusion of multiple "war-gods" (*gunshin*) in the Japanese elementary school songbooks after 1911. This not only gives us a glimpse of the sort of hero celebrated by the Japanese establishment, but also of the authorities' interest in weaponizing music in propaganda, education, and in the mobilization of imperial subjects in praise of the state. This process accelerated after 1925, which saw the widespread dissemination of radio and a broadening of the domestic gramophone industry. It was not merely military technology that drove the spread of Japanese militarism—radio, too, played a major part in holding the empire together.

The reader of history looks for reflections of themselves in the storyline, but I see only passing glimmers—the losers in the 1892 election, the "extremists" purged for "left-wing views," which apparently included unimpeded democratic elections and extended suffrage. When the Japanese authorities themselves kept up a constant barrage of claims for one nation, of one mind, with a single purpose, and foreign sources are often happy to swallow this image, the first casualty was nuance. In a recent paper about the early 20th century magazine *Wartime Graphic*, Yu Sakai argues that despite an outward appearance of approved patriotism, the

---

[10] Asada, *From Mahan to Pearl Harbor*, loc. 160. Asada suggests that the Japanese language, itself the product of a millennium of samurai intrigues, is partly to blame here. For the incompatible designs, see Goodwin and Starkings, *Japanese Aero Engines 1910–1945*, pp. 55–6.

magazine sustained an enduring *anti*-war message, deftly edging around the censor to offer subtle digs at a population gone mad with thoughts of heroes on distant battlefields. Sakai's account offers a rare glimpse of a group of Japanese little discussed: the pacifists for whom open dissent was fast becoming a dangerous act, risking public attack.[11]

It would be wonderful, to make a historian's life easier, if there were some single mastermind, cackling over his plans for world domination, but there wasn't. Japan was a ship sailing towards war for decades, captained not by one single Great Man of History, but by a rabble of dozens of changing governments, military factions, cliques and temporary alliances, influenced by overseas events, news (fake and real), and changes in circumstances or technology.

Nobody comes out of this well. There are few "good guys" in a story that chronicles the rise of extremism and a nationwide suicidal fanaticism, wartime atrocities and crimes against humanity. Behind every military blunder and casualty mentioned in this book, there is a tragedy of someone's son or daughter. Militarism spread from the armed forces, to the government, cartels and the people. What was first pitched as a plan to *avoid* war employed such belligerent and escalating means that it created ever larger military appropriations. An attempt to set a secure cordon of interest constantly expanded in reaction to the new threats it found on its own border. By 1937, it was too late—Japan had blundered into the middle of China's own civil conflict, committing the entire nation to total war in an effort to be prepared for... total war.

In fact, in the years between 1868 and 1945, we are witness to the prolonged death throes of a samurai elite that was proclaimed finished at the Meiji Restoration, but would endure in multiple forms in the shadows for decades to come. Its last victors, the power-brokers of Satsuma, Chōshū and their allied domains, presided over the foundation of a modern democracy to which they regarded themselves as somehow superior. Their influence persisted until the 1910s, when the unelected, unconstitutional council of imperial advisers, the *genrō* (the "original old men") died off, fatally leaving no checks or balances in place. In particular with the death in 1922 of Yamagata Aritomo, the father of the Imperial Japanese Army, new factions arose within the military, intent on smashing the domination of the old Satsuma and Chōshū cliques.

---

[11] Sakai, "Survive to be critical," p. 11.

Insubordination turned to mutiny, while the armed forces turned to the rhetoric of their forefathers—the idea that they were being loyal to the Emperor by being disloyal to his misguided officials. Fatally, they did so within a system that was set up to switch the entire nation onto a military footing.

The Japanese in the 1890s were lauded abroad as the "British of Asia," a plucky island nation with a strong navy and a constitutional monarch, bringing the light of civilization to the struggling, backward Chinese empire. Within a few decades, they were rebranded as the new Yellow Peril, an insidious, untrustworthy network of spies and predators, that had to be stopped with extreme prejudice before they conquered the world. In his book *Military Orientalism*, Patrick Porter asks how such mixed messages reflect the temptation to render an "Other" easily classifiable, when shifting political situations lead to sudden about-faces—the noble *mujahedeen* fighting the Soviets, for example, transform into the dastardly Taliban when fighting the Americans, but surely they can't be both? Sometimes, we even see people's opinions changing in the space of a single season. The author Jack London arrived in the Far East to cover the Russo-Japanese War, fulsome in praise for the "warrior race" of the Japanese. Three months later, he stomped home, frustrated with bureaucracy and strict censorship rules, calling the Japanese "ridiculously childish" and "savages."[12]

There were also, undoubtedly, matters of intercultural misunderstanding. Japanese officers regarded it as unmanly to shave more than once or twice a week, leading foreign military observers to characterize the ranks as unkempt and poorly disciplined, and not simply obeying their superiors' example. It may seem like such a minor issue amid such national crises, but as we shall see, the draconian rules of the Japanese Army barracks, in which officers ruled over their men with capricious brutality, would have implications elsewhere, particularly after the outbreak of the Pacific War.[13]

It's worth noting an additional issue, here: that of *auto*-orientalism. Some of the prime proponents of myth-making about Japan were not foreign pundits, clueless or otherwise, but the Japanese themselves, particularly the military authorities after 1895, keen to force a resolute

---

[12] Sweeney, "Delays and Vexation," p. 554.
[13] Harries and Harries, *Soldiers of the Sun*, p. 96.

national vision. We can witness the slow creep of this militarist agenda as it takes over factions within the armed forces, then the government, then institutions of the state, until it starts to force its way into people's homes and lives. The demands of the military ate up huge proportions of Japan's early twentieth century budgets; the Army and Navy's pursuit of their own security of funding and power, often in rivalry with each other, would steer the course of Japanese foreign policy and domestic planning. By the 1920s, Japan was preparing for a total war—against an enemy still to be decided, purging itself of any dissenters or doubters, and zoning out territories overseas to be acquired in order to secure the resources for its own protection.

Militarism also becomes entangled with other -isms—imperialism and colonialism. Mark Peattie argues in *The Japanese Colonial Empire* that Japan was a late-comer, arriving on the international scene right at the "apogee of the 'new imperialism,'" jostling for position with longer-established and better-equipped rivals. It did so at close hand—unlike, say, Britain or the United States, which were thousands of miles from their overseas possessions, many of Japan's acquisitions were right on its doorstep, with striking strategic implications.[14]

There are many other books about the economics of Japanese imperialism, and the Western response to Japanese expansion in the Far East. This book focuses on the mindset of the Japanese—the sight of European powers carving up China, or the creeping threat of Russia in north-east Asia, with the United States growing ever nearer across the Pacific. How did Japan, a nation that had spent 250 years in self-imposed isolation come to terms with the ideals, principles and hypocrisies of the Western powers that made broad claims of international harmony, yet still imposed racist policies at home? And how could it do so without provoking the foreign powers? This book attempts to convey at least some of the intricacies of the hair-trigger balances and shifts in power, not only of international politics, but of Japan's seething internal rivalries.

At times it may seem that I am glorifying acts of aggression, whereas I am merely reporting, faithfully, the enthusiasm and vainglory of the contemporary Japanese media. In historical terms, I am recounting "the story people tell themselves about themselves," which is to say that

---

[14] Myers and Peattie, *The Japanese Colonial Empire*, p. 6.

sometimes this book may appear to be distastefully celebratory of war crimes or parochially blinkered regarding events in world history. This is an account of militarism, which means it avoids pacifism, friendly international relations and, frankly, stories of hope, concentrating instead on the minds and personalities that predicted, prepared for and prosecuted total war. Presenting such a tale requires a degree of method-acting, by both writer and reader, in order to place ourselves within the contexts of very different times and attitudes—in particular the social-Darwinist attitudes prevalent in the late 19th century, when Japan was thrust back into the global community and found itself scrambling to keep its footing in a dog-eat-dog world.

I am not alone in feeling the need to point this out—many other works in and around this topic come with a certain apologetic tone, as if by merely opening ourselves to another perspective, we are somehow condoning it. Peter Duus, for example, feels the need in the introduction to *The Abacus and the Sword* to thank advisers who have stopped him providing "what might have appeared to be an endorsement of Japanese imperialism." Similarly, Mark Peattie, in *Nanyō*, apologizes for telling the story from the Japanese point of view, in a book with the express purpose of telling the story from the Japanese point of view.[15]

My computer tells me that one of the most common words I have used in writing this manuscript is "incident," owing to the frequent recurrence of the terms *jihen* and *jiken* in Japanese history books—words on a careful continuum of meaning. Both are usually translated as "incident," but one carries substantially more weight than the other.

A *jihen* is a crime or action that achieves wider crisis proportions, an emergency, usually overseas, that veritably demands intervention, possibly even named as such in a dog-whistle call to the military. In Japanese accounts, it frequently marks events that bring down governments, or likely acts of war, or sometimes conflicts that really should be called "wars," but are carefully *not* called that in order to avoid activating sanctions or intervention clauses in treaties with foreign powers. Some readers may already know of the Manchurian Incident or the Mukden Incident but there are at least a dozen more, including the Imo Incident (1882) a soldiers' mutiny in Korea, the Itsubi Incident (1895), in which Japanese agents stabbed the Korean queen and set fire to her corpse,

---

[15] Duus, *The Abacus and the Sword*, p. xii; Peattie, *Nanyō*, p. xv.

and the Boxer Uprising (1900), which was called the Hokushin ("North Qing") Incident in Japan. The last chronological *jihen* noted in this book is the undeclared war between Japan and the Soviet Union, fought in Mongolia over the summer of 1939 and known in English as the Battles of Khalkhin Gol, and in Japanese as the Nomonhan Incident. The conflict in China from 1937–1941, was known in Japanese as the China Incident, until the Japanese attack on Pearl Harbor escalated it into the Pacific War. There was, it seems, little need for weasel words after that.

A *jiken* is also an incident, but it is more like an "affair" that Sherlock Holmes might investigate, a common term to be found in the titles of crime novels, somehow less of a big deal than a national-emergency *jihen*. Early on, such scandals are often named simply by their date. By the early twentieth century, there are so many of them that they start to get individual titles. And yet, many of the "affairs" mentioned in this book could easily have escalated into full-blown crises; one wonders if their historical importance hasn't been played down somehow by being filed as lower-level events by historians or media. See for yourself, when this book gets to the little-known Amoy Incident of 1900, in which, but for some diplomatic brinkmanship, Japan might have invaded China three decades earlier than it did, or the Rape of Nanjing in 1937, a terrible holocaust that would surely be a *jihen* by anyone's standards, but is a mere *jiken* in Japanese historiography—presumably because the distant murders of tens of thousands of Chinese civilians presented no contemporary threat to the standing of either the Japanese Army or the Japanese government. In order to put such issues in perspective, the timeline at the back of this book marks those events regarded by Japanese posterity as full-blown emergency *jihen* with an asterisk.[16]

This book, too, is a product of its time and context, as is its author. I hope that my painting of a colossal story in broad strokes will encourage the interested reader to seek out more detailed accounts. This version has been conceived in the 2020s, amid global crisis, domestic political instability and the racial reconfigurations of post-colonial studies. I was drawn to see parallels, not only with the sight of a nation readily destroying itself while horrified moderates looked on, of robber barons making a killing while the weak suffered, of oligarchs and billionaires rushing

---

[16] O'Dwyer, *Significant Soil*, p. 277, notes that the Manchurian Incident started off as a mere *jiken* on September 18, but was renamed a *jihen* by the Japanese cabinet three days later, after it had turned into a crisis.

through new laws while hoping to remain beyond their reach, and of political opportunists ready to use extremist violence to either assert or combat "the will of the people," but also of a movement that sought to reclaim the agency and power of an entire race from its oppressors.

Leaning on Patrick Porter's ideas in *Military Orientalism*, Alexander Nordlund outlined another feature of the attitudes in the late 19th and early 20th century: that so many foreign correspondents "both admired and feared the Japanese as an exceptional Oriental nation." They were like "us" and not like "us"—they had a different diet; they had a weird penchant for atrocity not only to enemies, but to each other; they were inexplicable and, above all, *inscrutable*. They were, in the words of the British officer Ian Hamilton, dangerous throwbacks to "antique standards of military virtue," creatures out of time, ill-suited to the modern age, and ominously "more natural, less complex, and less nervous" in the face of battle.

Not to mention sneaky. Correspondents in the Russo-Japanese War were openly disdainful of the Japanese reliance on espionage, regarded at the time as a profession ill-suited for "a man of Western birth," but which "cost the Russians more lives in this war than Japanese strategy or Japanese leadership." Considering the decades of espionage in Central Asia, as part of the "Great Game" between Russia and Britain, the comment seems woefully lacking in self-awareness.[17]

Hirohito, of course, the Shōwa Emperor, is a recurring character in accounts of Japan's Pacific War—like generations of his ancestors, a monarch with grand authority, and yet a frustratingly oblique and fragile means to wield it. There are plenty of accounts, including Francis Pike's recent *Hirohito's War*, offering evidence that Hirohito was complicit in the actions of his generals. This, however, is not the story that Hirohito told himself, either in his 1946 confessional "Soliloquy," or in the archival *Veritable Record of the Shōwa Emperor* [Shōwa Tennō Jitsuroku], which commenced publication in 2015. The *Veritable Record*, yet to be translated into English, repeatedly shows the Emperor admonishing his generals, urging them for explanations and solutions, and expressing his annoyance with the upper ranks' inability to control their own underlings. The Hirohito of the *Veritable Record* is certainly a component in decision-making processes, but often only a participant in them, forced

---

[17] Nordlund, "A War of Others," pp. 32–3.

to mollify his rulings on the basis of the information he is fed—certainly, by 1933, he was being over-ruled by his own Army, when a chief of staff ominously warned him that an order to withdraw from Jehol could ignite a military coup. Then again, not even the *Veritable Record* is the definitive last word on the Shōwa Emperor's era—in 2019, red-faced officials from the Imperial Household admitted that there were over 5,000 errors in the first, limited-printing edition, thereby compromising the editorial integrity of the first wave of books that drew on it.

There is also a matter of perspective. We might recoil in horror at the deeds of the Japanese military machine in East Asia, but only because its actions were now possible to visualize, report and remember. Many of the awful happenings reported in Asia were not uncommon in Japan, where torture had long been used to extract confessions from prisoners, or to test the resolve of suspected undercover Christians.[18] While many millions of non-Japanese fell victim to Japanese militarism, so, too, did millions of Japanese. We hear their voices, intermittently, dimly through the noise—moments of protest like Yosano Akiko's exhortation to her brother not to die at Port Arthur, glimpses of tragedy, like the dead soldiers, buried in mass pauper's graves after the Bōshin War, while their leaders raided the "restored" Emperor's coffers to pay themselves a hefty reward.[19]

Something that I have found astonishing, even after more than twenty years writing about Japan, is the stories that the Japanese chose to remember. As part of the authorities' push for a nation dedicated to Total War, the establishment constantly favored narratives of tragic deaths and miserable mistakes, carrying Japan's reputation for "the nobility of failure" to new heights of ineptitude, blunders and defeats. In the early 20th century, the Japanese raised statues to a man who sunk his own ship, a man who disobeyed orders and got himself killed, and a man whose sole achievement on a cold mountainside was not dying after he had been marooned there by his own superiors' incompetence. But as we will see, this, too, has its origins in strange attractors and influences behind the scenes, as a military complex, somewhat at war with itself, tries to create an armed force, and a state behind it, that is ready for the ultimate sacrifice.

---

[18] Calman, *The Nature and Origins of Japanese Imperialism*, p. 181.
[19] Calman, *The Nature and Origins of Japanese Imperialism*, p. 231.

   The infamous 1941 attack on Pearl Harbor occurred partway through what is sometimes known in Japan as the Fifteen Years War—acknowledging precisely when it started remains a political act, as specific dates tend to shift blame between several potential agents—take your pick between 1937, or 1931, or 1928, or as this book may lead to you to wonder, perhaps even earlier.[20] Certainly, by the time of Japan's surrender in 1945, an entire generation had grown up knowing nothing but conflict. But the transformation of Japan into a militarist power began decades earlier, with the toppling of the old samurai regime, and the rush of the formerly isolated nation onto the world stage.

---

[20] Hotta, *Pan-Asianism and Japan's War*, pp. 4–5. For example, Gamsa, *Manchuria*, p. 87, notes that the People's Republic of China has insisted since 2017 that the start of the second Sino-Japanese War should be dated to 1931, not 1937 as had previously been widely accepted.

CHAPTER 1

Rich Nation, Strong Army

Afafter a decade of unrest and political in-fighting over the foreign threat, Japan erupted in civil conflict in 1868. The southern clans of Satsuma and Chōshū, claiming to be acting in the name of the new teenage Emperor, effectively declared war on the Shōgun.

The Tokugawa Shōgunate had ruled Japan in the Emperor's name ever since the Battle of Sekigahara in 1600. For the ensuing two and a half centuries, a samurai clan's allegiances at Sekigahara had determined its fortunes. Those who had fought on the Tokugawa side were trusted vassals, assigned the fiefs closest to the Shōgun's headquarters in Edo, or given smaller but strategically crucial domains. Those who had only defected to the Tokugawa cause at the last minute, or who had fought on the losing side, had been shunted into distant or unpromising domains.

Satsuma, Chōshū and a couple of smaller, allied domains, had been nursing their grievances ever since. Furthest from the center of power, they were notorious for edgy disobedience—Satsuma, for example, had an unofficial back-door to trade with China, along the nearby Ryūkyū archipelago, which was still officially a vassal state of China. Chōshū, according to legend, had an annual New Year tradition at which its nobles asked each other if the time had yet come to restart the war with the Tokugawa clan.

Historians are usually discouraged from such "primordialism," but in the case of the Satsuma and Chōshū, we can truly see the renewal of hostilities and settling of old scores that had lain dormant for two and a half centuries. In the war that broke out in 1868, Satsuma, Chōshū and their lesser allies, Tosa and Hizen, not only overthrew the old order, but established themselves firmly as the masters of the new. They would dominate not only Japanese political life for decades, but also the military and even the official story about Japan's modernization. Their influence did not truly wane until the 1910s, when the old guard started

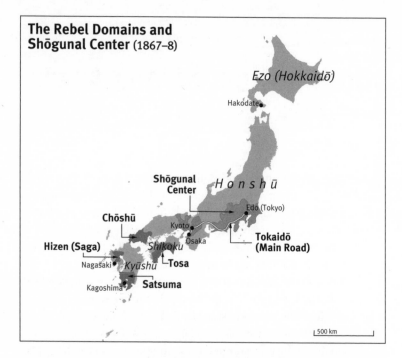

The Rebel Domains and Shōgunal Center (1867–8)

Ezo (Hokkaidō)

Hakodate

Shōgunal
Center   *H o n s h ū*

Chōshū   Edo (Tokyo)

Kyoto
Hizen (Saga)   *Shikoku*   Osaka   Tokaidō
(Main Road)
Nagasaki   *Kyūshū*   Tosa
Kagoshima   Satsuma

500 km

to die off along with the Emperor they had "restored," dismissed by one Edo newspaper as a "small boy of indolent character," manipulated by a clique of Satsuma and Chōshū puppet-masters.[1]

The marching song of the anti-Shōgun soldiers as they advanced on Edo is a fascinating historical curio, mixing old-time Japanese music with the modern newcomers of pipes and drums. There are echoes, in both its instrumentation and in its lyrics, of two songs introduced by the sailors on Perry's Black Ships: "Yankee Doodle Dandy" and "The Star-Spangled Banner." "Miya-san, Miya-san" has been credited to various authors, although the most likely candidates were a team comprising one of the Chōshū leaders and his Kyōto geisha, determined to create a song that would state the objectives of the army as it left behind the sympathetic south, and advanced through territory with a longer pedigree of loyalty to the Shōgun. It was increasingly important, as the army neared Edo, to establish that its cause met with imperial approval, calling attention to the fact that the army's leader was a prince, carrying

---

[1] Steele, "Edo in 1868," p. 136.

the young Emperor's own banner. Scouts rode ahead of the marching soldiers, distributing copies of the song to villages along the road, turning it into a national singing event that united not only the soldiers from the southern domains, but the crowds along the route.[2]

> Miya-san, Miya-san, onma no mae ni
> Hira-hira suru no wa nan jai na
> Tokoton yare tonyare na.

> Prince, oh prince, what is that that flutters in front of your noble horse?
>   Gonna get it done, done to the end.

The rest of the song provided an extensive resumé.

> Know you not, it is the imperial brocade, signifying punishment for rebels?
> [Gonna get it done, etc.]
> Those who defy the Emperor of this entire realm
> The warriors of Satsuma, Chōshū, Tosa, Hizen shoot on target, time and again
> [Gonna get it done, etc.]
> In battles at Fushimi, Toba, Yodo, Hashimoto and Kuzuha
> Skills of Satsuma, Chōshū, Tosa, Hizen in unison.
> [Gonna get it done, etc.]

There was something sassy about referring to their nominal leader, Prince Arisugawa, simply as *Miya-san*—some later variants of the song evolved into the more respectful *Miya-sama*. It was almost as if the southern samurai were so full of themselves and their mission that they regarded the imperial family as their *assistants* in the venture, rather than their superiors. A repeated refrain, occurring ten more times throughout the song, is thick with southern slang, and promises to get it done—"it" being the overthrow of the Shōgun and the restoration of the Emperor. Later lines repeatedly assert the unified resolve of the soldiers

---

[2] Taguchi, "Tokoton yare bushi ni tsuite," p. 127; Mitsui, *Popular Music in Japan*, loc. 202.

from the southern domains—the list of allies, "*Sat-Chō-To-Shi no*" is also a pun, on "[playing] each other's tunes." Despite stating regrets for the necessity of military action, the song is heavy with the contempt they feel for the menfolk of Edo, on the Kantō plain.

> Hearing the sound, where do the men of Kantō run?
> They fled to the east, leaving their castle and spirit behind.
> [Gonna get it done, etc.]
> Although nobody wants to drive them out of their country or kill them
> Because they resist, the first move comes from
> The men of Satsuma, Chōshū, Tosa, Hizen.
> [Gonna get it done, etc.]
> In the midst of bullets, raining down
> They charge, devoting their lives for your sake.
> [Gonna get it done, etc.][3]

Despite the boasts of the song, not all the enemy had fled to the east. A substantial number remained in Edo, based at the Kan'ei Temple, burial site of many a Tokugawa Shōgun. At dawn on the July 4, 1868, the Imperial forces attacked this last Tokugawa stronghold in the Shōgun's city, fighting for much of the day in heavy rain that nevertheless failed to stop the nearby temple burning down, and fire spreading out into the town.

The water turned red at Shinobazu Pond in Ueno, as loyalist forces from the southern domains, determined to "restore" the Emperor's authority, faced off against the *other* loyalists, fighting on behalf of the discredited Shōgun. The confusion over allegiances, with both sides claiming to be obeying what the teenage Emperor's will *really ought to be*, was nothing compared to the mismatched materials in use. The southern samurai were a confusing clash of styles and equipment, as if the soldiers had arrived from different centuries. Some were wielding state-of-the-art breech-loading Snider rifles; others had antique, muzzle-loaded muskets. Among their commanders, there were men dressed like 19th-century Europeans and men in samurai armor, wielding swords. The most striking were the officers, easily identified by their huge yak-hair fright-wigs like something out of the kabuki

---

[3] Osada, *Sensō ga Nokoshita Uta*, pp. 16–17.

theater—black for men from Satsuma, white for Chōshū, and a garish scarlet for samurai from Tosa.

The unity of the Imperial forces was not as complete as their battle hymn claimed. A pushy Chōshū military adviser had drawn up the battle plan for Ueno, in a hard-won fight that placed unnecessary pressure on the men from Satsuma, exacerbated when Chōshū reinforcements failed to show up. This, however, didn't seem to bother the Satsuma samurai Saigō Takamori, who had been frustrated by a lack of opportunities to fight, and welcomed the exhilarating chance to get his hands bloody at Ueno.

"With our ample preparations, we made short work of [the enemy]," he observed, his "our" referring to the battle-ready men of Satsuma, not their latecomer Chōshū comrades. "And this is an exceptional and extreme delight."[4]

But there was more at stake than control of Edo. The Battle of Ueno was also a fork in the historical road, the shutting down of a pretender to the throne who might otherwise have been a pro-Shōgun option. The abbot of the Kan'ei temple was Rinnōji no Miya (1847–1895) himself an imperial prince in his early twenties, and a candidate for an Emperor sure to be on the Shōgun's side. As his samurai died by the dozen to hold the temple's Black Gate against Saigō's men, he escaped to a ship waiting in Edo harbor, and remained at large for several months while his supporters issued vain proclamations in his name, that he was the new "Emperor Tōbu."[5]

Much of this story has been scrubbed from historical memory. Most of the Kan'ei Temple grounds were confiscated, and the site of the battle is now Ueno Park. Talk of a putative Emperor Tōbu was roundly ignored by the victors, while Rinnōji no Miya was himself pardoned, renamed, and after a probationary period, put to work for the new order, all comments on his brief flirtation with rebellion forgotten.

A local newspaper reported that the victory of the Satsuma-Chōshū forces was so complete that "men are even afraid to bury the dead Tokugawa men, whose bodies are allowed to lie, the prey of the wild dogs and the fowls of the air, in the sacred places of one of the holiest places of the defeated clan. The Tokugawa men are literally swept out of

---

[4] Ravina, *The Last Samurai*, loc. 2053.
[5] Keene, *Emperor of Japan*, pp. 151–5.

[Edo], and no man dare harbor one on pain of death."[6] On September 8, facing continued unrest and chaos in Edo, the imperial forces shipped the young emperor there, in the hope that his presence in the city would dissuade residents from thinking of themselves as the Shōgun's subjects. For the first and last time, they also changed his reign name, from Jubilant Answer (*Keiō*), to the name that would define the era: Bright Rule (*Meiji*).[7] Even then, there were rumblings of opposition among the locals, including the topical joke that if the words were read backwards, they came out as "nobody's in charge." Meiji soon won them over by declaring a two-day holiday and distributing free saké throughout the city.[8]

The war that overthrew the Shōgun is often glossed over in a few sentences. Japan experienced a revolution, but there are still sources prepared to call it a "bloodless coup."[9] And, to be sure, when compared with the wars Japan would fight over the next eight decades, a list of less than ten thousand dead seems almost inconsequential—it was not unusual, in some years in the 19th century, for similar numbers of Japanese to be killed annually by cholera.

Some of the Shōgunal loyalists evacuated by sea, heading north along the coast of Japan. Several strongholds held out against the imperial advance, but while there was still some fighting in places, many castle towns surrendered without a fight upon seeing the approach of the Emperor's banner—it would have been an act of insanity, and indeed disloyalty, to have led a charge against the very flag they claimed to serve. Eventually, the Shōgun's men made their last stand on the northern island of Ezo, in the wind-swept port of Hakodate, inside the star-shaped fortress known as Goryōkaku—the Pentacle. The fight over Hakodate stretched through the winter of 1868–9, while the stragglers attempted to claim their redoubt as a separate state, a "Republic of Ezo" where they should be left in peace.

The victors, newly installed in Edo, were described in the *Japan Times' Overland Mail* as "ravenous, sluggish and dronish usurpers" who

---

[6] Steele, "Edo in 1868," p. 147.

[7] The name derives from a phrase in the ancient Chinese *Book of Changes* (*Yi Jing*), from the Chapter on the Explanation of the Trigrams (*Shuogua Zhuan*): "The saint faces south and listens: an **enlightened rule**." This in turn appears to be an oblique reference to the Pole Star, which keeps in place while all revolve around it.

[8] Steele, "Edo in 1868," pp. 150–51. Read out backwards as *osamarumei*, the term literally means "not governed by anyone."

[9] Lone, *Provincial Life and the Military in Imperial Japan*, p. 15, for example.

had left the Shōgun's city in ruins.[10] They were even determined to give it a grandiose new name—the Eastern Capital (*Tōkyō*).

Edo castle, already damaged, suffered a landslip that pitched one of its walls into the moat. The district of old samurai mansions was stripped for parts, "the hinges and bronze ornaments torn off the doors, and in many cases, the timbers and stone houses pulled down and their stone and timber sold to builders."[11] One of the few new building ventures in the aftermath was a shrine to those who had died in the Emperor's service in the war. The Shrine to Summon the Souls (*Shōkonsha*) was one of several similarly named memorials dotted around Japan, but as the largest and best-known, would come to be seen as a national place of remembrance for Japan's war dead. In the decades that followed, it would form the center of many national rituals of mourning, and the enshrinement of the heroes of Japanese militarism.

Edo had once been a city of over two million, but over half of its residents had been samurai retainers, either in attendance on their lord or managing his affairs in his absence. Without the Shōgun, there was no longer any need for compulsory attendance, no family hostages kept in the capital to prevent rebellions. The population of Edo fell by up to 50 per cent, with entire districts left deserted, or occupied by vagrants— sometimes locals deprived of their livelihood by the loss of their samurai clients, sometimes the clients themselves, redundant, exiled or masterless after the upheavals. By 1869, the government was coming up with things for them to do—a new Pioneering Office (*kaikon kyoku*) introduced forced relocation schemes to "open up new lands" for convicts, the workhouse poor and the destitute, at first in nearby Shimōsa to the east, but soon further away, at a convenient arm's length, on a new frontier.

Wary of Russian interests in the north, and keen to develop the lands of Ezo, the new Japanese government took steps to bring the island firmly within Japanese territory. Ezo was renamed Hokkaidō ("the North Sea Way"), and subject to a new development commission, run by a succession of appointees from the victorious forces—its first director was a man from Hizen, its second a nobleman allied to Chōshū, its third a Satsuma man. There were fortunes to be made on the new Hokkaidō frontier: fishery contracts, wide plains ready for agriculture or cattle,

---

[10] Steele, "Edo in 1868," p. 149.
[11] Steele, "Edo in 1868," p. 148, quoting the *Japan Times' Overland Mail*.

railway concessions, and construction contracts for entire towns. Paramount among these was Sapporo, a new city, not created organically by the slow accretion of buildings over decades, but plotted out in huge, regular square grids on the wide Ishikari plain.

The renaming of Ezo was a success, and a propaganda coup that has muddied the waters for historians ever since. It was a land-grab with little thought for the indigenous inhabitants, the Ainu, while business interests with old samurai clan associations dueled over hotly contested licenses to exploit the new lands and resources. It was an early cash-cow for Mitsubishi, the shipping company set up by a man from Tosa, that would soon become the government's conveyor of choice for military transport and supplies. The opening of the new frontier generated immense wealth, sometimes through commerce and sometimes through corruption (there are tales of millions squandered on inappropriate farming equipment, sourced on glad-handing junkets to the United States), and sometimes through the exploitation of forced labor. In fact, Hokkaidō in the 1870s offered a miniature premonition of many of the processes that would characterize the Japanese empire overseas in decades to come, concealed as a domestic issue, and not the newly opened "foreign" territory that it truly was.

But while the Meiji Restoration had toppled the old order, it had yet to deal with the problem that had so destabilized Japan—the Unequal Treaties with the foreign powers. In order to do so, Japan needed to demonstrate to the foreign powers that it was a truly enlightened, modern state, not an unstable nation that had just emerged from a medieval time-warp.

As part of this reorganization in 1871, the old samurai domains were abolished—the clans were stripped of their authorities. The feudal lords were re-appointed as non-hereditary prefectural governors, and rebranded with a series of noble titles, as barons, dukes and counts. The effect has been regarded, not without justification, as a second *coup d'état* only a couple of years after the first, in which the architects of the Meiji Restoration began kicking away the ladder by which they had ascended, buying off rival clan leaders with short-term appointments and transfers of assets. They had, in effect, risen to power on the basis of "Revering the Emperor and Expelling the Barbarians," but now adopted the same policies of appeasement and modernization that the Shōgun had attempted to bring about, and for which they had overthrown him!

Some people felt short-changed. Chief among them was Saigō Taka-mori, the Satsuma man who had fought so hard for traditional values, only to find himself in the very Japan he had tried to avoid. As the new government prepared to send a research group, the Iwakura Mission, on a world tour to investigate possible reforms and innovations, Saigō was heard at the farewell party calling one of its leaders a corporate stooge, and expressing his hope that the ship carrying them would sink on its way to America.[12]

The abolition of the old domains severed the bonds between the old feudal lords and their standing armies of samurai—it effectively turned every samurai in Japan into a *rōnin*, a masterless warrior. For some, it was a chance to fade into the population, trying their luck in another field (not for nothing, the old-time Japanese slang of a "warrior's busi-ness," referring to a samurai blundering into commerce and discovering the hard way that it wasn't as easy as it looked). Others fell into crime or vagrancy. But by far the most attractive proposition was to re-enlist in the military, not as retainers of a provincial warlord, but as officers in the newly established Imperial Japanese Army and Imperial Japanese Navy. Under new 1872 conscription laws, men of all classes between seventeen and forty years of age were required for three years' military service, fol-lowed by two in the reserves and two more on standby—summonable in times of national emergency, but otherwise released. The former sa-murai naturally assumed that officer's postings waited for them, while the peasants could form the rank and file.[13]

A conscript army, drawn from all classes of Japanese men, amounted to a further abolition of the old associations and connections of the sa-murai era. It was presented in terms of an equality of opportunity:

On the one hand, warriors who have lived without labor for gen-erations have had their stipends reduced and are stripped of their swords; on the other hand, the four classes of the people are about to receive their freedom. This is the way to restore the balance between the high and low, and to grant equal rights to all. It is, in short, the basis of uniting the farmer and the soldier into one. The people are not the people of former days. They are now equally

---

[12] Calman, *The Nature and Origins of Japanese Imperialism*, p. 132.
[13] Harries and Harries, *Soldiers of the Sun*, p. 22.

the people of the empire, and there is no distinction between them and their obligations to the state.[14]

All nations had armies, noted the Emperor's decree, and Japan was merely modernizing by extending the honor of military service from the samurai to all men. The peasants, in fact, had little choice, and literally could not afford not to serve. The Army, in particular, scooped up many of Japan's poor, while only the sons of richer farmers and merchants could buy their way out of serving for 270 yen—more than a year's average salary.[15]

In an attempt to drum up enthusiasm, the authorities tried another exercise in rebranding. Perhaps it was easier to put things another way— it wasn't so much that the samurai were no more; better to say that we were *all* samurai now, an idea implied within the 1872 *Soldiers' Code* (*Toku-hō*), which demanded seven virtues of all servicemen: loyalty, obedience, courage, control, frugality, honor and respect [for superiors].

The idea managed to annoy almost everybody—the samurai were incensed at the loss of their traditional duty to wage war, while many of the common folk regarded it not as an opportunity, but as a "blood tax."[16] In one tall tale circulating around the provinces, it was suggested that the military was harvesting the blood of new recruits and somehow transmitting it down the new telegraph wires being set up across the country. In a factory at a secret location, the blood was said to be used to dye the new standard-issue hatbands for infantry uniforms.[17] Books on how to avoid the draft became best-sellers, offering various cunning ruses for the reluctant recruit. These included acquiring only-child exemption through adoption into an heirless family, bribing a corruptible doctor for a bogus medical waiver, or disappearing off to Hokkaidō, where someone might prove to be impossible to track down. An unlikely but apparently genuine ruse involved the draftee hosting a round-the-clock party that would stretch on for several days, with his friends attending in shifts. The idea was to leave the host thoroughly and convincingly

---

[14] Ravina, *The Last Samurai*, loc. 113–20.

[15] Perhaps out of an unwillingness to be stuck with recruits with no experience of the sea, the Navy was more reluctant to use conscripts, and preferred volunteers. Evans and Peattie, *Kaigun*, p. 11.

[16] Calman, *The Nature and Origins of Japanese Imperialism*, p. 6.

[17] Harries and Harries, *Soldiers of the Sun*, p. 23.

exhausted on the day of his medical.[18]

While these reforms were underway, the Iwakura Mission was conducting its extensive survey of foreign countries, in order to establish the primary models for further improvements. It was a grand tour for several bigwigs in the Meiji establishment. Its leader, Iwakura Tomomi, was a distant cousin of the Emperor, while his deputies included Ōkubo Toshimichi (Satsuma), Itō Hirobumi (Chōshū), Kido Takayoshi (Chōshū) and Kume Kunitake (Hizen), along with a rabble of disciples to be dropped off en *route* to study particular subjects. It was intended to fly the flag for Japan's presence on the world stage, to renegotiate some of the harsher treaties imposed on the Shōgun's government before the Meiji Restoration, and to cherry-pick the very best of the contending Western institutions and processes. It was hence a remarkably influential operation—its members wrestled with huge questions for Japan's future, such as whether the Meiji Emperor should consider becoming a Christian, or if the people of Japan should cast aside their native language and all speak English thereafter, or perhaps ditch Chinese characters in favor of Roman letters.

The Iwakura Mission spent six months in the United States of America, four months in Britain, and then ten European countries in the first half of 1873, before steaming home via the Suez Canal, Singapore, and Shanghai. They arrived back in Japan in September 1873, having witnessed all sorts of wonders—Kume, the mission's official diarist, was reprimanded by the time they reached Britain for having already used up all his superlatives describing America. On their return, the Iwakura Mission expected their hard-won intelligence to be heard and obeyed.

The Japanese government, however, was split between the heavyweight returnees and the "caretakers" who had run things while they were away. All were in agreement that Japan needed to modernize, but the returnees, mainly Satsuma and Chōshū men, soon found something to argue about with the caretakers, who could be said to represent a brief flourishing of minor Meiji Restoration domains, such as Saga and Tosa. Regardless, the Iwakura returnees now expected the caretakers to step aside and allow them to apply what they had learned. The caretakers were reluctant to do so, leading to a power struggle at the center of government, in which foreign policy would become the main point of contention.

The Iwakura Mission members were not all agreed about the best

---

[18] Lone, *Provincial Life and the Military in Imperial Japan*, pp. 17–18.

things they had seen, although they did concur that it would not be enough to merely modernize; unlike the Chinese, they would be better off adopting many Western institutions wholesale. Moreover, for thinkers like the writer Fukuzawa Yukichi (1835–1901), Japan also needed to find a way of becoming part of this modern world without becoming a slave to it.

> We want our learning independent, not licking up the lees and scum of the westerners. We want our commerce independent, not dominated by them. We want our law independent, not held in contempt by them. We want our religion independent, not trampled underfoot by them.[19]

Fukuzawa argued that Asia was in danger of crumbling beneath the onslaught of the western powers, but that Japan could be its savior. In order to do so, however, Japan would need to "quit Asia" (*datsu-A*). "We cannot wait for our neighbor countries to become so civilized that all may combine together to make Asia progress," he wrote. "We must rather break out of formation and behave the same way as the civilized countries of the West are doing."[20]

Part of the problem, argued Fukuzawa, was that Japan had "a government but no nation"—the scars of the Meiji Restoration were still apparent; there was nothing to unite the people behind a common goal.[21]

"Revere the Emperor, Expel the Barbarians" would no longer do. Instead, the Meiji oligarchs dredged up a new slogan from ancient China more appropriate for their era: "Rich Nation, Strong Army" (*fukoku kyōhei*).[22] To a scholar of classical Chinese, the phrase carries ominous implications, since it originated in Qin, the obscure state that adopted

---

[19] Blacker, *The Japanese Enlightenment*, pp. 11–12. Fukuzawa was not a member of the Iwakura Mission.

[20] Blacker, *The Japanese Enlightenment*, p. 136.

[21] Sakai, "Survive to be critical," p. 8.

[22] In Chinese *fuguo qiangbing*—a quote from the *Intrigues of the Warring States*. Few seem to have commented on the (perhaps inadvertent) switch in nuance. "Revere the Emperor, Expel the Barbarians" had been a slogan that identified the Japanese with the loyalists to the Chinese ruler, resisting incursions from the outside world. "Rich Nation, Strong Army" reconfigures the Japanese self-image as one of the upstarts and would-be usurpers, ready to take the throne from the ruler of China. It is, however, easy to read too much into such allusions, since all too often, it turns out that the Japanese weren't putting that much thought into them themselves.

a fierce policy of militarization until, after a century of intrigues and fighting, its king would proclaim himself the ruler of the known world. He is best known in our time for being the man whose tomb is guarded by the Terracotta Warriors. Were the Meiji oligarchs truly announcing, like the nobles of ancient Qin, that they were embarking upon a century-long mission to save China from itself by taking it over?

But since most of them were from the Satsuma-Chōshū alliance that had toppled the old order, they were in agreement about the paramount importance of their own Emperor. Despite agitations among the public for "Freedom and People's Rights," the drafters of Japan's forthcoming constitution did not recognize that power derived from the people—such an idea was a dangerous Western notion, already troubling the monarchies of Europe. As for the best model to follow, the Japanese were naturally drawn to the constitutional monarchies of Britain and Germany. Germany, in particular, a newly created nation built of multiple former domains under a single emperor (the Kaiser), seemed to offer an ideal example, although others in the council supported a more British model, in which the sovereign presided as a figurehead over a parliament. It was this that Japan would ultimately implement, albeit with some vital organizational differences. For a start, the Japanese Emperor would enjoy the advice of an extra-constitutional think-tank of grand old men (the *genrō*).

In this, the leaders of the Meiji Restoration were clinging to the rhetoric of their own rise to power—that the Emperor was the head of state, and his authority had been returned to its traditional conditions by the brave rebels... no, sorry, the brave *loyalists* of the Meiji Restoration. They had not been rebels, because they had been acting out of their sense of duty to their sovereign, who had been misled and poorly advised. And they, the grand old men of Satsuma and Chōshū, would remain at his side, dominating his Privy Council and the posts in his early Cabinets, to ensure that he was not misled and poorly advised ever again. This was all very well, but it would turn into a constitutional dilemma, in which the *genrō* papered over all the imperfections in the Meiji constitution, postponing any problems for a generation until there was nobody left to take their place.[23]

There were unexpected consequences of the abolition of the feudal

[23] Oka, *Five Political Leaders of Modern Japan*, p. 23.

domains, the most pressing of which was the sudden breakdown of back-channel communication between Japan and Korea. During the Shōgunate, the Sō samurai clan on the island of Tsūshima had been permitted to dock at a specific harbor near Busan, Korea, forming a shadowy trade corridor between the supposedly "closed" nations of Korea and Japan. Now, their docking station was rebranded as the Japanese Legation, intended as a consulate for the new Meiji government. The reimagining of Japan's trading post as a foreign embassy ran contrary to the Korean kingdom's own policies—Korea still banned foreign contact, as had Japan until only recently. A local Korean official noted that the Japanese, by throwing aside old customs and loyalties and by shamelessly trashing centuries of tradition, had become a "lawless nation." It was if Japan had put itself through a decade of upheaval, only to be told by its closest neighbor that it had ideas above its station.[24]

The Japanese had not made their lives easier by notifying the Koreans of this shift in policy with a high-minded communiqué that referred to His Majesty, the *Emperor* of Japan.

The Korean response leapt on the language. Korea was a loyal vassal state of China, and hence could only recognize the existence of a single Emperor—there could never be, as Confucius had once said, "two suns in the sky." Nor was the ruler of Korea, a king, about to cede precedence to the ruler of Japan, whose overseas communications for centuries had been happy to refer to himself by a term better translated as "Great Prince."

Korea refused to acknowledge the regime change brought about by the men of Satsuma and Chōshū, reminding the Japanese, in the process, that Korea's allegiances lay to its west, in Beijing. The quibble over terminology was only an excuse. The Korean authorities remained disapproving and dismissive of Japan's willingness to kowtow to foreigners. It was, as one teasing poster on the consulate wall suggested in May 1873, as if the Japanese weren't worthy of being called Japanese any more.[25]

Korea was set to become Japan's first big foreign policy issue. One gets the sense, reading the arguments over the "Subdue Korea" debate that broke out in 1873, that every faction within the Japanese government saw it as a vital test of policy and processes. The more

---

[24] Ravina, *The Last Samurai*, loc. 2395.
[25] Duus, *The Abacus and the Sword*, p. 37.

diplomatically minded wanted to settle it with a specially-appointed negotiator, to prove that Japan could be tactful. The more aggressive wanted to see Korea chastened with a military expedition. Still others cautioned against a violent reaction, since the last thing Japan needed was to encourage further foreign intervention. Japan's response to Korea was sure to become the basis of an ongoing foreign policy, so what was it to be? An attempt to establish cordial and friendly relations, or the first move of an attempt to make Korea subordinate to Japan? And if it were the latter, was Japan actually ready to fight that war? Whatever Japan did at this historical moment, it needed to handle it well and without foreign help or hindrance.[26]

While the Korea debate dragged on, Japan faced another foreign policy problem in Taiwan—events preceded the Korea issue, but had taken many months to percolate. On a stormy night in November 1871, a ship from the Ryūkyū Islands had capsized off Taiwan's south-east coast. Sixty-six survivors struggled ashore, where local Chinese warned them of "savage" tribesmen in the forest, and under the pretext of helping them, relieved them of all their valuables. Distrusting their erstwhile saviors, the Ryūkyūans left them behind and marched into the forbidden forest, where they met local villagers, who made a ritual friendship offer of water and food.

The story, as told back in Japan, was that the sailors were massacred by head-hunters. The story back in Taiwan, was that they had met local villagers, and inadvertently insulted them by dining and dashing. Possibly, the villagers had expected a "reward" that was not forthcoming; possibly their extraction of this ransom from their charges was regarded by the Ryūkyūans as robbery. Whatever happened, fifty-four of the fleeing Ryūkyūans were tracked down the following day and slaughtered.[27]

There were multiple chances to settle the incident at a local level. But the Ryūkyū islands were in a territorially unclear position, and deliberately so. Ever since 1655, the "kings" of the Ryūkyū islands had only existed in order to keep up the pretense of Ryūkyū being a Chinese vassal state—such a performance thereby avoided antagonizing the Chinese and provoking military action. Now, however, the Japanese state wanted Ryūkyū officially acknowledged as part of its own territory, and

---

[26] Duus, *The Abacus and the Sword*, p. 41.
[27] Barclay, *Outcasts of Empire*, pp. 52–3.

the deaths of the fishermen on Taiwan were a priceless opportunity to enforce this idea.

The Japanese were encouraged in this by Charles Le Gendre (1830–99), the former American consul in Amoy, China, who pushed himself on the Japanese as an adviser in Taiwanese aboriginal matters, and urged them to use the incident as a political lever. A Civil War veteran and a fearsome sight, having lost an eye and part of his nose to a bullet in Virginia, the French-born Le Gendre had advanced as far as he could in his diplomatic career. He was calling in on Japan on his way home to the United States, having been reprimanded for over-stepping his authority, and refused promotion to a higher position.

Le Gendre regarded his main achievement to have been a successful resolution of an earlier situation on Taiwan, where he had secured an agreement from aborigines to never attack men on ships that flew the American flag. He had done so by inviting himself along as an "observer" on a Chinese expedition, seizing command from the hapless Chinese general, and marching into the hinterland to parley with the local chieftain Toketok.

Le Gendre regarded Taiwan as a microcosm of all China, and hence that his limited knowledge of the island made him an expert on the entire country. In 1871, he summarized his ideas in a "letter" to a colleague, to which he subsequently appended 160 pages of memoranda and essays, and self-published in Amoy under the title *How to Deal With China*. Now couched as learned advice to the U.S. Secretary of State, who had openly rejected such counsel, the book's one hundred copies were liberally strewn around the diplomatic community, where its title page cunningly alluded to Le Gendre as both a general and a consul, neither of which was really true at the time it was printed. It would be, however, the perfect calling card in Japan.[28]

Le Gendre arrived in Tokyo bragging about his military record and his achievements in Taiwan as if he were a returning hero, and not a mild embarrassment being edged towards early retirement. Talking himself up as an expert on matters Taiwanese, Le Gendre observed that China's hold on the island was tenuous at best, and that it would be in Japan's interest to seize the island, along with Korea and Manchuria (northeast

---

[28] Gordon, "Taiwan and the Powers," p. 101. The U.S. Secretary of State, William H. Seward, had decreed in 1867 that there was "no case" in which the U.S. desired the acquisition of Taiwan.

China, the homeland of the Manchu Emperors), in order to become the master of all Asia.[29]

> Formosa [i.e. Taiwan] must change hands in the interest of civilization and humanity, no nation would be better qualified than Japan to step in and take the place of China... Unless the Formosan tribes are reconciled or else subdued and exterminated either by China or Japan, the impending evil cannot be averted; and therefore, if China neglects the task, Japan, in self-protection, must perform it herself.[30]

Le Gendre's confidence on Taiwanese matters led to his new position with the Japanese government, as a diplomatic adviser. In that capacity, he prepared *Notes of Travel in Formosa*, a compendium of everything he knew about the island, with legal commentary on the international politics of an invasion. It amounted to a guide to how Japan in East Asia might best imitate America's manifest destiny, and remained under-the-table reading in Japanese diplomatic circles for decades to come.

Le Gendre accompanied the Japanese foreign minister Soejima Taneomi to Beijing to discuss the Taiwan issue, much to the annoyance of the Chinese negotiator, Li Hongzhang, who objected to the presence of a white man at a discussion of a Sino-Japanese issue. But by June 1872, Le Gendre had what he wanted: an admission by the Chinese that China had little real authority over the Taiwanese aborigines. If the Chinese were unable to control the territory, observed Soejima, then the Japanese reserved the right to take action of their own.[31]

While Soejima was in China negotiating over the Taiwanese issue, there was an attempt by his deputy back in Tokyo to send Saigō Takamori, the bullet-headed bruiser last seen laughing off the blood and gore of the battle of Ueno, to negotiate with the Koreans, over the issue of the Legation and international relations.

An enthusiastic volunteer for the mission, Saigō was planning on his own spectacular demise. He wrote that he was by far the best choice of ambassador, but that since his mission was to die at the hands of an assassin, thereby provoking an international incident, he would do his

[29] Caruthers, "Anodyne for Expansion," p. 139.
[30] Le Gendre, *Notes of Travel in Formosa*, p. 329.
[31] Gordon, "Japan's Abortive Colonial Venture," pp. 173–4.

best. So, at least he confessed in private letters—in public, he claimed
that he would do his best to achieve a diplomatic solution.[32]

Fortunately for regional peace, at least in the short-term, Saigō's departure was delayed while the government bickered about the best way
to deal with Korea. Japan had plenty of overseas issues to deal with—
some, like the Taiwan issue, were relatively minor, but hawks in favor of
a Korean war tried to play up the threat presented by Russia. This, too,
was a matter of some contention—one could just as easily argue that
Russia would use unrest in Korea as an excuse to *increase* its presence
in the region, and that hence war was best avoided.

Amid a whirl of resignations in protest, and the sudden taking ill
of the Chancellor of the Realm, Iwakura Tomomi was ordered by the
Emperor to take over the deliberations. Iwakura issued a firm ruling,
phrased as a memorial to the Emperor, regarding Japan's lack of readi-
ness to embark on a foreign adventure. It had only been five years since
the Restoration, he noted, and Japan remained politically insecure and
institutionally inexperienced. Security appeared to have been established at home, but it was best to tread carefully. "Under such circumstances," he wrote, "dealing with foreign countries should not be viewed
lightly."[33]

While many in the government were in agreement about the need
to take action, the time was not yet right. Japan needed to juggle one
threat of foreign interference against another—much of the young Meiji
state was shored up by loans from Britain, and Ōkubo Toshimichi, now
the equivalent of the minister of home affairs, was concerned that Britain would intervene if Japan leapt into a frivolous overseas expedition
before properly settling its debts at home.

It took a while for the implications to sink in—it was over a week before a heated argument between Saigō and Iwakura at the latter's home,
in which even Saigō got the message. He was not going to be sent overseas to cause trouble. Realizing that he was deeply unwelcome in the
government, Saigō and his supporters resigned, ending the rule of the
"caretakers" and leaving Ōkubo's faction free to take over. Ōkubo and
his allies planned to pursue a robustly imperialist foreign policy—there

---

[32] de Bary et al., *Sources of Japanese Tradition*, loc. 19170–19181.

[33] Duus, *The Abacus and the Sword*, p. 42. "Chancellor of the Realm" (*daijō-daijin*) is
a position roughly equivalent to Prime Minister, although Japan did not have an
official "Prime Minister" until the appointment of the first, Itō Hirobumi, in 1885.

were plans for an expedition to Taiwan in 1874, and a tougher stance to be taken on Korea in 1875.

This was not good enough for Saigō, who expressed his frustration with the aid of a classical Chinese allusion.

"A true man would be a shattered jewel," he said, "ashamed to be an intact tile."[34] The phrasing was drawn from a story some 1,300 years old, from the time of the collapse of the Northern Qi, one of several contending Chinese dynasties in a period of medieval unrest. Faced with the prospect of execution or living on with a usurper's surname in 550 AD, one Qi nobleman proclaimed: "Better to be shattered jade than a whole tile" (*ning ke yu sui, bu neng wa quan*). Jade, the imperial stone, could famously be broken but never twisted, making it a symbol of constancy and, to some extent, suicidal loyalty to an ideal—the jade/jewel mix-up is a feature of the sheer antiquity of the language involved, as if a U.S. politician giving a speech today suddenly dropped a reference in medieval Latin.

By February 1874, the Japanese cabinet had come around to Le Gendre's way of thinking, while he continued to press that aboriginal territory in Taiwan should be annexed by Japan "for the benefit of the whole civilized world." Le Gendre was seconded to Japan's newly established Taiwan Aborigines Land Affairs Bureau, run by Ōkuma Shigenobu (a man from Hizen). With Le Gendre's encouragement, Ōkuma arranged with his contacts in the Mitsubishi shipping company to arrange a task force to occupy Taiwan, with a manpower roster that suggested less a punitive military action than the opening phase of a colonization effort. Despite protests from the U.S. ambassador to Japan, who disapproved not only of Le Gendre's involvement, but of the presence of two American military advisers and a rented U.S. ship, the expedition set out in May 1874. It was commanded by Saigō Takamori's brother, Saigō Tsugumichi, and left in a hurry, before the government could issue a countermand.

Accounts of the expedition demonstrate just how confusing the island's diversity was. The Japanese soldiers established friendly relations with the local chieftain Toketok, who claimed suzerainty over 16 tribes, but not the Botan people on his borders, whom he hoped the Japanese would suppress. While one group of Japanese soldiers was literally

---

[34] Fraleigh, "Songs of the Righteous Spirit," p. 118, notes that the poet Hirano Kuniomi used the same allusion in 1862—Saigō was not the first, but he is the most famous.

having a cook-out with friendly tribesmen, presenting them with rifles as gifts, along with a Japanese flag for them to fly as a sign of their co-operation (or alliance, or subjugation, depending on whom one asked), another group of aborigines opened fire with rifles on a Japanese ship.

The Botan tribe killed a Japanese soldier on a scouting mission, and six more in an ambush of the party sent to investigate, in a battle that claimed dozens of aboriginal lives, including that of Chief Toketok, who was presumably fighting on the same side as the Japanese. Further military action was curtailed by an outbreak of malaria among the invaders, which claimed 550 lives.

In spite of such disasters, the Taiwan expedition was an immense and underhand success. Not only did China pay the Japanese to go away—in the words of the British diplomat Harry Parkes, demonstrating a "willingness to pay to be invaded"—the Chinese admitted that they had little control over the east of Taiwan, creating the potential for further interference. More cunningly, in managing to wheedle even a single penny of compensation from China for the maltreatment of the shipwrecked Ryūkyū sailors, Japan had made the Chinese concede that the Ryūkyūans were Japanese subjects. Ryūkyū had enjoyed a dual status for centuries but had now been snipped away from Chinese authority. The invasion of Taiwan might have appeared to be a failure but had successfully locked Ryūkyū into a Japanese orbit. Wrangling about the implications would drag on for the next half-decade, but by 1880, the Ryūkyū islands had been branded first a domain, and then a full-fledged Japanese prefecture.[35]

Now there was less of a fear of foreign intervention. Japan had recently signed a treaty with Russia, while no foreign power had bothered to intervene when Japan landed soldiers on Taiwan in 1874. Behind the scenes, Charles Le Gendre advised that Korea should be next.[36] It was not until September 20, 1875 that Japan made its move, when the *Un'yō*, a Japanese surveying vessel illegally in Korean waters, sent a provisioning party ashore at Ganghwa island, near the mouth of the Han river that led to Seoul. When Korean shore batteries opened fire on the intruders, the *Un'yō* shot back from its shipboard guns and landed a raiding party.

Facing surprised Korean soldiers with nothing but matchlock

[35] Paine, *The Sino-Japanese War*, p. 96.
[36] Duus, *The Abacus and the Sword*, p. 45.

muskets, the Japanese marines killed thirty-five. Japan then notified the British and French that Korea had started it, and that this was an insult that needed to be answered.

If the "surveying" actions of the Japanese vessel seemed oddly similar to those of Commodore Matthew Perry in Japanese waters twenty years earlier, that was no coincidence. The U.S. had literally provided Japan with a playbook for gunboat diplomacy, when the U.S. minister John Armor Bingham presented Inoue Kaoru, then the vice-minister of Japan's legation in Korea, with a copy of Perry's memoirs.[37]

At least officially, the whole thing was a misunderstanding, although the ship's commander, Inoue Yoshika, was a staunch supporter of Saigō Takamori's anti-Korean stance, with a bright career ahead of him that would see him ultimately retire as an admiral and viscount, it is difficult to believe that he was not aware of Korean coastal interdictions, nor indeed that he had put to sea without enough food and water to get home again. Regardless, within a week of the Ganghwa Incident, Japan had dispatched gunboats to Korea to "protect" Japanese subjects there from Korean reprisals.

The Treaty of Ganghwa, negotiated over the summer of 1876, heavily imitated the unequal treaties that Japan had been made to sign itself. It was negotiated with many of the tricks from Commodore Perry's strategy, including the sight of an impressive looking flotilla of ships that, in truth, scraped up almost everything in the Japanese Navy, along with a couple of rented foreign transports to bulk out the numbers. Negotiators were also carefully inaccurate with the numbers they mentioned, falsely claiming that there were four thousand Japanese soldiers aboard the ships, ready to come ashore in case of trouble—in fact, there were only eight hundred.

As with the Unequal Treaties that the Japanese themselves had signed, there were clauses regarding the right to come ashore to restock "wood and water," and demands that Korea deal with Japan on an equal footing, as per "the law of nations." Like the Europeans and Americans in Japan, Japanese in Korea were granted extraterritoriality, outside the rule of Korean law. At least the treaty asserted that Korea was an independent state, although such a point was a matter of some contention. For the Japanese, it implied that Korean's independence was a claim that

---

[37] Kim, "The Sino-Japanese War," p. 5.

needed to be supported with modernization suitable enough to ensure that Korea did not fall prey to another foreign power—Japan, naturally, was ready to help with such developments. But this only created a new problem elsewhere, since the apparent "independence" of Korea would come as something of a surprise to the Chinese.

The Ganghwa Treaty was not a simple copy of Japan's foreign treaties. The differences were more palpable than the similarities. Unlike Japan's foreign treaties, there was no "most-favored nation status," so Japan was not obliged to share any of these concessions with any other country. Moreover, Japanese imports and exports were not only completely exempt from tariffs, but could be bought and sold in Korea using Japanese currency.[38]

However, concerns that Japan's foreign policy required peace at home were well founded. There were those among the former samurai who saw themselves excluded from the adventures of the new order, short-changed by the reforms and betrayed by their former allies. Such men formed a new nest of unrest, in those same, fractious southern domains that had once started the Meiji Restoration.

Already in February 1874, government troops had been sent to Saga (the old Hizen domain), in order to prevent one of the resigned ministers from organizing an unspecified attack—possibly on Korea itself, or even on the Japanese government. Saigō Takamori himself put on a show of setting up schools in Satsuma, purportedly dedicated to promoting a universal Confucian education and the increasingly outmoded virtues of a traditional samurai. Suspiciously, by 1875, when the Japanese Navy was winning new victories in Korea, the students of the Satsuma schools were forbidden from leaving to study in Tokyo—it was as if Satsuma was walling itself away from the new government it had helped to found.

Tensions between the modernizing government and the samurai who had put it in power continued to grow. In 1876, the samurai were stripped of their traditional right to wear swords in public, which was now an honor restricted to state ceremonies, soldiers and police. In same year, annual stipends, previously a guaranteed income samurai regarded as their birth right, were transferred into thirty-year government bonds. There was no need for the samurai in public life—they had lost their

---

[38] Duus, *The Abacus and the Sword*, p. 48.

income, their swords and even their haircuts were out of fashion.[39]

Some had faded into the Army and Navy, and could be found among the officer class. But the likes of Saigō had talked themselves out of any such role in the new order, and soon fought back. In one insurrection in Satsuma, 200 samurai attacked Kumamoto castle and killed the governor. They called themselves the *Shinpūren*—the League of the Divine Wind, itself a reference to the *Kamikaze* storm that had once shielded south Japan from invaders. Five days later in Chōshū, several hundred disaffected samurai seized a local arsenal and raided a local treasury—it was thereby possible, just about, to spin such an action more as a bank robbery than an uprising. Saigō himself did not make a move until the early months of 1877, when some of his schools uncovered government agents, sent to infiltrate them on the suspicion that they were training grounds for anti-government action.

Saigō's ill-fated Satsuma Rebellion did not have a clear plan. It seemed framed as a replay of the victorious march on the Shōgun's capital of 1868, although not all of his recruits were aware that his grand gesture of "loyalty" to traditional values would involve moving against the government in Tokyo.

In the meantime, however, they were bogged down at Kumamoto Castle, in a long siege of the government troops within. Several unrelated groups also rose up, filling in the gaps in Saigō's plan with false claims that support for him would lead to such innovations as tax-free townships and local devolution of power. By March, there were unfounded newspaper reports that Saigō carried a banner demanding "a New Government, Rich in Virtue" (*shinsei kōtoku*), but while that was precisely the sort of thing one might expect Saigō to say, it wasn't true.[40]

Saigō's grand gesture, vaguely imagined to be a long march on Tokyo, where he intended to "question" the government, never made it more than ten kilometers outside of Kumamoto. Government troops arrived to relieve the siege, and a break-out assault was turned back at Taburazaka—barely four stops on today's local railway.

Heavily outnumbered, Saigō's men still held off the imperial forces for some weeks, aided in part by the local terrain—strongholds, redoubts

---

[39] Ravina, *The Last Samurai*, loc. 2585. A thirty-year government bond would have matured in 1906, shortly after Japan nearly bankrupted itself in the Russo-Japanese War.

[40] Ravina, *The Last Samurai*, loc. 2672.

and levees illegally designed to make the entire area around Kumamoto an extension of its castle defenses. Tokugawa era law forbade each domain having more than one castle, but the area around Kumamoto was festooned with fortified "schools," and something that one observer called "rifle pits"—forerunners of the trenches that would come to distinguish wars to come, easily defensible and hastily constructed with shovels and sandbags.[41]

In one turnabout, the Satsuma rebels purloined the banner of the 14th Infantry Regiment and waved it mockingly at its former owners. Despite his samurai leanings, Saigō expected his opponents to behave like gentleman—he ordered his field hospitals marked with customary white flags, only for the government troops to raid one of them and butcher the wounded. It was, behind the scenes, not merely the last stand of the samurai, but the first victory of the conscript troops—Saigō's traditional organization had been overcome by trained farm boys and fishermen.[42] Or that, at least, was how the tale would eventually be spun. A media clampdown prevented the newspapers from reporting heavy casualties among the government forces. Foreign observers were less impressed, noting that the government officers were often too timid to commit to large-scale battle, they were usually old-school samurai like Saigō himself, inexperienced in the use of modern weaponry and tactics. With nothing left to lose, and fighting on their home ground, Saigō and his men held out for longer than expected thanks to local support and guerrilla tactics.

But it was all over by September, with Saigō and his last 500 men outnumbered sixty to one by the government forces. Wounded, Saigō was beheaded by one of his lieutenants in a *seppuku* ceremony, true to the last to his samurai beliefs.

Saigō's failed rebellion made him one of Japanese history's great underdogs. He never had to compromise; never had to come up with a solution to save lives instead of wasting them. He had fought his way into the new order, thrown his weight around when his attitude and beliefs were no longer fit for purpose, and plotted to start a distracting war with Korea. Finally, he had led an insurrection and died for his beliefs,

---

[41] Harries and Harries, *Soldiers of the Sun*, p. 31.
[42] Calman, *The Nature and Origins of Japanese Imperialism*, p. 175. It should be noted that the best reference Calman can find for this is the work of a historical novelist, Shiba Ryōtarō.

which were already disregarded by a state intent on putting the days of the samurai behind it.

But Saigō still had allies and supporters, seven of whom would murder the statesman Ōkubo Toshimichi in 1878, in reprisal for "betraying" his Satsuma countrymen by ordering the suppression of the rebellion. Saigō's younger brother, Tsugumichi, went on to lead the life that Saigō could have had as a more pragmatic member of the establishment, becoming a cabinet minister, admiral and eventually a Marquis. It is thanks, in part, to the continued presence of Satsuma men in the Japanese government that Saigō's insurrection came to be regarded with a degree of sheepish embarrassment, as if, for all his faults and his useful idiocy, he had been the only man to cling to his beliefs. Folk legends persisted that he had somehow escaped his enemies and was in hiding, plotting his revenge, or that he had been raised to the heavens, appearing as a comet in the year of his death—albeit, somewhat inconveniently, a month before he actually died.[43]

The Emperor Meiji tried to draw a line under the seditious leanings of some of those in his service. Meaningfully, in 1879, he changed the name of the "Tokyo Shrine to Summon the Spirits" to the "Shrine to Quiet the State" (*Yasukuni Jinja*). Like many of the other classical Chinese allusions in 19th-century Japanese politics, this reference tends to be cited out of context, without much consideration of the original being quoted. In the original Chinese, the term is found in an official's defense of his decision to put a soldier into a government position:

> I have done it to secure the **quiet of the State**. When you have men who have rendered great service, and you do not give them the noblest offices, are they likely to remain quiet? There are few who can do so.[44]

The Emperor and his advisers would continue to dismantle the foundations of the old samurai order, and to carefully mark out expectations for soldierly conduct. The 1882 *Imperial Rescript to Soldiers and Sailors* began with a long pre-amble in which the Emperor recited a potted history of martial matters in Japan, beginning with the legendary Emperor

---

[43] Ravina, *The Last Samurai*, loc. 188.

[44] The comment is made in the *Zuo Zhuan* (23rd year of Duke Xi: 637 BCE) by an official who appointed a loyal soldier as a chief minister. In Chinese: *jing guo*.

Jinmu, who had personally led his men to put down opponents of the throne. The samurai were blamed for 700 years of "politicking," which was now apparently cured by the restoration of true tradition, which meant that all men were able to fight for their Emperor, not merely a privileged few. And it was a privilege, since the multi-part decree, which all military personnel were obliged to memorize, began with an announcement that service to the nation was a righteous way to repay one's debt to the state for being born in it in the first place.

> As it is the military that defends a nation and maintains state power, bear in mind that the strength of the military determines the fortune of the nation. Instead of getting confused by the public opinions or meddling in politics, simply offer the nation your allegiance, and be prepared for a duty that is heavier than a mountain and a death that is lighter than a feather.

The *Rescript* informed all soldiers to respect rank and seniority (senior officers at the time, of course, usually being members of the Satsuma and Chōshū cliques), and instructed them to regard the order of any superior officer as a direct command from the Emperor himself. "There is a difference," it warns, "between foolhardiness and courage. Hot-blooded violence is not bravery. A serviceman must always know his duty, maintain his courage, and consider matters prudently. True courage may be found in devotion to military duty, without despising weak enemies, or fearing strong ones."

As a blueprint for military protocol, it was a wonderfully clear document. In Japan's battles and intrigues over the next sixty years, it would be repeatedly ignored.

A soldier's life, for many a mid-19th century samurai, had been one of relative idleness, devoted to one-on-one training in the martial arts. Histories of warfare tend to concentrate on the battles won and lost, and dramatic tales of bravery. They tend not to pay attention to the dull, humdrum realities of everyday life for soldiers—exercises, training drills, endless practice. There was, observed the French military attachés, an awful lot of kendō practice, pomp, ceremony and staged mock battles, but very little practical experience of how it might feel to be on a twenty-mile route-march or confronted by an enemy like Saigō, who refused to play by the rules of a war game.

But even here, there were politics. The Japanese were still debating how best to sample European knowledge, and a faction behind the scenes was pushing a different country as the best example. For a decade, the Japanese had been leaning on the advice of French military experts, but as the Iwakura Mission had returned home to report, France might have once been the nation of Napoleon, but that was far in the past. Why was Japan taking advice from French soldiers, when French soldiers had been the losers in the Franco-Prussian War of 1870?

Clearly, Japan had hitched itself to the wrong wagon—leading to the dismissal of the French advisers in 1880, and a sudden love for all things German: a heftier concentration on a General Staff, better able to manage longer-term planning in place of the relatively local focus of the French tacticians.[45] The leading influencer on Army development in the decade that followed was Jakob Meckel (1842–1906), a Prussian military adviser brought in to reorganize the Japanese Army.

Meckel was a salesman for authoritarian government—his native Prussia had, after all, originally began as the lands of the military order of the Teutonic Knights before merging with Germany, and the old samurai guard were eager to agree with his suggestions for total obedience to the Emperor.

Meckel was also a big-picture guy, keen to encourage the Japanese to consider large-scale operations. For years, the Japanese had pursued a samurai-era obstructionism, fearful of introducing any new measures that might make it easier for an invader to get around. Meckel turned this idea on its head, insisting that Japanese domestic transport networks allow swift and efficient connection of strategic points—by 1891, all military installations were linked by rail. If there were ever an event like the Satsuma Rebellion again, domestic forces could rush to deal with it. Prussian troops were trained in repeated war games, military exercises that Meckel encouraged the Japanese to try. It was hence under his tutelage that the Army staged an elaborate three-day exercise in 1890, based on the premise that a foreign power had blockaded Japan's coastline and landed an invasion force in Nagoya, which had to be contained while Japanese reinforcements arrived to bolster a counter-attack. One lesson learned was the crucial contribution of rail transport—a division that had marched overland from Osaka was left with feet so swollen that they

---

[45] Harries and Harries, *Soldiers of the Sun*, pp. 33–4.

had to switch their boots for sandals.[46]

On Meckel's advice, Japanese soldiers were no longer billeted in long-term barracks like a super-police force to keep order. Instead, they were organized into divisions that could be redeployed—effectively, Meckel's reforms switched the Army from an essentially defensive or constabulary role to an offensive one.[47]

Meckel's *tactical* experience, however, was less beneficial to the Japanese. He was a veteran of the Franco-Prussian War, which meant his experience of direct military technology was already over a decade out of date. His emphasis on an authoritarian state, fielding an army that unquestioningly followed orders, carried at the sharp end the concept of soldiers fearlessly advancing on enemy positions in a column, the sheer weight of numbers allowing for victory despite a high loss of life. This emphasis on the importance and disposability of infantry, in an age of ever-increasing rate-of-fire for defenders' small-arms, would waste many Japanese lives in future wars.[48]

As lawyers drafted Japan's new constitution, the Emperor's role as commander-in-chief was circumscribed—although, yes, he was the leader of the Japanese military, his responsibilities were at least constitutionally limited to issuing approved commands, and determining the size and budgets of the military. Just as civilians could not be trusted to command military forces in the field, the Emperor could not be expected to make strategic or tactical decisions without expert advice. The Army Minister and Navy Minister, posts created in 1872 as part of the general military reforms, could continue to advise him in his cabinet, but he now also received the attentions of a Chief of Staff, outside of cabinet protocols, who would offer advice and report to him directly on military matters, regardless of the political party in power, or faction dominating in the cabinet.[49]

As part of the general proclamation of the Meiji Constitution in 1889, the late Saigō Takamori was pardoned for his actions, and lauded as the "last true samurai." Later the same year, a statue of him was

---

[46] Lone, *Provincial Life and the Military in Imperial Japan*, pp. 18, 20–21.

[47] Lone, *Japan's First Modern War*, p. 21.

[48] Harries and Harries, *Soldiers of the Sun*, p. 50.

[49] The Army Minister was sometimes referred to as the War Minister—it was not until the 1890s that the Navy began to emerge from under the Army's shadow, ceasing to be subordinate to it.

unveiled in Ueno Park, the site of his famous victory, although in a sop to his enemies, it depicted him not in uniform but in civilian dress with a hunting dog at his side. Or at least, it was supposed to depict him—nobody was sure any more what he looked like. Having shunned all photography during his lifetime as an unwelcome foreign imposition, there were no surviving images of Saigō, and his appearance was guessed at by artists who created a collage based on images of his closest relatives.

An editorial in *Taiyō* magazine warned of the dangerous precedent in honoring such a man in such a prominent public fashion, more likely to weasel its way into the public consciousness than "ten volumes of historical biography":

> But honestly speaking, we feel that the building of a statue for him in Ueno Park is an immoral act. Our private opinions aside, it is a historical fact that his life ended with an act of treason… Ueno Park is one of the finest and largest parks in the empire. If a statue is to be built in such a location, it ought to depict a person worth of veneration…[50]

After all, Saigō had not died in the service of the state, which was why his spirit was not to be worshipped at the Yasukuni Shrine. Surely, some suggested, the state should be venerating those men who were loyal soldiers to the Emperor—men like Japan's Army Chief of Staff, Yamagata Aritomo (Chōshū), who was so loyal he was about to rig an election in the name of national security.

[50] Saaler, *Men in Metal*, p. 148.

Japan's Closest Neighbors (1871-95)

Beijing

Tianjin

Dalian
(Port Arthur)

Pyongyang

KOREA

Seoul

Incheon

Busan

CHINA

JAPAN

Kagoshi

Shanghai

Okinawa

Ryūkyū Islands

Amoy

Taiwan

Tainan

200 km

CHAPTER 2

A Dagger to the Heart

Jakob Meckel, the Prussian military adviser, described Korea as a "dagger pointed at the heart of Japan"—a marshaling point for a potential invasion force, tantalizingly close to Japanese territory.[1] It had, after all, been the location of the Mongol invasion fleet in the Middle Ages, that had only been defeated by suicidal on-shore resistance by the samurai, and by the legendary Kamikaze, "Divine Winds" that had destroyed the invading fleets in catastrophic storms.

Yamagata Aritomo, Army Chief of Staff for much of the 1880s, and the man who had urged the Emperor to release the *Imperial Rescript to Soldiers and Sailors*, argued that Japan had a "cordon of interest" in East Asia, and a "cordon of sovereignty" and needed to secure both these outer and inner zones before Russian plans to complete a Trans-Siberian Railway reached fruition. A stronger Russia connection to East Asia was sure to inspire a stronger Chinese militarization, which would mean increased Chinese attentions to Korea, and the possibility that China would form an alliance with another foreign power in order to counteract the influence of Russia. In the ensuing scramble for power and influence, the resources and territories of East Asia would become hotly contested, like "a pile of meat among tigers."[2] A stable Korea was hence crucial to Japan's national security. In order to deal with Chinese and Russian influence on the peninsula, Japan would ultimately fight two wars.

Korea was in a remarkably similar position to Japan. It, too, had a young monarch, King Gojong (1852–1919)—so young, in fact, that when as a teenager in 1873 he asserted his right to rule in his own name, he had already been king for eight years. He had, until that point, been

---

[1] Harries and Harries, *Soldiers of the Sun*, p. 49.
[2] Duus, *The Abacus and the Sword*, p. 64. The memo was dated 1890. I shuffle it a little out of chronology here.

represented by his father, Prince Heungseong (1820–1898), usually mentioned in historical sources as the *Daewongun* ("Grand Archduke"). Things were tense between the two—the Daewongun was resentful for being ousted from power; his son was ever wary that his father might stage a comeback. Japan, China and also Russia would merrily exploit the conflict both between father and son, and also their in-laws, the powerful Min clan, which had provided King Gojong with his influential pro-Chinese wife, Queen Min (1851–1895). Conflict soon ensued within the Korean court between these factions, which were broadly divided into pro-Chinese traditionalists, and reformers favoring aid from either Russia or Japan.

By 1881, Japan was actively courting Korean reformers, hosting a Korean research mission for four months in order to demonstrate the achievements of modern Japan. Japan's military attaché, Horimoto Reizō, was invited to train a new elite Korean force with modern weapons and tactics, but this Special Skills Force (*byeolgigun*) soon caused problems of its own.

The old Korean military was under-funded and often unpaid. As part of the further cut-backs brought in to make space for the hundred-man Special Skills Force, a thousand older soldiers were discharged, many of them still waiting for over a year for their back-pay. The rest of the Korean army resented the Special Skills Force for its better treatment and new equipment, particularly since it did not take a master strategist to see that it was incubating the officers of the future Korean army—aristocratic, privileged and above all, pro-Japanese.

The situation blew up in July 1882, when King Gojong ordered for the discharged soldiers to receive a month's pay. This itself was nowhere near what they were owed, but the real problem was that the soldiers were supposed to be paid in rice. The Min family, members of which were in charge of finances, left payment in the hands of a corrupt official who sold off best supplies and paid the soldiers with inferior rice that had been cut with millet, sand and bran. Fermenting in the summer heat, the mixture was soon inedible, leading the soldiers to riot. Joined by disaffected members of the public, the mob attacked members of the Min family, targeted Japanese businesses and residents, and began a search for Queen Min, presumed to be the mastermind of all her family's intrigues and corruption. Lieutenant Horimoto, leader of the Special Skills Force, was ambushed in his home and slowly murdered by a group of men taking turns to stab him. At the Japanese Legation, diplomat Hanabusa Yoshimoto ordered his staff to burn their documents and set fire to the building in order to cover their escape.

Hanabusa and his men fled downriver from Seoul, briefly holing up in Incheon before having to run again, in a rainstorm, chased through the streets by Korean soldiers. Six Japanese were killed in the street-to-street fighting, before the survivors commandeered a boat and fled out to sea. Three days later, they were picked up by a British survey ship, which brought them home to Japan.[3]

Hanabusa returned the following month, backed by four warships—the entire Japanese Navy at the time. In his absence, the Daewongun had retaken control, restored to power on the grounds that he, alone, stood against King Gojong and the hated Min clan. Hanabusa demanded half a million yen in compensation for the burning of the legation (which he himself had set alight), and threatened war if his demands were not met.

Queen Min, however, had other ideas, leaning on King Gojong to ask for help from China. Li Hongzhang, the Viceroy of Zhili, sent three warships from Tianjin, along with 4,000 soldiers in transport vessels, leading to a new stand-off between China, there to protect its vassal state, and Japan, there to protect a supposedly independent Korea. Amid the deadlock, officers from the Chinese navy kidnapped the Daewongun, locking him inside his palanquin and not letting him out until the ship reached Tianjin. He would remain under house arrest in Beijing for the next three years, leaving his son King Gojong, as well as the Min in-laws back in charge in Korea, bolstered with Japanese assistance. The resultant Treaty of Chemulpo saw Korea agreeing to pay damages to the victims of the insurrection, the half-million for the legation, as well as Japan's expenses for the costs of the return expedition—the money was such a huge proportion of Korea's annual budget that it would have to be paid in five annual installments. In recognition of the possibility of another uprising, Japan was granted the right to protect its Korean legation with "a few" soldiers.

However, despite the concessions made to Japan, Gojong and the Min family remained a pro-Chinese government. Incensed at Japan's "cunning tricks" (the actual words used in a Chinese communiqué) China replaced the ill-fated Lieutenant Horimoto with its own officers,

---

[3] Keene, *Emperor of Japan*, pp. 373–4.

placed a German official in charge of Korean customs tariffs, and awarded itself special trading concessions and extraterritorial rights in Korea even better than those enjoyed by the Japanese.

Korea would not officially become a battleground between China and Japan for another decade, but the factors were all in place by 1882, including a little-mentioned sidebar to the incident. The *Gen'yōsha* (Dark Ocean Society), had started off as a group agitating for the return of samurai rights and respect in the style of Saigō Takamori. With samurai nostalgia out of favor after the Satsuma Rebellion, it pivoted briefly to become an advocate for "Freedom and People's Rights." By 1881, it had switched allegiance again, proclaiming itself to be a nationalist organization, "honoring the Emperor and respecting the Empire." In fact, its interests were tied intimately to carrying "empire" to mainland Asia, where some of its founders already had developing business interests, and embracing a far more belligerent interest in Japanese expansionism. In this capacity, frustrated with what they regarded as a "lackluster" response by the Japanese military, a group from the Gen'yōsha society formed an armed task force, hijacked a steamship and set out for Korea. This venture, reminiscent of Saigō Takamori's old plans to provoke conflict in Korea, only fizzled out because the 1882 incident had been settled by the time the would-be private army arrived.[4]

Much as Japan had been torn by conservative Shōgun and reformist Restoration forces, Korea was now in contention between a traditionalist pro-China lobby and a modernist pro-Japan lobby. By 1884, Japan had "forgiven" the remaining indemnity payments owed by Korea, replacing them with loans to the independence faction and backing a pro-Japanese Korean newspaper.

King Gojong's love of China was waning, particularly after 1885, when he was forced to let Beijing handle Korea's foreign policy. Caught between Japan and China, he sought help from Russia—a scheme quickly suspended when China warningly sent the Daewongun home from his Beijing exile.

Japan had been outgunned by the Chinese. Even with the inefficiency

---

[4] Iguchi, "Gen'yōsha Nationalism," p. 91. The name derived from the *Genkai Nada* ("Dark Open Sea") that separated Korea from Japan. Its successor, the Black Dragon Society, in 1901 when Korea was effectively won, was similarly named for a geopolitical feature, the Black Dragon River (*Heilong Jiang*) that marked the border between Manchuria and Russia, also known as the Amur River.

of its military organization, which remained fragmented and inefficient on account of the Manchus' fear of facing a revolt from their own troops, China still had thousands more troops at its disposal than Japan. By 1886, the Japanese Army's China expert, Ogawa Masaji, had drawn up a plan for war with China, to commence within five years, aimed at carving China into multiple sectors under Japanese influence, thereby dismembering the empire of the Manchus and protecting Japan from a united Chinese threat. It was, however, little more than an ill-conceived war game, failing to recognize the likelihood of foreign intervention or local resistance.[5]

The Chinese were keen to demonstrate their power. In August 1886, Admiral Ding Ruchang, commander of China's northern fleet, arrived in Japanese waters on a "goodwill" cruise intended to show off his latest acquisitions, the massive German-built warships *Dingyuan* and *Zhenyuan* (the Decider and the Suppressor). Each was twice the size of anything the Japanese could put in the water—heavily armored, lumbering fortresses with guns so huge that the noise in early tests had blown out their own portholes. Ding hoped that the sight of his ships would persuade the Japanese to avoid any conflict in the first place, although his plans backfired in Nagasaki.

Ding's problem was not his ships, but his sailors, several hundred of whom swarmed ashore on Friday 13th. Inevitably, there were scuffles, and a Japanese policeman was attacked with a sword after he tried to arrest five men who had been accused of smashing furniture in a brothel.

Although there were apologies all round, Ding allowed another 400 sailors ashore two days later, whereupon several got into an altercation after they were caught urinating on a police box. Although the sailors had disembarked unarmed, they were soon equipped with makeshift weapons—it was implied, by friends within Nagasaki's Chinese community—turning them into a fighting force twice the size of Nagasaki's entire police complement. By Monday morning, two policemen and five sailors were dead, with many others injured, after both the sailors and police brought countrymen as reinforcements to the street-fight.

This "Nagasaki Incident" sufficiently spooked the Japanese—fake news in the local press implied that the Chinese had arrived to recapture the Ryūkyū islands, and the mere sight of the two huge vessels

---

[5] Duus, *The Abacus and the Sword*, p. 63.

made China appear to be a foe to be taken seriously. Wrangles over the blame, delayed by foreign lawyers on lucrative day-rates, would stretch into the following year, and it would prove to be merely the most visible manifestation of a decade of petty antagonisms, lynchings and assaults, perpetrated by the Chinese and Japanese upon each other in port towns in both nations, in a long undercurrent of mutual antagonism. The ultranationalist Gen'yōsha society, in particular, was infuriated by the "insult" that the Chinese had delivered against Japan, instigating multiple retaliatory actions in its wake.[6]

Yamagata Aritomo served as Home Minister for the five years leading up to the proclamation of the Meiji Constitution in 1890. For the year preceding the Constitution, and the democratically elected government it brought with it, he introduced a number of new domestic policies. Discipline was tightened up in the police force; local officials were urged to think of themselves not as servants of the people, but conscripts appointed to government service. Even as the *Imperial Rescript to Soldiers and Sailors* had forbidden the military from meddling in politics, Yamagata's reforms attempted to impose a similar restriction on many other figures in public life, including schoolteachers and students.

To hear Yamagata talk about the Meiji Constitution, you could be forgiven for thinking it was some kind of liberal free-for-all. In fact, the right to vote in 1890 only extended to five per cent of the population—adult males who met a certain level of property qualification. Regardless, wary of the influence of elected officials, Yamagata enacted policies that ran counter to the very idea of democracy and liberalism. "Foreign ideas" were not to be discussed, even though the very concept of the new Constitution was itself a foreign idea—not that you would know it, as its wording clung as closely as possible to ancient forerunners. The new laws were not to be debated. In 1887, a Peace Preservation Ordinance

---

[6] Cassel, *Grounds of Judgement*, loc. 3019–26. Ding would return on another cruise in 1891, but did not allow any sailors ashore. His attempts to impress also backfired, as a young Tōgō Heihachirō got a closer look at his ships, and adjudged that poor discipline and maintenance would defeat them before the Japanese Navy ever got in firing range. See Clements, *Admiral Tōgō*, pp. 76–8. For the Gen'yōsha involvement, see Norman, "The Genyosha," p. 276.

made it illegal to form a secret society or assembly.[7]

By 1889, Yamagata became Prime Minister in addition to Home Minister, demanding money for military appropriations from a parliament with a liberal majority that wanted to curtail military expansion. Yamagata's message to the people of Japan was that even as they were offered their own parliament and limited suffrage, it would still be business as usual. Yamagata's actions gave him the ability to shut down suspicious schools like those that had harbored Saigō Takamori's rebels, to arrest and interrogate anyone holding the sort of meeting that had led to the Meiji Restoration in the first place. For anyone planning to found a political party or society, Yamagata's reforms all but encouraged them to double down on secrecy or sedition.

Some secret societies, however, existed with the collusion of the military and police. The Gen'yōsha, for example, strongly agreed with Yamagata that there had been a failure in popular democracy—or rather, a failure of the Meiji Restoration to deliver the kind of Japan that the Gen'yōsha activists wanted. As some of its own pamphlets argued:

> Once the Constitution was promulgated and the Diet [Parliament] established, the popular rights parties failed to realize that the state was being surrounded on all sides by formidable enemies, and increasingly looked down upon by foreigners. They remained absorbed in futile debate. Thus, the Gen'yōsha cast away the theory of popular rights like a worn-out pair of sandals. This time it decided to rely on a statist doctrine, and strove to fend of foreign enemies by preparing the country for military action and strengthening its army.[8]

In fact, the "statist" doctrine, based on the Prussian model in which the entire nation formed a loyal workforce directed at preparations for war, was exactly what Yamagata was hoping for. But like the "loyalists" of the Meiji Restoration, who could not agree what principle they were supposed to be loyal to, the Gen'yōsha embraced the idea that they would need to interfere in politics in order to create the state they wished to be loyal to. They would set aside the performance of democracy, and

---

[7] Harries and Harries, *Soldiers of the Sun*, p. 39.
[8] Joos, "The Gen'yōsha (1881) and Premodern Roots of Japanese Expansionism," p. 65.

pursue a more underhand agenda—Gen'yōsha activists, admitted or suspected, were implicated in many of the intimidations and assassinations that would come to infest Japanese politics over the next twenty years.

The Gen'yōsha, and its successor organization the Black Dragon Society (*Kōryūkai*), managed to dig up military theorists from decades earlier, suggesting that Japan was destined to lead the world, starting with easy pickings such as Korea and Manchuria, the two closest mainland territories, as well as Kamchatka, north of the Kurile Islands, and the Ryūkyū Islands to the south, now already in Japanese hands. Using inflammatory and frankly medieval language, one of the Gen'yōsha's founders spoke of restoring Japan's ancient Mimana protectorate in Korea, seizing the mouth of the River Yangtze and Hong Kong. The Koreans, apparently, were to be used as frontline troops in further Japanese expansion:

> ...we shall thus subdue that unruly bunch, chasing them as falcons chase sparrows—straddling huge warships, we shall trample the hordes of barbarians, we shall overturn the present world order and turn the "resplendent center" [China] into vile barbarians. We shall bring down Heaven and put Earth at the top, we shall punish and kill in every region.[9]

In 1889, Gen'yōsha terrorists grievously wounded the Japanese statesman Ōkuma Shigenobu, who was then attempting to renegotiate Japan's Unequal Treaties with the foreign powers. The bomb attack on Ōkuma caused him to lose a leg, although he put on a chillingly brave face while he was recovering.

"I am glad I was injured by a progressive Western invention," he quipped, "and not a sword or some old-fashioned device."[10]

It was believed (wrongly, as it transpired), that the injury spelled the end of the 51-year-old Ōkuma's career. He did, for a while, announce his retirement, propelling his American assistant of the previous fifteen years to seek employment elsewhere. The 60-year-old Charles Le Gendre, architect of Japan's earliest imperialist adventures, consequently left Japan for Korea, where he would spend the last nine years of his life

---

[9] Joos, "The Gen'yōsha (1881) and Premodern Roots of Japanese Expansionism," p. 68.
[10] Oka, *Five Political Leaders of Modern Japan*, p. 33.

offering what was presumably the world's worst advice to his new master, King Gojong.

Japanese extremists, albeit with no known affiliation, also got the blame for an embarrassing incident that may have steered Russo-Japanese relations forever into enmity. In 1891, Prince Nicholas, heir to the Russian throne, arrived in Nagasaki with his cousin, Prince George of Greece, arrived in Nagasaki, where they charmed the local dignitaries by day and chased prostitutes at night. Nicholas got a dragon tattoo, and travelled onward to Kagoshima in what was once Satsuma, where the traditionally-minded local ruler put on a show of samurai martial prowess and archery. Their entourage steamed across the Inland Sea to Kobe, and then up towards Kyōto, the former imperial capital. But amid breathless reports of the affinity felt by the young prince for the similarly-aged Meiji Emperor, and the chances for international friendship, there was an attempt on the prince's life in the lakeside resort of Ōtsu, near Kyōto. One of the police bodyguards drew his own sword and attacked Nicholas, only thwarted by the intervention of George and some rickshaw coolies. The incident left the prince shaken, and sporting a scar on the right of his face that would be with him for the rest of his life.

The motives of the would-be assassin, Tsuda Sanzō, were never clear. He claimed in his trial that he had felt ashamed, reduced from his former samurai status to that of a lowly policeman, playing bodyguard to a couple of foreigners who failed to show the correct degree of respect when viewing a monument to the fallen of the Satsuma Rebellion. There were speculations in the press that he had deeper motives—anger over the Russian acquisition of Sakhalin island from Japan, or fear that Nicholas would be the instigator of a future war against Japan.

Regardless, it was an incident of national shame and widespread performances of grief and contrition, including a letter-writing campaign of apology, and even a woman who committed suicide in atonement. It was an embarrassment to the Japanese nation, rumored to have ever after left Nicholas nursing a quiet hatred of the Japanese. For years to come, the date of the "Ōtsu Incident" was marked in the calendar of the Russian Navy, as if it were an insult that would one day demand revenge.[11]

Tsuda was sentenced to life imprisonment—the death penalty for attacking royalty having been adjudged to only apply to the *Japanese*

---

[11] Keene, *Emperor of Japan*, pp. 447–57.

variety. But he was dead anyway, within the year, having suspiciously succumbed to "pneumonia" in a Hokkaidō jail.

As for Nicholas, he went on to Vladivostok, where he participated in the grand ceremony to break ground on a railway that would ultimately stretch all the way across Asia, back to Moscow. Just as American sea power had once brought it within ten days of Japan's coast, Russia was now on the verge of an engineering project that would make it much easier for Russia to pursue a war in the Far East.

The commencement of work on what would become the Trans-Siberian Railway animated the Japanese Army like no other issue. Russia was liable to take an interest in Korea, not only in terms of maintaining political stability in the region, but in search of trading concessions and a warm-water port—Vladivostok remained ice-bound for several months a year.

The tone of martial exuberance in Japan had reached a new height (albeit a height that would soon be surpassed). "Myriad Enemies" (1891, *Teki wa Ikuman*), a preposterously gung-ho anthem, would set the tone at military events for decades to come.

> Tens of thousands of enemies may come
> But they are merely a rabble like so many crows
> But even if they are not like crows
> Absolute justice is sure to prevail.
> Wrong cannot defeat Right
> The Straight shall conquer Crooked
> The honorable heart is unbending
> Just like an arrow piercing a stone
> Just like an arrow piercing a stone
> What is there for us to fear?[12]

Later verses go on to boast that greater glories await those whose Rising Sun banners are torn by enemy fire, and exhort the fighting men of Japan to advance, even unto their deaths in battle.

---

[12] Osada, *Sensō ga Nokoshita Uta*, p. 26. An arrow piercing a stone is a reference to the Chinese Han-dynasty general Li Guang, who not only is supposed to have performed such a feat, but committed suicide after failing to be allowed to acquit himself on the battlefield. The song used lyrics written in 1886, but not set to music until 1891.

If you are routed, it will disgrace our country
Dying in the advance is the honorable thing to do
Rather than endure as a roof tile
Be **shattered like a jewel**
Dying on a mat [i.e. at home] is not the way of the warrior
Trampled by horseshoes, your body left on the battlefield
Only then will the people of the world will speak of your honor.

The words were a startling return to the stoic, suicidal heroism characterized by Saigō Takamori in the Satsuma Rebellion. Although Saigō had failed in his venture, his desire to be a "shattered jewel" (*gyokusai*) was referenced in countless performances of the song over the next fifty years.

It should come as no surprise that societies like the Gen'yōsha, and supposed "lone wolves" like Tsuda turned underground, and enjoyed a tacit reciprocity with the military and its allies in government. From the very outset, Japanese democracy was a dirty conflict between the military and the wider population. Military influence on education was already underway, billeting student-teachers in barracks and drilling them like soldiers. The new education system was aimed at producing a "nation-at-arms" mindset by the time the current generation of elementary schoolchildren reached adulthood around 1900. But there still remained the men of their parents' generation, expectant of democratic rights and influence, just about to vote in the 1892 general election.

Now out of office but still heavily influential through his Army connections, Yamagata Aritomo feared that the voters would return a government that did not see things as the military did—a deluded, liberal-leaning Diet that would refuse to approve budget hikes that the military deemed to be absolutely necessary. He was, in his own mind, already in the preamble to a foreign war to secure Japan's security, and prepared to do anything in order to keep the upper hand.

The 1892 election was the most troubled in Japanese political history. Military sympathizers within the government tried to purge provincial offices of anyone with unwelcome party connections, arresting several dozen on trumped-up charges, and thereby depriving them of the chance to campaign. Armed toughs (from the Gen'yōsha, among others) were sent to intimidate candidates at their homes, and to dissuade voters from making the "wrong" decision at voting booths, particularly in those districts where liberal parties had already shown strong support. They did so with the tacit cooperation of the police, who allowed the non-uniformed, unidentified toughs to start trouble, and then could be counted upon to arrive and arrest only the enemies of the Gen'yōsha.[13] The resistance was strongest in areas associated with the prime movers in the Meiji Restoration—voting was not even possible in some parts of Saga (formerly Hizen), while the ballot boxes went missing in Kōchi (formerly Tosa). Court action was required to overturn victories based on misreported counts; a judge had to overturn a victory based on fake votes in Toyama.

Despite all these subterfuges, including one candidate losing by only six votes, having been detained on false charges and unable to campaign in his district, the election still returned a liberal majority, including 130 Diet members who had been accused by the authorities of being "extremists." As Yamagata had feared, many of the new politicians were reluctant to approve higher military budgets.

Meanwhile, the stand-off in Korea, between the pro-China traditionalists and the pro-Japan modernists, began to escalate. But Japanese factions were playing both sides. In the provinces, local officials had to contend with the Eastern Learning (*donghak*) sect, an organization proclaiming itself to be traditionalists, promoting a return to old-school values, before the days of the hated, modern Western Learning (*seohak*).

"Others," wrote the Japanese Foreign Minister Mutsu Munemitsu, "have seen them merely as a lawless gang spoiling for a fight."[14]

With no sense of irony whatsoever, the *donghak* agitators were backed by Japanese ultranationalists, promoting a sense of traditionalism redolent of the Satsuma Rebellion, but in such a fashion that was sure to drive the Korean government further into the arms of the Japanese.

The *donghak* rebels had multiple concerns, many of them born from simple poverty and deprivation, or from the disruption caused by unwanted modern projects, such as compulsory labor on dam-building and new public works. In echoes of the rhetoric of the Meiji Restoration, they petitioned the Korean king to demand the execution of corrupt officials, the expulsion of foreigners (including the Japanese), and the removal from power of the influential Min family. They did so, again like the Meiji revolutionaries, while proclaiming their "loyalty" not only

---

[13] Calman, *The Nature and Origin of Japanese Imperialism*, p. 8; Norman, "The Genyosha," p. 277.

[14] Berger, *Kenkenroku*, p. 5.

to a ruler who was misguided, but to their ancestors, whose traditions were under threat.

Sure enough, after a *donghak* "peasant army" began raiding and robbing provincial officials and landlords, King Gojong instituted a crackdown, appealing to the Chinese for help. The prospect of an increased Chinese troop presence in Korea allowed the Japanese, under the terms of the Treaty of Ganghwa, to send a "matching" force. Even though the *donghak* rebels had been put down by the time the forces arrived, neither side was ready to leave. The stand-off between traditionalists and modernists now escalated into two foreign military presences. The Japanese, in fact, would have sent even more troops initially if Yamagata had got his way. Mindful of the stand-offs in earlier Korean crises, Yamagata thought it best if the Army fielded overwhelming forces from the very start, in order to secure Seoul and the ear of the King. He was over-ruled, however, by the Navy Minister Yamamoto Gonnohyōe, who reminded him that the Army could not move to Korea without the Navy, and the Navy was unprepared to move so many troops that it might attract foreign attention and a foreign intervention.[15]

The Western powers, in fact, were broadly in agreement that while Japan's methods were often devious and brutal, wresting control from the Chinese would ultimately be the best possible thing for Korea. Even though the editorials of the British-owned *North-China Herald* had no qualms about calling out Japan for manufacturing the war under a pretext, it was ready to suggest that the ends justified the means:

> [There] can be little question that it would be much better for the Coreans [sic] if their country came under Japanese control. China does nothing to mitigate the intolerable misgovernment and oppression under which, as every traveller and writer tells us, the whole country groans and travails.[16]

The Japanese demanded that King Gojong take steps to reform his failing state, proposing huge fixes to the Korean police, military, education system, judiciary and taxation, all based on Japan's own modernist model, and requiring extensive Japanese investment. Such "investment"

---

[15] Duus, *The Abacus and the Sword*, p. 178.
[16] Kim, "The Sino-Japanese War," p. 9.

was already underway—when representatives of Korea's modernist faction travelled to Tokyo to discuss possible direction for reform, the Japanese government paid all their expenses.

China refused to allow such meddling, but Japan was already taking steps.

The Japanese Foreign Minister, Mutsu Munemitsu, hoping to rally the Japanese people into a nationwide distraction from politics and economic depression, doubled down on the military presence in Korea, advising his ministerial representative in Korea that the time had come to manufacture an excuse for war.

"You will commence active movement on some pretext," he wrote in July 1894, "taking care to do what is least liable to criticism in the eyes of the world."[17]

Mutsu himself was the middle man in an elaborate deception. He had neglected to tell the Prime Minister, Itō Hirobumi (again), that the *donghak* threat had already been dispelled. He also carefully worded his communications with Itō to conceal the fact that he was sending not a brigade of 2,000 men, but a "mixed brigade" of 7,000, which his Army contact, General Kawakami, had determined to be the necessary number of men to seize control. In doing so, he provoked the Chinese, who sent more men to match, with 8,000 reinforcements landing at the Taedong river, ready to march on Pyongyang in mid-June.

Li Hongzhang, the strategist of the Chinese response, regarded the Japanese troop build-up as an idle threat, designed to bluff the Chinese into making concessions in Korea. He consequently called the Japanese bluff by increasing the troop presence even more, commissioning several civilian transports to bring even more reinforcements from further afield.

Even as the troop transports were underway, the Japanese struck at the heart of the Korean government, seizing the royal palace in Seoul, deposing King Gojong, and installing his father-regent, the Daewongun, once again. Two days later, Japanese Navy ships sunk the *Kowshing*, a civilian ship flying the British flag, and with a British captain, commissioned by the Chinese to transport soldiers from Shanghai to Korea.[18]

---

[17] Harries and Harries, *Soldiers of the Sun*, p. 55. See also Lone, *Japan's First Modern War*, p. 25.

[18] I lack the space here to go into detail over the incredibly tense confrontation over the *Kowshing*, although interested readers can read about it further in my *Admiral Tōgō*, pp. 91–101.

The Sino-Japanese War (1894–5)

It was only then, on August 1, with Japanese troops already in Korea for over a month, and a thousand men drowned on the *Kowshing*, that the Meiji Emperor somewhat tardily announced the official declaration of war.[19] The Sino-Japanese War, as it is known in English, was referred to in Japanese as the Japan-Qing War (*nisshin sensō*)—implying that the Japanese were not fighting the people of China themselves, but there to rescue the people of Korea from China's ruling clique, the Qing *dynasty* of Manchus.

Until the Sino-Japanese War, the Japanese Navy had been stuck in a subordinate position, beneath the authority of the Army Minister (whose official designation might also be translated as War Minister). Events in 1894 made it clear just how crucial the Navy was to operations in mainland Asia, curtailing Chinese troop movements, commanding the coastlines of Korea so completely, that the Chinese suffered from severe constriction of their lines of supply, communication and reinforcement. The Japanese Army was able to cross over to Korea in vast numbers,

---

[19] Lone, *Japan's First Modern War*, p. 1.

advance with constant resupply and a secure rear. It faced timid, and often poorly equipped Chinese soldiers, with doubtful levels of allegiance to their Manchu masters, ready to discharge their ammunition, thereby literally discharging their duties, and then flee. With such limited resistance in the initial stages, the Japanese Army's dispatches home amounted to a series of stirring victories, as if the troops were enjoying divine support.

Mutsu was a sharp judge of his people. Before the outbreak of hostilities, the Japanese media seemed indifferent to the prospect of war. Nor were all the Japanese troops necessarily spoiling for a fight. Several soldiers in Hiroshima were shot as deserters after they fled the camp from which they were expecting to embark for Korea. Others seem to have been taken aback by the outbreak of war, believing, like Li Hongzhang, that the whole thing was a bluff.[20]

However, later in the summer, Japan was so overrun with popular organizations and pro-war pressure groups, soliciting donations of money and materials, that the authorities were obliged to issue a public order in August 1894, asking people to return to their regular jobs and leave war to the military. Schools enthusiastically embraced government-sponsored songbooks packed with verses celebrating Japan's early victories and heroes, while a new directive in September changed boys' school uniforms so that they were better suited to exercise routines and military drills. Wooden, reduced-size models of the standard-issue Murata rifle went on sale to help with school ceremonies in imitation of military drills. Newly established youth groups such as the Righteous Corps of Patriots (*Hōkoku Gidan*) were collecting money and organizing recruitment drives for a war with China, even though they had no power or authority to do so. Most importantly for Mutsu, however, they were doing so across party lines, forgetting any liberal or conservative enmity, and uniting behind a new cause.[21] Once the war was actually underway, in a gesture of national solidarity, all of the usual bickering that had characterized the previous few years of party politics was suspended. A cynic might have come out of the Sino-Japanese War thinking that the best way to keep Japan running smoothly was to keep it on a constant war-footing whenever possible.[22]

---

[20] Lone, *Provincial Life and the Military in Imperial Japan*, p. 27–8, 36.

[21] Kim, "The Sino-Japanese War," p. 14.

[22] Oka, *Five Political Leaders of Modern Japan*, p. 28 notes that Itō Hirobumi's experience in wartime politics greatly shook his support of "transcendence politics" and

Newspaper reportage enjoyed a new boom, boosted by embedded correspondents and up-to-date news reaching Japan by telegraph, as well a custom for printing soldiers' letters to their families in local newspapers. Shopkeepers were heard to complain that so many people were staying indoors to catch up on daily "extras" that the war was proving to be a threat to business. Eventually, they began retooling their products to take on a military theme—there was a rise in hairpins shaped like rifles or military sabers, and other products rebranded with a Medal or a Victory in their names.[23] The press enthusiastically reported the war, although there were substantial problems finding something suitably martial to say about so many battles that were routs for the enemy. While the authorities continued to celebrate the generals and the admirals, the press concentrated on the common men who had so famously been ordered to take the place of the samurai in the 1873 conscription notices—the beginning of a new strand of commemoration, favoring the patriot soldier, and forming the basis of the next generation's model Japanese subjects.

A tougher time experienced by the Japanese at Ansong helpfully supplied one of the war's great *causes célèbres*: a young bugler, found dead in the aftermath of the battle with his bugle still pressed to his lips.

The sight was soon celebrated in poems and prose, and became the subject of several songs, full of breathless enthusiasm about the nobility of sacrifice, and failing to note that he had died for nothing. The "Sounding of the Bugle" (*Rappa no Hibiki*) was typical:

> Although the bullet pierced his throat
> Although hot blood filled his windpipe
> He held on to his bugle
> Using a Murata rifle in his left hand as a walking stick
>
> Shattered jewel and shattered body
> Yet his spirit still marches on
> To defeat the enemy.
> Oh, what a courageous bugler.[24]

---

put him on a collision course with his own former allies in the old guard.

[23] Lone, *Provincial Life and the Military in Imperial Japan*, pp. 28, 39.

[24] This song does not appear in Osada. I found it online at http://tensyofleet.sakura.ne.jp/band/midi/rappa.html

Even foreign correspondents were whipped up into fervor about it, with one translating a eulogy about how this brave boy's bugle "drives the dragon screaming / makes the pig-tails yield."[25] Initially identified as the 25-year-old Shirakami Genjirō from Okayama, the man became one of the model heroes incorporated into Japanese textbooks for schools, only for two newspapers to duke it out over his true identity, when it was revealed that the real Shirakami had actually drowned during the assault on Seonghwan, and that the celebrated bugler was more likely to have been Kiguchi Kohei, whose demise more fitted that in the song. Government-approved textbooks would later switch the hero's name.

Although there were complaints that the Navy had been reduced to little more than a transport service to get the Army across the strait to Korea, it had scored the initial victories that made the Army's swift advance possible. Thanks to swift naval action at the start of the war, Korea's ports were in Japanese hands, making it impossible for the Chinese to land reinforcements by sea. Nor was Admiral Ding presenting much of a threat—rightly believing that he would be cashiered or executed for losing ships, even in a victory, he remained timidly out of range, not daring to risk any of his grand vessels.

By mid-September, the Japanese Army had taken Pyongyang, the last defensible strongpoint before the Chinese border at the Yalu River. They did so under the nominal command of Yamagata Aritomo, who had pestered headquarters to send him into the field as a "real" commander. Shortly after the battle, Yamagata fell ill, putting him out of action. The Battle of the Yellow Sea, two days later, was the Navy's next move, sailing into Chinese waters in pursuit of Admiral Ding's fleet.

Korea was effectively secured in Japanese hands, leading to a second-wave advance into Chinese territory, with the notional ultimate objective of Beijing. In October, the Japanese crossed the Yalu River into Manchuria, and made amphibious landings at the ports of Dalian and Port Arthur on the end of the Liaodong peninsula.

Port Arthur and the Liaodong campaign as a whole was the grand exoneration of Nogi Maresuke (1849–1912), a man whose previous claim to fame had been losing his regimental banner to the Satsuma rebels in 1877. He had been so ashamed at his dereliction of duty that he had

---

[25] Kim, "The Sino-Japanese War," p. 16.

only been dissuaded from committing suicide by the order of a superior officer. Reading between the lines, Nogi was a Chōshū man who somehow clung to the promotional ladder out of seniority and connections, and through his willingness to travel abroad in 1887 to Germany, where he had become an enthusiastic student of the sort of Prussian military tactics favored by Jakob Meckel.

Against the Chinese troops, who were disorganized and under-motivated, Meckel's policy of relentless advance paid high dividends. There were heavy casualties among the officers, whom Nogi had ordered to lead from the front, but the Japanese gained swift ground in the face of Chinese infantry who tended to fire off all their ammunition and then run.

The killing did not stop with the fall of Port Arthur. As Japanese soldiers entered the town, they found the corpse of one of their own, impaled on a wooden stake. He had apparently been killed in answer to a decree by the local magistrate, offering bounties on captured Japanese troops, and lesser fees for a head or right hand. This was far from the first example of Chinese atrocities—there had been earlier mutilations reported in Pyongyang, as well as Chinese attacks on Red Cross tents in both Pyongyang and Jinzhou. On this occasion, however, the soldiers were not restrained from reprisals.[26]

"Corpses were still hanging on the trees when the fortress fell," wrote the British seaman James Allan, "and it is not surprising that their former comrades should have been maddened by the sight, though of course the officers are greatly to blame for permitting the fearful retaliation… to be carried to such lengths."[27]

"This filled us with rage and a desire to crush any Chinese soldier," admitted one Japanese participant.

> Anyone we saw in the town, we killed. The streets were filled with corpses, so many they blocked our way. We killed people in their homes; by and large, there wasn't a single house without from three to six dead. Blood was flowing and the smell was awful. We sent out search parties. We shot some, hacked at others.

---

[26] Lone, *Japan's First Modern War*, p. 144. I say this not to excuse Japanese behavior, but to contextualize it.

[27] Allan, *Under the Dragon Flag*, p. 35.

The Chinese troops just dropped their arms and fled. Firing and slashing, it was unbounded joy.[28]

The Port Arthur Massacre was a turning point in accounts of Japanese militarism. Although none dared try to file a report of the events in place, where the Japanese censor might intercept it, within a few weeks, accounts were appearing in the foreign press.

The Japanese press remained silent on the matter or dismissed it, either as fake news drummed up by China-lovers, or as Western hypocrisy. Some even argued it was fitting behavior for a civilized nation. "Our empire," stated the *Gifu Nichinichi* newspaper, "should apply to [the Chinese] the same laws of engagement as are applied to the savages of Africa."[29] However, internationally, the scandal was damaging enough to Japan's diplomatic reputation to warrant official comment from the government. The Japanese Foreign Ministry announced that there would be an enquiry (for which nobody would be punished), and pleaded that Japanese soldiers had been "transported with rage at the mutilation of their comrades," and that the vast bulk of the victims of the massacre had been Chinese soldiers attempting to escape in civilian disguises.

James Creelman of the *New York World*, who was ultimately accused of vastly over-inflating his own report on the number of deaths from hundreds to thousands, nevertheless appears to have had the last word. "It was the first stain upon Japanese civilization. The Japanese in this instance relapsed into barbarism."[30]

Alleged eyewitness accounts also made it clear that this was far from misreporting of the hunting down of deserters and fleeing enemies. James Allan observed Japanese soldiers butchering people, including many women and children in a lake:

[They] had driven large numbers of the fugitives into the water, and were firing on them from every side, and driving back with

---

[28] Lone, *Japan's First Modern War*, p. 155. Lone goes on to note (p. 160) that the Japanese press did report the execution of Chinese not in uniform, but claimed that they were soldiers in disguise.

[29] Lone, *Japan's First Modern War*, p. 144.

[30] Paine, *The Sino-Japanese War of 1894–5*, p. 213. For criticism of Creelman, including the observations made even at the time that Japanese behavior had been little different from that of Americans avenging the defeat of Custer at Wounded Knee, see Dorwart "James Creelman…," p. 700.

the bayonet those who attempted to struggle out. The dead floated on the water, which was reddened with blood. The soldiers, yelling and laughing with vengeful glee, seemed to gloat over the agonies of their victims.[31]

The Port Arthur Massacre risked ruining decades of careful negotiation and development, intended to qualify Japan for a removal of the Unequal Treaties. After news of it broke in America, senators openly questioned whether the Japanese were ready to be admitted to the world of civilized nations.

The war correspondent Francis McCullagh found in the behavior of the Japanese in Manchuria a terrifying portent of things to come.

> I often discover myself muttering, "What terrible fellows these Japs are! What superhuman perseverance! What incredible bravery! How little did I think that the awkward, smooth-faced lads in uniform that I used to so often meet walking hand-in-hand in [Ueno] Park like Dresden shepherdesses, would prove to be such demons for warfare? What can we, any of us… do against a race which fears no more the supreme dolour of death than we fear a shower of rain?[32]

In December 1894, celebrations in Tokyo acted as if the war was already over. Mary Haggard, wife of the Belgian ambassador, wrote in her diary about the party-like atmosphere at Shinobazu Pond in Ueno Park, where high-spirited locals ceremonially sunk a model Chinese warship with toy torpedoes.[33] Children were directly involved in expressions of military matters and morale, sent out to greet troop trains, brought along to military funerals and celebrations, and subjected to many a classroom talk by returning soldiers—militarism began to wheedle its way into the classroom. The Yasukuni Shrine overtook the entertainment districts of Asakusa and Ueno as the first place visited by provincial tourists—some to pray, others to poke around the growing number of trophies from the China war in the shrine's Yūshūkan gallery.[34]

---

[31] Allan, *Under the Dragon Flag*, p. 41.

[32] McCullagh, *With the Cossacks*, p. 234.

[33] d'Anethan, *Fourteen Years of Diplomatic Life in Japan*, loc. 1258.

[34] Lone, *Provincial Life and the Military in Imperial Japan*, pp. 35, 109.

But the Japanese soldiers were still bogged down in Manchuria, writing letters home about a winter so piercing that a cup of water drawn from a well would be frozen before it could be brought indoors, and where continued supply-line difficulties were leaving some soldiers forced to share a single blanket between three.[35]

China, however, was on the defensive. The last of the northern fleet was stuck in the port of Weihaiwei, on which the Japanese were closing from both land and sea. Popular historical memory of the battle over Weihaiwei revolves around the sad fate of Admiral Ding, his great warships the *Dingyuan* and *Zhenyuan* reduced to little more than artillery platforms trapped in the harbor, as the Japanese Army advanced ever closer.

The Japanese media of the time, however, preferred to concentrate on the tale of one Captain Higuchi Seizaburō, who took pity on a lost Chinese infant during the advance on Weihaiwei, and picked it up to keep it safe. He was immortalized in a number of prints doing so, even though "keeping it safe" meant carrying the baby on one arm, like a human shield, while he wielded a sword with the other. The child was said to have been returned to its mother after the attack, although some variants of the Higuchi story suggest that it had been abandoned by one of the Weihaiwei commander's concubines as she fled through Japanese lines. Higuchi subsequently became the subject of many an adoring woodblock print and poster, on the grounds that he was more compassionate to the Chinese than the Chinese themselves.[36]

Itō Hirobumi and Mutsu Munemitsu, the Japanese Prime Minister and Foreign Minister, were obliged to manage the end of the war at a political level. Using a command from the Emperor to "hear about the battles" as his excuse, Itō had his over-eager rival, Yamagata Aritomo, transferred home, ostensibly on the grounds of his continued ill health, but in fact to keep him from marching on Beijing.

Japan had spent two years' worth of its national budget on the war, and could not afford to continue—only the payment of its costs by a defeated China would prevent an economic collapse.[37] Japan could not afford to further agitate any foreign powers—the war had been ostensibly over Korea, and had achieved its objective. There was a very real danger that if the Japanese marched on Beijing, they might take it, leading

---

[35] Lone, *Provincial Life and the Military in Imperial Japan*, p. 29.

[36] Rzadek, "Field Manual of Valor," pp. 136–9.

[37] Kim, "The Sino-Japanese War," p. 20.

to a greater risk of the collapse of the Manchu imperial rule, and chaos in China. Such a victory was sure to be opposed by the foreign powers, since it would risk annulling every treaty signed with the Manchu regime. Japan's advance hence needed to stop right where it was, and even then, it might be a step too far.

The war had been officially about control of Korea, but now found the Japanese also occupying the two strategic peninsulas, Shandong and Liaodong, that guarded the sea-road towards Tianjin. While the Army and Navy had performed well, their successes risked plunging Japan into a wider conflict—already, Russian and German ambassadors had warned Itō that Japan could not hold onto such territory. Mutsu did not need to read between the lines of the increasingly stern diplomatic communiqués; he could even read about it in the foreign press. Korea was fair game, but the London *Times* ran an article reporting that "the European nations were determined to prevent Japan from seizing a single inch of Chinese territory in the peace settlement."[38]

Li Hongzhang was invited to peace talks in Shimonoseki, where Itō and Mutsu hoped to make some sort of deal. Mutsu had previously regarded Chinese negotiators of low rank and little authority, and assumed that they were being sent merely to put on a performance of negotiation. Li, however, was an official of a high-enough rank to actively pursue peace, and possessed of a disarming charm that even seemed to worm its way into Mutsu's good graces. Li observed, as negotiations began, that the war had "fortunately awakened China from her long slumber" and that he hoped that Japan and China, "the two great powers of Asia," might ultimately unite their respective ingenuity and resources in order to hold off further Western incursions.[39]

However, the news that Japan was *negotiating* instead of demanding to keep what it had taken did not sit well with ultranationalists. "The Japanese people as a whole," wrote Mutsu, "had not yet wearied of the war and argued that peace was still premature."[40]

One of them, a university drop-out called Koyama Toyotarō, waited for Li on his way back to his temple lodgings in Shimonoseki, and shot him in the face.

Li survived the attack with bullet lodged in his cheek, and Koyama

---

[38] Berger, *Kenkenroku*, pp. 164–5.
[39] Berger, *Kenkenroku*, pp. 168–9.
[40] Berger, *Kenkenroku*, p. 152.

was bundled away into prison. He would claim in his trial that he had acted because he had wanted the war to continue, but his act was such an embarrassment to the Japanese negotiators that it only made them hasten towards a deal. In fact, Li was ready to agree to all of Japan's demands, and signed the Treaty of Shimonoseki on April 17, only for news to reach Itō that all Russian warships had been placed on 24-hour alert. Ambassadors from Russia, France and Germany all offered ominous and threatening "advice" that even though China had agreed to hand over Liaodong to Japan, Japan should not take it.

This "Triple Intervention" led Japan to the brink of an all-new war, in which the combined fleets of three European powers would have easily bottled up almost the entire Japanese fighting force on the mainland. On May 5, Itō backed down, took a higher indemnity payment from the Chinese, and agreed to pull the troops out of Chinese territory. Korea no longer qualified as such.

The brief eight-month war had depleted much of Japan's arsenal and supplies. The Japanese newspapers spun the end of the war as a victory over all China, but the Japanese had only engaged with a fraction of China's military manpower, in three relatively small theaters—Korea, which was already partly occupied before hostilities broke out, Manchuria, and a final action in Taiwan (discussed below). The government tried not to let it show, but the war over Korea had maxed out the country's current military strength. Had the war gone on, Japan would have been ill-prepared to advance further.

In his memoirs, Mutsu argued that negotiations had been less troubled by international pressure than by domestic expectations. He seethed at the way that the Japanese press had whipped up the public into anti-Chinese sentiment, and scoffed at the way that racist rhetoric had suddenly turned shame-faced and apologetic when someone had shot Li Hongzhang. He admitted that he had only granted the ceasefire in China that Li had been demanding because Li had been shot while under the protection of the Japanese, and that he needed to somehow drag Japan back to the moral high ground.[41]

Mutsu's deputy summed up the wider sense of grievance:

At present, Japan must keep calm and sit tight so as to lull

---
[41] Berger, *Kenkenroku*, pp. 174–7.

suspicions nurtured against her. During this time, the foundations of national power must be consolidated, and we must watch and wait for the opportunity in the Orient that will surely come one day. When this day arrives, Japan will decide her own fate, and she will be able not only to put in their place the powers who seek to meddle in her affairs, she will even be able, should this be necessary, to meddle in their affairs.[42]

The indemnity from China accounted for almost twice as much as Japan's war expenses, and much of that money was ploughed back into the military-industrial complex. Little of it trickled down to the common folk, since rises in the costs of living and a hike in taxes wiped out any likely benefit.

There was, it seemed, one rule for the Europeans and another for the Japanese. In 1896, the former Crown Prince Nicholas was crowned as Tsar Nicholas II. At his Moscow enthronement, the Chinese guests were accorded pride of place and order of precedence, ahead of the Japanese attendees—although possibly the Japanese did not notice quite how feted the Chinese were. Within a month of Nicholas ascending the throne, Russia and China had signed a secret treaty, in which Russia offered protection to China on its East Asian flank, in return for permission to shorten the Trans-Siberian Railway by driving it right through the middle of Manchuria.

Within two years of the Triple Intervention, Germany had grabbed concessions for itself on the Shandong Peninsula, Britain had snatched the "New Territories" adjacent to Hong Kong, and Russia had taken advantage of China's weak possession by demanding and receiving a 25-year lease on the entire Liaodong Peninsula (the same place Japan had been forced to give up), giving the Tsar's fleet a warm-water harbor in Port Arthur, and control of the railway that led from Dalian to Harbin. When China turned out to be unable to pay its war-debt to Japan, Russia stepped in with a loan, demanding a hefty price by taking the rights to the Chinese Eastern Railway, which stretched from Harbin to Vladivostok.

The Russian ambassador even tried to offer an explanation—that different rules applied because Japan was too close to Korea and China, and hence would have enjoyed an unfair strategic and commercial

---

[42] Storry, *Japan and the Decline of the West in Asia, 1894–1943*, p. 30.

advantage. Mutsu noted at the time that the argument was "glaringly inconsistent." That advantage was now handed to Russia instead, which now had a railway head and a port that was actually closer to China than Japan.

Japan's sole long-term gain from the Sino-Japanese War was a last-minute land-grab in the south, which was underway even as Li Hongzhang was signing the Treaty of Shimonoseki. A fleet seized the Pescadores islands off the coast of Fujian, cutting off Taiwan from the mainland. Japanese forces then seized the entire island of Taiwan, which had been specifically excluded from the peace treaty negotiations.

The acquisition of Taiwan was some small solace—as Mutsu sourly observed, it meant that the best of Japan's Navy was off on an adventure to the south, and hence unable to help hold off the Triple Intervention. Large-scale resistance on Taiwan would stretch on for five months, while sporadic guerrilla attacks continued for another seven years.[43] Although Taiwan's first governor, an admiral from Satsuma, would proclaim the island to be under Japanese control the moment his soldiers marched into the administrative center in Tainan, he faced a strong resistance, including an attempt by local Chinese to proclaim Taiwan a republic and seek foreign aid, as well as local partisan fighting among the Hakka Chinese ethnic subgroup and Taiwanese aborigines.

Little of this was mentioned back in Japan, where, if anything, the media was floundering to find anything positive to report. The victories seemed a little too swift, the Chinese a little too easy to overcome. Print artists cranked out garish images of bold Japanese heroes, imagined in moments of daring or battling the elements, but turned a blind eye to the unvarnished truth about Japan's casualties. It was true that the Japanese had only suffered 1,000 soldiers killed in action in the Sino-Japanese War, but another 17,000 had died of disease, including 1,500 lost in Taiwan to cholera and malaria, among them the imperial prince who had, in a different time and with a different name, once been fielded as a pretender to the throne by the Shōgunal loyalists.[44] Cholera was also spread throughout Japan by soldiers returning with infections—unlisted among the war dead are some 36,000 civilians in Japan, who died from outbreaks in the summer of 1895 that were associated, even at the time,

---

[43] Lamley, "Taiwan Under Japanese Rule," p. 205.

[44] Harries and Harries, *Soldiers of the Sun*, p. 61. Compare the figures with Kim, "Sino-Japanese War," p. 20 which has 11,894 (disease) to 1,418 (KIA).

with the return of military transports.[45]

Just as in Port Arthur, there were reports of extreme brutality shown by the Japanese towards the natives in Taiwan, although in that regard they were hardly any worse than the Chinese, who had not only butchered the Taiwanese in the 1890s in their own suppression campaigns, but had been seen selling the meat from dead natives for human consumption in local marketplaces, both as food and as a cure for malaria.[46]

Perhaps Li Hongzhang had the last laugh. He joked that Taiwan was an awful territory, that had proved to be nothing but trouble to the Chinese. He even joked that he had suggested to his Manchu masters in 1873 that they sell it to Britain, and if the British refused, make a gift of it to them, in subtle revenge for their seizure of Hong Kong.[47] There were stories of young Japanese men, fearful of being posted there to die of disease, holding celebratory parties if they failed their conscription medical, while Buddhist priests in one sect offered to say prayers to get men out of the draft.[48] There were serious discussions in the Japanese government as to whether Japan would be better off just selling the whole island to the French. Instead, more strategic heads prevailed, and a college was set up in far Hokkaidō, Japan's previous frontier, to train the technicians and administrators who would be needed to drag Taiwan bodily into the Japanese empire. Ultimately, the college would grow into Takushoku University, the alma mater that would supply much of the technical know-how for Japan's ever-expanding empire in the early twentieth century.

The resolution of the war did not put an end to Korea's internal struggles. The Min family still wielded an unwelcome influence over the restored King Gojong and the machineries of state. The Daewongun, however, was ready to do a deal with the Japanese in order to oust them, in which he enlisted the aid of Miura Gorō, Japan's new minister in Seoul.

Miura had arrived without any explicit instructions from Tokyo, and hence seems to have been working on his own initiative when he

---

[45] Lone, *Provincial Life and the Military in Imperial Japan*, p. 33. Such issues were not solely a problem for the Japanese. In the Boer War, 58% of Britain's casualties had been due to sickness, not combat. See Best, *British Engagement with Japan*, p. 219.

[46] Davidson, *The Island of Formosa*, pp. 254–5; Mackay, *From Far Formosa*, pp. 275-6.

[47] Chaïkin, *The Sino-Japanese War*, p. 31.

[48] Kim, "The Sino-Japanese War," p. 12.

hatched a plan to stage a coup, using the newly formed Military Training Division (*hullyeondae*), a thousand-strong successor to the earlier
Special Skills Force, schooled by Japanese officers but led by Koreans.
With news that King Gojong was planning to disband the division, Miura moved forward his plans and struck in the early hours of October 8,
1895. Disguised in Korean uniforms, Gen'yōsha agents scaled the walls
of the palace to open the gates to a larger force. In the ensuing fight, the
Japanese killed the minister of the royal household, and burst into the
chambers of Queen Min herself. There, they stabbed the queen to death
(along with two of her maids), before dragging her body out into the
courtyard, soaking it with kerosene, and setting fire to it.[49]

Miura openly lied in his initial dispatches that the entire affair had
been a coup attempt backed by the Daewongun against his own son
and daughter-in-law. Any reports of Japanese involvement, he claimed,
were confused, because the Koreans of the Military Training Division
had *disguised* themselves as Japanese, and the Japanese who arrived on
the scene had only done so to protect King Gojong from the rebels. Unfortunately for Miura, his men had left far too many witnesses alive—
including ladies in waiting who knew the sound of Japanese when they
heard it, as well as two American bystanders. As for King Gojong, he
was fearful enough of his Japanese "rescuers" to flee from them to seek
asylum at the Russian legation, where he would develop a love of coffee,
and plot with new Russian allies to counter the Japanese influence on
his country. He would eventually signal his country's uncoupling from
China by proclaiming in 1897 that he, too, was now an Emperor, fit to
deal on equal terms not only with the ruler of China, but also with the
rulers of Russia and Japan.

Miura's actions were a colossal embarrassment to the Japanese authorities, who shipped him and forty-seven accomplices home for a
show trial, conducted to give the appearance to Western powers that
Japan was holding its subjects to account by the rule of law. Miura initially denied any knowledge of the incident, only to admit that he had
been involved, when his attorney suggested that an action of "political

---

[49] Iguchi, "Gen'yōsha Nationalism," p. 91; Norman, "The Genyosha," p. 281 comes
close to framing the entire Sino-Japanese War as a feud between Queen Min and
the Gen'yōsha, beginning with the murder in Shanghai in 1894 of one of their Korean activist allies, supposedly by an assassin in the Queen's service, and ending with
their retaliatory strike on her in her palace a year later.

supremacy" could not be regarded as murder in the traditional sense. The court eventually ruled that there was insufficient evidence that any of the accused men had definitely taken part in the killings, and they were released.

The Chinese had been driven out of Korea, and their greatest allies in the local aristocracy terminated with extreme prejudice. But for the hawks of Japan's military ministries, the securing of Korea had merely extended Japan's potential site of conflict to a new frontier—that which it shared with Manchuria, an area increasingly under Russian influence.

CHAPTER 3

The White Peril

Japan's victory over China led to much bragging, both at home and abroad, about the courageous and successful Japanese. Within the Japanese military, it led to a swift reappraisal and approval of the potential offered by the Navy, particularly after a number of high-ranking leaders, including Saigō Tsugumichi, arranged the translation and publication of Alfred Thayer Mahan's *The Influence of Sea Power on History* (1890). In wars to come, it was understood, Japan's Navy would play a crucial role in securing the routes for both conquest and resupply, best achieved through a single, crushing destruction of the enemy's seaborne forces: a decisive naval battle (*kantai kassen*).[1]

The Japanese were not the only fans. Mahan's book was required reading for every other would-be colonialist leader, including Kaiser Wilhelm II. The German ruler, hoping to keep the new Tsar of Russia busy in the East, sent him an allegorical painting of the races of the West, facing a new enemy in the east, titled "Peoples of Europe, Guard Your Dearest Goods." The following year, the Russian sociologist Jacques Novikow coined a new term for the rising power in the East, the Yellow Peril. Far from seeing Japan accepted into the family of modern nations, its success only saw further moves against it internationally.

Konoe Atsumaro, president of the House of Peers at the turn of the century, saw such obstructions as the opening moves of a racial conflict.

> As I see it, in the future East Asia cannot avoid becoming a stage for a contest between the races. Even if fleeting considerations of foreign policy should produce a different environment, this will yield no more than a temporary result. The final outcome will be a contest between the yellow and white races, and in this contest,

---

[1] Asada, *From Mahan to Pearl Harbor*, loc. 188.

the Chinese people and the Japanese people will be placed in the same position, being both considered as the sworn enemy of the white race.[2]

Much of the rhetoric of the ensuing two decades would involve Japan's prevarications over which role to play in mainland Asia—as a champion of Asian peoples against outsiders, or as an apparently unwelcome accomplice to the "Anglo-Saxons" of Britain and America. The first flashpoint was Hawaii, where an attempt to curtail Japanese immigration in 1897 led to the arrival of Japan's British-built warship *Naniwa* as a show of force. Alfred Thayer Mahan, the grand strategist of sea power, wrote to the U.S. president Theodore Roosevelt:

Of course, Japan is a small and poor state, as compared to ourselves; but the question is are we going to allow her to dominate the future of those most important islands because of our lethargy?[3]

Mahan's advice was that the U.S. needed to annex Hawaii as soon as possible. The U.S. would do so in 1898, not ostensibly to outmaneuver Japan, but in the interests of a mercantile imperialism. This, however, was interpreted in Japan as an American advance towards Asia. Much as the *Times* had predicted in 1852, Hawaii was seen as a stepping stone to China.

In 1899, the U.S. Secretary of State John Hay wrote a series of memos that would ultimately be enshrined as America's Open Door policy—an insistence that China not be broken up into colonies, but maintained as a single state, to which all interested parties had equal and free access. A cartoon in *Puck* magazine ably summarized Hay's position, presenting Uncle Sam as a stern, fatherly figure brandishing a piece of paper, and hectoring an assembly of European figureheads, including representatives of France, Italy, Britain, Russia and Germany.

"Gentleman," says Uncle Sam, "you may cut up this map as much as

---

[2] Zachmann, "Konoe Atsumaro and the Idea of an Alliance of the Yellow Race, 1898" p. 89.

[3] Asada, *From Mahan to Pearl Harbor*, loc. 327. Japanese military strategy and political policy was partly founded on Mahan's own published writings. Both Japanese and American strategists were leaning on Mahan's ideas in expecting they would ultimately end up fighting each other over China.

you like, but remember that I am here to stay, and that you can't divide *me* up into spheres of influence."

The cartoon, by J.S. Pugh, is notable firstly for the apparent confidence it has in America's power of persuasion—Uncle Sam towers above the Europeans, who look up at him sheepishly like naughty children. In the background, Austria-Hungary is sharpening its own pair of shears, indicating that more raiders are on their way, but Japan is not one of them. Popular opinion simply did not consider Japan to be a contender in the race to carve up China, although the Senate Committee on Foreign Relations in the U.S. was already discussing Hawaii as the "key to the Pacific" in a possible future conflict with Japan.[4]

Things would change only a year later, with Japan's involvement in the suppression of the Boxer Uprising. Amid a summer drought sure to lead to frayed tempers, rebels in Shandong rose up in an anti-foreign movement that was carefully co-opted by the Manchus to exclude the Manchus themselves. Proclaiming that they were "supporting the Qing and exterminating the foreigners," the Boxer rebels marched on Beijing itself, where they laid siege to the Foreign Legation quarter just outside the Forbidden City.

Japanese soldiers formed part of the Eight-Nation Alliance sent to rescue missionaries and diplomats in Beijing, alongside American, Austro-Hungarian, British, French, German, Italian and Russian brigades. Despite claims in the press that everybody got along, there were tensions among the forces. There was, for example, considerable disagreement about the way to fight. The Japanese, still true to the close-ranks ideas of Jakob Meckel, made easy targets for Chinese riflemen, and stood so close together than even a miss would be sure to hit someone else. The British military attaché looked on aghast as the Japanese suffered heavy losses charging the Chinese, and further casualties in their eagerness to engage in close-quarters combat. It was, he wrote, as if they had a fixed idea that a battle was not properly fought unless both sides suffered heavy casualties. The Russian military attaché was similarly mocking, observing that one Japanese company suffered 90% casualties attacking the arsenal at Tianjin, pointlessly charging head-on while a more tactically minded Russian squad flanked and neutralized the Chinese

---

[4] *From Mahan to Pearl Harbor*, loc. 381.

strong-point, suffering only six losses.[5]

Conversely, the Japanese press were openly disdainful of Britain's troops, well-trained Sikhs who knew to scatter and take cover, who wore away enemy positions from a distance, and who only engaged in hand-to-hand combat as a last resort. It was, in fact, a Sikh who had been the first man of the relief forces into the Legation Quarter, cunningly sneaking in through the sewer. But to read the Japanese press, one would think these accomplished soldiers were ineffectual cowards.

Many of the residents of Beijing had fled ahead of the relief forces. Of those that remained, many Manchus and Chinese supporters of the Boxers committed suicide instead of trusting in their fate at the hands of the new arrivals. "It is to be feared," wrote the correspondent for the *Daily Telegraph*, "that they were right."[6]

According to the American missionary, Luella Miner:

> The conduct of the Russian soldiers is *atrocious*, the French are not much better, and the Japanese are looting and burning without mercy… Women and girls by hundreds have committed suicide to escape a worse fate at the hands of Russian and Japanese brutes.[7]

With so much of the city abandoned in a hurry, looting was an inevitable temptation. Anecdotes from the fall of the city are indiscriminate in the account of the atrocities committed by men of all nationalities—the Indian soldiers flogged for molesting Chinese Christian converts; the British infantrymen found testing their ammunition on an old Chinese man begging for his life, and the American marine shrugging off looting on the grounds of the "excitement of a campaign." Amid all this, the Japanese were swiftly absented, in part, claimed one observer, because their commanding officers had lured them away back to their "regimental wives" in brothels newly set up in Beijing and Tianjin—one of the first extant references in English to the presence of what would come to be referred to as "comfort women" among the Japanese Army.[8]

---

[5] Menning, "Miscalculating One's Enemies," p. 158.

[6] Preston, *A Brief History of the Boxer Rebellion*, p. 298.

[7] Preston, *A Brief History of the Boxer Rebellion*, p. 298.

[8] Preston, *A Brief History of the Boxer Rebellion*, pp. 298–300. It has been claimed by some that these military brothels were staffed by "volunteers," and hence not part of the continuum of "comfort women." It is difficult to imagine the women's state being particularly voluntary.

The Japanese soldiers were performatively cooperative in Beijing, doing nothing to rock the boat, at least with their foreign allies. To some, their presence there was a tardy opportunity to enact the plans for Beijing in the war of 1895—thanks in part to an affinity for the Chinese language, they were regarded as the most successful looters, able to target places and artifacts far more competently than the average European. Except perhaps, the Germans, who wrenched the priceless bronze astronomical instruments from the roof of the Old Observatory and shipped them back to Berlin. Among the British, a small Pekinese dog was one of the spoils of war, carefully looked after on the long voyage home, and eventually presented to Queen Victoria, who named it Looty.

Despite outnumbering the other contingents, the Japanese raised no official complaint about overall leadership going to a European officer, nor did they protest when the Russians, falsely claiming to have more troops than everybody else, demanded the biggest victory parade. The Japanese did not outstay their welcome, sending many of their troops home as soon as the troubles were dispelled. There was, it was understood, no hope of any tactical advantages when multiple foreign countries had troops on the scene.

However, while international attention was focused on Beijing, the time was ideal to try it on elsewhere. Yamagata Aritomo, now Prime Minister again, was incensed that the Russians were lingering with an increased presence in Manchuria, the British had found an excuse to build up troops on the Yangtze, and the French and Germans were similarly lurking with what he called "evil intentions."[9]

Yamagata saw no reason not to try some maneuvers of his own—an opportunity to pursue a "southern project," increasing Japan's influence across the Taiwan Strait in the mainland provinces of Fujian and Zhejiang. "By this means," he argued, "we can in future opposite Taiwan build up special strength which will serve in time of peace as the focus for trade and industry within China. Thus, we can hold in our grasp 'the throat of the Far East' and keep in check any intrusion by an enemy."[10] Nor was Yamagata even the first to express such views—schemes had been proposed for expansion into Fujian by the very first Japanese governor-general of Taiwan in 1896, mere months after the island was occupied.[11]

---

[9] Harries and Harries, *Soldiers of the Sun*. p. 71.
[10] Nish, "Japan's Indecision During the Boxer Disturbances," p. 450.
[11] Jansen, "Opportunists in South China," p. 243.

Japan's moves on Fujian went on throughout 1900. A treaty for railway development, openly based on the one the Germans had made the Chinese sign in Shandong, failed to get approval from Chinese officials in June. Even as the international force was reaching Beijing to relieve the siege of the Legations, Japanese officers in Taiwan were warned to expect orders for an operation on the Fujian mainland, to deal with an unspecified incident.

The incident eventually supplied itself on August 23, when Takamatsu Sei, a Japanese nationalist and sometime Buddhist priest, arrived at the Amoy consulate, claiming that his temple had just been burned down by a Chinese mob. The U.S. consul Burlingame Johnson had a different story, claiming that the "temple" was little more than the house where Takamatsu lived with two other "priests," who were often behind on their rent. On the night before the alleged arson, the men had been seen carrying their valuables out of the house, and the only person on the premises when the fire started was Takamatsu himself.[12]

Regardless, Japanese marines were dispatched to Amoy, where their mere presence handily stirred up some further protests and provocations. By August 28, the Japanese were ready to authorize a full-scale task force—mail ships were impounded on Taiwan to prevent any warning, the international undersea cable connection to Amoy was mysteriously cut off, and Japanese ships and transports began arriving in Amoy harbor. However, a sudden message arrived from Tokyo, calling off the mission, and ordering everyone home. The officers already on shore, including the governor-general's assistant, Gotō Shinpei, were left fuming—however, unlike the belligerent Saigō Tsugumichi in 1874, they did not ignore their orders to stand down.

Back in Tokyo, Itō Hirobumi had persuaded the cabinet to cancel the mission, on the grounds that he had word that the Russian anti-Boxer forces were finally leaving Manchuria. This later turned out to be untrue, but by the time this became apparent, the United States, Britain, France and Russia had also sent ships to Amoy. Facetiously taking the Japanese at their word, that they had sent their troops ashore to deal with local disturbances, the British landed marines of their own on September 5. There not being any disturbances to speak of, the local foreign consuls treated their Japanese counterpart to dinner on September 8, in

---

[12] Jansen, "Opportunists in South China," p. 246.

an attempt to smooth over any sense that he had been caught with his own raiding party. The official line, as reported by the Japanese consul in Shanghai, was that the troops had been landed "solely to protect consulate and foreign residents."[13]

Feeling that he had been betrayed by his own government, Governor-General Kodama threatened to resign, and was only dissuaded when an imperial envoy was sent to plead with him. When it became clear that the Japanese probably had missed a critical window in Amoy, for precisely the sort of land-grab that had characterized the acquisition of Taiwan itself in 1895, thanks to Itō's untrue claims, the entire Yamagata cabinet resigned. The new prime minister would be Itō Hirobumi, although he was obliged to appoint Taiwan's Governor-General Kodama, still smarting from the "Amoy Incident," as his Army Minister.

The Amoy Incident could have easily escalated into something far more explosive. Asides in memoirs and reports suggest that Kodama had also been liaising with Chinese secret societies planning a revolt of their own. History records an abortive uprising at Huizhou, about a hundred miles from Guangzhou, where Qing troops surprised six hundred rebel partisans assembling on the coast in September. The fighting in the hills would drag on for two weeks, with the rebels briefly gaining ground— aided by strong local support, and a significant number of troops defecting from the Qing side. This operation was *also* being directed from Taiwan, but by the Chinese revolutionary Sun Yat-sen, who got word to his local commanders that the rebel forces should march for Amoy, where they were sure of unspecified help. However, the rebels were cut off by Qing reinforcements and never made it to Amoy, thereby not quite embroiling the city in precisely the kind of local unrest in which Gotō and the Japanese were earnestly hoping to intervene. When Sun was let down by a Japanese arms dealer, who failed to deliver promised weapons, he ordered his Huizhou rebels to flee.[14]

The incompetence of the Japanese Army became a matter of international gossip in January 1902, after 199 Japanese soldiers froze to

---

[13] Jansen, "Opportunists in South China," p. 247.

[14] Jansen, "Opportunists in South China," pp. 244–5. Jansen uses the old, Cantonese-accented spelling of Waichow for Huizhou. Considering the people involved in the Amoy Incident, it seems likely that the "arms dealer" who let Sun down was the same organization that had been caught trying to run guns to anti-American rebels in the Philippines the previous year—a group of Japanese businessmen dealing in Japanese-made hardware, whose ship, the *Nunobiki Maru*, had sunk.

death in a mountain training exercise in northern Honshū. Stuck in a blizzard four kilometers from their objective, they were missing for five days before a search party uncovered Corporal Gotō Fusanosuke, buried in the snow. For simply staying alive, Gotō would be memorialized with a statue on Mount Hakkōda, although his career was over—like seven others among the eleven survivors, he lost his arms and legs to frostbite. The incident would subsequently be celebrated multiple times in the Japanese media as an example of Japanese fortitude in the face of adversity, although a cynic might interpret it as a case of gross negligence.

Although a rehearsal exercise had been carried out in more favorable weather, none of its participants were in attendance on the actual march. The commanding officer was a last-minute replacement, pushed into his role after the original leader went home to see his wife and newborn child. Extreme temperatures dropped below minus 40 degrees Celsius, whereas the soldiers were ill-equipped for conditions below minus 20. One captain only evaded frostbite because he was wearing non-standard-issue rubber shoes, and many of the soldiers had no spare dry gloves or socks. Many doomed themselves by wandering away from their encampment in the dark, thereby becoming separated and lost.

Observing that the soldiers were in training for winter combat against an enemy that could only be Russia, Gleb Vannovskii, the Russian military attaché, scornfully reported that the Japanese were poorly trained and inexperienced at dealing with the cold. The incident on Mount Hakkōda, in fact, was such an incredible blunder that it would leave some in the Russian military *over*-confident about their chances against the Japanese in any future conflict. Vannovskii was recalled soon afterwards, in part because of the irregularity of his reports, leaving his replacement little time to adequately assess reforms and improvements to a military that Vannovskii had done little but ridicule.[15]

A few years later, in a gesture that was presumably well-intentioned and not outrageous trolling, King Haakon VII of Norway presented the Meiji Emperor with a pair of skis in sympathy.

Among the military clique in Japan, there was a stark choice to be argued. Itō Hirobumi argued that Japan's best policy was to befriend Russia, and cooperate in their Manchurian sphere of mutual interest.

---

[15] Menning, "Miscalculating One's Enemies," p. 152. For the statue, Saaler, *Men in Metal*, p. 313.

Yamagata Aritomo thought that conflict with Russia was inevitable unless Japan truly wanted its own influence to stop at the Yalu River, and Japan's best hope against Russia was to team up with Great Britain, not necessarily in war, but as a guarantor of peace.

Certainly, the Japanese and the British had been mutual admirers for decades, notwithstanding the lampooning of the Japanese in the good-natured operetta *The Mikado* (1885), into which the writers Gilbert and Sullivan had even worked a recognizable pastiche of the old battle-hymn, "Miya-san, Miya-san"—a tune they had overheard sung by Japanese ex-pats in a model village erected in Knightsbridge, London.[16] In the 1902 Anglo-Japanese Alliance, fated to last for the next twenty years, Britain agreed to enter any war on Japan's side if any two powers united against Japan.[17]

Had such an agreement had been in place in 1895, the Triple Intervention would have been impossible, because the Russians, Germans and French would have been unable to threaten Japan without staring a war with Britain. The British admiral Sir Cyprian Bridge thought it was sure to be a good thing:

> I presume to think the Anglo-Japanese Alliance is a good thing. Anyone who knows anything of Japan must have seen that she was determined to range herself on the side of some Power, and it would have been deplorable had she been left to range herself with those who are against us.[18]

But if the British had intended the Anglo-Japanese Alliance as a warning to Russia to avoid conflict with Japan, it is possible that they had not considered the implications. The idea of an ally on the other side of the world, distracting Russia from committing resources to Europe, was as attractive to the British as it was for the Germans. For Britain's overseas dominions, however, it was less appealing—already, Australia had imposed written tests for potential immigrants, as a means of curtailing the

---

[16] Cortazzi, *Japan in Late Victorian London*, p. 60 regards this as "a myth" because the village opened only two months before the opening night of the show. I regard that as ample time for wily impresarios to drop in a few phrases of local color to a work in progress, but concede that they may have heard it somewhere else.

[17] Oka, *Five Political Leaders of Modern Japan*, p. 14.

[18] Lindgren, "A Station in Transition," p. 465.

influx of Asians, while racial tensions were also running high in Canada. Neither of those British possessions, however, had much say in decisions made back in London. Moreover, while the Alliance offered the potential of British intervention if Russia attacked Japan, it also handed the Japanese a free pass to start a war with Russia, sure that none of Russia's allies would come to its aid. It also supplied the Japanese with a vital commodity that would palpably improve the performance of the Japanese Navy—British coal.

Although Japan had been self-sufficient in coal production, its local supply was not of military grade—it was bituminous, and tended to create such black, billowing clouds from smokestacks that Japanese ships were visible at a substantially greater distance than those of other nations. Cardiff coal, however, burned more efficiently than the Japanese variety, effectively and palpably upgrading the Navy's ships, speed and range at a vital moment. By the eve of the conflict with Russia, Cardiff coal from Britain accounted for a quarter of the Japanese Navy's fuel stocks.[19]

By 1903, the Russian forces sent to China to deal with the Boxer Uprising had still not left Manchuria. They had effectively become a large and threatening garrison sitting on the border with Korea. Encouraged by the German Kaiser, but also by his own festering dislike for the Japanese, Tsar Nicolas II reneged on promises to remove his men, effectively goading the Japanese to attack his troops if they dared.

Emperor Meiji was informed of the decision to go to war with Russia on 1st February, although no direct action was taken for another week. Diplomats in Tokyo would have got some sense of impending disaster when the telegraph offices suddenly stopped working, thereby making it impossible for the Russian ambassador to warn his countrymen in the event of an attack. Bafflingly, the Russians were wrong-footed by signs they really should have noticed. War Minister Kuropatkin had received reports of suspicious behavior as early as Christmas Eve 1903. By December 29, he was asking his advisers about previous Japanese actions against China in 1894, querying if there were any precedents for mobilizing forces and then attacking before a declaration of war was officially issued. He was not only told that this was exactly what had happened, but also informed about the sinking of the *Kowshing*, again

---

[19] Evans and Peattie, *Kaigun*, p. 66.

before war had been declared.[20]

As if this were not enough of a clue, a Russian military intelligence officer had reported on December 31 that the Japanese had requisitioned so many civilian transport vessels that all exports were halted from Japan to Australia, the United States and Europe. He reported two further impressments of a further hundred vessels in January—what did the Russians *think* the Japanese were going to do with all that tonnage?

Japan would not give Russia further opportunity to prepare. The first strike would fall to the same Tōgō who had sunk the *Kowshing* a decade earlier. Now an Admiral, Tōgō launched a surprise attack on the Russian fleet in Port Arthur on the morning of the 8th February.

Russia, it seemed, had learned nothing from Japan's surprise attack on the Chinese in 1894. It was a peculiarity of Port Arthur that the harbor was so tight, and its entrance too small, that deploying all the ships out of it would take two tides. Any commander who wanted vessels ready for combat needed to station them *outside* the harbor, unprotected from a torpedo attack. The officer in charge of the Pacific Fleet, Stepan Makarov, had warned his superiors that "if we do not now shift the fleet to the interior anchorage, then we will have to do so following the first night attack, after paying dearly for the mistake."[21]

Strategists had estimated that a full-on naval confrontation with Russia was sure to cost Japan half its Navy, but Tōgō's attack disabled three enemy ships in the first hours. By daybreak, the rest of the Russian fleet had time enough to stoke boilers to mount a counter-attack. Technically, the Russians had shooed the Japanese away, with both sides taking some damage, but Tōgō was within a day's journey of his home dockyards at Sasebo, while the Russians had only limited repair facilities at Port Arthur.

Regardless, over the next few months, the Navy's war in the Far East revolved around repeated attempts by the Russians to break out of Port Arthur. By April, when Tōgō scuttled several old ships to further block the harbor entrance, he was ready to declare the Russians unable to bring their ships out.

Eventually, the Russian fleet was ordered by Tsar Nicolas II to break out and run for Vladivostok, or else its admiral would face legal action.

---

[20] Menning, "Misjudging One's Enemies," pp. 168–9.
[21] Menning, "Misjudging One's Enemies," p. 169.

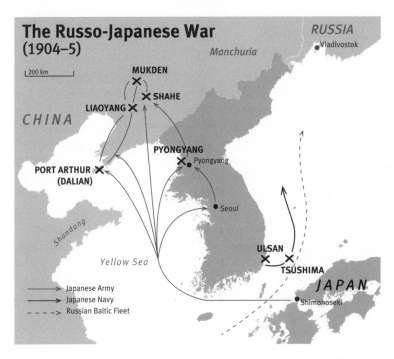

The subsequent Battle of the Yellow Sea was another victory for the Japanese, with most of the Russians pushed back into Port Arthur. A handful of ships did make it out, but were impounded by the Germans in Qingdao or the British in Shanghai. A sole Russian cruiser made it as far as Sakhalin Island, before her captain scuttled her as the Japanese closed in.

The outbreak of the Russo-Japanese War could not have been better planned. Russia's four new state-of-the-art warships were still incomplete in European shipyards. The Trans-Siberian Railway still required a ship to move its rolling stock across Lake Baikal, drastically slowing troop deployment. And best of all, the bulk of Russia's Pacific fleet were sitting ducks in the harbor.

Japan fielded 1.1 million men, almost five times as many combatants as in the Sino-Japanese War, of which at least fifty thousand would be killed. The sheer size of the mobilization had a significant effect on agricultural manpower in rural communities, but also in the number of families with a relative involved in the fighting. Those with memories of the previous war were ready to run benefit drives, particularly to supply soldiers with blankets. A 1904 austerity initiative called for a reduction in the consumption of tobacco or alcohol, as well as lavish celebrations of weddings or birthdays. A government directive tried to discourage the proliferation of good-luck charms, including the "thousand-stitch belt" (*sennin-bari*)—a folk belief that invulnerability could be imparted to soldiers by soliciting multiple female passers-by to add a stitch to a cloth talisman.[22]

The war against Russia also saw the revival of "Miya-san, Miya-san," the old 1868 battle hymn of the Meiji Restoration, its opening call now replaced with "*Minna-san, Minna-san*" (Everyone, Everyone), but retaining the "Gonna get it done" refrain at the end of every line, as it recounted the major battle locations:

> Everyone, Everyone, what is that flurry behind the battleship?
> Don't you know that's Russian soldiers surrendering?
> [Gonna get it done, etc.]
> Everyone, Everyone, what's that lurking in the Tsugaru Strait?
> Don't you know that's Russian warships on the prowl?
> [Gonna get it done, etc.]
> Everyone, Everyone, what's that sea battle off Incheon?
> Don't you know that's Japanese vessels shelling the Russians?
> [Gonna get it done, etc.]
> Everyone, Everyone, what's that cannon-fire near Port Arthur?
> Don't you know that's Japanese ships firing at Russian ships?
> [Gonna get it done, etc.]
> Everyone, Everyone, what was the Russian ship sunk in this battle?
> Don't you know it was the *Varyag*?[23]

Another version, placing a different emphasis on the "it" that needed to get done, highlighted the remuneration of the troops:

> Everyone, Everyone, what is it that we contribute to this war?
> Don't you know that is the reward money for expedition soldiers?

The Russo-Japanese War has attained the nickname among historians of "World War Zero," mainly because it was the testing ground for much

---

[22] Ōe, *Chōhei-sei*, p. 124.
[23] Taguchi, "Tokoton yare bushi ni tsuite," pp. 134–5.

of the tactics and technology that would distinguish the First World War—new advances in weaponry and communications, barbed wire, sea mines, wireless telegraphy, wired telephony (for artillery spotters) and trenches. It was also heavily observed by foreign correspondents, giving many of them, and their readers, a first glimpse of what the industrialization of military machinery signified for the twentieth century battlefield. In many cases, the correspondents were brought over in the expectation that they would only need a couple of days to witness an inevitable Japanese victory. Instead, as the siege dragged on for weeks, Port Arthur became a macabre joke—back in Japan "...and Port Arthur will fall in days" became a comic response to anyone who promised that the check was in the mail.[24]

It also marked the end of an era—it was the last hurrah for that generation of soldiers in the modern army who could still remember the days of the samurai. Both General Nogi and Admiral Tōgō, for example, had served as teenagers in the last battles of the samurai era, and were now old men. The old samurai stipends, which had been converted into thirty-year government bonds, were now maturing. Whatever form Japan's next war would take, it would be prosecuted by soldiers, sailors and officers who *only* remembered the modern military, and not the disruptions that had brought it into being.

General Nogi, victor of 1894, had been called out of retirement to return to Port Arthur—a terrible decision, since he was depressed, suicidal and a decade behind the times in his assessment of the terrain and the technology. Over-confident in his men's ability to breach the Russian defenses on the narrow peninsula that led to the city, he sent successive waves of Japanese soldiers to face barbed wire, landmines and heavy artillery. His tactics would have been more successful had Nogi not been deprived of 18 vital siege howitzers, which had been lost at sea in a June sortie from the Russians operating out of Vladivostok.

Foreign correspondents noted that the Japanese Army seemed unwilling to do anything except charge. One noted that "sapping" operations—the digging of trenches and tunnels—would have permitted the Japanese to get closer to Russian fortifications before having to advance across open ground, but the Japanese seemed to lose interest in working too long with picks and shovels. Another was shocked at the sight

---

[24] Lone, *Provincial Life and the Military in Imperial Japan*, p. 59.

of Japanese soldiers willingly obeying orders to impale themselves on Russian bayonets, allowing a second wave of soldiers to overwhelm the trench while the enemy struggled to disentangle themselves.[25]

Prefiguring the hell of a war to come, the correspondent of the London *Times* likened it to the Charge of the Light Brigade, with the fateful difference that this was not a solitary military blunder, but a lethal mistake made repeatedly, several times a day, for weeks "with the scientific destructiveness of modern weapons thrown into the scale."

> The Japanese soldiers were called upon to face death in so many different ways that each soldier could make choice of what he considered to be the most honourable method, and succumb accordingly. There were bullets... there were common shells, shrapnel and pom-poms. There were mines, hand grenades and torpedoes; pits filled with fire, and with stakes pointed at the end; masses of rock and poisonous gases.[26]

Facing Russian enemies who had been promised that they would receive a year's wages for every month they served at Port Arthur, decimated by *beri beri* in the summer and exposure in the winter, the Japanese took immense losses, sometimes discharging as much ammunition in a single day as they had during the entire Sino-Japanese War. One of General Nogi's own sons died during one of the assaults, but with little effect on his antiquated tactics. In one incident, an entire column of Japanese soldiers was found dead, with no sign of injury—later found to have been the victims of electrocution, in a Russian experiment with live electric wires.[27]

In desperation, the Army began recruiting volunteers for suicide missions, sending in "human bullets" (*nikudan*, literally "meat bullets") to carry explosive charges into enemy lines in repeated attempts to blow a path through.

For those whose loved ones were present at the conflict, the recruitment of "human bullets" was a terrifying prospect. The idea prompted the poet Yosano Akiko to write to her brother in Port Arthur, and to

---

[25] Nordlund, "A War of Others," pp. 37–8.
[26] Ashmead-Bartlett, *Port Arthur*, pp. 184–5.
[27] Ashmead-Bartlett, *Port Arthur*, p. 185. The experiment was not repeated, on the grounds that it was difficult to maintain a circuit amid bombardment.

reprint her words to him in verse form in the September 1904 issue of *Myōjō* magazine.

Oh, my brother, I weep for you
Do not lay down your life
You are our last-born
Most dear to our parents
But did they teach you to wield a sword
To take a life
To kill or be killed
At twenty-four?[28]

Yosano goes on to lament the future her brother might be throwing away—he's supposed to be taking over the family store, becoming a merchant, not involving himself in a pointless battle. And then, perhaps, she goes too far.

Do not lay down your life
His Majesty the Emperor does not go into battle.
The path to spilling another's blood
To dying like a beast
Cannot be considered a glorious demise
By his august and noble mind?

True enough, it was not an attack on the Emperor himself—there are plenty of precedents in Japanese history in which dissent was couched in terms of the Emperor's true wishes, ignored by his incumbent advisers. Yosano turns to the subject of her recently widowed mother, whose hair "grows whiter by the day," even in a time of imperial proclamations of peace and prosperity.

"Do Not Lay Down Your Life" was an explosive work in twentieth century Japan. It challenged the prevailing wisdom not only of Japan's modern expansion, but of the very ethics of the samurai. It was not merely a dissenting voice amid all the gung-ho patriotic songs of 1904, but the voice of a *woman*, asserting that family and love were

---

[28] Rabson, "Yosano Akiko on War," p. 46. See also Humphreys, *Way of the Heavenly Sword*, p. 203 for a discussion of the term "human bullets."

more important than politics and duty. Yosano's words led to a public argument in the media between critics, some of whom regarded them as reasonable concerns expressed for the safety of a loved one, while others denounced her for "dangerous thinking." It all really depended on where one stood on her comments on the Emperor—was she calling him a coward, or simply wondering if he had all the facts?

Yosano was not the sole critic of the war, nor even the first. People threw rocks at her house, but despite her open challenge to the authorities, she escaped the imprisonment that already awaited the socialist editor of *Heimin Shinbun* (*The People's Paper*), whose anti-war stance had stood in vain against a rising tide of fanaticism. Even *Myōjō* magazine had published other voices critical of the war in preceding months, including a grimly evocative poem by Tamano Hanako that August:

> In this war / wearing black / he stands shrouded in stars.
> "This is my world" / says the god of night.[29]

But for most of the press, the war was a fantastic distraction and a national obsession. One magazine, the *Wartime Graphic* (*Senji Gahō*) even ran a cartoon chronicling those people who had been left idle by the war effort—not merely builders left without new houses to work on and drapers without customers, but geisha girls with nobody to entertain, and a theater doorman with no shoes to collect.[30]

General Nogi was under pressure to take Port Arthur, and not merely because of the remnants of the Russian Pacific Fleet inside it. In an act of outstanding desperation, the Russian Baltic Fleet was on its way from Europe, on an 18,000-mile journey that threatened to tip the balance once more in Russia's favor. Thanks to the Anglo-Japanese Alliance, the Baltic Fleet's ability to put into foreign ports for resupply or repair was limited, but it was vital to shut down any chance of it reaching Port Arthur.

Eventually, Port Arthur's fate was sealed by the hard-won capture of one of the hill forts surrounding it. The Japanese were able to turn captured siege guns on the harbor itself, pounding the Pacific Fleet until it was sunk at anchor. The leader of the Russians within the town agreed

---

[29] Rabson, "Yosano Akiko on War," p. 50.
[30] Sakai, "Survive to be critical," p. 5.

to discuss surrender with General Nogi.

The Russians retreated north, for the grand showdown at the old Manchu capital of Mukden—at the time, possibly the largest land battle fought in world history, although it would be eclipsed within the decade. With only minimal racist epithets, Britain's Lord Curzon had noted of the Japanese victory, comparing them to England's medieval heyday:

> [W]e could not have done what the Japs have done: for as a nation, we are growing stale, flaccid and nerveless. In a point of national ardour and power of self-sacrifice, the Japs stand about where we did at Agincourt.[31]

Despite a Japanese victory, logistical cracks were starting to show. Supply lines were over-stretched, ammunition was running low, and disease was on the rise. Moreover, the wartime conditions were taxing the home economy, accounting for 53% of the year's national budget, and causing the home factories to run low on steel.[32] As in the Sino-Japanese War of a decade earlier, Japan had reached its limits, and tentatively put out feelers, through the United States, for peace negotiations. Russia, however, did not respond, still pinning its hopes on the arrival of the Baltic Fleet, then somewhere in the Indian Ocean and heading ever eastwards.

The Russo-Japanese War repeated much of the tactics, and indeed the locations, of the Sino-Japanese War of ten years earlier. A Japanese surprise attack, a swift naval domination of local waters, while one section of the Army marched through Korea and over the Yalu, and another landed on the Liaodong peninsula to take Port Arthur. If anything was different, it was the logistics. As Louis Seaman, an American surgeon observed, the Japanese Army was not only armed against the Russians, but against the "silent foe" of disease and discomfort that had claimed so many more casualties ten years earlier.

The Japanese soldiers, he wrote, were well supplied and bivouacked, and had no need to risk being poisoned by captured enemy supplies or bad food. They were adequately equipped and informed to deal with the extremes of Manchurian heat and cold. He was, in this assessment, a trifle optimistic.[33]

---

[31] Best, *British Engagement with Japan*, p. 186.

[32] Harries and Harries, *Soldiers of the Sun*, p. 90.

[33] Harries and Harries, *Soldiers of the Sun*, p. 83.

There were some missteps that the media tried to downplay. The mud banks and shorelines of the fast-flowing Yalu River had changed so much since the Sino-Japanese War that Army maps were next to useless. The Russians helped by failing to adequately camouflage their artillery positions, so that Japanese spies were able to work out who was where, and to draw up new plans on the spot.

The Japanese, too, were over-confident. While the Russians were constantly forced to respond, rather than take the initiative, they were at least a unified and somewhat modern military force. They were not predisposed to fire off all their ammunition and flee, nor did they stand much chance of blending into the local population if they deserted. Instead, they stayed at their posts, shooting rifles with better accuracy and a quicker rate of fire, into close-packed ranks of Japanese soldiers whose blue uniforms made them easy targets. As had been noted in the Boxer Uprising, the Japanese took higher casualties then they really needed to—a thousand men lost in the crossing of the Yalu and its tributaries.

"Here was an infantry charge," wrote Ellis Ashmead-Bartlett of Port Arthur, "after the manner of the wars a hundred years ago—something supposed to have disappeared forever from modern battlefields."[34]

As for the Baltic Fleet, its grand tour of the world would end in tragedy. Disorganized and ramshackle, and comprising many ships that were frankly unsuitable for the task at hand, it limped all the way around the world, the subject of many a press speculation as it tried to avoid giving away its position. By the time it reached the China Sea, Port Arthur had fallen, leaving it with the unenviable task of somehow running for Vladivostok, through Japanese waters.

Admiral Tōgō's ships were lying in wait on both sides of the Tsūshima Strait, listening for coded telegraph reports of the Baltic Fleet's location, speed and vector. Once he was sure where the Baltic Fleet not only was, but where it was shortly about to be, he hoisted the signal flag "Z," which had a specific meaning in his captains' code books:

> The rise or fall of the empire depends on this battle. Let each man do his utmost.[35]

---

[34] Ashmead-Bartlett, *Port Arthur*, p. 148.

[35] Clements, *Admiral Tōgō*, p. 198. According to Hotta, *Japan 1941*, p. 126, the crucial tip-off to Admiral Tōgō came from a young official at Japan's Shanghai consulate, that same Matsuoka Yōsuke, who would become the Foreign Minister on the eve of

It was Tōgō's gesture towards the words of one of his personal heroes, the British Admiral Horatio Nelson, who had issued a similar command ("England expects every man to do his duty") before the Battle of Trafalgar. Associated forever with Tōgō's victory at Tsushima, the Z-flag would be seen on many later occasions in the history of Japanese militarism, not necessarily at sea, where its over-use could confuse more practical signaling, but on land, where it would be flown in factories as a signal of national resolve.

The destruction of the Baltic Fleet would become one of the touchstones of Japanese military pride in the years that came. It made a reluctant international celebrity out of Tōgō, an unassuming man whose true achievement could be found in the preceding decade, spent on the unglamorous tasks of training his crew. Such diligence does not make for good press, leading his victory at Tsushima to be valorized, as ever, with songs celebrating suicidal heroism, and unlikely portents of divine intervention. A century later, it is now incredibly difficult to separate genuine reportage from fictional accounts that the Japanese media has subsequently come to regard as true. Both Japanese and foreign media concentrated specifically on the decisive naval battles and tales of romantic heroism, often ignoring niggling issues that would return to bite Japan in future.

In particular, there was remarkably little said about the handful of cruisers and torpedo boats of Russia's Vladivostok Squadron, that had mounted several attacks on Japanese positions on the Korean coast in 1904, killed over a thousand soldiers before they even reached the front line, and sank Nogi's siege cannons, as well as enough coastal transports to create food shortages on the Japanese home islands. Its actions almost ended the career of Admiral Kamimura Hikonojō of the 2nd Fleet, who found his home besieged by angry members of the public, amid calls in the newspapers for him to kill himself. On one occasion, the Vladivostok fleet even managed to sneak out into the Pacific and raid Japan's east coast, steaming home while flying a British flag as a disguise.[36] It is hardly a tale that sits easily with the main narrative of stirring Japanese victories at sea, which led to it being fatally ignored by later strategic planners.

Pearl Harbor. She also suggests that the near fatal injuries sustained by a young Yamamoto Isoroku at Tsushima may have pushed him into onshore strategy instead of active service.

[36] Kitamura, *A Forgotten Lesson of the Russo-Japanese War*, p. 21.

Kamimura would eventually acquit himself at the Battle off Ulsan, which saw one Russian cruiser scuttled and two more damaged beyond the capabilities of the Vladivostok shipyard to repair them. Kamimura got a song in his honor, which has much to say about the froth on the waves and the red setting sun, but not a whole lot about five months in which the Russians had terrorized Japanese domestic shipping.[37]

Two days after the Battle of Tsūshima, Tsar Nicholas II agreed to peace talks to be arranged by the United States, which would stretch on at Portsmouth, New Hampshire, throughout August 1905. The Japanese got some of what they wanted—a Russian withdrawal from Manchuria, and possession of the Russian territories in Liaodong, as well as the railways. But Japan had driven itself close to bankruptcy in the expectation that victory would mean a cash pay-out.

The Russian negotiators refused, secure in the knowledge that Japan could not afford to restart hostilities. Already, four new divisions of Russian soldiers had been shipped to Manchuria. They would leave, but only if Japan agreed to waive any demands for Russia to pay out. Instead, Japan was fobbed off with a donation of territory that Russia could afford to lose. The Japanese people were told that their supreme sacrifice was worth it all because now they were the proud owners of the southern two-fifths of Sakhalin Island.

It was a moment of supreme shock, as if the world had been turned upside-down. "In a world where the loser defeats the victor in peace talks," commented one newspaper, "one almost expects leaves to sink and rocks to float!"[38]

The people were not pleased. After swallowing a decade of government propaganda about the will of the masses and the united resolve of the Japanese people, they took to the streets in September at the news that they would have to pay their own bills for the war. In the ensuing disruption, known as the Hibiya Riots, more than 350 buildings were wrecked or burned down, including thirteen churches and nine police stations. The writer Kunikida Doppo, editor of the subtly subversive *Wartime Graphic*, was heard to say that he thought the revolution had finally begun.[39] During the riots elsewhere in Japan, an angry mob even

[37] Osada, *Sensō ga Nokoshita Uta*, pp. 136–7.
[38] Lone, *Provincial Life and the Military in Imperial Japan*, p. 55.
[39] Sakai, "Survive to be critical," pp. 22–3.

pulled down the statue of Itō Hirobumi in Kobe.[40]

There are, however, doubts about the extent of such "mass" protest. Focusing on provincial life, the historian Stewart Lone argues instead that many such moments of public dissent were staged by tub-thumping politicians, who did not truly want the war to continue, but still wished to score points against the sitting government that had, in their eyes, mismanaged its end. Komura Jūtarō, the Foreign Minister who signed the Treaty on Japan's behalf, soon found his name appropriated in Yokohama business slang, where "doing a Komura" became a new term for bungling an apparently sure thing.[41]

And, indeed, the terms of the Treaty of Portsmouth did eventually bring down the government of the prime minister Katsura Tarō, who was obliged to resign in favor of his rival, Saionji Kinmochi. The new Cabinet came packed with ministers with strong ties to business and industry, ready to get to work on Japan's new sphere of influence, over the Yalu River and into Manchuria.

Among the spoils of war agreed at the Portsmouth conference, Japan acquired the South Manchuria Railway company and its assets, effectively extending its influence all the way from Port Arthur up to Changchun—the line onwards to Harbin remained in Russian hands. Less of a railway company than an all-controlling industrial concern, dominating logistics and the local economy, the South Manchuria Railway was put under the command of Gotō Shinpei, the efficient administrator who had already turned around the fortunes of Japan's possessions in Taiwan (as well as almost invading Fujian in 1900). The supposedly incompetent Foreign Minister Komura quietly and unobtrusively changed the course of history by adding a clause to the treaty that restricted ownership of shares in the South Manchuria Railway to Chinese or Japanese subjects. This, in turn, headed off an attempt by the U.S. railroad baron E.H. Harriman to buy into the Manchurian transport network. In decades to come, this would allow Manchuria to become a sphere of wholly Japanese influence, and eventually a puppet state.[42]

To protect Japanese interests in its new holding on the Liaodong peninsula, a new military unit was formed in 1906—the Kwantung Garrison (later renamed the Kwantung Army). Ostensibly, it was there

---

[40] Saaler, *Men in Metal*, p. 219.
[41] Lone, *Provincial Life and the Military in Imperial Japan*, pp. 60–61.
[42] Lu, *Agony of Choice*, pp. 19–20.

to provide security in Port Arthur, Dalian and environs. In practice, it was a rail-borne task force able to ship itself anywhere along the tracks from Dalian to Changchun.[43]

With Russia successfully held at bay, the true treasure was Korea, signed over as a Japanese protectorate in 1905, not without resistance from former King, now Emperor Gojong, whose palace was menacingly surrounded by Japanese troops. His prime minister similarly refused to cooperate, leading to the Japanese regarding the treaty as officially "signed" when physical threats and arm-twisting had managed to secure a five-man quorum among the reluctant cabinet ministers. The deal made Japan responsible for Korea's borders, harbors and foreign policy, and made Itō Hirobumi, the newly appointed Resident-General in Seoul, the de facto master of the kingdom in the name of the Japanese emperor. The helpless Gojong wrote to several foreign monarchs, pleading for assistance, but received none—the foreign powers had agreed to look the other way over Japan's "special interests" in Korea, particularly since the prime minister of Japan, Katsura Tarō had agreed in principle with the Secretary of War, William Howard Taft in July 1905 that Japan would not contest America's presence in the Philippines if America remained similarly hands-off over Korea.[44]

Japan's victory also alerted the international community to its potential as a threat. In 1906, the San Francisco school board refused to allow Japanese pupils to attend classes with white students, the reaction in Japan was one of indignation at what was seen to be a breaking of earlier

---

[43] The term derives from "East of the Pass" (*Guan dong*), common among Chinese migrant laborers in the region, as Manchuria was beyond the Shanhai Pass that marked the coastal terminus of the Great Wall; see Gamsa, *Manchuria*, p. 70. It can still be heard in modern slang, but the region is more commonly known as Liaodong, i.e. "East of the [River] Liao." The reasoning is geopolitical—the modern-day People's Republic discourages any discussion of Manchuria that implies, however obliquely, it was once not part of China, which was surely part of the Japanese rationale for using the name Kwantung Army in the first place. For similar reasons, I have learned never to use the term Manchukuo in conversations with Chinese without prefacing it with *wei* (false).

[44] Esthus, "The Taft-Katsura Agreement," p. 50. Esthus wrestles with the degree to which the conversation between Taft and Katsura was in any way legally binding, or a representation of actual U.S. policy, but that is a story for another time.

agreements over immigration.

"The only sin the Japanese have ever committed," commented the nationalist Tokutomi Sohō, "is that of being Japanese. If this is the case, we must break down the white domination [of the world]."[45]

Friction over immigration to the U.S. west coast reached the point that U.S. strategists drew up the first draft of what would become known as *War Plan Orange*, a strategy document to be held in reserve in case of open conflict with Japan. But for the decade following the end of the Russo-Japanese War, the only enemies faced by the Japanese military were ideological and attitudinal. Newspapers ran stories about the listlessness of modern youth, draft-dodging remained a common pursuit, and strategists fretted about the rise of pernicious doctrines. Socialism, in particular, was regarded as a dangerous way of thinking, not merely because of its opposition to monarchy, but because it was widely believed that socialist agitation had contributed to the weakness of Russia. The very ideals that had helped Japan in 1905 by undermining Nicholas II, now risked undermining the Japanese Emperor at home.

The Army would never be as popular as it was at the close of the Russo-Japanese War, when its victories were celebrated, and before its gains were eroded. In the years that followed, it might attempt to assert it still enjoyed popular support, through propaganda and declaration, but from 1905 onwards such statements became increasingly shrill, defensive and demanding. Popular opinion, particularly in the press, came to describe the Japanese Army as a "haunted house."[46]

Both the Army and Navy turned to public spaces in their attempts to win over the people. Sven Saaler writes:

> While only three statues were commissioned in 1904 and six in 1905, the count rose to eleven in 1906, fourteen in 1907, eleven in 1908 and sixteen in 1909. The increase was remarkable enough to be noticed by... the *New York Times*, [which] posed the rhetorical question: "Is it possible that Japan has caught our modern mania for putting up statues to people whenever there is the slightest justification?"[47]

---

[45] Asada, *From Mahan to Pearl Harbor*, loc. 580.

[46] Harries and Harries, *Soldiers of the Sun*, pp. 94 and 103.

[47] Saaler, *Men in Metal*, p. 168.

The statues, often attended by platoons of day-tripping schoolchildren with mops and scrubbing brushes, were not the only ongoing memorials of the war. Memorial forests were planted all over Japan, as a
means of keeping construction workers busy, while many a community
gained a war memorial library room, as well as a supply of Army-surplus
rifles and ammunition—sold off to cadet or reservist associations in a
drive to clear out superfluous and outmoded equipment.

Such celebrations could not hide the ongoing costs. The exceptional
wartime tax hikes stayed in place for years to come, while sharp price
rises in everything from fuel to clothing had long-term impacts on the
general population. The price of food went up by thirty per cent. Facing
virtual black-outs in towns that could not even afford oil lamps in their
shops, the post-war period saw an increase in urban and rural Japanese
giving up on stagnant home life and seeking their fortunes elsewhere,
on the Hokkaidō frontier, or even in the colony of Taiwan or the protectorate of Korea. This became an even more attractive proposition in
1907, when Japan officially took over Korea's internal affairs, forcing the
abdication of Emperor Gojong.[48]

"The Japanese," writes S.C.M. Paine, "ultimately derived the wrong
lesson from their turn-of-the-century wars with China and Russia. They
concluded that they had won. Actually, their adversaries had lost."[49] In
the case of China, Japan had been fighting a fading Manchu leadership
fearful of assigning too much power to its Chinese lackeys, hemor-
rhaging supplies to corruption, and with officers reluctant to take any
risk—more afraid of their Manchu masters than the enemy they were
supposed to be fighting. Against Russia, they faced a Tsar undermined
by revolutionary intrigues on his home ground, at the far end of the
longest supply line in the world. Reading between the lines, the Army
in particular seems to have been all too aware that victory in the Russo-Japanese War had been an incredibly close affair, and by no means
guaranteed a repeat performance in the event of renewed hostilities.

As for the Navy, it was winning friends at home and abroad. When
Prince Fushimi Sadanaru made a state visit to Britain, ostensibly to
thank the British for their "advice" during the Russo-Japanese War, the
timorous authorities slapped a universal ban on performances of *The*

---

[48] Lone, *Provincial Life and the Military in Imperial Japan*, p. 63.
[49] Paine, *The Sino-Japanese War*, p. 369.

Mikado lest it cause offense. Navy and marine bands were prohibited from even playing the music, amateur productions were similarly forbidden, and when an impresario in Sheffield flouted the rules and put on a performance to a packed house (commenting to the London *Times* that he wished the government banned a play *every* week), his theatrical license was revoked. A Japanese journalist, dispatched to the UK to cover the Prince's arrival, bought a ticket for the Sheffield show and reported that the show was superb fun.[50]

The press had a field day, asking whether such political correctness now also extended to a ban on *Hamlet*, at its plot suggested that the ruler of another allied nation, Denmark, might be a murderer. Questions were asked in Parliament, as to who precisely—the Lord Chamberlain, the Foreign Office, perhaps the King himself?—had ordered the ban, while voices in the print media began a campaign to drag Fushimi himself into the drama by asking him if he really would have objected to an operetta that used "Japan" merely as a foil for skewering British foibles.

On arrival, Prince Fushimi confounded expectations, steaming into the Royal Navy docks at Chatham while his own military band on deck serenaded the dignitaries waiting onshore with a medley from *The Mikado*—or at least, so the British believed. The Japanese musicians were more likely to have been playing the original 1868 battle hymn "Miya-san, Miya-san," a suitable anthem for a prince's flagship, unaware of its associations for their hosts. Far from being insulted at the portrayal of the Japanese in the Gilbert and Sullivan musical, Prince Fushimi expressed regret that he would be unable to see it while he was in London; it was banned in Japan, on the grounds that it was probably disrespectful to the imperial institution, although he had heard it was "delightful and harmless."[51]

Back home in Japan, Tanaka Giichi, commander of the Third Infantry Regiment, saw the integration of military and civilian concerns

---

[50] Lawrence, "The Banned Mikado," p. 156. The revocation of the licence is not mentioned in Lawrence, but reported in Goodman, "The Fushimi Incident," p. 299.

[51] Goodman, "The Fushimi Incident," p. 302. His comments were reported in the *New York Times*, May 7, 1907; Rodman, "A More Humane *Mikado*," p. 289. Cortazzi, *Japan in Late Victorian London*, pp. 69–71, suggests a more precise timeline, to the effect that *The Mikado* was performable in Yokohama in 1887 with a name-change, presumably frowned upon after the Public Order Law of 1900, openly refused permission by the Tokyo police in 1923, and out of the question after the Public Security Preservation Law of 1925.

as a vital part of preparation for the next war, on the grounds that "the age when wars are fought by the military alone is over." Only one in five, Tanaka observed, of the one million men mobilized for the war in Russia, were soldiers. The rest were reservists, merchant seamen, the kind of people that the nation needed to count in the next war. In order to make his point, he took the unusual step of sending two platoons of his own men to assist at the meeting of the Tokyo Patriotic Women's Society—the military and the civilians, he argued, needed to get used to each other.[52]

Tanaka was instrumental in reforms to Army regulations, which had remained unrevised since they were lifted from the Prussian military manual in 1894. His reforms focused on "spiritual education" (*seishin kyōiku*), to ensure that soldiers were inculcated with a will to sacrifice themselves in achieving strategic goals. In 1908, Army life was sharply regulated by the introduction of *The Barracks Handbook* (*Guntai Naimusho*), an officer's manual aimed at combating lax discipline and poor performance in peacetime, in the vain hope of creating a more efficient fighting force in war. This reform was aimed at protecting the Army from some of the temptations and distractions of civilian life, but within fifteen years, it was regarded in hindsight as a sharp turning point—a directive that separated military men from civilian life, sealing them off in an increasingly anachronistic and out-of-touch bubble, even restricting and controlling their media access, focused only on their own concerns, preparing, and indeed waiting for a war that would reassert their winning status.[53]

The new code firmly locked soldiers into the whims of their officers. The barracks "family" was now ruled by task-masters with an iron will, the soldiers pitilessly subordinate to any scheme that their officers deemed sufficient to make a spirited man of them. In 1909, the first inkling of what such fanaticism might wreak became apparent in Ōsaka, when two soldiers died on a forced march in July heat. They had not been permitted to remove their helmets or uniforms, to drink water or to rest and eat, for twenty-four hours straight. Eighty of their comrades had collapsed, and nine were hospitalized. This, then, was the new "fighting spirit" of the Japanese military—a self-directed brutality that was fated to find tragic outlets in the way the Japanese military treated others.[54]

---

[52] Victoria, *Zen at War*, p. 18.

[53] Lone, *Provincial Life and the Military in Imperial Japan*, p. 117.

[54] Harries and Harries, *Soldiers of the Sun*, p. 102.

All of which, allegedly, was for the benefit of Japan's new colonial subjects. Not everybody played along. Sin Chae-ho, a Confucian scholar who had resigned from his teaching position in protest at Korea becoming a Japanese protectorate, summarized the way in which the Japanese were using Pan-Asian rhetoric to conceal their conquests.

> When we are angry at Japan for depriving Korea of its rights, they tell us that "All Eastern countries are one, and you should not be upset." When we are infuriated by Japanese exploitation, they lie to us: "All of the yellow race is one, so you should not complain." They are trying to make people forget about nationalism by intoxicating them with Easternism. It is these bandits who have been propagating the slogan of Easternism.[55]

Itō Hirobumi, as the Resident-General for Japan in Korea, saw himself as a buffer keeping the protectorate from sliding further under Japanese control. By June 1909, however, he had given up fighting the Army on the issue of home-rule, and resigned his post.[56] A few months later in October, the thirty-year-old Thomas An Jung-geun, a Christian convert and Russia-trained resistance fighter, ambushed him on the train platform at Harbin station, Manchuria, where Itō had been meeting a Russian emissary in October 1909. An shot Itō three times, yelling that he was acting on behalf of Korea.

The dying Itō muttered: "Whoever shot me was an idiot."[57]

An believed, mistakenly, that Itō had ordered the assassination of Queen Min in 1895, and that Itō had criminally misinformed the Meiji Emperor about the extent to which Koreans welcomed the protectorate. He believed that Meiji would intercede if he knew the extent to which the Koreans were suffering under Japanese rule. Much like the samurai who led the Meiji Restoration, he believed that he was fighting for what the Emperor *would order*, if only the Emperor had the right facts. Among the list of Itō's crimes against Koreans, An added a crime against the Japanese themselves, suggesting that Meiji's father Emperor Kōmei, who had died at 35 from smallpox, had in fact been poisoned by Itō and

---

[55] Kim, "Sin Ch'ae-ho," p. 192.
[56] Duus, *The Abacus and the Sword*, p. 235. Duus notes that Itō faced criticism at home, and armed guerilla resistance in Korea.
[57] Itō, *Itō Hirobumi*, pp. 564–76.

the anti-Shōgunal clique.

Awaiting his execution some months later—and irritated that he was being tried as a common criminal and not as a prisoner of war—An wrote a manifesto of his beliefs, arguing that his actions were intended to wake up the people of Asia before Japanese crimes caused their land to be "burned to cinders." He argued that Itō had been the master of a secret cabal of power-hungry conspirators who had seized control of Japan, turned Korea into his own private fiefdom, and was now busily perverting the cause of Pan-Asian brotherhood as a cloak for Japanese imperialism.

> If Japan fails to change its political strategy and if oppression continues to increase daily, then the Chinese and the Koreans will no longer endure the humiliations inflicted upon them by the people of the same race, but will prefer defeat at the hands of another race. The consequences are clear. The oppressed inhabitants of China and Korea will collaborate with the white people.[58]

An's dream of a united Asia called for a combined Sino-Japanese-Korean bank, a peace conference between the three countries, and for Port Arthur to become a free city. He was executed in 1910, still believing fervently that Asia could be united under Japanese guidance, without the need for a Japanese imperium.

Instead, the assassination of Itō provided the Japanese with the perfect excuse to tighten their grip on Korea. Uniforms and swords became obligatory not only for the armed services, but for officials, including teachers in elementary schools. Dissident political organizations (which would be nearly all of them) were forbidden, and the press was strictly censored. The Japan-Korea Annexation Treaty of 1910 made Korea officially *part of* Japan—the two countries are the same color, one unified realm, on all maps printed in Japan for the next thirty-five years. Gojong's son, Sunjong, was downgraded to kingly status, and confined to his palace, a subject of the Japanese Emperor.

---

[58] Lee, "An Chung-gun: 'A Discourse on Peace in East Asia', 1910," p. 210.

Commodore Matthew Perry. Perry (1794–1858), who led the "Black Ships" that opened Japan to the outside world, commemorated in a statue in modern-day Hakodate, Japan. *Photo: Kati Clements.*

ABOVE: **The Battle of Ueno.** A painted screen depicting the Battle of Ueno at the Kan'ei Temple, now at the Tōshōgū shrine in Ueno. *Photo: PHGCOM.*

LEFT: **Saigō Takamori.** The controversial "last samurai," as depicted in his statue in what is now Ueno Park, site of the Battle of Ueno. Owing to his death as a rebel in 1877, he is shown wearing civilian dress, not armor or a uniform. *Photo: Kati Clements.*

LEFT: **The Meji Emperor.** Mutsuhito (1852–1912), was the teenage prince whose "restoration" as emperor cloaked the seizure of power by the Satsuma and Chōshū domains, and the onset of Japan's modern era. Engraving by Edoardo Chiosonne (1888). *Photo: Maruki Riyō.*

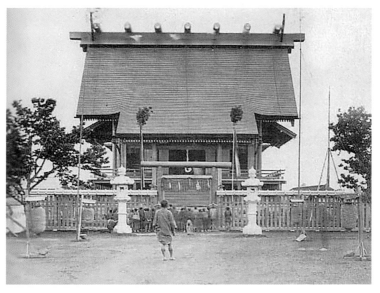

Summoning Souls. The original modest form of the Shōkonsha (Shrine to Summon the Souls), established by the Meiji Emperor to commemorate Japan's war dead. It was renamed the Yasukuni (Shrine to Pacify the Nation) in 1879. *Photo: Sekai Bunka.*

The Mikado. Poster by John Hassall for Gilbert & Sullivan's *The Mikado* (1885), which lifted lyrics and music from "Miya-san, Miya-san," the marching song of the Meiji Restoration rebels. *Photo: Public Domain.*

The Murder of Queen Min.
Queen Min of Korea's
assassination, as reported
in the French press in 1895.
Photo: Le Journal illustré.

Yasukuni Completed. A celebration
in 1895 of the completed
Yasukuni Shrine, as depicted by
Shinohara Kiyo'oki, shows Japan's
ultra-modern army, a world away
from the samurai of a generation
before. *Photo: Melikian Collection.*

Captain Higuchi. Much celebrated in multiple woodblock prints of 1895, Higuchi Seizaburō leads an assault on Weihaiwei while carrying an abandoned Chinese baby. *Photo: Boston Museum of Fine Art.*

Winter Warfare. In an 1895 print by Taguchi Beisaku, Japanese troops brave a blizzard to scout enemy positions. A generation later at Mount Hakkōda, inadequate preparation for winter maneuvers would prove to be one of the worst peacetime disasters in Japanese military history. *Photo: British Museum.*

The Surrender of Weihaiwei. A woodblock print by Migita Toshi-
hide uses perspective to make the Japanese in modern uniforms tower over the Chinese and their foreign advisers. The
picture shows Admiral Ding Ruchang surrendering, although
he had already committed suicide by this point. *Photo: Jonathan Clements.*

威海衛陥落北洋艦隊提督丁汝降伏圖

The Yellow Peril. A lithograph commissioned by Kaiser Wilhelm II depicts a vivid imagery of European civilization under threat from an oriental menace. *Photo: Harper's Magazine.*

Putting His Foot Down. A British cartoon by J.S. Pughe depicts Uncle Sam issuing a stern warning to the other imperial powers. *Photo: Puck magazine.*

Making a Meal of It. In a 1904 cartoon by Kobayashi Kiyochika, defeated Russian soldiers are made to eat their own ammunition. *Photo: Library of Congress.*

Lieutenant Hirose. Remembered as the first of Japan's modern "war gods" (*gunshin*), Hirose Takeo (1868–1904) was killed in action while scuttling a block ship at the entrance to Port Arthur and subsequently commemorated in a children's song in an increasingly militaristic school system. Woodblock print by Ōkura Kōtō (1904). *Photo: Rijksmuseum.*

The Boxer Uprising. A commemorative saké cup adorned with the flags of the international alliance that marched on Beijing in 1900 to relieve the besieged Foreign Legations: Japan, the United States, Italy, Austria-Hungary, Russia, France, Germany and the United Kingdom. *Photo: Melikian Collection.*

The Silent Admiral. Statue of Admiral Tōgō Heihachirō (1848–1934) on the dockside in contemporary Yokosuka. In the background is his flagship from the Battle of Tsūshima, the *Mikasa*. *Photo: Jonathan Clements.*

CHAPTER 4

The War Gods

Revolution was in the air. In May 1910, a factory worker in Nagano was arrested with bomb-making materials, and swiftly (perhaps too swiftly) implicated in a wider conspiracy of leftists, allegedly plotting to kill the Meiji Emperor. Twenty-four "radicals" were executed for the plot, on shaky evidence.[1]

The Japanese authorities were mindful of the damage that activism could achieve, particularly in China, where revolutionaries, many of them ironically funded by Japanese money, successfully overthrew the Qing dynasty in 1911. The removal of the "Last Emperor" ushered in even further disintegration of China, with rival governments, local warlords and other interest groups contending to gain control of the infant republic. Having spent decades pretending to have an interest in preserving the integrity of China, foreign powers now openly wondered where the borders of true China should now be drawn. A large faction within the new Republic of China clung to the notion of China as a multi-ethnic state, with a five-striped flag incorporating not only the 90% Han Chinese majority, but also the Manchus, Tibetans, Mongols, and other races. But others argued that the Han had no claim over territories acquired during the era of Manchu expansion and conquest—separatist movements rose up in the Muslim-majority Xinjiang, and in non-Han ethnic areas such as Tibet and Mongolia, often with support from foreign powers who saw tantalizing prospects for new colonial gains, on the edges of a new, reduced-size Republic of China. Britain, for example, saw opportunities for investment and mineral exploitation in an independent Tibet, while Russia eyed both Xinjiang and Mongolia.

Japan's position, as outlined by its Foreign Minister, Uchida Yasuya, in 1911, was that Japan had no particular objection to the creation of

---

[1] Huffman, "High Treason Incident," p. 118.

a Chinese Republic. This was not actually true; Japan would have preferred a constitutional monarchy on its doorstep, as it would eventually
fabricate in Manchuria twenty years later. However, for the meantime,
Japan and Britain would prefer it if the new China did not include
Manchuria, Tibet or Mongolia.[2] This attempt to detach the non-Han
regions failed, although it did lead to Japanese interests in Manchuria
being recognized by Britain, allowing Japan to station troops along the
Beijing-Mukden railway.

Manchuria remained, at least on paper, part of China. But the authority of the Republic was impossible to enforce there without local
military muscle. The Kwantung Army, with control of the all-important railway, had effectively become one more power-broker in a lawless
region with immense potential.

When Emperor Meiji passed away in 1912, he was joined in death
by General Nogi, that military paragon who had repeatedly asked to be
allowed to kill himself in atonement for various misdeeds. Refused permission to die over a lost battle flag or a mishandled siege, Nogi finally
got his wish after the death of the Emperor, leaving a suicide note that
restated his sense of deep shame over the number of lives lost in the Russo-Japanese War—both his sons had died in the conflict. Nogi's death
would eventually be spun by the media not as the last self-destructive
act of a mediocre general, but as a traditionalist sensation—the daring
return of a style of samurai suicide that had been illegal since 1663, and
a glorious reassertion of virtue and military honor.

The Taishō era, named for Meiji's son, the Taishō Emperor (1879–
1926), began with a political crisis indicative of future military moves
within the government. Over-stretched in Korea and Manchuria, the
Army demanded two more divisions to defend its new area of interest.
Prime Minister Saionji Kinmochi refused to come up with the funds,
leading his Army Minister, Uehara Yūsaku, to resign in protest.

Uehara's decision exposed a dangerous loophole in the organization of the Japanese government. Army and Navy Ministers had to be
serving officers, supplied by the armed forces themselves. The Army
was supposed to nominate a replacement for Uehara, but refused to do
so, making it impossible for Saionji to form a cabinet—it was a critical

---

[2] Gates, "Out with the New and in with the Old," p. 67. For constitutional monarchy,
see Best, *British Engagement with Japan*, p. 252.

moment, demonstrating that irrespective of the Prime Minister in power or the political party with a majority, Japan's constitutional protocols made it possible for the Army or Navy to bring down any government that would not agree to their wishes. Constitutionally, the Army and Navy did not take orders from the government, but from the Emperor himself, encouraging them to act, much like the Meiji Restorationists, in accordance with what they imagined the Emperor's wishes to be.

Faced with such a rebellion, Saionji's government collapsed, in a move seen by much of the media as a devious power-play by old Chōshū men, clinging to their hold on military power. In a note of praise from the history books, Saionji's refusal to bend to the Army's will was praised by much of the popular press as a noble sacrifice, like a "shattered jewel" (*gyokusai*). He was, inevitably, replaced by a Chōshū man, Katsura Tarō, the protégé of Yamagata Aritomo.[3]

As part of the new domination by the military, the Japanese government began to lay the groundwork of what would eventually come to be known as State Shintō—a careful foregrounding of Emperor-worship and a martial spirit.[4] Between 1911 and 1914, the Ministry of Education issued an all-new songbook series for use in elementary schools, designed to turn schoolchildren into "good Japanese" less liable to support a revolution against their monarch. Whereas the previous songbooks, in use since the 1880s, had concentrated on figures from folktales and samurai history, including the doomed samurai Kusunoki Masashige, who rode willingly to his death at the behest of a medieval Emperor, the new edition came crammed with songs about the heroes of Japan's recent wars, including the suicidal General Nogi. In fact, Nogi appears as little more than an aside in actual school history books of the time, his Port Arthur debacle swept under the carpet, but had a much larger footprint in songbooks and moral education. He was celebrated not for his actions, but for his ethical purity, with songs accompanied by romanticized commentary on his childhood stoicism. He would remain prominent in Japanese school song books until 1945, while his deeds, as celebrated in song, would also become attached to school plays and poetry recitals.[5]

Nogi was joined in the school books by a gaggle of other newly minted heroes, chiefly from the glory days of the Russo-Japanese War, although

[3] Person, *Arbiters of Patriotism*, pp. 76–77.
[4] Best, *British Engagement with Japan*, p. 229.
[5] Cave, "Story, song and ceremony," pp. 16–17.

some were lauded for their peacetime achievements. One such new hero was the commander of one of Japan's first submarines.

Arriving too late to make any contribution to the Russo-Japanese War, submarines now formed a new component of the Navy. The first five were Holland-type submarines from the United States. The sixth *Kaigun Holland #6*, was a copy built in the Kawasaki dockyards with the cooperation of American engineers, and achieved lasting infamy when it sank during sea trials in April 1910. While testing the gasoline engine, with a snorkel-like ventilation pipe extending above the surface, Lieutenant Sakuma Tsutomu brought his sub fatally too low in the water, causing water to rush in. A chain broke on the emergency ventilator slide, making it impossible to stop the flow of water, and causing the sub to sink to the sea bottom. Trapped sixty feet below the surface, with the electrics shorted, the 14 men aboard the #6 frantically tried to pump water out in the darkness. They slowly suffocated.

The sinking of the #6 would have been a forgotten naval accident were it not for Lieutenant Sakuma, who calmly kept a diary of his last hours. In it, he dispassionately apologized for his mistake, noting to Navy technicians that it was human error, not the submarine that had failed. He listed precise details of their attempted counter-measures, and told his commanding officer where to find his last will and testament in his house. He praised his men for the steadfast calmness in the face of certain death, and with handwriting that became increasingly spidery and indistinct, observed that his eardrums had popped under the pressure, and that breathing was becoming difficult as petrol fumes filled the conning tower.

Sakuma's letter, retrieved from the wreck the following day, was reprinted in newspapers, and soon celebrated as an example of Japanese fortitude, a captain going down with his ship. Of crucial importance to the Japanese press, and many a foreign journalist, was the fact that the sailors had remained at their posts, instead of panicking or turning on each other, as had been reported in some similar incidents outside Japan. Despite having sunk his own ship, Sakuma's stiff upper lip made him a hero to a generation of cadets, and the full text of his dying words would be reprinted for study in Japanese schools. He would also be memorialized as a statue and the subject of a song, although "Skipper Sakuma" (*Sakuma Teichō*), struggles visibly across ten plodding verses to find something positive to say.

Flowers fall but leave their scent
Men fall but leave their names.
Well done, Skipper Sakuma,
A paragon of Japanese manhood. [...]

Death on the battlefield where bullets fly
Is not the only form of courage.
Hearing about this fearless, loyal demise
Even cowards will be uplifted.

The skipper was born in Fukui
A Navy lieutenant called Tsutomu.
Promoted by imperial order.
The dead conferred with glorious honor.[6]

Similarly commemorated with a schoolbook song was Hirose Takeo, a naval officer in the Russo-Japanese War who had volunteered to command one of the block ships—aging hulks that were sunk at the entrance of Port Arthur harbor in order to keep the Russians bottled in. His ship was struck as it approached the harbor, and Hirose died while searching onboard for survivors.

By 1912, Lieutenant Hirose had been immortalized in multiple prints and engravings, had gained a bust and two statues dotted around Japan, and become the subject of a song that became part of the music curriculum for Japanese schoolchildren. He had been acclaimed by the media as a War God (*gunshin*). This designation was later made official, and he became the first of Japan's twentieth-century war heroes to be granted his own shrine.

The cannons thunder, the bullets fly
Upon the deck awash with wild waves
Shrouded in darkness, the lieutenant calls
Where is Sugino? Sugino isn't there.

---

[6] Osada, *Sensō ga Nokoshita Uta*, pp. 148–50. For his statue, see Saaler, *Men in Metal*, p. 313.

None found within the ship, three times he searches
He calls but no answer, he searches but no sign
The ship is slipping soon beneath the waves
Among the many enemy shells, one hits its mark

The lieutenant is struck, there within the boat
Slain by the flying shell
In the hateful depths beyond Lushun [Port Arthur] harbor
Hirose the War God, preserved in the rolls of honor.[7]

The sudden cult over Hirose represented an attempt by the Navy to outmaneuver the Army on the public celebration of war heroes. Of the statues mushrooming all over Japan to commemorate great military men, the vast majority were of senior Army figures—generals and field marshals—whereas the Navy pushed a more engaging agenda, of celebrating lower-ranking officers with whom the public might be more expected to empathize and identify. The Navy also pioneered the placing of such statues in places with heavy through-traffic, such as in the streets facing train stations.[8]

The Army fought back with its own Russo-Japanese War hero in the new songbook, Major Tachibana Shūta, an officer killed in action at the Battle of Liaoyang in 1904. Tachibana's achievement was somewhat questionable—he had refused orders to take cover in a trench during an assault on Russian positions. Instead, he had announced that he was going to charge them, at which point he was riddled with bullets and killed. This brief moment in military history somehow managed to take up eighteen verses in the original 1906 version, but was edited down to just three for the children's sing-along:

Dead bodies piled up like a mountain.
Blood flows like a river.
A scene of carnage, the Xiangyang Temple
The moon filtered blue through the clouds.

---

[7] Osada, *Sensō ga Nokoshita Uta*, p. 639. Note that this version is the one sung by children in Japanese schools, not the 14-verse epic as originally conceived.
[8] Saaler, *Men in Metal*, pp. 169–71.

"Most of our side has been defeated.
Wait here for a while," so he was told, yet
His courage affronted.
"Now is the time to die.

For the sake of our country.
For the honour of the army."
While speaking thus, he fell.
In glory, Tachibana![9]

For a repeat of the endless waves of doomed soldiery that had characterized Port Arthur, the Japanese military wanted to maintain a fighting stance based less on skill and tactics than on straightforward, blind obedience. Soldiers needed to maintain the utmost, unquestioning confidence in their divine mission and their Army's invulnerability, even at the expense of individual lives—civilian life was hence dragged further towards the alien concerns of the military. In 1913, in an effort to counter a sense of generational apathy among the young, the Ministry of Education adopted the Army's physical educational manual for use in boys' exercises at schools. The following year, magazine articles encouraged mothers to teach their children martial songs, to counteract the rise of popular music, and to buy toy swords and bugles for their sons to play with.[10]

As for the infantry themselves, "A Foot Soldier's Duty" (*Hohei no Honryō*) was destined to become one of the Army's evergreen songs, written by a young cadet in 1911, and spreading from schools to men on active service. It introduced the image of the falling petals of cherry blossoms (*sakura*), liable to be seen around the time of graduation from military academies, and most famously seen on the slopes of Mount Yoshino. The song goes on to compare the red flashes on a soldier's dress uniform collar to the color of cherries.

Weeping cherry is the color of the collar
The flowers in Yoshino blown in the storm

---

[9] Osada, *Sensō ga Nokoshita Uta*, p. 642. For the original 18-verse monster, see pp. 120–30. Note that the song is called Lieutenant-Colonel Tachibana (*Tachibana Chūsa*), anachronistically assigning him his posthumous promotion.

[10] Lone, *Provincial Life and the Military in Imperial Japan*, pp. 98–9.

Born as a Japanese man
Be a fallen petal in a skirmish battle

An arm-length gun is not good as a weapon
A finger-length knife would not do
Don't you know that for two thousand years
The Japanese spirit has been forged?

Warriors protecting the battle flag
The number is 200,000 in all
Gathered in eighty places
They will never disarm even in their dreams

Once stepping into an enemy territory
You are the leader
The final break is your mission
Cavalrymen, artillerymen, cooperate

Traversing the Alps
Old history, white snow
The Battle of Mukden
Shows the elegance of the Japanese infantry.

This is the foot soldier's duty.
Oh, our brave infantry arm
Congenial spirits,
Let's carry out our duties together.[11]

Although Japanese soldiers had seen plenty of grim action fighting
Korean guerrillas in the years since the Russo-Japanese War, "A Foot
Soldier's Duty" clung to the more romantic imagery of the Army's last
grand victory, the Battle of Mukden. Just as the earlier "Myriad Enemies" established the "shattered jewel" in the romanticized imagery of

---

[11] Osada, *Sensō ga Nokoshita Uta*, pp. 154–5. I am substituting arm and finger for
the archaic measurements *shaku* and *sun*. A different final verse was only sung on
school occasions: "Oh, our brave infantry / Congenial friends, come on now / Let's
talk at the hundred-day anniversary. / Reflecting our collar color in a cup of sake."
There were several other variants, including a 1932 rewrite.

Japanese militarism, "A Foot Soldier's Duty" reinforced the image of the cherry blossom as another analogy for a heroic death—the term *Sakura* frequently recurs hereafter in Japanese militarist discourse, not only in songs and poetry, but also in unit names, insignia, medals and equipment designations.

Throughout the 1910s, Japanese governments alternated between cabinets with civilian sympathies and those dominated by military concerns. This led to an odd oscillation in tensions between these interest groups. The ever-increasing costs of the empire required more money spent on the military. But the military needed to find some common ground with the civilian governments that approved its funding. Increased funding for the military pushed up taxes, causing resentment among the common people. The pay-off for military funding was often an uneasy increase in political suffrage, increasing the threat that the military perceived towards its own plans.[12] There were further frictions, particularly when military considerations impinged on public life.

For the people's own good, Army planners argued, it was better for railways to run in the hinterland, not along the coastline where they would be more vulnerable to bombardment from the sea. This was all very well, but most people in Japan lived on the coastline, where the railways were most needed. Similarly, Army interference in apparently everyday matters poked into many areas of civil life, affecting even the design of tram lines, which had to be wide enough to permit the passage of a gun carriage.[13]

In January 1914, the Navy had been severely discredited in a local crisis, in which leaked papers from the Siemens corporation were found to prove that officials had been widely bribed to secure lucrative shore facility and shipbuilding contracts.[14] The scandal seemed likely to sink many of the Navy's plans for budgetary requisitions—it was hence incredibly convenient for the Navy that war with Germany should break out in August of that same year.

At the time of the outbreak of the First World War, Prime Minister Ōkuma Shigenobu, architect of many a previous cunning plan, characterized it as "the chance of a millennium."[15] However, many Japanese

---

[12] Dunscomb, *Japan's Siberian Intervention*, p. 2.

[13] Harries and Harries, *Soldiers of the Sun*, p. 103.

[14] Schencking, "The Imperial Japanese Navy and the First World War," p. 86.

[15] Clements, "The Chance of a Millennium," p. 146.

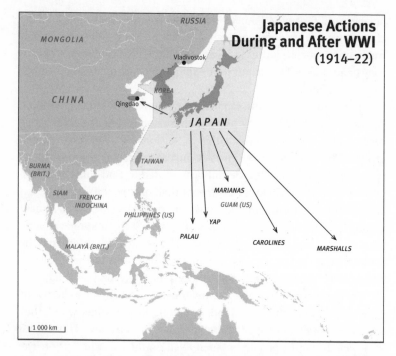

Japanese Actions During and After WWI (1914–22)

were unsure of what was at stake. There were reports of schoolchildren and their teachers assuming that this was some sort of delayed revenge on Germany for the Triple Intervention of 1895. Others confused Austria, Germany's ally, with *Australia*, assuming that the war was being fought over recent Australian efforts to exclude Japanese immigrants. It was, perhaps, fortunate that German commerce raiding in the Pacific gave the Japanese something to focus on as the act of a belligerent foe.[16]

The British were keen to secure limited Japanese assistance in the Pacific, but were wary of encouraging too intense a Japanese involvement on the Chinese mainland. They asked the Japanese to keep to hunting operations against armed German merchant convoys. The Navy Minister, Yashiro Rokurō, surprised the Japanese parliament on September 4 by claiming that even this innocuous-sounding task would require more funding. Yes, he told a supplementary war budget committee, it was true that Japan possessed fifty destroyers, but forty-two of them were over nine years old, which made them vulnerable against

---

[16] Lone, *Provincial Life and the Military in Imperial Japan*, p. 104.

newer German ships. Even to meet the constabulary request of the government, to simply look for trouble at sea, he required, and received, immediate approval for the construction of ten new destroyers.[17]

However, this was economical with the truth, as some of his serving officers would soon demonstrate. Many of the Navy top brass were long-term supporters of the Southern Advance (*nanshin*) policy, a strategic plan to conquer the South Pacific, both to the benefit of the Japanese Empire, and in demonstration of the Navy's capabilities and usefulness. They saw the outbreak of war as the perfect opportunity to seize German colonial possessions in the Pacific, and to justify the vast expense that the navy had already incurred. Moreover, as noted by Admiral Akiyama Saneyuki, it would be poor tactics indeed to send Japanese fleets to steam around the Pacific, hoping to run into a German convoy. It made far greater sense, both strategically and logistically, to begin by seizing the bases that the Germans would themselves be using, all the better to restrict German movements and expand Japanese range.[18]

On September 30, sixteen days after he had been put in command of the First South Seas Task Force, Vice-Admiral Yamaya Tanin took matters into his own hands, landing troops at Jaliut Atoll in the Marshall Islands. Similar landings soon followed at Yap, the nexus of Germany's telegraph cables, and the Caroline Islands. These seizures went largely unopposed.

The sole major battle in the East Asian theater in the First World War was a joint British-Japanese siege of the German colony at Qingdao, the city that overlooked Jiaozhou Bay, the best harbor in north China. British accounts of the Japanese at Qingdao were guarded but impressed, praising their discipline and their skills in artillery, although one correspondent was a little troubled at the sight of one Japanese soldier in a newly captured redoubt, "laughing like a schoolboy after a huge prank."[19]

The German commander gave notice of his intention to capitulate on November 7, but he was kept waiting another week before the document was signed. The German surrender was hence made official on November 14, the seventeenth anniversary of the Triple Intervention, an anniversary that the British appear not to have noticed, but well appreciated by the Japanese.

[17] Schencking, "The Imperial Japanese Navy and the First World War," p. 93.
[18] Schencking, "The Imperial Japanese Navy and the First World War," p. 92.
[19] Fenby, *The Siege of Tsingtao*, loc. 470, 494.

As the British marched into the town, the Germans turned their backs on them and pulled down their pants—a gesture of derision at the idea of European forces fighting alongside Asian allies.[20]

Although the Navy would see some action elsewhere, Qingdao was the only place the Japanese Army saw large-scale action in the First World War—a fact that contributed to the sardonic and weary tone of the most popular song about it, which finishes every stanza with the infantry slang for "no good" (*natchoran*). After expressing his surprise that anyone could have thought Qingdao was a good place, populated as it is by "tail-less foxes," the singer pauses to ridicule the smartly dressed sailors who brought him to the siege, and to facetiously claim that although he is ready to die, he only ducks from the bullets because it is a matter of honor that he lives to see Qingdao fall.

> Abandoning my parents, wife and children
> I became a soldier.
> With tears, I completed three years of service.
> When I got home, the roof was leaking.
> *Natchoran*.[21]

It has become customary for historians to downplay Japan's involvement in the First World War as a thinly disguised land-grab and a few desultory patrols. This is certainly not how it was viewed at the time by many British subjects, particularly the residents of Canada's west coast, who were relieved to hear that Japanese warships were patrolling Pacific sea lanes—until the completion of the Panama Canal, British Columbia's handful of gunboats were effectively 15,000 sea-miles away from any likely reinforcements. In one incident of touching bravado in August 1914, the nascent Canadian navy was so under-supplied that HMCS *Rainbow*, its sole light cruiser, was obliged to put to sea to watch for possible German invaders, despite not having any ammunition for its guns.[22]

Similarly, since neither the Japanese Navy nor media, nor even many Japanese historians, ever expressed much interest in the unglamorous world of escort duty, the actions of the Japanese in Mediterranean waters tend to be dismissed. Far from aimlessly sailing around

---

[20] Fenby, *The Siege of Tsingtao*, loc. 509.
[21] Osada, *Sensō ga Nokoshita Uta*, pp. 259–61.
[22] Meehan, "From Alliance to Conference," p. 50.

in circles, which is the impression one might get from many a history book, the Japanese cruisers based out of Malta successfully kept 788 Allied transports safe from German attack, and rescued 1,800 British subjects from a sinking vessel, an action in which 54 Japanese sailors lost their lives to a U-boat attack.[23]

The buzzword in military circles after the summer of 1915 was *autarky*—the need to be self-sufficient. Wars were no longer matters of limited campaigns by small armies, supplied by neutral countries nearby. They were becoming *total* conflicts, enmeshing entire national populations in austerity measures and supply chains. The British, for example, had discovered far too late that 90% of the optical glass in their binoculars came from either Germany or France, and by 1915 were commandeering all the samples left in local stores and pleading with the public to donate binoculars for the war effort. Conversely, the Germans had relied so heavily on rubber imported from the British colonies that by 1915, they were suffering from a severe shortage of materials for tires and cables. The two enemies were so beholden to each other for such mundane items that they were even prepared to arrange an underhand exchange of the materials on neutral territory, so they could both continue fighting each other. The United States, with an entire continent of resources close at hand, was the ideal that Japan sought to emulate.[24]

It was not enough that Japan had its own shipyards and weapons factories—to fight in a twentieth century war, it would need ready access to coal, and as ships switched over to new engines, oil. It would need iron ore and rare metals, and the surety of a food supply, or risk being shut down as Germany had been. It would need rubber, sourced from the same South-East Asian plantations as much of the rubber already in such short supply in Europe. To keep itself secure in the twentieth century, Japan needed either a guaranteed, safe and unbreakable trade in such materials, or to incorporate the territories that produced them within the borders of its empire.

---

[23] Kitamura, *A Forgotten Lesson of the Russo-Japanese War*, p. 13. As noted in Collingham, *The Taste of War*, loc. 4634, the Navy's concentration on warship construction for a "decisive battle" would cripple Japan's capabilities for safe seaborn transportation, and ultimately contribute to starvation and deprivation in the latter days of the Pacific War.

[24] Barnhart, *Japan Prepares for Total War*, p. 42. The importance of a "territorial base for wealth and resource" was a crucial pillar of Mahan's *The Influence of Sea Power on History*, compulsory reading at both the Army and Navy staff colleges.

Colonel Koiso Kuniaki (1880–1950) was tasked with compiling a report on Japan's chances in such a conflict. He concluded, after an extensive tour of Japan and its possessions, that neither Korea nor Taiwan would provide enough of a buffer, since they were *agricultural* territories, and that it was vital for Japan to obtain secure resource nodes further afield, most obviously in China. He also recommended that the Japanese military be granted a mandate to seize control of vital domestic industries in times of national crisis, in order to have direct access to war materials.[25]

The Japanese government had already been on the case for six months. While the war raged on in Europe, Japan began to consolidate its territorial gains in China, with Ōkuma Shigenobu and Katō Takaaki concocting a list of "Twenty-One Demands" to impose upon the Chinese. The Demands came in five groups. The first, centered on Shandong, recognized that control of the former German colony was now in Japanese hands, locking Japan in as the master of the peninsula's rail network and industries. The second pursued similar expansion in Manchuria, calling for the Japanese to have settlement rights and extraterritoriality, as well as the right to pursue their interests in Inner Mongolia, now regarded as an essential buffer with Russia. The third set of demands targeted three mining concerns in the Chinese hinterland, already deeply in debt to Japanese investors, and demanded that they were handed over to full Japanese control. Any of the above proposals were liable to meet with reluctant assent from Japan's own allies, as being belligerent but understandable in terms of the current policies of imperialism being pursued elsewhere.

The final two Demands aimed to make Japan's influence in China greater than that of any other colonial power. One called for China to agree not to grant any more coastal concessions to other foreign countries. The last, the most startlingly pushy, demanded that China hand over its financial policy and internal policing to Japanese "advisers," allow Japan to build three extensive new railways, sure to amount to underhand invasion conduits like the South Manchuria Railway, as well as Buddhist temples and schools—this seemingly innocent clause would open the door to propaganda and indoctrination. It was, the reader may recall, an alleged attack on a Buddhist temple that led to the abortive

---

[25] Barnhart, *Japan Prepares for Total War*, p. 17.

Amoy Incident. In fact, the combined railways, schools, and policing initiatives would amount to a takeover not only of Amoy, but of all of Fujian province, extending Japan's influence across the Taiwan Strait and onto the Chinese mainland.

On hearing the Demands, the irate Chinese President Yuan Shi-kai asked his adviser "why the Japanese government were dealing with China as if it were a slave."[26]

He was not alone in this opinion—even Yamagata Aritomo, now retired but consulted by Katō, thought that the final set of demands was going too far, since they did, indeed, treat China like a subject state.

Yuan was either unaware, or all *too* aware that the Demands were actually a step up from earlier offers proposed by his own predecessor as President, Sun Yat-sen. In 1905, frustrated in his ambitions for revolution, Sun had speculated on the possibility of offering Manchuria to the Japanese in exchange for supporting his revolution. In 1912, with the Republic of China in its infancy, he suggested that it lop off the Manchurian provinces, which were, after all, merely the homeland of the ousted Qing emperors, in exchange for massive loans fit to build a new nation. It is not as if the Japanese were springing the situation on the Chinese at all—they were entering a new round of negotiation on something that the Chinese, or at least a faction now out of power, had proposed themselves.[27]

Somewhat naively, Katō had hoped that details of the 21 Demands would not leak from the Chinese. President Yuan had no such qualms, immediately supplying the foreign and domestic press with a précis, and whipping up a frenzy of anti-Japanese sentiment. Precise details were not forthcoming for another month, at which time it became apparent that the Japanese had not admitted the full scope of the Demands to their allies. This would return to haunt them in the peace conference that ended the war.

The opening of the Panama Canal, overshadowed in the news by the outbreak of war, would also have a long-lasting effect on national policy. In drastically shortening the distance for shipping between the Atlantic and Pacific oceans, it made Pacific trade a far more lucrative and desirable option for both the United States and Britain, increasing

---

[26] Naraoka, "A New Look at Japan's Twenty-One Demands," p. 191.
[27] Kwong, *War and Geopolitics in Interwar Manchuria*, p. 42.

their level of engagement with Pacific sea routes.

"Between 1890 and 1914," writes Kimura Masato, "Britain's mer-chant navy carried up to 60 percent of the world's trade, and built two thirds of its ships."[28] America's own merchant marine had been in decline since the Civil War, owing to a concentration on America's own coastal waters, instead of longer distance traffic. The opening of the Panama Canal, however, shortened the journey from New York to the Chinese coast by 3,768 miles (nine days' travel), not only opening the under-de-veloped Pacific coast of the United States to trade and commerce, but making it possible for heavy goods—oil, metals, and machinery—to be transported more economically to Asian markets. The bonuses were just as lucrative to the Japanese, for whom the American east coast was the largest export market, now ten days closer with attendant reductions in shipping costs that could make Japanese goods even more competitive. Furthermore, the Canal brought Brazil, with a growing Japanese immi-grant population, ten days closer to Japan, opening up the possibility of more frequent trade and migrant contacts. Attempts by the United States to impose a transit tax on shipping through the Panama Canal would have eaten into Japanese profits, but were suspended after British protests, and by other considerations related to the outbreak of the war.[29]

Japan's physical seizure of former German colonies was merely the most obvious manifestation of its rise in the Pacific. By 1917, with American shipping concentrating heavily on the more lucrative Atlan-tic supply-run, Japan already represented 55% of merchant shipping in the Pacific. Although American entrepreneurs were making short-term profits shipping goods to Europe, Japanese shipping lines had come to dominate much of the Pacific trade corridors, and hence freight pric-ing, everywhere from South America to Australia and along the coast of China.[30]

By 1917, Japan was relying on the United States for more than 90% of the high-grade steel required for building ships. Under the pretext of securing essential materials for its own entry into the war, President Woodrow Wilson shut down steel and iron exports to Japan on July 9, even though some Japanese factory owners had already paid for their orders. The decision amounted to an embargo on the Japan trade, and

[28] Kimura, "Securing the Maritime Trade," p. 108.
[29] Kimura, "Securing the Maritime Trade," pp. 118–20.
[30] Safford, "Experiment in Containment," p. 440.

was seen as such by the Japanese media. Pundits in both Japan and the U.S. described it as a ruse designed to force Japan to divert more of its merchant shipping to the Atlantic, helping the European war effort while also reducing Japan's long-term influence in Asia.

"The embargo problem… is a life and death problem to the Japanese," commented the *Osaka Asahi* newspaper. "It is like giving a cold bath to the prosperity-intoxicated people of Japan."[31] It use of the term "prosperity" is interesting—with German possessions secured, almost all the "global" conflict was now in Europe. Japan was an ally in the war against Germany, but enjoying the fruits of a peaceful and uncontested Pacific. There had already been complaints from Britain that Japan had been openly lying about the amount of merchant shipping required for wartime essentials, and that much of its Pacific trade amounted to profiteering.

The lack of new merchant ships placed a strain on simple logistics—goods and materials started to pile up in warehouses and on docksides, while prices began to rise because of shortages and scarcity.

Paul Reinsch, the U.S. ambassador in Beijing, was soon reporting precisely the opposite—that the Japanese had realized that their old European suppliers would be tied up in war and recovery for the next decade, and that the U.S. was already twisting their arm over raw materials. In fact, the existence of the U.S. embargo proved to be the best possible argument for Colonel Koiso's self-sufficiency recommendations. If this was how America treated Japan when they were on the same side, it was clear that if they were ever to become opponents, America could strangle Japan's military capability at a distance.[32]

Less than six weeks after Wilson imposed the embargo, Japan sent the first of many survey expeditions into the Chinese hinterland, hoping to secure a new, local supply of iron ore in Shandong. By the time that the U.S. relented in March 1918, agreeing to release thousands of tons of steel stockpiled in California shipyards, on the understanding that the Japanese would send a merchant fleet to help out in the Atlantic, Japanese investors were even investigating the possibility of buying up abandoned mines in the U.S. itself.[33] Moreover, the crisis allowed the Army Ministry to push through its Munitions Mobilization Law (*Gunju*

---

[31] Safford, "Experiment in Containment," p. 442.

[32] As noted in Miller, *Bankrupting the Enemy*, loc. 145, this had effectively been U.S. strategy for any potential war with Japan since 1906.

[33] Safford, "Experiment in Containment," pp. 449–50.

dōin-hō), a piece of legislation allowing the commandeering of vital industries in time of war, and which would sit, like a time-bomb, on the Japanese statute books for the next twenty years until it went off in 1938.

It is likely that the bill would never have passed, at least not in that form, had not the U.S. offered such overwhelming evidence that Colonel Koiso's recommendations were justified. The new law was mitigated only in the language that would activate it—a mere "international incident" would not be enough; Japan would have to be actually "at war." Nevertheless, the threat now existed that disruptive or seditious officers in the Army or Navy could precipitate a conflict that would then allow their own organizations to take over the government.[34]

Far from stunting Japan's ambitions in Asia, the American embargo had only reminded Japan of the unreliability of its fair-weather friends, and given it, in the words of the U.S. ambassador to Tokyo, further "motive for territorial expansion."[35] It also turned into a win-win situation for the Japanese Navy—criticized for not being modern *enough* at the outset of the war, the Navy now argued for more investment. Having disobeyed orders and seized German possessions, it now demanded extra funding to protect them. For the politicians, another lesson to take home from the war was that Japan was critically beholden to other countries for raw materials. It needed more influence in Asia and the south seas, not less.

In the first two weeks of the First World War, the seizure of German island possessions increased the size of the Japanese empire by 8,000 square kilometers, most of which was open sea. It also vastly extended the responsibilities of Japan's Navy by a similar degree, leading to a huge drain on the national treasury. By 1921, when Japan arrived ready to make concessions at the Washington Naval Conference, the Imperial Japanese Navy would be eating up 32% of the national budget.[36]

If Japan did not secure resources, warned Navy minister Katō Tomosaburō, then its ally across the Pacific could readily outpace it in any arms race, and "it would lead to such an extreme disparity as to reduce the Pacific Ocean to an American lake."[37]

---

[34] Barnhart, *Japan Prepares for Total War*, p. 17. The scheme is reminiscent of that of Britain's Ministry of Munitions, which was created in 1915 to streamline supply chains in wartime. Britain's ministry, however, was abolished in 1921 with the end of the Siberian Intervention, whereas Japan's remained in place.

[35] Safford, "Experiment in Containment," p. 450.

[36] Schencking, "The Imperial Japanese Navy and the First World War," p. 84.

[37] Asada, *From Mahan to Pearl Harbor*, loc. 1267. The term "American lake" seems to

The First World War had taught the Navy that if pitched into an arms race with the United States, Japan was sure to lose through lack of access to resources and factories. Chinese possessions could mitigate the problem a little, but in the short-term, Japan was better off agreeing to physical limits on the size of its fleet, in order to hold the Americans at arm's length for a generation. And... then what?

"In Europe after the Great War," wrote Miyazaki Tōten, "there will be a clash of imperialism and non-imperialism and, if imperialism does not perish, it is easy to see the starving tigers [of Europe] will turn around on their heels and fight over scraps of meat in the Orient."[38] Such suspicions had been part of scholarly discourse in Asia since the beginning of the Taishō era, if not before, and echoed warnings of a "white peril." Despite the ongoing Anglo-Japanese Alliance, the former politician and prominent Christian Nagai Ryūtarō had said in a 1913 speech:

> The English and the Americans profess the principles of democracy, and they claim to be rebuilding the world through democracy, but in fact Anglo-American democracy is the money politics of a cabal of financial combines who provide the government and political parties with secret funds and election expenses. In a drive to secure dominant control over the world's resources by invading smaller countries and exploiting ethnic minorities, these financial combines have finally plunged the world into a great conflict. Claims to be rebuilding the world through democracy made by those who ought to be condemned for upsetting world peace are like claims by a criminal that he is a policeman protecting law and order. I believe there is no greater threat to the whole human race.[39]

"I am afraid," wrote the Indian Pan-Asianist Taraknath Das, "Asia will be the battleground of the next gigantic war for which the diplomats of the First Class Powers are now preparing."[40] Das lamented the weakness of China, which, in his view, with a population of 400 million, could

---

deliberately evoke the use of the term in naval strategy documents by Satō Tetsutarō as early as 1912.

[38] Szpilman, "Miyazaki Tōten's Pan-Asianism, 1915–1919," p. 137.

[39] Duus, "Nagai Ryūtarō: The White Peril, 1913," p. 160.

[40] Aydin, "Taraknath Das: Pan-Asian Solidarity as a 'Realist' Grand Strategy," p. 308.

have easily forced a more conciliatory attitude if only it were not so disorganized and backward. Das predicted that the world order would remain mired in past conflicts for as long as the British maintained their "absurd" colonial presence in India, but he also envisaged that Japan's expanding influence, either through military aggression or economic success, was sure to bring it into conflict with the European powers. Das looked forward to a stronger China, thanks to Japanese investment and support, that might be able to exert a more forceful position on the international stage. His ideals ironically came out sounding oddly similar to those of the Japanese ultra-nationalists, who similarly called for Japan to lead Asia into the future.

"The threat that the White people pose to the Yellow people is now imminent," stated the inaugural issue of the ultra-nationalist Black Dragon Society's journal in 1917. "The Japanese Empire, as the last [independent] representative of Asia, is the only one that can fight and face the West as the backbone of the Yellow race."[41]

Other Pan-Asianists were more mollifying in tone. "We do not hold so narrow-minded a view as to drive the Whites out of Asia," wrote the politician and editor Tokutomi Sohō. "What we want is simply that we become independent of the Whites, or Yellows free of the rampancy of the Whites."[42]

As the war drew to a close, Japan was dragged into an unexpected epilogue, as part of a new multinational intervention on the Asian mainland. The Tsar's Russia having collapsed in its own revolution in 1917, the closing days of the war saw calls to come to the aid of the last "White" Russians in Siberia, fighting a losing action against the advance eastward of the "Red" Bolsheviks.

On paper, it seemed like a dream come true—the chance to join the British, French, Canadians, Italians, Americans and even a contingent of Chinese, in a police action that could establish a buffer state in Siberia, forever walling off the revolutionary Russians from the Pacific coast. In practice, it was a colossal waste of time and money, a four-year drain on already-stretched resources, with wavering support from changing governments back in Tokyo, bringing home little but a deadly second wave of "Spanish" influenza.[43]

---

[41] Saaler, "The Kokuryūkai, 1901–1920," p. 122.

[42] Swale, "Tokutomi Sohō and the 'Asiatic Monroe Doctrine', 1917," p. 282.

[43] Humphreys, *Way of the Heavenly Sword*, p. 24. For the flu, see Otsubo, "Fighting on

With an overwhelming majority of the manpower present, the Japanese general Ōtani Kikuzō was made the nominal leader of the Siberian expedition, although the British contingent refused to accept his authority. The British were already on shaky ground, since most of their troops were actually Canadian conscripts, reporting to both Ōtani and the British command, while political leaders back in the UK debated the very relevance of the Siberian Expedition. Since the war was now officially over, the continued presence of Allied troops in Siberia could no longer be justified as part of the Allied mission. It was, instead, tantamount to an invasion of Russia, or at very least, interference in Russia's internal affairs.

The Siberian Intervention was an epilogue to the war, an irritation to many of its participants, many of whom just wanted to go home. But it was real enough to those who were there—you can still find a memorial to the "Great War" in San Francisco's Golden Gate Park, established by bereaved families, which gives very America-centric dates for the conflict that include losses in Siberia: "1917–21."

Japan's participation in Siberia met with a mixed reception among the population—anticipating resistance to an overseas action that had been tacked onto a war that was supposed to be over, the government banned media commentary on the enterprise, including unapproved war reporting and even accounts of troop movements. The first soldiers to depart, in August 1918, were waved off by cheering crowds with flags, but within a couple of weeks, civil unrest had broken out over sky-rocketing rice prices. Martial law was declared amid claims that the Siberian mission was a profiteering boondoggle, and later troop trains leaving for the ports were met with jeers and booing.[44]

The domestic rice shortage was exacerbated by wartime appropriations overseas—where the Japanese might have fixed the shortfall in the past by importing rice from elsewhere, Chinese farmers were growing tobacco for the European market, and farmers in French Indochina were exporting their produce to Europe. What little rice there was often had to be requisitioned from across the Korean Strait—"The problem of urban hunger," writes the food historian Lizzie Collingham, "had now been

---

Two Fronts," pp. 471–8.

[44] Dunscomb, *Japan's Siberian Intervention*, pp. 68–70. See also Lu, *Agony of Choice*, p. 33 for the Japanese government's attempts to drag in participants by offering investment subsidies.

successfully exported to the peasants of Korea."[45] By the end of August, anti-government feeling over "rice riots" all around Japan had reached such a fever pitch that an Osaka newspaper dared to write "The age that dazzled the people with majestic brilliance has long passed; who can respect the crown of a monkey? The people suffer in misery, hungry sparrows weep in empty storehouses." Amid talk that Japan was approaching a "day of final judgment," journalist Ōnishi Toshio pushed one step too far, by noting that he and his fellow writers were musing about the ancient Chinese portent: "a white rainbow pierced the sun." It was a reference, as in the days of the Meiji Restoration, to an ancient Chinese crisis, probably intended as a demand for political resignations, but interpreted by the authorities (in something of an over-reaction), as a call to kill the Emperor.[46]

Both the disappointments of the Great War, and the expense of the ongoing Siberian Intervention could hopefully be mitigated by the Paris Peace Conference, where the victors in the conflict hoped to settle as many international issues as possible, and to set up an international league that would, somewhat optisuyin

mistically, ensure that there would be no more need for wars. Japan, obviously, would be at the conference table as one of the victorious allies, although inconveniently, so was China.

The former Prime Minister, Saionji Kinmochi, was sent at the head of the Japanese delegation to the Paris Peace Conference, with orders to secure Japan's interests in the Pacific and its new acquisition in Shandong, as well as to push the white nations into dismantling barriers to Japanese commerce and immigration—a "racial equality" clause in the charter of the mooted League of Nations.

Saionji faced considerable resistance among his own entourage, including the 29-year-old aristocrat and future Prime Minister, Konoe Fumimaro (1891–1945), son of Konoe Atsumaro, who had strong doubts about the willingness of the Europeans and Americans to cooperate. Konoe was careful to stress that he did not have something against all Europeans or Americans—plenty of them were honorable men, or at least thought they were. Some pushed an agenda of "democratic

---

[45] Collingham, *The Taste of War*, loc. 1068.
[46] Huffman, *Creating a Public*, p. 367. The reference is to "*bai hong guan ri*," a saying from the *Intrigues of the Warring* States regarding the assassination of a chancellor in the state of Han. Anyone who knew enough Chinese to understand the phrase would also know it was unlikely to have been aimed at the emperor.

humanitarianism," fully aware that it was a cover for their own imperialist schemes. Others genuinely believed in the idea, which was why
Konoe thought it important to distinguish between Westerners who
were conscious of their "egoism," and those who were not.

"The European War," he wrote, "was a battle between existing great
powers and great powers in the making. It was a battle between those
who found it convenient to maintain the status quo, and those who
found it convenient to destroy it." In this argument, Konoe regarded
Germany as a late-comer like Japan, unable to secure adequate colonies
because, as he put it, the British and the French had already sewn up so
much of the world for themselves.

Germany, argued Konoe, had followed the wrong path by taking
an aggressive military position. He did not want Japan to make the
same mistake, but he was also worried at the degree of "fawning" he
saw among the Japanese, giddy with the high-handed notions of the
proposed peace conference and the League of Nations. If, wrote Konoe,
the League of Nations would *really* turn out to be an organization dedicated to justice and humanity, he would be all for it. But he suspected it
would turn into a toothless body, rubber-stamping the unjust decisions
of Britain and the United States.

Despite being only a junior member of the delegation—scolded by
Saionji on the way to the conference for picking flowers in a Ceylon park—
Konoe wrote as if he would be standing at a podium, thundering at the in-
ternational community about Japans requirements for the post-war world.

He would demand, he promised, decolonization and the opening
of free markets. He would demand an end to racism and racist policies,
not solely those aimed at the Japanese, but at all non-whites.

> Japanese and other yellow races are regarded as inferior and are
> being persecuted... The yellow man is prevented from securing a
> job or renting a house or land. One even needs a white guarantor
> in order to stay just one night in some hotels. Such a situation is,
> from the point of view of humanitarianism, a grave problem...[47]

---

[47] Hotta, "Konoe Fumimaro: 'A Call to Reject the Anglo-American Peace', 1918," p. 317.

Konoe offered no clue as to how he would achieve such aims—he was so peripheral to the delegation that on one occasion he had to sneak into a meeting using press credentials from a newspaper his family owned. Nor did he really explain how Japan would square its own mission on the Asian mainland—its annexing of Korea and its ongoing plans in the north-east, with his own calls for decolonization. Would Konoe's justice-minded Japan be pulling out of Korea, for example? The most sardonic critique of Konoe comes from the modern Pan-Asian historian Eri Hotta, who sums up his earnest rhetoric as if it were a Groucho Marx routine:

> We reject your exclusive club because you don't want us as a member, even though we really deserve to be one. If you change your mind, we would reconsider accepting your offer of membership (and we would probably end up excluding other non-members because it feels good to be privileged, though we might be nicer to them than you have been to us). If you don't take us seriously, you will regret it, because we might resort to forceful means just like the Germans.[48]

Colonel Koiso's explosive report, coupled with Japan's own experience in the war, seemed to have left the country with two options. Supporting the idea of a League of Nations, with truly free trade and truly free migration, was the peaceful solution. But if the League of Nations failed to deliver on its promise, then the only option for national security would be a vigorous pursuit of empire.

Japan's behavior in the Pacific had concerned its Allies from the outset, particularly after all foreign vessels, even those of Japan's allies, were forbidden from approaching the Japanese-protected Pacific islands without prior permission. Both the U.S. army and navy planning divisions issued memos expressing their concerns that if the Japanese fortified islands such as Kwajalein, Truk and Saipan, they would be almost invulnerable. Such objections were discounted by negotiators at the Paris Peace Conference, on the grounds that the U.S. Navy was *obliged* to be paranoid about other nations.

One U.S. navy commander, William Sims, waved away the fears on

---

[48] Hotta, "Konoe Fumimaro: 'A Call to Reject the Anglo-American Peace', 1918," p. 313.

the grounds that even if Japan did use the Pacific islands for military purposes, all it would be realistically able to manage would be a "surprise attack" of some sort, "not a full-scale war."[49]

America's apprehensions were folded into a more general set of stipulations for Japan's continued presence on the former German islands of the Pacific, with an insistence that Japan's presence be under the auspices of a League of Nations mandate, and that Japan agreed not to fortify the islands. There was particular argument over Yap, a tiny cluster of islands some 380 km southeast of Guam, which happened to be the nexus for the undersea telegraph cables connecting Guam, Manado and Shanghai. If Yap remained in Japanese hands, argued Woodrow Wilson, then the Japanese could cut off trans-Pacific telegraph communications at will. However, he received little support, and the Japan retained the strategically important territory.

The province of Shandong was the major sticking point. China would not sign the treaty if Shandong was not handed back to the Chinese. Japan would not sign if it was. Japan got its way, winning itself status as a founder member of the League of Nations as a result, but also twisting Woodrow Wilson's arm from the very outset. Wilson resignedly regarded the League of Nations plan as the "best deal that could be gotten out of a dirty past," noting:

> The only hope, was, somehow, to keep the world together, get the League of Nations with Japan in it, and then try to secure justice for the Chinese not only regards Japan, but as regarding England, Russia, France and America, all of whom had concessions in China.[50]

China had lost the entire peninsula of Shandong to Japan, and was expected to be satisfied with one small bonus—the return of the astronomical instruments looted by the Germans during the Boxer Uprising. China's delegate refused to sign the Treaty of Versailles, and the "May Fourth" protests that broke out in China over the poor terms were a turning point in Chinese history, in which many republican Chinese thinkers and leaders gave up on the idea of European values, turning

---

[49] Takahara, "The Wilson Administration and the Mandate Question," pp. 151–2.
[50] Nakatani, "What Peace Meant to Japan," p. 186.

instead to Communism.

But the Japanese, too, were deeply dissatisfied with the outcome, having acquired *some* territorial gains, but not the vital anti-racism clause that would have re-opened markets and immigration. Despite having gained Shandong at China's expense, the Japanese press still scolded the Chinese for including the Japanese among the targets of the protests.

"How many times," wrote the *Osaka Mainichi*, "has Japan unsuccessfully attempted to tell the Chinese of the error of their anti-Japanese behavior? Yet it has happened once again, like a recurring fit of female hysteria."[51]

Korea, too, erupted in protests. The death of the former King Gojong in January 1919 had been a cause for much national reflection, particularly over the fact that Korea's interests in a post-war world were being handled by their Japanese masters at the Paris conference. In a series of protests that came to be known as the "March 1st Movement," Koreans demanded that the Japanese recognize that they, too, deserved to benefit from the sentiments of Woodrow Wilson's fourteen-point plan for international peace, which included a call for national self-determination.

Music in Korea was already heavily under the influence of Japan's colonization scheme, which was pushing many of the songs from Japan's increasingly militaristic school curriculum upon classes in Korean schools. One protest song, which may have sneaked initially under the noses of the Japanese authorities, was the "Korean Anthem" (*Aegukga*—literally "Patriotic Song"), which was then sung to the tune of "Auld Lang Syne," and may therefore have seemed harmless unless one understood the lyrics.

> Until the day when the waters of the Eastern Sea run dry
> And Mount Baekdu is worn away,
> May God protect our nation.
> Three thousand *li* of splendid rivers and mountains
> Filled with Roses of Sharon
> Great Korean People, stay true to the Great Korean Way.[52]

---

[51] Iida, "Fleeing the West, Making Asia Home," p. 423.
[52] Kim, "Rethinking Colonialism," pp. 34–5.

The ban on singing protest songs in Korea led to the seditious use of a folk song, "Arirang," as a symbol of Korean resistance. Today there are over 3600 variants of 60 songs that bear the name, but the basic version was understood by the 1919 protestors to be a reference to a lone pine tree on a hill outside Seoul, used for centuries as a place of execution. It was hence a song of doomed defiance, and a hope for better things.[53]

> Arirang, Arirang, Arariyo
> You are going over Arirang hill
> My love you are leaving me
> Your feet will be sore before you go ten leagues
> Just as there are many stars in the sky
> There are many dreams in my heart
> There, over there, that mountain is Baekdu
> Where, even in the middle of winter days, flowers bloom.

Meanwhile, the anti-Japanese feeling expressed on the mainland was to have a transformative effect on the ideology of Kita Ikki (1883–1937), a "continental adventurer" and would-be supporter of revolution in China, who came home to Japan, disenchanted, after suffering at the hands of Chinese protestors. The experience would cause him to propose a new program for pushing Western influence out of Asia, which would require radical reforms at home before Japan could be expected to turn its attention to helping China. In *An Outline Plan for the Reconstruction of Japan* (*Nihon Kaizō Hōan Taikō*), Kita suggested that the only way to achieve true success would be to stage a military coup, suspend the constitution for three years of martial law, and then turn the newly purged nation towards Asian conquest, thereby to save China and, eventually, India, by incorporating them within a Japanese empire. Conceding that Japanese was a hard language for foreigners to learn, he also made the modest proposal that everybody should learn Esperanto. "Peace without war," he added, "is not the way of Heaven."[54]

---

[53] Atkins, "The Dual Career of 'Arirang,'" pp. 644–5.
[54] Grunden, "Kita Ikki," p. 180. Usui, "Prelego pri Esperanto por japanoj en Pekino." Quote from Szpilman's translation in Saaler and Szpilman, op. cit., p. I: 278.

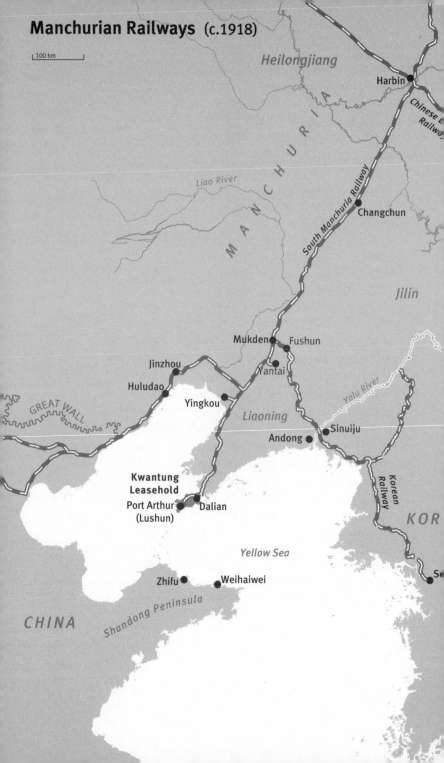

Manchurian Railways (c.1918)

100 km

Heilongjiang

Harbin

Chinese E.
Railway

MANCHURIA

Liao River

Jilin

South Manchuria Railway

Changchun

Mukden · Fushun

Jinzhou

Yantai

Huludao

Yingkou

Liaoning

Yalu River

Sinuiju

Andong

Korean
Railway

GREAT WALL

*Kwantung
Leasehold*

Port Arthur
(Lushun)

Dalian

KOR

Zhifu · Weihaiwei

Yellow Sea

S

CHINA

Shandong Peninsula

CHAPTER 5

The Promised Land

J apan's experience of the "Great War" had been nothing like the apocalypse endured by some other powers. Only 300 Japanese lost their lives in the conflict, versus, for example, over 116,000 Americans, and nearly 888,000 from Britain and its dominions. Although Japan had done more in the war than was often admitted, it was nevertheless at arm's length from many of the innovations and advances that characterized other nations' experience. In the aftermath, Japan was still fielding an army with pre-war weapons and tactics, ill-suited for whatever the next conflict might be. The Japanese had little experience of the big new war machines—airplanes and tanks, nor of radical new artillery that could be placed miles behind the front line. The growing importance of portable machine guns profoundly changed infantry tactics, favoring squads that could act on their own initiative, not wait meekly for orders from above. In the words of Horike Kazumaro, who served in the Army from 1916–44:

> Up till this time [post World War I] the core of our tactics was close combat relying on the bayonet. This became the decisive force in battle, and since the so-called close combat principle of tactics was traditional after the Russo-Japanese War, they weren't able to switch easily to these new tactics based on firepower. Worse yet, they continued close combat tactical principles right up until World War II… When machine guns fired all about you, there had to be leaders who would call for the assault element to attack precisely at the opportune moment. Up until this time, the platoon leader had just stood at the head of his platoon, brandished his sword and cried out: "Follow me!"[1]

---

[1] Humphreys, "Crisis and Reaction," p. 72.

The problem resided within the high command—the generation of soldiers who had been promoted to their positions during Japan's defeat-free years since 1894—why change doctrine now?

The general population was much more in favor of change, with a growing interest in socialism and left-wing politics, and even the voting-in of Japan's first Christian prime minister, and first "commoner" (unlike his predecessors, he was not a baron or count or similar noble rank) Hara Kei, elected in 1918 with the slogan "Militarism is Dead." Hara was precisely the sort of democrat that reformers of the previous decade had wanted—a party leader, reflecting the concerns of voters. This made him the worst kind of politician in the eyes of the militarists—he encouraged a appeasing attitude towards unrest in Japan's colonies and offered the worryingly reformist slogan of "Wipe the Slate Clean," removing the military appointees who had previously governed Korea and Taiwan, and even musing that the governor of the Liaodong peninsula could be a civilian if necessary. Hara's cabinet approved an electoral reform bill that would extend the voting franchise even further down towards the general population. At the time, this still extended to a mere 5% of the population, three million men paying the requisite amount of tax.[2]

In 1921, Hara was stabbed to death at a train station by a railway switchman angry with his lack of military backbone. Among several corruption scandals perpetrated by his party, Hara had also, claimed his assassin, failed to deal with the Russians appropriately over 700 Japanese massacred by Russian partisans at Nikolaievsk the previous year, and let the Japanese people down by withdrawing from Siberia and handing back Qingdao to China.

It was an assassination that found ghoulish support in many parts of the country—newsboys were heard cheering as they announced the extra edition about Hara's death, while one newspaper ran with the headline: "Prime Minister Hara Punished by Death."[3]

In the 1920s, Japan gained a Socialist party and a Communist party, both of considerable concern to conservatives who regarded such ideologies as factors in the downfall of Japan's enemies. There was also a growing sense of apathy towards the old order—one political agitator

---

[2] Oka, *Five Political Leaders of Modern Japan*, pp. 114–5.
[3] Oka, *Five Political Leaders of Modern Japan*, p. 122. For Nicolaievsk, see Bisher, *White Terror*, pp. 258–9.

described his shock at a cinema in the 1920s, when the audience did not bother to follow the onscreen instructions to remove their hats for the image of the Emperor.[4]

Nationalism, an increased emphasis on the veneration of the Emperor, and loyalty to Japan's "national spirit," began to be actively promoted as an alternative to socialism. But in the words of John Person:

> The policing of political activities in the early twentieth century, particularly since the 1917 October Revolution in Russia, had been aimed at containing socialism. In this effort, nationalism had served as the answer to revolutionary politics. But by the 1930s the cure served as the poison—nationalism was now revolutionary, at least in the sense that it was a threat to the government.[5]

The threat of war in the Pacific was mollified by the Washington Naval Conference of 1921, in which the powers agreed on limits in certain classes of warship. At the very least, caps on new ships helped reduce the expense of constantly attempting to outdo the imaginary innovations of a prospective enemy, although the Navy continued to look for loopholes. The Anglo-Japanese Alliance was brought to an end with a new "Four Power Treaty," in which Britain, Japan, the United States and France agreed a notional consultancy process with each other in the event of any disputes over Pacific possessions.

A year later in 1922, the Nine Power Treaty between all of the attendees of the Washington Conference effectively wrote the Open Door Policy into international law. In doing so, it obliged Japan to return Shandong to its fellow signatory, China, and also to have withdrawn from Manchuria. Manchuria remained in Japanese hands, with Japan clinging to the idea of its "special interests" as agreed in 1917.

Such deals had been concluded under the auspices of the League of Nations, an international body that would attempt, over the next twenty years, to resolve conflicts through dialogue and disarmament. Some on the Japanese political scene embraced this idea—after twenty years dancing to the tune of Yamagata and his supporters, they now avenged themselves on the military. It was even suggested in the Diet that Japan

---

[4] Lone, *Provincial Life and the Military in Imperial Japan*, p. 128.
[5] Person, *Arbiters of Patriotism*, p. 164.

had exhausted its supply of enemies—Soviet Russia was weak in the east, China was no threat, Germany was in ruins, and deals had just been struck with the U.S. and Britain. The Army had wasted millions of yen in Siberia, to no good end; it was now interfering in attempts to find a diplomatic solution in China. The Navy was a huge expense that constantly demanded more money for better ships, mercifully limited in the near future by the Washington Conference. The League of Nations now promised to settle disputes by negotiations—perhaps it was a time to call a halt to the huge amounts of money being poured into the Japanese military?

For the officers of the Japanese Army the victory of the Allied Powers was of less concern than the defeat of Germany. Germany had, after all, provided much of the organization and ideology of the Japanese Army. Amid much punditry regarding what went wrong, Army leaders came to accept the explanation of Erich von Ludendorff, who argued that the German military had not been *defeated*, but let down by its own people, who had caved in because of the prolonged and draining nature of the war. It was the people, not the soldiers who had been at fault—which meant that the Army's best strategy for the future was not to reform itself, but to ensure that doctrines such as socialism and communism did not undermine its home support. For Ludendorff, a military preparing for future war needed to win not only on the battlefield, but in the provision of its supply lines, the actions of its government's foreign policy, and most importantly, the hearts and minds of its people—complete autarky. Ideology would now be a crucial factor in preparation for war, not just among the soldiers, but among the people at home. If left unchecked, socialist ideals risked threatening the Emperor himself, as they had done in Russia. Increasingly strident calls to defund the military would hence be perceived by the military itself in the 1920s as a strategic threat.[6]

Some of the scheming came not from the upper echelons, but from activists in the lower ranks, such as Tōjō Hideki (1884–1948), a young officer in the Army. His father, Tōjō Hidenori (1855–1913) had been a minor officer in Japan's early wars, a student of Jakob Meckel, well-educated in matters of military theory, returning from a German posting to serve many years as an instructor at the Army staff college, but out

---

[6] Humphreys, "Crisis and Reaction," p. 78; Person, *Arbiters of Patriotism*, p. 221.

of place in the Army's aggressive, unimaginative battlefield style. After the Sino-Japanese War, the elder Tōjō had made the mistake of openly complaining to Yamagata Aritomo about the influence of the Chōshū clique on promotions, believing that he had been passed over because he came from a region that had initially opposed the imperial forces during the Meiji Restoration. Given the chance to prove himself in the field as a brigade commander in the Russo-Japanese War, the elder Tōjō twice took action on his own initiative that caused trouble for his superiors—once retreating against orders, and then refusing to commence a night attack with insufficient reconnaissance. In the both cases, his decisions may well have saved his men's lives, at the expense of a wider strategic advantages. For these actions, he was adjudged to be "unsuitable to command soldiers on active duty," and shunted into the reserves on health grounds.[7]

This was not how the story was remembered by his son. The younger Tōjō believed that his father's unimpressive career, ending with a grudging promotion to lieutenant-general just before retirement, was hampered by the Chōshū power-brokers within the Army. The younger Tōjō regarded the Chōshū faction's domination of Army careers to be not only flawed, but also dangerous, since he, like his father, was heavily influenced by German military thought, and believed that the people of Japan needed to construct some sort of variant of the German *Wehrstaat*—a unified national polity committed to defense.

The younger Tōjō returned to Japan from Switzerland and Germany in 1922, to take up a new position at the Army staff college. His journey took him on a train through the Prohibition-era United States, which he dismissed without leaving his carriage as morally bankrupt. Back in Japan, Tōjō presided over a four-year period in which the Army college's acceptance rate plummeted for applicants from the old Chōshū domains. Major Tōjō and other staff officers accepted written applications from all over Japan, but used the oral examination in Tokyo to determine if a candidate came from the area now known as Yamaguchi Prefecture. Some officials did observe at the time that it was odd so few men from the region were making it to the college, but Yamagata Aritomo, the one figure who might have had the muscle to initiate an investigation, had died shortly before Tōjō's arrival in 1922. It had been five decades since

---

[7] Chōnan, *Shin Shiryō ni yoru Nichi-Ro Sensō Rikusen-shi*, pp. 702–4.

the Meiji Restoration—the young leaders of that coup were dying off. Their protégés in the upper ranks now faced a concerted challenge from their own underlings, determined to break the last connections shared by the elite of yesteryear.[8]

The death of Yamagata, who had dominated Army policy and politics since the 1870s, marked the slow fade of the original Satsuma and Chōshū influence on the military. True enough there was still a second generation of officers appointed with the approval of the Satsuma and Chōshū cliques, but a growing number of younger officers had risen through the ranks from other parts of the country.

Now there were three generations represented in the Army—the old-school former samurai, diminishing by the year; the first generation of their modern recruits, now rising to high positions, and an increasingly fanatical coterie of young junior officers, determined to inflict radical change. Like their predecessors, some began to envisage the necessity for a military coup: a "Shōwa Restoration."

Ugaki Kazushige (1868–1956), the new Army Minister in 1924, did his best to shake things up—he shut down four of the twenty-one infantry divisions, hoping to use the savings to better equip the remainder with modern weapons. He slashed the requirements for conscription by a third, to only two years, and established a new staff section dedicated to mobilization in the event of a total war.

Optimism about Japan's position in the world was fading once again by the mid-1920s. The Siberian Expedition had led nowhere and cost more than the Sino-Japanese War; the Kantō Earthquake of 1923 had dealt a savage blow to the domestic economy, so much so that the first half of the 1920s saw further cuts in the military, The Army alone lost nine divisions, leading to many career officers fretting about their job security.[9] Social scientists in 1924 reported another issue with young soldiery—permanently impoverished, at risk to life and limb and prone to sudden repostings and dangerous duties, military men were the sole career group that Japanese women did not want to marry; while no gentleman, it was claimed, would marry the daughter of a soldier or sailor.

---

[8] Humphreys, *The Way of the Heavenly Sword*, p. 40. See also Hotta, *Japan 1941*, p. 119 for details of Tōjō's accomplices and co-conspirators from among the Japanese officers in Germany.

[9] Lone, *Provincial Life and the Military in Imperial Japan*, p. 116. The Army also lost more than 13,000 horses, a sign of further modernization.

"Only drunkards on trains," it was claimed, were prepared to publicly praise the military. Street altercations between military men and angry civilians became commonplace enough that some soldiers were reported as going to work out of uniform, in order to avoid trouble.[10]

Soviet Russia was agitating for more influence in Manchuria once more, while the Chinese, with Russian support, were contesting some of Japan's footholds on the Asian mainland. Arguably the worst assault came from an unexpected quarter when the United States, facing increased financial recession, imposed a new Immigration Law in 1924 that slashed quotas and effectively shut down all immigration from Asia.

This was not the borderless, harmonious world that the League of Nations had been promising. It was assumed, by many in both Japan and the U.S., that the bill would never make it through the Senate. The Japanese ambassador had warned Washington of the "grave consequences" that the bill would introduce to what had previously been, in his words, "the otherwise happy and mutually advantageous relations" that the two countries had enjoyed. But with the successful passage of the bill, the Japanese reaction escalated to a level not seen since the death of General Nogi in 1912.

Before dawn on the May 21, 1924, an unidentified Japanese man slipped into a Tokyo garden, sliced open his own stomach with a dagger, and then slit his own throat. The body was found later that day, together with three letters of protest, which made it clear that he had intended to kill himself in the garden of the U.S. ambassador, but that he had got the wrong address, and consequently spilled his intestines over the shrubbery of Japan's former finance minister.

The letter to the U.S. ambassador, Cyrus Woods, as reprinted in the *New York Times*, laid out his grievances:

> I greatly regret that your country… enacted the Japanese exclusion clause in complete disregard of humanity… I am a Japanese. We are now humiliated by your country in the eyes of the world without justification… I prefer death rather than to feel resentment.[11]

In fact, Woods, a man much respected by the Japanese, had already

---

[10] Lone, *Provincial Life and the Military in Imperial Japan*, pp. 116–7.
[11] Stalker, "Suicide, Boycotts and Embracing Tagore," pp. 153–4.

resigned in protest at the Immigration Law, as would his Japanese counterpart in Washington. The protestor went on to promise to intercede
with Jesus Christ in the afterlife, in order to get something remedied,
perhaps unaware of the Bible's position on suicide. His death was not the
last. Soon afterwards, two students threw themselves in front of trains,
one bearing a note calling for a boycott of American goods. A cadet at
a military academy swallowed rat poison and hanged himself, writing
in his suicide note another plea to the departing Woods, to deal with
this "racial insult." Taid O'Conroy, a lecturer at Keiō University, offered
a first-hand report:

> During the first days of the United States' decision Japan was in a
> state of hysteria. … All the superb sacrifice of money… of food,
> clothes bedding and first-aid materials by America at the time
> of the great earthquake, only one year before, was forgotten: the
> country of the Gods had been insulted… Where previously dis-
> dain and distrust were the strongest ingredients now hatred takes
> precedent.[12]

By early June, the protest movement had swelled to such an extent that
it could fill a stadium with a mock funeral for the first suicide, an event
proclaimed as the inaugural meeting of the Anti-American Citizens
Convention. Posters calling for a boycott on American goods sprang up
on street corners, while the Tokyo City Medical Association broke its
own code of ethics in advocating a refusal to treat American patients.[13]

On June 7, sword-wielding activists took the fight directly to which-
ever hapless foreigners happened to be staying at the Imperial Hotel
in Tokyo, barging into the ballroom in protest at the sight of frivolous
dancing at a time of national crisis.

> While the [Saturday] afternoon dance at the Imperial Hotel was
> in full swing, a body of armed men forced their way into the hotel,

---

[12] O'Conroy, *The Menace of Japan*, pp. 46–7. Ambassador Woods was loved by the
Japanese in part for his contributions to the relief efforts following the 1923 Kantō
earthquake. His official reason for resignation was the declining health of his moth-
er-in-law, although even the American press of the day saw through this excuse. See
New York Times, May 19, 1924, "Woods Resigns," p. 1.

[13] Stalker, "Suicide, Boycotts and Embracing Tagore," p. 157.

> armed with swords and wearing black masks over their faces, de-
> termined to start a massacre, the only thing that prevented the
> "race protectors" from carrying out their scheme was the inspira-
> tion of the manager, He told the band to play the national anthem,
> and to keep on playing it. No Japanese will insult the Emperor by
> moving during its performance, and the situation was saved.[14]

Their protest hence extended to little more than shouting and the scattering of pamphlets bearing the slogan "Punish Tyrannical America,"
but the weapons in their hands gave their protest a frisson of terrorist
action for the tabloid press. As a result, Japanese guests were banned
from dances at other hotels with western clientele, further aggravating
the general population's sense of being treated as second-class citizens.

That month, the boycotts began to bite, particularly in the cosmetics and toiletries market, with women rejecting American hair products,
and 50 geisha girls praised in the local media for refusing American
make-up. By mid-summer, sales in Japan of American canned goods
fell 30%; cosmetics by 50%.[15]

Stores began to favor non-American products—there was a surge
in German camera sales, and a boom in locally-made toothpaste. English-language signs in some stores turned away American customers,
noting that it must be "rather unpleasant" for them anyway, to have to
buy products from a race that their own nation had excluded.

Amid protests from politicians and vested business interests, the
anti-American fervor extended into the movie business. Racketeers,
lurking in the doorways, threatened patrons of American films at picture houses, while local film companies, seeing the chance to seize a
larger market share from U.S. studios, announced they would not be
distributing any American films. The *benshi* impresarios, whose job
was to turn "silent" movies into dramatic talkies, refused to show up for
work at theaters showing American movies. Hollywood fought back by
threatening to close cinemas down, a viable threat owing to the lack of
available product in the domestic industry.

Just as the movie madness subsided, anti-American sentiment

---

[14] O'Conroy, *The Menace of Japan*, p. 49. I have corrected the day of the week, which is
given as Sunday in O'Conroy's book—the *Japan Advertiser* report was written several years after the event, quite possibly after it had grown with the telling.
[15] Stalker, "Suicide, Boycotts and Embracing Tagore," pp. 158–9.

rose in the schools and among the religious community, which had long prided itself on the moral high ground of Christianity. Claiming to be a supporter only of "the two J's, Japan and Jesus," noted maverick Uchimura Kanzō wrote an inflammatory letter to a Tokyo newspaper.

> Whatever material benefit the Japanese may have derived from Americans, they have lost more spiritually. It is a fact patent to all that the reason for the Japan of today being a slave to materialistic lust can be traced to the evil influence of Americans. The Christianity of Americans is, in the majority of cases, shallow to the extreme. It is materialistic and partisan. It differs entirely in its fundamental spirit from that of Christ.[16]

Newspapers in Japan, which had previously turned a blind eye to anti-Japanese discrimination in America, now made lynchings and victimization front-page news. July 1 was proclaimed to be "National Humiliation Day," at which flags flew at half-mast, and in a protest that was blown all out proportion by the media and politicians, a 22-year-old student sneaked into the U.S. embassy and lowered the flag on its roof.

By 1925, the government had issued an even firmer clampdown on public dissent, the Peace Preservation Law, which made it a criminal act to join an organization that rejected the notion of private property (i.e. Communists), or which posed a threat to the *kokutai*, a term usually translated as the "national polity." The word had first appeared in Japanese in the *Imperial Rescript on Education* in 1890—now it had become a fundamental, pivotal and dangerously undefined term in the new law. Where the Communists were concerned, their desire to abolish the monarchy was a clear threat to the imperial institution. But the term *kokutai* seemed to extent further than the Emperor himself, to some nebulous idea of Japan and the Japanese, as a nation.

"Although everybody understands what *kokutai* is," said one Japanese politician, "when asked to clearly explain it, this becomes something extremely difficult to do, and there is certainly no-one who can speak of it precisely."[17]

The *Rescript* had intended *kokutai* to mean some sort of traditional,

---

[16] Stalker, "Suicide, Boycotts and Embracing Tagore," p. 162.

[17] Ward, *Thought Crime*, p. 225.

conservative sense of Japan's fundamental character, but even then, it was impossible to say for sure what that meant. Was it Japan's "fundamental character" on the day that the Shōgun was ordered to throw out the foreigners? Or perhaps on the day that forces of Satsuma and Chōshū marched, singing, against their supposed leader? Was it Japan's fundamental character on the day before or after the promulgation of the Meiji constitution? Nobody could say—*kokutai* now meant whatever those in power thought it did, and anyone "threatening" it could be arrested, with no ceiling on the level of punishment.

It was then, and only then, with socialism and Communism effectively abolished from Japanese political discourse, that the government passed the General Election Law, granting the vote to all men over twenty-five years of age. Japanese menfolk could now participate in the political process, but only in a playing field that spanned center to right, to far-right.[18]

A subtle resistance persisted in the empire. Sadly, no prints survive today of Na Un-gyu's silent Korean film *Arirang* (1926), making it impossible to assess just how radical its subject matter was. For the Japanese, it was an innocuous melodrama about thwarted love, but whenever the police were not present in a Korean movie theater, the local narrator or *byeonsa* (Japanese: *benshi*) would concoct a different story, making the whole thing out to be about a man sentenced to death for murdering a Japanese collaborator who has raped his fiancée. "Arirang" became the song sung by the condemned man as he went to his execution, brought to life in the cinema by the house orchestra. The film, which in its raw state was considered harmless by the Japanese authorities, became for the Koreans a subversive assertion of anti-Japanese feeling. The song "Arirang" became even more associated with the resistance.[19]

Dissidence even extended to the capital of Japan. In 1927, a conscript at a military parade broke ranks to hand a letter to the Emperor, protesting about the treatment of Japan's *burakumin* underclass. For this show of "disrespect" to the *kokutai*, he served a year in military jail, and his regiment was made to walk home instead of getting the train. Over the next twenty years, offences against the *kokutai* would be cited as grounds for arrest and imprisonment of more than 70,000 Japanese,

[18] Person, *Arbiters of Patriotism*, p. 95.
[19] Atkins, "The Dual Career of 'Arirang,'" p. 652.

and many more subjects in the Empire at large.[20]

The greatest offence against the *kokutai*, it seemed, came in 1928, when the first general election with universal suffrage for men over twenty-five returned a number of politicians regarded by the authorities as dangerously liberal or even closeted leftists. In reaction, the Ministry of Education founded a Students Division, intended to police potential dissidents on university campuses. Derided almost immediately as "thought police," these new on-campus "counselors" were charged with ensuring that young minds were not corrupted by un-Japanese ideas.[21]

Amid such bold talk, there was an odd historical irony, that much of Japan's economy was bolstered by sales of a single commodity—silk. From the 1890s, when the U.S. overtook France as the main export market, a huge proportion of Japan's foreign currency earnings derived from the export of raw silk and related products to the United States. Fully 10% of Japan's arable land was taken up with mulberry orchards to feed silk worms, while by 1929, the United States accounted for 95% of Japan's silk trade, and the silk trade accounted for up to 54% of all Japan's exports. The introduction of Coco Chanel's "Little Black Dress" in 1926 was not merely a revolution in fashion, but in international commerce, delivering a sharp blow to Japan's export prospects, which had previously relied on intricate and bulky gowns. So, too, was the widening availability of rayon, an artificial fiber perfected in 1924 and soon undercutting silk on the market. The onset of a global depression, which impacted the United States in 1929, had a predictable effect on the sales of luxury items, including silk clothing, causing Japan's silk exports to the U.S. to plummet during the 1930s to a mere eighth of their former level. Only the rise of the silk stocking, a mass-production item after the invention of all-in-one knitting machine, offered any respite to Japan's troubled export market.

Still, economically and romantically, there was always the prospect of new commodities and opportunities on the Asian mainland. America, Australia and Canada might have closed their doors to Japanese immigrants, but much was made of the potential of what *National Geographic* magazine would call "the Promised Land of Asia."[22]

Much of China might have been in chaos, split between rival

---

[20] Lone, *Provincial Life and the Military in Imperial Japan*, p. 118.

[21] Person, *Arbiters of Patriotism*, p. 126.

[22] Gamsa, *Manchuria*, p. 75.

regimes and a growing Communist insurgency, but the north-eastern plains of Manchuria were presented as a thriving melting pot. Knitted together by its railways, home to Russian and Jewish émigrés, a growing population of Chinese laborers in search of a safer life, Mongols and Manchus, along with Japanese settlers (including many Korean subjects of the Japanese empire). Popular culture in the Japanese home islands was inundated with orientalist fantasies, with Chinese melodies and buzzwords sneaking into the gramophone hits of the period. In 1924, fresh-faced starlet Fukube Tomiko made her singing debut with "A Manchuria Girl" (*Manshū Musume*), in which she sung enthusiastically of a 16-year-old girl waiting for her betrothed, Mr. Wang, beneath the winter jasmine. The following year, in "Spring on the Border" (*Kunizakai no Haru*), Oka Haruo peppered his debut song with Russian terms—not merely the Amur River over which he gazes, but the sound of a balalaika, the heat of the *pechka* (a Russian stove), and the taste of vodka.

The railways in Manchuria remained the prime agents of Japanese power, as transport networks, as vectors for troop movements, and also for links between enclaves of industry and commerce, separated by the often-lawless wilderness. The South Manchuria Railway (*Mantetsu*) was a hugely profitable, vertically integrated corporation offering high returns for its investors and generating up to a third of Japan's "domestic" tax revenue. Despite not actually being *in* Japan, the South Manchuria Railway was Japan's largest corporation, already supplying 75% of the world's soybean market with far-flung additional ventures including its own coal mines in Shandong, thereby reducing the cost of the fuel for its own locomotives, its own ports, warehouses and even hotels.[23]

The company song, a regular staff sing-along throughout the 1920s, made the corporation's mission clear.

> From the East, the Light comes
> Shining over the lands of East Asia
> We are sent, that is our mission
>
> See! The Pole Star is shining prominently
> On wide plains, on open country
> On ten thousand leagues of open country

---

[23] Young, *Japan's Total Empire*, p. 31.

The bell at daybreak announces it is tomorrow
On the plains of *Man-Mō* [Manchuria and Mongolia]
Together in prosperity, together in hope
[Fields of] sorghum like rippling waves, like a flood
The wide plains, the open country
The sun rises on open country

Happy that the people of East Asia
And the Land of Japan
Are forging ahead together in cooperation
Hark! Our song of harmony
Rings out until it shakes the Kunlun peak
The wide plains, the open country
The hills and rivers sing
Of open country.[24]

Amid all the talk of nationalism and bringing hope to the East, the company song refers to its employees as if they are emissaries of the Emperor, and chillingly suggests that its impact is intended to spread far beyond the tracks up to Changchun. Kunlun is a handily ambiguous term—it could refer to the mountain range that borders the Taklamakan desert, or as a poetic term for the legendary peak at the edge of China. Either way, the song proclaims a mission statement that stretches far, far to the west. Nine times, it refers to *kōgen*—the wide plains or open country—as if to suggest that Manchuria is empty land, there for the taking.

Takushoku University in Hokkaidō, originally founded as a school to produce graduates to work in the development and industrialization of Taiwan, became increasingly involved with the provision of workers to feed Japan's growing military-industrial expansion in Manchuria. By the 1920s, its student parties were the early venues for a new song, not about lost love or difficult studies, but about the prospects awaiting bold men on the Manchurian frontier. "Continental adventurers" (*tairiku rōnin*) was one term for these mercenaries and chancers, roaming the mainland in search of plunder, although they also embraced the somewhat more pejorative description of "horse bandits" (*bazoku*).

---

[24] *Manshū no Uta*; CD booklet, pp. 14–15 and 30–31. Not technically a "military" song, so not included in Osada.

Like the company song of the South Manchuria Railway, the "Horse Bandit Song" (*Bazoku no Uta*) depicted Manchuria as a land of golden opportunity, but also rugged adventure. The song takes the singer from the mountains on the border of Korea, through the major cities of Manchuria, to the Gobi Desert that stretches through Mongolia to the edge of Tibet. As to the rewards on offer, there is nothing but fighting and plunder (the *tael* is a unit of Chinese currency).

I'm going, so you go, too / I'm tired of living in narrow Japan.
Beyond the waves is a great wilderness of 400,000 people. [...]

When I left the country, I had skin smooth like jade
Now scarred by spears and swords, I truly am a man
A beard like needles on my smiling face
Against the morning wind of Mount Baekdu
I raise my sword up high and look below
Upon the great plains of north Manchuria
Still too small to be my home. [...]

Today I hide the hooves of horses
Outside the walls of Jilin
Tomorrow I shall attack Mukden
With my long hair blown in the wind.
In a flash of lightning
Today's prey is fifty thousand *taels*.

From the tip of drawn spears
The large dragon vomits blood on the Amur River.
The silver moon high in the clear sky
The grass of the Gobi Desert is my pillow.[25]

Such men were officially identified in a 1928 communiqué from Japan's Mukden consulate as "masterless warriors" (*rōnin*), drawn from a population of "decommissioned soldiers, veteran drug-dealers, second generation pimps and traffickers, and... 'hustlers,'" estimated to number at

---

[25] Osada, *Sensō ga Nokoshita Uta*, pp. 262–4. See also Lu, *Agony of Choice*, p. 19 for the concept of "developing the continent" (*tairiku keiei*)—an issue within Japanese foreign policy since the 1890s, if not before.

least ten thousand people, forming a shadowy underclass to the military and business interests already visible in Manchuria.[26]

The local warlord, Zhang Zuolin, enjoyed a monopoly on sales of both alcohol and tobacco—the city of Harbin alone was producing 4.3 million bottles of beer a year. Opium, illegal under the laws of the nominal authorities of Republican China, flourished as a major component of the Manchurian economy, occupying up to one in four Japanese expat workers in some element of the production and distribution chain, and bankrolling Zhang's ongoing scheme to become the ruler of more than just Manchuria.[27]

We should bear in mind that the term "warlord" is a pejorative, applied retroactively to the rulers of Manchuria and many other unstable regions in twentieth century, because they would ultimately be defeated. A warlord that becomes, say, the president of a country, is remembered differently by posterity.[28] True enough, some were glorified gangsters, and others renegade military officers, but when we are discussing a man like Zhang Zuolin in the mid-1920s, we are speaking of the leader of an army of 100,000 men, appointed as the "governor" of three Chinese provinces by a fragile central government in recognition of the power he had already taken for himself. Zhang, like many other warlords in Chinese history, came within a hair's breadth of snatching a longer, more enduring legitimacy. He minted his own currency, he commanded a regime with a huge budget, and as the 1920s wore on, he appropriated ever larger sectors of Manchuria's revenue to bankroll a bid for greater power—the takeover of Beijing itself and the Chinese republic. Among his allies, Zhang counted several other army commanders in Manchuria, including a non-Chinese player in the game, the Kwantung Army, Japan's

---

[26] Driscoll, *Absolute Erotic, Absolute Grotesque*, p. 233. He notes that the same consulate had issued a warning about Japanese traffickers and criminals in Manchuria ten years earlier, in 1918. Iguchi "Continental Adventurers," p. 62 has no qualms about linking them directly to the Black Dragon Society. The translation of *rōnin* as "adventurer" assumes a sly admiration on the part of the identifier, justifiable in terms of their own self-description, whereas the Mukden communiqué was using its more traditional, pejorative sense, of "masterless warriors." I hence translate the same word in two different ways here.

[27] Smith, *Intoxicating Manchuria*, pp. 28–9.

[28] Gamsa, *Manchuria*, p. 79; Kwong, *War and Geopolitics in Interwar Manchuria*, p. 7. The term in Chinese for warlord, *junfa*, was a loanword derived from the Japanese *gunbatsu* (military clique), as distinguished from a *zaibatsu*, a clique of commercial or industrial connections. Often, the one was soon allied with the other.

own military force, there to guard the South Manchuria Railway. At the beginning of the 1930s, the Kwantung Army's military strength was only a little over 12,000 men, dwarfed by the local warlord contingents.[29]

Manchuria's hinterland was lawless, but Japan had been a heavy contributor to such lawlessness for many years. It had not merely funded and supplied many of the partisans that fought the Russians in 1904, but continued to do so even after the war was over and the Russians had gone home, creating an ongoing outlaw problem for the Chinese. Outside the railway zone of heavy industries, Manchuria's black economy was even more robust, growing rich on the lucrative opium trade. By the South Manchuria Railway's own admission, up to a quarter of all the weapons seized from captured bandits were of Japanese manufacture—Japan was not merely fighting the outlaw problem in Manchuria, it was also shoring it up.[30]

Russia was on the mind of the Army's general staff, who decided to arrange for five new railway lines through northern Manchuria in order to have strong supply lines in case of a war with the Soviet Union. Japan was expecting ready cooperation from Zhang Zuolin, particularly after deploying troops along the railway lines in order to help him neutralize a rival. Their price for this rescue mission would be his assent to further concessions—he happily agreed, since Zhang was ever ready to make promises he did not necessarily expect to keep. This one, however, was soon contested publicly by the Chinese generalissimo Chiang Kai-shek, who refused to agree to any decisions not decided in consultation with the *actual* government of China. Was Zhang a Chinese official or a stooge of the Japanese? He could not be both.

It was a fateful and fatal moment. Zhang was forced to choose if he was an independent ruler in alliance with the Japanese, and risk the wrath of China, or if he were a subject of the Chinese, and risk the wrath of Japan. He chose to stick with China, leading to increasingly frosty relations with the Japanese.

As part of the South Manchuria Railway's drive to bring in new

---

[29] Kitamura, *The Causes of the Manchurian Incident*, p. 136.

[30] O'Conroy, *The Menace of Japan*, p. 176. To be fair, however, both Russia and Japan had left thousands of discarded weapons on Manchurian battlefields, so O'Conroy's claims of continued gun-running may lose a little water. The report was dated 1930; I shuffle it a little bit out of chronology here on the grounds that it would have been true several years earlier, too.

investors, it was prepared to bankroll celebrity tourists. In 1928, it funded Yosano Akiko, author of the controversial poem "Do Not Lay Down Your Life," now a prominent educator and writer, along with her similarly famous husband Hiroshi. The couple were ferried to Dalian, a port just down the coast from Port Arthur, to the edge of Inner Mongolia, and as far north as Harbin. But if South Manchuria Railway publicity representatives were hoping for an enthusiastic, romantic view of their territory, they would be disappointed.

Yosano faced renewed criticism back in Japan over "Do Not Lay Down Your Life," not for its pacifism, but for what one critic regarded as her naivety regarding the cause of wars. In a critical essay on anti-war literature, Kuroshima Denji singled out Yosano's poem for its "bourgeois worldview," emptily asserting personal issues and individual freedoms while displaying little understanding of what had actually caused the war, or how, in a Marxist sense, even Yosano's dreamy-eyed vision of running a little shop side-stepped the true nature of society.[31]

If Kuroshima's attack seemed picky or ungallant, it was a reasonable reflection of a general shift to the right, as leftists like Yosano were edged out of public life, their opinions belittled and ignored beneath a rising tide of performative patriotism. Yosano's journey on the South Manchuria Railway was the first overt sign that she was coming to an accommodation with the institutions she had once opposed. Or, at least, she tried.

Yosano's travelogue is strangely stilted, as if an author unsure of what she should be saying is simply writing out facts and hoping that a narrative arises. There are long recitations of places that she went, followed by other places that she went, occasionally leavened with info-dumps dropped into the text after she got home and had time to look them up. Occasionally, however, one can pick through the dispassionate text to find telling moments, such as a tense twenty minutes spent waiting for her driver, while a Chinese crowd stared ominously at her clothes, which marked her out as Japanese. In almost every occasion, the only people she truly interacts with are other Japanese.

Yosano didn't think much of the food, but she was impressed at how cheaply the workers of Manchuria could eat, and that it was possible to buy Japanese Morinaga-brand candy on the train. She found local Buddhist ceremonies impressively devout, observing that it made her feel

---

[31] Rabson, "Yosano Akiko on War," p. 53.

that the priests in her native Japan were often just droning out phrases by rote, devoid of any real passion. She disapproved of the teenage prostitutes and the regulated opium trade, and fumed that she was not permitted to go near Beijing, because of increased unrest and the danger presented to Japanese citizenry. This was an understatement—Chiang Kai-shek's National Revolutionary Army, on an expedition to reunite China under a single authority, had marched into Jinan in Shandong, and clashed in open conflict with Japanese troops. The Japanese soldiers were purportedly there to protect Japanese nationals, although in an ominous foretaste of insubordinations to come, they had set out for Jinan before being ordered to do so.

Yosano was, in fact, lucky not to have been on the wrong train. While she and her husband were in Mukden on June 4, 1928, they heard the sound of an explosion on the nearby railway. A bomb had gone off as the carriage of Zhang Zuolin passed by, mortally wounding him and several members of his entourage.

"There was a rumor," wrote the fearful Yosano, "that Chinese troops throughout the city were going to assault the Japanese [district]."[32] This, however, didn't stop her heading off for the day to see an open-cast mine in Fushun, where thirty to forty feet of shale had been stripped away from the surface to be pressed into crude oil, and to allow miners to get at the coal beneath.

Yosano did not see the bigger picture, that the mine and the death of Zhang were related. 1928 was the last year that Japan was self-sufficient in oil production. Over the next five years, the increased requirements for shipping and rail, heating and engine fuel would triple the demand.[33] The underhand grab for land and resources came within a period that saw Japan's very requirements for controlling those resources push it into over-reliance on foreign imports. Japan needed Manchuria to remain "self-sufficient" but the coming seizure of Manchuria would also doom the empire to search further afield for the fuel to maintain it.

Yosano did not wonder just who would have stood to benefit from blowing up Zhang's train. In the years since, the blame has been pinned variously on Communist agents and on Chinese rivals, although it is widely believed to have been the work of Kōmoto Daisaku, a young

---

[32] Yosano, *Travels in Manchuria and Mongolia*, loc. 1810.
[33] Miller, *Bankrupting the Enemy*, loc. 3257.

officer in the Kwantung Army.[34] Ironically, if it were Kōmoto (as Kōmoto claimed himself), he would have been acting against the wishes even of his famously insubordinate superiors. The Kwantung Army had, in fact, been grooming a replacement for Zhang, but their substitute was not yet ready. The murder set off a series of reprisals and putsches among the locals, in which Japan's preferred successor was executed, and Zhang's staunchly anti-Japanese son, Zhang Xueliang (1901–2001) eventually took over. The situation managed to ruin *everybody's* plans—it effectively put the Kwantung Army's scheme to seize control of Manchuria back by three years. Back in Tokyo, it would also bring down a government, when Prime Minister Tanaka Giichi was unable to bring the murderers to justice.[35]

A war in China was looming. The fighting in Jinan and the murder of Zhang Zuolin were fated to escalate into a full-scale conflict with China. But was Japan in any fit state to carry out such operations?

By 1929, the Planning Bureau that had been set up to manage the implications of the 1918 Munitions Mobilization Law was actively drawing up strategies for a two-year conflict so all-consuming that it would "gamble the fate of the nation." To do so, it demanded austerity-level budgets from every government ministry, in order to ascertain what would be necessary to keep the country running for 24 months of total war.

In summer 1929, the Bureau ran a full-scale exercise in the Osaka area, imagining an unspecified conflict on mainland Asia, as well as enemy landings with poison gas support on north Kyūshū as if there had been a counter-attack from Korea. But this war-game was not military, it was industrial. Factories were placed under military command and switched over to military materials production, while observers assessed efficiency and output. Factory owners happily played along, secure in the knowledge that the off-brand aspirin and military-grade fuel oil they were suddenly producing had a captive and guaranteed market—the government bought all products created during the exercise. Indeed, there was later something of a jurisdictional conflict as ministries fought over the right to oversee certain products—the Home Ministry outflanked the Ministry of Commerce and Industry

---

[34] Gamsa, *Manchuria*, p. 83.
[35] Mauch, "The Shōwa Political Crisis," p. 4.

over subsequent alcohol test runs, on the grounds it was necessary for "medicinal purposes." [36]

Music continued to function as a barometer of how the military wanted to shape public opinions. At movie theaters, "silent" films were still the primary medium, although they remained anything but silent, accompanied by a live orchestra and a *benshi* showman at the front of the cinema, sometimes even attired as one of the stars, bellowing plot-points and supplying dialogue. In the 1930s, however, a new vogue arose for a multi-media experience, with new films being prefaced by gramophone record releases. Some were played in sync with a gramophone accompaniment, others simply promoted through gramophone releases of the movie's main themes. The big hit of 1930 was *Marching On* (*Shin-gun*) a film that transplanted the action of James Boyd's 1927 American Civil War novel of the same name to an Asian battlefield. Its namesake theme song came with Japanese Army-approved lyrics.

> Brave men of the nation of the Rising Sun
> Now going into battle
> Flags fly and the blood rises
> The flags are flying and people excited.
> Cheers and the sound of the bugle.
>
> Unless we are victorious
> We cannot return to the land of our parents
> Without the decoration of the cherry blossom of distinguished service
> I will fall and never return home. […]
>
> Our warring selves and our birds overhead.
> Where will the airplanes end up?
> Brothers in the sky, we count on you.
> You can leave the ground to our Japanese swords.
>
> When attacking with the bullets of the Japanese spirit
> We see the shadow of the enemy.

---

[36] Barnhart, *Japan Prepares for Total War*, p. 19.

They magically disappear like cloud or mist
And the emperor's army glimmers.[37]

In April 1931, the Planning Bureau reported that Japan was *not* prepared for total war. It would, it was estimated, take a solid five years
of unimpeded peace-time growth to put Japan in a position where it
could fulfill its nation-gambling targets. And there remained the issue
of raw materials, for which the Bureau hoped to have a better plan by
the following year.

Members of the Kwantung Army, however, had ideas about
fast-tracking the situation. Two of its leaders, Lt-Col. Ishiwara Kanji
and Col. Itagaki Seishirō, had dusted off the sort of claims made in the
1915 Koiso report, and argued that the global depression risked shutting forever a window of golden opportunity. Manchuria could, indeed
should become a hive of industry, a thriving supply-house for Japan and,
in a vaguely defined trickle-down effect, some sort of benefit for China
as well. But only the Japanese had the resources, know-how and manpower to make Manchuria the best it could be. Manchuria needed to be
cut out of China's immediate authority.

Ishiwara, in particular, was committed to future war. He arrived in
Manchuria after serving four years as a lecturer in war theory at the Japanese Army's staff college, where he outlined detailed concepts, including
his belief that some wars were "wars of exhaustion," which ended like the
Russo-Japanese conflict when neither side was able to fight any longer,
while others were "wars of annihilation," in which one side was utterly
destroyed. He believed that the ultimate war of annihilation was nearing,
a "Very" World War, in which the advance of technology would reach
such a pinnacle that total and enduring victory would bring permanent
world peace at a terrible price.[38] He also believed that in the coming war,
Manchuria would be the key to Japan's survival, and that if the Chinese
were physically unable to run it in Japan's interests, the Japanese would
be obliged to take it from them.

Just to the southeast of the Kwantung Army's headquarters, new
lyrics to an old song offered a dire portent. The use of the folk song

---

[37] Osada, *Sensō ga Nokoshita Uta*, pp. 215–6 notes that the tune is reminiscent of one
of the imported musical hits of the Taishō era, "It's a Long Way to Tipperary" (1912),
itself popular as a marching song in the First World War.

[38] Kitamura, *The Causes of the Manchurian Incident*, p. 44.

"Arirang" as a protest anthem was gaining ground, with multiple variants inserting lyrics more openly critical of the Koreans' colonial masters and their intentions in Manchuria. The most blatant warned the people of Korea to beware the Rising Sun.

> Arirang, Arirang, Arariyo
> Friends, wake up from your shallow dream
> The crimson sun is rising over Arirang hill
> With two arms stretched wide.[39]

---

[39] Atkins, "The Dual Career of 'Arirang,'" p. 656. Such resonances, however, appear to have been lost on the Japanese, who were encouraged to regard the song as a harmless bit of local color, particularly after it was appropriated for the domestic market. Saijō Yaso, lyricist for many of twentieth-century Japan's best-loved popular songs, translated it into Japanese in 1931, turning it into an anthem of the empire throughout the next fifteen years.

CHAPTER 6

The Dark Valley

Leaders of the Kwantung Army, including Ishiwara's superior Colonel Itagaki Seishirō, believed that without a pliable local warlord, and without the support of the Japanese government, the only viable option to keep to the resource plan was for Manchuria to proclaim itself an independent state. Lieutenant Colonel Ishiwara decided, on his own initiative in 1931, to draft a *War Plan for the Conquest of Manchuria*, utilizing Kwantung Army staff resources, and statistical information acquired from the South Manchuria Railway. His argument was a little confused, arguing that Japan needed to invade China in order to save China, but also to save Japan.

> Japan needs to gain possession of Manchuria for the following reasons. First, Manchuria will be indispensable as a rear base for Japan in the event of the "American-Japanese War." Second, the Japanese who have been influenced by western ideas such as communism, socialism and liberalism, will be awakened and become conscious of the "national polity of Japan" (*kokutai*) by opening war between the [Imperial Japanese Army] and the North-eastern Army. Third, Japanese occupation of Manchuria will prevent Communism from permeating East Asia. Finally, Manchuria should be under Japanese control… in order to promote the political unification of the Republic of China, which is essential for the peace of Asia.[1]

Ishiwara did not regard Manchuria as part of China. It was, he argued, the homeland of the Manchus, and they, like the Mongols, had much more in common with the Japanese than the Chinese. The Chinese

---

[1] Kitamura, *The Causes of the Manchurian Incident*, pp. 58–9.

presence in Manchuria was a recent immigrant phenomenon, lured in by all the achievements of the Japanese in Manchuria, and it was only right, he argued, that Japan should reap the benefits. Ishiwara also regarded Manchuria as a window of opportunity—the Soviet Union was not yet strong enough to field an army to take it back, nor was the U.S. Navy in a position to intervene, but both of these capabilities were likely within a few years.

Ishiwara proposed that the Kwantung Army and the Imperial Japanese Army would manufacture a "pretext" to overthrow Zhang Xueliang and seize control of Manchuria, hopefully by persuading the locals that it was in their best interest. Citing a 1930 Kwantung Army strategy report, Ishiwara admitted that such an action would, in the long run, lead to a war with the United States, but such a war would be something that Japan could win, *if* it maintained its Manchurian gains for the long term, which would require the setting up of a tame local regime.[2]

Even the hawks of the Army and government administration found Ishiwara's ideas to be too aggressive. A speech by the Japanese politician Matsuoka Yōsuke, in January 1931 coined a new catchphrase that Japan needed to defend its Manchurian "lifeline" (*seimeisen*), but hopes remained that the Chiang Kai-shek's Republic of China, struggling against warlords and Communist insurgents further to the south, could be persuaded to simply give Manchuria up without a fight. Japan's military affairs policy-makers ultimately recommended putting the idea of an independent Manchuria directly to Chiang Kai-shek, in an attempt to secure his agreement, however reluctantly, that Manchuria was beyond his control, much as western Taiwan had been outside the authority of the Qing emperor. If Chiang did not concede, it was agreed, then the Army Ministry would raise the topic with the rest of the Cabinet, in an attempt to secure a more direct occupation of Manchuria. Japan would definitely be invading Manchuria, but hoped to do so with the public assent of the Chinese, thereby avoiding any diplomatic protests from other nations.[3]

In the meantime, a general was dispatched from Tokyo to Manchuria, to officially reprimand Ishiwara and his colleagues over their willingness to take matters into their own hands—or at least, to be publicly

[2] Kitamura, *The Causes of the Manchurian Incident*, pp. 62–4.
[3] Barnhart, *Japan Prepares for Total War*, pp. 22–3.

seen to be doing so, in order to allow Tokyo conspirators a little more room for denial.

Propaganda began to whip up during the summer of 1931, after soldiers of Zhang Xueliang's army captured, tortured and executed Captain Nakamura Shintarō and his four travelling companions near Suegongfu. The party was "missing" for several weeks before the story of their disappearance came to light, albeit reported very differently. The Japanese press called it an outrage against innocent men. Reporting in China hinged more on the notion that Captain Nakamura had been shot as a spy—his original travel documents had not given him permission to travel in the area, he had surveying equipment in his bags, and he had been posing as an agricultural engineer, possibly scouting water sources for a prospective invasion force. Whatever the truth of Nakamura's activities, the Chinese forces did themselves no favor by summarily executing him and then burning the evidence.[4]

The Japanese media seized upon the incident. A movie about Nakamura's last days was rushed into production, as well as two songs celebrating his apparent heroism. One "Ah, Captain Nakamura (*Aa, Nakamura Taii*) alluded to a lonely bivouac under the night sky a thousand leagues from home, a sneaky ambush, and four characters carved into his chest with a whip:

> Dying at the hands of cruel and disobedient devils
> His heroic spirit endures for eternity.
> Incarnated as a god that protects our nation.[5]

Ishiwara thought the Nakamura Incident was the ideal chance to escalate events, and pleaded with his commanders to be allowed to send an "investigation" up to Changchun, in the form of two infantry battalions, an

---

[4] Young, *Japan's Total Empire*, p. 39.

[5] This song was not in Osada, but there are several sources online, e.g. https://youtu.be/M4QvPAikv_c. Before Nakamura's posthumous celebrity really took off, a second incident also inflamed public opinion, although Ishiwara made no attempt to exploit it. At Wanbaoshan near Changchun, Chinese farmers got into a fight with a band of Korean share-croppers, who had illegally dug an irrigation ditch that stretched several kilometers across other people's land. This would actually prove to be far more inflammatory than the Nakamura Incident, and led to lynchings of Chinese by Koreans in Korea, with more than a hundred deaths. Retaliatory actions against Koreans in China allegedly led to *thousands* more deaths in 1931.

artillery unit and an armored train. Instead, he was infuriated not only by the refusal of his request, but by the resolution of the issue through diplomatic channels, after the Japanese consul in Mukden secured a promise from the Chinese that the matter would be investigated locally.[6]

It was only then that Ishiwara and his co-conspirators accepted that they would not enjoy the open support of the Japanese government, the Army or even the Kwantung Army. Accordingly, in September 1931, they took matters into their own hands, and manufactured their own pretext. The degree to which they did so with tacit approval from their own superiors, and the degree to which that approval extended up through the ranks and back to Tokyo, remains a controversial issue to this day.

Soldiers of the Kwantung Army, disguised in Chinese uniforms, blew up a section of the South Manchuria Railway outside Mukden. They did so with exaggerated care—for maximum tactical value, any soldier knows it is best to place one's bomb on a curved piece of track, which is harder to replace, or even better, at a bridge or tunnel which itself will have to be repaired. Ishiwara's men instead planted their bomb in such a way as to create the absolute minimum of inconvenience for the South Manchuria Railway engineers who would have to fix it later. The explosion broke off a 31-inch section of straight rail on a piece of flat ground, so inconsequential that the train from Changchun, running a few minutes behind, was able to pass over the damage without difficulty.[7]

This was not how the Kwantung Army reported it. Amid a heavy clampdown on the media, soldiers from Zhang's army had, it was claimed, blown up the railway. Japanese soldiers coincidentally on a nearby night exercise had chased them through the long sorghum grass by the railway. Pursuing them into a nearby barracks, they were fired upon by the bombers' comrades inside, and returned fire, not only with small-arms, but with the two howitzers they happened to have in the unfilled swimming pool of the Mukden officers' club. As the number of Chinese soldiers returning fire grew, the Japanese telephoned for re-inforcements.

That morning, the Kwantung Army chief of staff did not waste too

---

[6] Kitamura, *The Causes of the Manchurian Incident*, p. 150.

[7] Bulwer-Lytton, *Report of the Commission of Enquiry*, p. 66. In a moment of additional disbelief, the Lytton Report observes (p. 68) that the valiant Japanese soldiers attempting to warn the oncoming train "placed detonators" on the line to do so.

much time wondering how the Kwantung Army, outnumbered twenty-to-one by Chinese warlord forces, might fare in the new conflict. Instead, he telegrammed Tokyo in search of reinforcements from Korea. South Manchuria Railway officials sprang into action, setting up eight field offices along its network, with a further 40 telegraph stations. By the next day, Japanese forces had occupied half a dozen Manchurian cities, including the major population centers on the South Manchuria Railway: Changchun and Mukden. Three further cities were in Japanese control within the week, and as the fighting wore on, over 7,000 railway employees were co-opted into the military machine as support staff.[8]

On September 22, 1931, four days after the Incident was underway, the Shōwa Emperor ordered his Prime Minister to restrain the army in order to keep hold of the government's strict policy of not escalating the situation. But the situation had *already* escalated, with hand-wringing reports drifting back to Tokyo that officers had exceeded their authority, but nothing was to be done. In December, the government's inability to restrain its own Army led to the resignation of yet another Cabinet.[9]

However, the Kwantung Army, aided by the rolling stock of the South Manchuria Railway, sped through Manchuria seizing multiple strategic sites and encountering relatively little resistance from Zhang Xueliang's men—there would be prolonged guerrilla warfare for years, but most of Zhang's regular troops stood down. Even with a harder-fought resistance in the north, Manchuria had essentially fallen to the Kwantung Army by the early days of 1932. City by city, local governments were either persuaded to announce they were seceding from the Republic of China, or replaced with councilors who would. Harbin was one of the last places to hold out, but even that was in Japanese hands by February 1932, falling not to the Kwantung Army, who had started the Incident, but to a division of their colleagues in the Imperial Japanese Army, now lending support to the "insubordinate" activists.

China appealed to the League of Nations for intervention, leading to the dispatch of the Lytton Commission, a fact-finding team. But even as the Lytton Commission was setting out to gather materials in Manchuria, the next phase of Ishiwara's plan was underway. With the support of several Chinese warlords who had been persuaded to come over to

---

[8] O'Dwyer, *Significant Soil*, pp. 278–9.
[9] Mauch, "The Shōwa Political Crisis," p. 7.

the Kwantung Army's side, Manchuria was proclaimed as a newly independent state, "Manchukuo."[10]

"Henry" Puyi, the Last Emperor of China, living in relative obscurity for seven years since being thrown out of his Beijing residence, had been brought to Port Arthur in November 1931, and was proclaimed in February 1932 as the new president of Manchukuo. With Japanese help, the new state gained a flag, in which the five stripes of the original Chinese republic, representing a melting-pot of five races, was rearranged to form a canton of four minorities, above a field expanded from the original fifth stripe—the yellow earth of the Han Chinese majority. Manchukuo also acquired a government packed with Chinese ministers and Japanese "advisers," and its own army (again with Japanese advisers).

Anti-Japanese demonstrations in Shanghai, site of multiple foreign concessions with extraterritorial status, were soon met with pro-Japanese protests from within the Japanese concession.[11] Five militant Buddhist monks, chanting pro-Japanese slogans outside a Chinese factory, were assaulted by locals. One died from his injuries, leading to swift Japanese reprisals, including an arson attack on a Chinese factory. Both Japanese and Chinese military forces began assembling on the outskirts of the city—the Chinese from the landward side, and the Japanese fielding a flotilla of thirty ships, disembarking 7,000 troops.

On January 28, a midnight sortie from a Japanese aircraft carrier dropped bombs on civilian targets in Shanghai. Three thousand Japanese soldiers began seizing strategic targets across the city, including railway stations and post offices, meeting unexpectedly fierce resistance from soldiers of the Chinese 19th Route Army.

The fighting in Shanghai wore on throughout February, with ever-escalating troop commitments from both the Chinese and Japanese, while the foreign community feebly protested about the risks of danger and damage to French, British and American lives and properties in the

---

[10] Strictly speaking, *Manzhouguo*, or the "land of the Manchus." I have retained the *Manchukuo* romanization here, and throughout this book, because it is commonplace in historical coverage of the state.

[11] In an unexpected side-effect of the Shanghai protests, in 1934 the Japanese consul in Bruxelles complained to the Belgian authorities about the appearance of anti-Japanese slogans in the *Tintin* comic *The Blue Lotus*. The artist, Hergé, appeared to have copied a street scene from photos of Shanghai, unaware that he had faithfully reproduced signs declaring "Boycott Japanese Products" and "Down with Imperialism." De Weyer, "Censorship in Belgian Comics," p. 1.

city. The presence of so many Americans and Europeans, in fact, led to substantially more foreign media attention paid to the Shanghai Incident than to the ongoing Manchurian Incident to the north.[12]

The poet Yosano Akiko, apparently convinced by her own sojourn in Manchuria that Japan had China's best interests at heart, wrote about the deluded beliefs of the Chinese resistance fighters. Her "Rosy-Cheeked Death" revisited the concerns of her famous "Do Not Lay Down Your Life," lamenting 200 teenage Chinese student-soldiers who died in the fighting, and sympathizing with the feelings of their bereaved mothers, or the fiancées she presumed to have already been chosen for some of them.

> Perhaps they had read a little / But lacked sufficient knowledge of the world / And never knew the name of Sun Yat-sen / Who prayed for the peace of their nation.

> Who is that deceives them / with their youthful, naïve hearts / teaching them to hate / their good neighbor, Japan?[13]

But while Yosano mulled over the sight of dead Chinese boys and blamed their corrupt general for leading them astray, this new poem lacked her earlier concerns about whether or not there was any point to the conflict. Japan's role on the Asian mainland, she now implied, was benign and justified, and those Chinese that could not see it were being duped by their leaders.

The most famous moment in the Shanghai fighting was an odd choice for celebration. Three Japanese soldiers were killed carrying a "Bangalore torpedo" (a long explosive cylinder for clearing barbed wire, known in Japanese as a *hakaitō* or "destruction tube"). For this, they were celebrated as "the three bomb heroes" (*bakudan sanyūshi*) by Army Minister Araki Sadao—a term subsequently taken up by several newspapers, although others preferred the term "three heroic human bullets" (*nikudan sanyūshi*). Their sacrifice was front-page news back in Japan, and soon the subject of a competition to write a song in their praise, to be set to music provided by a military academy band. The most

---

[12] Lu, *Agony of Choice*, p. 71.
[13] Rabson, "Yosano Akiko at War," pp. 56–7.

famous, "The Three Bomb Heroes" (*Bakudan Sanyūshi*) of at least seven released that year, included the following lines:

> Now is the time / to show that the courage of Japanese men is stronger than forged iron.

> They kick the ground and run / determined smiles on their faces / Leaving but a word to their comrades / a brisk farewell.

> No time to lose / the *hakaitō* they embrace is lit / arriving at the barbed wire, they throw themselves upon it.

> With the sound of a roaring explosion / they breach a pathway through / now our squads charge in / like a surge of foaming brine.

> Not the plum blossoms of Jiangnan / but the flesh of torn and fallen bodies / these three men are national flowers / offered to a righteous army [*jingi no gun*]

> Their pure, loyal spirit will be discussed for eternity / Forever under heaven shall they be an inspiration / Peerlessly courageous three heroes / Shiningly honorable three heroes.[14]

The author of the winning lyrics was Yosano Akiko's husband, the celebrity poet Yosano Hiroshi, founder of the *Myōjo* literary magazine, who threw in several Chinese allusions, including the plum blossoms of Jiangnan (the region around Shanghai), the classical term "under heaven" (also a term for the Emperor), and *jingi*—the first two Confucian virtues: benevolence and justice. Even he seemed a tad embarrassed by his entry, noting that he had dashed it off in a limited amount of time, but figured it would suffice because "military songs are hardly literary."

His wife would also publish a poem on the incident, "Citizens of Japan, A Morning Song," several months later, but presumably also originally scribbled in haste in the hope of winning the 500-yen prize. In it, she celebrated the soldiers' deaths, as they "dance through the barbed wire" and scatter their bodies "like flowers." Twice, in her 1932 poem,

---

[14] Osada, *Sensō ga Nokoshita Uta*, pp. 225–6.

she repeated a declaration of loyalty to the Emperor: "Ah, the August-ness of His Majesty's reign / that inspires people's hearts / it is a time that ignites our sense of duty." As for the Emperor's subjects, Yosano had now forgotten all thought of doubting her imperial masters. The soldiers on the front line, in Yosano's change of heart, now enjoyed the full support of the nation.

> And they are but one example.
> For we, too, the people behind the guns,
> Redouble our courage many times over
> And rally everyone to the cause.[15]

Posthumously promoted, immortalized in several statues, played by actors in five movies that year, and the subject of a nationally organized charity for their dependents, the three "human bullet" heroes are an important point on the continuum celebrating suicidal loyalty to the Emperor. In a cash-in of questionable taste, their images were also appropriated for Three Human Bullet-branded saké and candy.[16] However, their true story may not have been quite so valiant as the media claimed. Certainly, they were picked from 36 volunteers to undertake the task, although the danger they faced was not strategically vital, and was a frankly unnecessary mission. Moreover, there were whispers even at the time that their deaths were a dreadful accident, and that far from knowingly charging to their deaths, they had been blown up before they could escape to safety, due to a fuse that had been lethally cut too short. Seen in that light, Araki Sadao's prominent praise of their actions, and the whole media storm ensuing, starts to look more like a cynical spin on a terrible military blunder.

Any large-scale opposition in Japan to military adventures on the mainland was crushed by several terrorist actions committed by young officers and cadets—Manchuria and Shanghai had ushered in the era that later historians would term the "dark valley" (*kurai tanima*), in

---

[15] Rabson, "Yosano Akiko at War," p. 59.

[16] Young, *Japan's Total Empire*, p. 77. Such propaganda was also a useful distraction from domestic issues. Even as the Japanese media was crowing about successes in China, poverty levels in recession-hit Japan were climbing to alarming levels. A government survey in 1932 reported that 200,000 children were showing up to school each day with no food to eat. See Collingham, *The Taste of War*, loc. 1099.

which democracy was terrorized into silence by militarist terrorism.[17] One conspiracy, the League of Blood Incident of February 1932, did not go according to plan, with only two of its plotters actually following through with their aim of killing major public figures. Activists were more successful in their aims on May 15, when a group of young Navy officers killed the Prime Minister, Inukai Tsuyoshi, after breaking into his house. Accomplices also created minor incidents elsewhere, including a hand-grenade attack on a bank, an abortive attack on another minister, and in what was planned as a deliberate attempt to drag America into war, a failed plan to assassinate the movie star Charlie Chaplin, who was in Tokyo at the time watching a sumo wrestling match—the conspirators do not appear to have realized that Chaplin was actually British.

As a result of the government doubling down on the situation in Manchuria, there was a boom in songs from the days of the Russo-Japanese War, returning popular culture to Manchurian subjects and themes. The big domestic hit of 1932 was the "Manchurian March" (*Manshū Kōshinkyoku*), rushed out in February to remind the Japanese that northeast Asia had been within Japan's cordon of interest for a generation, used in March as the main theme to a feature film of the same name. It referred to the "buried bones of brave men" left in the region from the Russo-Japanese War, as well as freezing cold, soldiers missing home, camping out under the night stars and boiling rice in "muddy yellow water." It is only with the final verse that it turns to modern concerns, and Manchuria's strategic role.

> For peace in the East, we do not regret giving up our lives
> For this is Japan's lifeline (*Nihon no seimeisen*)
> With 90 million brothers and sisters
> Let's protect Manchuria together.[18]

That September, the Japanese government officially recognized Manchukuo as an independent state, while the Lytton Commission was still

---

[17] The concept was popularized by Ōkouchi Kazuo with his 1970 book *Kurai Tanima no Rōdō Undō: Taishō, Shōwa* [*Labor Movements in the Dark Valley: Taishō/Shōwa*]. The term, however, derives ultimately from the Japanese translation of Psalm 23:4— "Yea, though I walk through the shadow of the valley of death, I will fear no evil."

[18] Gamsa, *Manchuria*, p. 87; Osada, *Sensō ga Nokoshita Uta*, pp. 230–31; Mitsui, *Popular Music in Japan*, loc. 224.

investigating. This, in fact, was a cause of some irritation to the Lytton investigators, since not only were they now guests in a state they did not yet recognize, but their Japanese hosts refused to guarantee their safety beyond the railway zone, thereby impeding their ability to gather evidence.[19]

Regardless, the Lytton Report ruled that the Kwantung Army's actions "cannot be regarded as measures of legitimate self-defense" and that the damage to the railway track was so minimal that it was hardly "sufficient to justify military action."[20] The report was, at least officially, careful not to assign blame, after the French committee member refused to condemn Japan. However, if that was his belief, he must have missed the tone of the English-language report, which flippantly chronicles the many unlikely claims of the Japanese, including the apparent bravery of one Lieutenant Kawamoto in ordering his 500-strong team to attack a barracks estimated to contain 10,000 Chinese soldiers ("because offence is the best defense"), the outstanding efficiency of the Kwantung Army in deploying so fast, and the claim of the Chinese that the sentries in the barracks, having been ordered to do nothing to aggravate the Japanese, were armed only with dummy rifles.

Japan's answer to the League of Nations was that its rules and regulations only applied to actual *nations*, and that before the foundation of Manchukuo, north-east China had been a lawless wilderness, a "divided community" occupied by several races, over which China had no control, and which, without Japan's intervention, might easily have fallen to Communism. Appealing to a historical precedent, Japanese arguments even pointed out the unavoidable fact that Manchuria was *north* of the Great Wall, which marked the historical borders of China.[21] There was hence no state to invade, nor any reasonable jurisdiction in international law. Matsuoka Yōsuke, the former vice-president of the South Manchuria Railway, was on hand in the Geneva chamber to present a somewhat histrionic case for Japan, noting that Japan would accept no interference in its interests in Manchukuo, just as surely as the U.S. would not permit meddling in the Panama Canal Zone, and Britain in Egypt.

Humanity crucified Jesus of Nazareth two thousand years ago...
We Japanese feel that we are now put on trial. Some of the people

[19] Kuhn, "The Lytton Report," p. 97.
[20] Bulwer-Lytton, *Report of the Commission of Enquiry*, p. 71.
[21] Gamsa, *Manchuria*, p. 90.

in Europe and America may wish even to crucify Japan in the twentieth century. Gentlemen, Japan stands ready to be crucified! But we do believe, and firmly believe, that in a very few years, world opinion will be changed and that we also shall be understood by the world as Jesus of Nazareth was.[22]

Such arguments failed to persuade the council of the League of Nations, which voted in early 1933 to condemn Japan as an aggressor. The Japanese delegation, however, walked out of the conference chamber and never came back. Back in Japan, Matsuoka gave a radio broadcast in which he explained his reasons: that East and West would always be fundamentally opposed, that foreigners "needed to understand the spirit of our nation without equivocation," and that a noble, poetic image of sacrifice was called for. "I wanted," he said, "to be like a cherry-blossom in its graceful parting."[23]

The walk-out at the League of Nations was a turning-point in Japanese politics. For decades, Japan had played along with the internationalist game, for fear of foreign intervention. Now, Japan entered an era of "autonomous diplomacy," making decisions regarding Manchukuo and, as subsequent years would show, the rest of China as well as South-East Asia, with a distinct lack of regard for whether it angered foreign powers or not.[24]

In 1934, Puyi was upgraded, from President of Manchukuo, to Emperor of Manchukuo, a nation that continued to fail to be recognized by most of the international community—a tin-pot "puppet" regime with a somewhat tin-eared national anthem.

> Twixt Heaven and Earth, now there is the new Manchuria
> The new Manchuria is the new land
> Let us make our nation fine, upstanding and free of sadness
> With only love and no hatred
> Thirty million people, thirty million people
> And at ten times that shall we yet be free

---

[22] Lu, *Agony of Choice*, p. 85. Back in Japan, Matsuoka's speech was greatly admired, released as a gramophone record, and adopted by some schools as a supplementary English exercise, alongside the works of Shakespeare. See also Hotta, *Japan 1941*, p. 88.

[23] Lu, *Agony of Choice*, p. 95.

[24] Young, *Japan's Total Empire*, p. 46.

Righteous (*renyi*) and devout (*lirang*), we shall be rectified
Family in order and state well ruled, we shall want for nothing
Now let us join the world,
And in future, Heaven and Earth.[25]

Sung in Chinese, the Manchukuo national anthem made dog-whistle allusions to Confucian thought, using the terminology of Confucian virtues, particularly "righteous," which would become a buzzword for ultra-nationalism throughout the 1930s—*renyi* in Chinese is the Japanese *jingi*, that same "benevolence and justice" alluded to in Yosano Hiroshi's poem, above. Its final two lines, contrasting two words for the wider world, carry the ominous tone of "today Manchuria, tomorrow the world."

The Kwantung Army had claimed to act to secure the Japanese nation's access to vital resources, but also dragged the concerns of Japan further along Army lines. Policy advisers in the United States scoffed at the whole idea, predicting that Manchukuo would turn into a money pit, requiring huge amount of investment with no sign of the promised returns. It was hoped by the Americans that this would prove to be such an embarrassment to the Army that it lost all support back in Japan, and cleared the way for more level-headed moderates. However, the leaders of the Manchukuo coup surely knew this themselves, and that they were now gambling their own reputations and futures on Manchukuo becoming a success.[26]

Manchukuo now had to deliver on the promise outlined by the previous generation of explorers and researchers. Its open plains had been turned into vast agribusinesses; it was producing huge quantities of soy and soybean products. It had the largest timber reserves of any Chinese or former Chinese province, and was an industrial powerhouse producing tiles, ceramics, matches, salt, iron, dye, soap and medical products.[27] Compare the largesse and potential of Manchuria with Japan's poverty-stricken home economy, exacerbated in 1934 by a crop failure in the northern rice fields. The acquisition of Manchuria had unexpected consequences back in Japan, where a sense of the need to vastly increase Japan's available manpower completely overturned previous

[25] https://tanken.com/mankokka.html
[26] Barnhart, *Japan Prepares for Total War*, p. 102.
[27] O'Conroy, *The Menace of Japan*, p. 174.

Manchukuo

SOVIET UNION

SOVIET UNION

ONGOLIA

MANCHUKUO

● Harbin

Changchun
(Xinjing) ●

JEHOL
1933

● Mukden

▲ Mount Baekdu

KWANTUNG
Leased Japan 1905

KOREA
Annexed Japan 1910

CHINA

JAPAN

scare-mongering about overpopulation. Now, the new buzzwords were "give birth and multiply" (*umeyo, fuyaseyo*), while discussion of legal birth control or abortion were now regarded as subversive to state policy. The disconnection between government policy and life for the common people was glaring—infant mortality rates were climbing, and in 1934 alone, 11,000 Japanese girls were sold into prostitution by families that could not afford to support them.[28]

The new state of Manchukuo, no longer concerned about Chinese factionalism, rubber-stamped agreements with Japan securing previous commercial and mining agreements in perpetuity.[29] But it also confronted Japan with a new issue—a physical border with the Soviet Union, which the top brass in the Japanese Army universally agreed was the most likely enemy for Japan to face in a future conflict... even though it was their men's own actions that had made this more likely. Among the Kwantung Army's preparations for a coming war, its Epidemic Prevention and Water Purification Department gained a new, secret unit, ostensibly dedicated to fighting disease. Sometimes named the Ishii Unit after its leader, Ishii Shirō, but better known today by the designation Unit 731, the team conducted intensive experiments into diseases, blood-loss, frostbite, amputations and wounds, the effectiveness of grenades and the potential of chemical and bacteriological weapons. To do so, they used human test subjects, euphemistically termed "Manchurian monkeys" in some of their published research papers, or *maruta* (logs) in the grim slang of the facility staff.[30]

Ishii was a protégé of Lieutenant General Araki Sadao, the main proponent of the Soviet threat, although since Araki was the Russian-speaking former military attaché to St Petersburg, and a major player in the Siberian Intervention, who regarded Siberia as within Japan's sphere of interest, one might be forgiven that he was simply pushing for a policy agenda that favored his own skillset. Araki's admiration for the

---

[28] Otsubo, "Feminist Maternal Eugenics," p. 43. Like the "dark valley" itself, this quote appears to derive from the Bible, in this case Genesis 9:7 "be fruitful and multiply," which in Japanese is the very close *umeyo, fueyo*. For infant mortality and prostitution, see Young, *Japan's Total Empire*, p. 324.

[29] Many of these mines would become crucial to the Japanese war effort. See Wang, "Cuncun Heshan, Cuncun Jin," a quirky account of the Sino-Japanese conflict as revealed through geological documents.

[30] Harris, *Factories of Death*, is the most accessible source on the history of Unit 731 and its multiple atrocities.

insubordinate officers was blatant—he had been Army Minister in the Inukai cabinet in 1932, but that had not stopped him calling Inukai's assassins "irrepressible patriots." The son of a former Tokugawa clan samurai, Araki was determined to drag samurai values back into public life in the 20th century, and regarded them as highly compatible with the philosophy of fascism. In September 1932, when speaking to the press, Araki first coined the term that would come to be associated with his ideals: the Imperial Way (*Kōdōha*). Over the years that followed, the Imperial Way would form a substantial faction within the armed forces, an arch-conservative force demanding a return to "traditional values," meaning samurai-style obedience to the Emperor. Araki, in fact, often seemed to be calling for a return to Japan's samurai-era exclusion from the outside world—his sole concession to modernity was that in order for Japan to enjoy blissful isolation, it needed to extend its borders a little into mainland Asia to secure the necessary supplies.

As part of Araki's focus on north-east Asia and the perceived Soviet threat, the Imperial Way faction advocated a pre-emptive strike against the Soviet Union. It also drew dangerously on the philosophy of Kita Ikki, particularly his seditious *Outline Plan for the Reconstruction of Japan* (*Nihon Kaizō Hōan Taikō*)—talk began, among the army, of a need to drag Japan back onto the *correct* course, and to eliminate the dangerously liberal ideas that were undermining the state. The means of doing so was couched in the same terms as those of the samurai who had masterminded the coup of 1868—the time was approaching for a "Shōwa Restoration."

Just as the Meiji rebels had proclaimed their loyalty to the presumed wishes of a teenage emperor, the would-be Shōwa rebels regarded themselves as the true instruments of the will of the Shōwa Emperor, even though his own archives show him repeatedly castigating them for their actions. The rise of such an ultra-nationalist clique within the Army led to the formation of an opposition faction, although to call them "moderates" would be misleading. The enemies of the Imperial Way faction were a group officers similarly convinced of an impending war, but believing that the best way to prepare to it was not to undertake unilateral action on the mainland, but to cultivate the cooperation and support of the government and the industrial combines, not merely in Japan, but in China. They were sticking to the original plan as conceived in the Koiso report of 1915, and wanted to continue to work within the existing political system, all the better to ensure a smoothly running military machine. The Imperial Way zealots called them, contemptuously, the Control Faction (*Tōseiha*), and the tension between these two cliques would steer the first half of the 1930s in Japanese political life.

In early 1933, the fighting in Manchukuo spilled over into Jehol, Inner Mongolia. The Shōwa Emperor reluctantly gave his assent to further "strategic operations" in Jehol, on the understanding that they would be necessary to secure the territory that the Army already held in Manchuria. However, warned by his Prime Minister that fighting in Jehol might prove to be the last straw with the League of Nations, the Emperor tried to countermand his own order in mid-February.

The Army, however, was not going to listen to him. Now, the Emperor was warned by his Chief Aide de Camp that any attempt to stop the Jehol operation would "give rise to a commotion, and may well be the cause of a *coup d'état*."[31] The Army's loyalty to the Emperor was now contingent on the Emperor giving the orders that the Army wanted to hear, and the Army was utterly convinced not only that the Soviet Union was the next enemy, but that its influence extended to the home front, and was responsible for much of the political agitation and unrest back home in Japan. An internal Army pamphlet, distributed to officers in 1933, made its position clear:

> Is there a single Soviet citizen in Soviet Russia who would propagate the idea of Japanese imperial morality? We have not yet been able to influence a single Soviet person and make him believe in the Japanese national policy and imperial virtue; but hundreds of thousands of Japanese are acting as the agents of the Soviets in spreading Communist ideas in our Empire, and are rapidly destroying our national basis. It is due to them that Japan has become the arena of revolutionary struggle.[32]

Konoe Fumimaro, the stern critic of the Paris Peace Conference, leapt to the defense of Japan's position in 1933:

> Japanese actions [in Manchuria] have been questioned many

---

[31] Mauch, "The Shōwa Political Crisis," p. 7.
[32] Tanin and Yohan, *When Japan Goes to War*, p. 262.

times by the League of Nations. Japan seems to be in the position of a defendant being tried in the name of world peace before an international court. It is time now that we explain to the world why Japan's national survival compels to act this way, and state our honest convictions about how true world peace can be achieved.[33]

Konoe vented his frustrations at the "so-called pacifists in the West" who criticized Japan for simply pursuing resources and land. Japan, he argued was being unfairly confined by international rules, while other nations, with smaller populations and less pressing needs, were being granted room to grow and expand.

"World War I had little to do with justice versus brute force," he observed. "It was a conflict between the advanced nations that would benefit from maintaining the status quo, and the less developed nations that sought to destroy it. What can we do to remove these conditions and achieve true peace? At the least, freedom of economic transactions must be secured, and freedom of migration must be reorganized."[34] Japan, he pleaded, was a nation that saw its population rise by a million people every year.

The Army and the Navy had come to a mutual understanding. Each predicted a crisis within three years—the former on the frontier with the Soviet Union, the latter when arms limitation treaties came up for renegotiation. Consequently, both supported each other's concerns in the Cabinet, and the budget agreed in late 1933 to increase the military's share of the national budget from 36% to 45%.[35]

Even within these appropriations, there were arguments. Araki and his Imperial Way clique wanted weapons and ammunition. Those within the Control clique thought that the money was better spent on longer-term investments, such as more factories able to provide larger quantities of necessary items in the future. Araki was gone by 1934, having made too many enemies in the administration, and leaving things briefly in the hands of the Control-faction, major-general Nagata Tetsuzan.

Nagata inherited a series of fires to fight, including a Navy determined to rapidly expand with the end of the arms limitation treaty in 1936, and a Kwantung Army clamoring for more resources to deal with a

[33] Oka, *Konoe Fumimaro*, p. 31.

[34] Oka, *Konoe Fumimaro*, p. 31.

[35] Barnhart, *Japan Prepares for Total War*, p. 26.

Russian military build-up that had been caused by its own actions. There was plenty of talk in the Japanese government and military about the need to secure northern China in some similar fashion to the manner in which Manchukuo had been secured—the creation of some sort of national territory that could be held at arm's length from Chiang Kai-shek's government in the south. Matsuoka Yōsuke, the new president of the South Manchuria Railway, already had helpful suggestions about how to extend his corporation's pernicious influence southwards, and had sent Tokyo a wish-list of places in north China that might be targeted for their potential to supply Japan with coal, iron-ore, oil and cotton.[36]

In May 1934, Major-General Nagata also took delivery of the 54-volume policy document for mobilizing the nation in the event of a total war. Delayed and effectively superseded by the actions of the Kwantung Army, it was good for only eighteen months before it would need to be substantially revised—the Planning Bureau was already working on a second edition that would be applicable to the year 1937.

Nagata, however, would not live to see it. Aggrieved young Army officers, some utterly convinced that arrests and expulsions of a cadet conspiracy (the "Military Academy Incident" of 1934) had been fake news designed to purge unwelcome extremists from the military, were gunning for him. He narrowly escaped an assassination attempt in June 1935, but his luck ran out two months later.

In August 1935, Nagata was stabbed to death in his office by a young lieutenant-colonel who regarded him as a traitor to Araki's careful schemes—the Control-clique toady who had fired or elbowed aside some of the Imperial Way's best men, and left the Army "in the paws of high finance." The assassin was a textbook Imperial Way fanatic; he had stopped off on the way to pray at both the Ise and Meiji shrines, sure that if he succeeded, his murderous act would have met with divine approval. He calmly handed himself over to the authorities, spouting weaponized Zen to the effect that there was "no good or evil." As he was walked off into custody, a high-ranking officer stopped and silently shook his hand—it was notable that in a building full of officers wearing swords and side-arms, only one colonel seemed to have rushed to Nagata's defense. The assassin's trial, which stretched on until the following July, hinged for much of its deliberation on the matter of whether the

[36] Barnhart, *Japan Prepares for Total War*, p. 30.

assassin was a lone-wolf, or an agent of a wider conspiracy within the Japanese military.[37]

The Justice Minister, Ōhara Naoshi, expressed his serious concern about the continued flouting of military discipline and Japanese law.

> Hiding behind the pretext of emperorism [sic] and patriotism, they make the world a sullen place by illegally suppressing the freedom of speech of others and constraining their actions, privileging a violent demeanor, and bringing about a social environment in which the general citizen cannot say what they want to say. This is a major cause of social anxiety.[38]

The Emperor's own *Veritable Record* again notes Hirohito expressing his concern to his Army Chief of Staff in September 1935 about insubordination in the ranks, and the obvious deceit inherent in repeated incidents of apparently hot-headed young officers "dragging" their apparently powerless superiors along with them after initiating acts of war.[39] But the Emperor did not actually say "insubordination" (*kōmei*). The term he chose to use was *gekokujō*, "the low dominating the high," a phrase previously used by historians to describe the period of Japan's 15th and 16th century. The Emperor's phrasing implies a genuine fear that Japan was on the brink of a civil war.[40]

He had his answer four months later, on February 26, 1936.

Even as the trial was underway, a group of Imperial Way officers led 1,500 men in a drastic action, proclaiming themselves to be the Righteous Army (*gigun*), shouting a slogan loaded with allusions to the Meiji Restoration: "Revere the Emperor, Destroy the Traitors" (*sonnō tōkan*).

In a series of raids at dawn in the snowy capital, several companies of soldiers led armed assaults on the residences of key figures associated with budget cuts and purges in the military, including the Prime Minister, the Finance Minister, and the recently retired Lord of the Privy Seal, all key advisers to the Emperor. Five hundred men seized the Tokyo

---

[37] Victoria, *Zen War Stories*, pp. 27–38; Hotta, *Japan 1941*, p. 121.

[38] Person, *Arbiters of Patriotism*, p. 184.

[39] Mauch, "The Shōwa Political Crisis," p. 7.

[40] Perez, *Japan at War*, p. 51 notes that *gekokujō* is a less commonly used descriptor for the period 1467–1570, usually referred to as *sengoku*—literally "the Warring States." The term itself originated in Sui dynasty China, in the early 7th century AD, as *xia ke shang*.

police headquarters without resistance, successfully shutting down any likely civilian emergency response. 160 others occupied the Ministry of War building, and made a series of demands to the War Minister, making it plain what their motives were. Among their demands were the War Minister's assent to the notion of a Shōwa Restoration, no force to be used against the "Righteous Army," a number of arrests and dismissals of prominent officers opposed to the Imperial Way faction, and the immediate appointment of Araki Sadao, not to a government office or Tokyo position, but to the command of the Kwantung Army.[41]

A group of the soldiers that had previously attacked the Prime Minister's house then took on a second mission, raiding the offices of the *Asahi Shinbun* newspaper and wrecking the typesetting trays, thereby making it impossible for the newspaper to put together a new edition.

In the afternoon, the Army Minister issued a response to the soldiers in his offices, agreeing with them that the national spirit faced a serious threat, and that their grievances had been reported to the Emperor. Beyond that, it remained a matter of the Emperor's approval.

It was this final clause that would set the threads unraveling. The Imperial Way faction regarded the Emperor as divine and benign presence, and themselves as the interpreter of his handily unstated will. But their uprising, while surgically targeted at the heart of Tokyo's institutions, had not been quite as successful as they thought. Of their seven assassination targets, only three were dead, including the Finance Minister who approved military budget cuts, shot while he slept, and the Inspector General of Military Education, machine-gunned in front of his nine-year-old daughter.

The others survived through a variety of dramatic circumstances, including the former Prime Minister Saionji Kinmochi, who embarked upon a desperate car-chase to avoid pursuers, only to discover that he had long evaded his would-be murderers, and that the car following him was instead full of journalists.

Makino Nobuaki, a former Foreign Minister, was spirited to safety by one of his bodyguards while others delayed the attackers in a prolonged gunfight.[42] Hearing a single gunshot from within the burning hotel, the attackers assumed that it was Makino committing suicide, and

---

[41] Chaen, *Zusetsu Ni Niroku Jiken*, pp. 120–24.

[42] Makino was also the son of the statesman Ōkubo Toshimichi, adopted into another family as a child.

wrongly reported their mission as a success.

The Grand Chamberlain, Suzuki Kantarō, was shot twice in his bedroom. Believing him to be mortally wounded, one of his attackers prepared to finish the job with a sword, but in a moment of samurai drama, Suzuki's weeping wife, Taka, pleaded to be allowed to kill him herself. The soldiers saluted and withdrew, although Mrs. Suzuki never got around to her task of the day, and Suzuki survived.

Prime Minister Okada Keisuke had been alerted to the attack on his mansion by the gunshots of his four police bodyguards mounting a foolhardy defense against 280 armed men from the 1st Infantry Regiment. The deaths of the bodyguards bought him enough time to find a hiding place, while his brother-in-law, a military officer who looked enough like him to fool the attackers, died in his place.

Okada remained in hiding for the duration of the uprising, which only made matters worse for his alleged killers, as he was a former admiral, as was Saitō Makoto, shot repeatedly as his wife Haruko tried to shield his body, as was Suzuki, whose wife had forgotten to cut his throat that morning. All of which served to make news of the uprising sound less like a "righteous" coup in some quarters, and more like a declaration of war by the Army on the Navy. Consequently, the 40 warships mustered in Tokyo Bay began landing marines to secure and defend onshore naval installations against a possible attack by the rebels, and the Tokyo Police began plotting an extremist response of their own, canvassing 300 volunteers to prepare for a suicidal assault on the entrenched soldiers.[43]

Meanwhile, the unflappable Mrs. Suzuki formed an unexpected new fighting front of her own, by phoning the Imperial Palace, where before her marriage she had been the nanny and governess to three princes, including the young Hirohito. The conspirators had presumably not expected her to be able to place a direct call to the Shōwa Emperor describing the attack on her husband—already fuming at news of the uprising, His Majesty was heard to mutter: "Taka is like a mother to me." An hour after midnight, the Emperor signed a declaration of martial law, effectively pitting one faction of the Army against another on the streets of Tokyo.

The next morning, the rebels found themselves in political limbo.

---

[43] Person, *Arbiters of Patriotism*, p. 187. Fortunately, the services of the kamikaze cops were not required.

The last man standing with the power to form a new Cabinet was a Control-faction man, who refused to accept a new government stuffed with rebel appointees—at least, that was how the rebels heard the news. In fact, the Emperor himself had refused to accept a new Cabinet until the "insurgents" (his unequivocal choice of word, not reported to the rebels themselves) had been dealt with, and even threatened to go out in person to fight them.

> Why should we forgive them when these brutal officers kill our right-hand advisors? [...] All my most trusted retainers are dead and their actions are aimed directly at me... We ourselves will lead the Imperial Guards and suppress them.[44]

General Araki himself visited the besieged rebels at the War Ministry, and sheepishly requested that they stand down. So, too, did General Mazaki, another of the rebel's heroes, who similarly asked them to return to their barracks and leave the negotiations to the grown-ups. They said they would do so as soon as the Emperor ordered them to, secure in the belief that he would not dare.

The Emperor, however, was having none of it. That morning, he had authorized the use of force against the rebels, accusing them of "trying to put a silk noose around my neck." By dawn on the 28th, forty-eight hours after the initial attacks, the wording of government documents had ominously begun referring to the officers' actions not as an "uprising," but as a "rebellion." Other units had failed to join with the 1,500 original rebels, who now found themselves surrounded by more than ten times as many government troops.

Their bluff had been called over the nature of loyalty. Like the Shōgunal troops of the Meiji Restoration, who had been dared to charge against the Emperor's own banner, the rebels in the War Ministry had been out-maneuvered. To make things even clearer, a trio of aircraft dropped flyers on the rebel positions, while a hot-air balloon unfurled a long banner proclaiming: "The Imperial Command has been issued. Do not resist the Army colors."

Arguments broke out among the rebel soldiers, some 70% of whom were not Imperial Way idealists at all, but young recruits who had been

---

[44] Connors, *The Emperor's Adviser*, p. 168.

following the orders of their superiors, unaware that their actions would be branded as *disloyal* to the Emperor. The non-commissioned officers were ordered to take the enlisted men back to the barracks, while the ringleaders prepared to face the consequences of their actions. Several committed suicide, others were apprehended, stripped of their rank, and put on trial. Controversially, the philosopher Kita Ikki, author of the pamphlets said to have inspired the rebels, was included among the court martial defendants, despite not being an officer in the military. Ultimately, he, along with eighteen other conspirators, was executed by a firing squad at the Shibuya military prison.

The February 26th Incident spelled the end of the influence of the Imperial Way faction, and the culling of a significant number of idealist officers not only from the Army, but also from historical memory. Since they had not died "in the service of the Emperor," the remains of the executed soldiers and their suicidal comrades were excluded from the Yasukuni Shrine, and were instead interred at the Kensōji temple, where a modern gravestone, erected by some of their descendants, commemorates them as "the twenty-two samurai."

The Emperor's decision was a moment of powerful political brinkmanship. His adviser, Saionji Kinmochi, warned him that if the soldiers had refused to obey, he would have forced a constitutional crisis. Saionji was particularly concerned over the possibility of a ready-made replacement waiting in the wings—over the previous few years, the Emperor's younger brother Prince Chichibu had repeatedly voiced support for some of the young officers' more drastic actions, and was known to have consorted with the ultra-nationalist thinker Kita Ikki. Posted out of the way for the previous three years, in part to keep him at arm's length from possible conspirators, Prince Chichibu had suspiciously returned to Tokyo on February 27. Saionji continued to fret that any further direct action by the Shōwa Emperor would encourage "Japanese history to repeat itself"—the precedents he cited were centuries old, but he warned that there were plenty of cases of a younger prince, wittingly or otherwise, becoming the focus for the murder of a ruling monarch.[45]

The Emperor's act served as a sudden, albeit brief, halt to the rise of certain war-mongering factions within his military and government, and a cessation to the previous decade's trend for political assassinations.

---

[45] Connors, *The Emperor's Adviser*, p. 170.

In the Japanese Diet, it led to the politician Saitō Takao boldly taking a stance against the military, and suggesting that the young idealists, spurred on by demagogues like Kita Ikki, had fatally over-simplified complex issues.

> These irresponsible and reckless ideas had easily convinced the young officers that 'the political parties, the *zaibatsu* [industrial combines] and the ruling class were rotten' and that only a drastic transformation could rescue Japan from its looming destruction. They became fanatics, certain that the only way to end 'Japan's weak foreign policy' and 'the humiliating London Naval Treaty' was to murder the prime minister and impose military rule.[46]

However, in its zeal to prevent the ousted generals from re-entering political life, the government fatefully followed Army advice to insist that, hereafter, all Army and Navy ministers be officers on active service. Far from limiting the power of the military within the government, this new policy would ensure that the concerns of soldiers in the field were prioritized among their representatives in the Cabinet. The Control faction might have won the tussle over influence in the military, but it was frankly the lesser of two evils—its officers' interest in long-term planning made them just as likely to favor strong connections to Manchukuo, and sympathies with the rising power of Nazi Germany.[47]

---

[46] Fouraker, "Saitō Takao," p. 7. See also Yoshimi, *Grassroots Fascism*, p. 42.
[47] Mauch, "The Shōwa Political Crisis," p. 4.

CHAPTER 7

An Octopus Eating Its Own Tentacles

In 1936, while Japan had been distracted by the attempted coup in Tokyo, the Kwantung Army and the Manchukuo Army had supported a Mongol prince's attempt to seize control of part of Inner Mongolia, on the Manchukuo border. It was a force of 10,000 Mongols under Prince Demchugdongrub, backed by 6,000 soldiers from Manchukuo, a claim that overlooked the fact that the "Manchukuo" forces were staffed with Japanese officers.

Demchugdongrub, usually referred to, for obvious reasons, as Prince De, became the nominal leader of the "Mongol Military Government" in February 1936, "advised" by his Japanese deputy Yamauchi Tōyōnori. It was a textbook repeat of the set-up for Manchukuo, bootstrapping yet another state into existence in the Chinese hinterland. As with Manchukuo, Demchugdongrub's ambition extended somewhat further than his reach—there was talk of his putative Mongol union extending all the way to the edges of Tibet, but it remained a small territory nestled against the borders of Manchukuo. He was, however, an ideal case—a local figure, reliant on Japanese support, who could be leaned upon to seize a portion of Chinese territory in the name of "independence" that could then form a secret Japanese possession.

Japan was caught in a strategic bind—it would take an estimated five years to build Manchuria up into the required bastion of self-sufficiency, but it would take five years of *peace*. If Manchuria were constantly on a war-footing, or facing Chinese counter-insurgency, it would never have the chance.[1]

---

[1] Hotta, *Pan-Asianism and Japan's War*, p. 125.

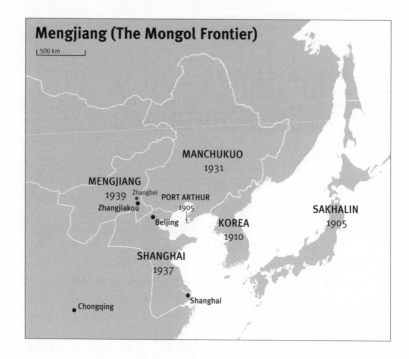

Arguments among the Army leaders reveal a wide-ranging difference of views regarding the situation. Ishiwara Kanji argued for pulling Japanese forces out of north China to concentrate on securing Manchukuo. His rivals argued that Manchukuo could not be secure without a further push into China, a strike that would destroy the capability of the Chinese to mount an effective counter-attack. General Tanaka Giichi promised Tokyo decision-makers that he could accomplish everything with three divisions in just three months. It would cost 100 million yen, and tie up a huge proportion of Japan's civilian shipping tonnage to transport all the necessary equipment, but it would all be over by the end of the year. A suitably dangerous "incident," it was hoped, could be used to provoke a series of uprisings, establish Demchugdongrub deeper in Inner Mongolia, and similar puppets to the south, and to then link these newly "independent" regions into a new Chinese republic to rival Chiang Kai-shek's. The sooner this could be done, the sooner these pacified territories could be put to work supplying the Japanese war effort.

An official in the Foreign Ministry called it out for what it was, a ludicrous war to fund more war, like "an octopus eating its own tentacles."[2]

Ishiwara, oddly becoming the voice of reason six years after provoking the Manchurian Incident, pleaded that the budget for the assault scheme would not be enough—that his own projections suggested that Japan did not yet have the manpower or resources to adequately carry out the mission, and that any attack would drag the country deeper and deeper into an unwinnable war on the Asian mainland.

"It will be what Spain was for Napoleon: an endless bog," he said.[3]

Ishiwara was ignored. If there was going to be a war with the United States, or Russia, or another European power, Japan needed Manchukuo, which meant Japan needed China pacified. Japan had to gamble in China in 1937, in order to stand a chance of gambling elsewhere in the war to come.

Tōjō Hideki always claimed that the suitable "incident" that presented itself in July 1937, shortly after he had been promoted to Chief of Staff on the Kwantung Army, was nothing to do with him. This was despite the fact that one of his first acts in his new role was to send a secret telegram to the Army Vice-Minister in Tokyo, suggesting that the rising threat of a Soviet attack on Manchukuo made it imperative to have a secure southern flank, to avoid also having to fight China at the same time. Echoing the plans of his Kwantung Army colleagues, Tōjō strongly advocated actions against China, both to protect Japanese subjects under potential threat in the north, and to incapacitate Chiang Kai-shek's regime in Nanjing further to the south.[4]

Nevertheless, a suitable incident did arise on July 7, thanks to the rules and rights in place among the foreign powers since the Boxer Uprising of 1900. Ever since, foreign powers had retained the right to garrison troops in Beijing to protect their Legations from a repeat occurrence—these rights extended to the railway lines linking Beijing to the sea, as well as additional rights to go on military exercises without the need to inform the Chinese. But whereas most powers had a relatively small troop contingent in Beijing, consistent with the spirit of the agreement signed after the Boxer Uprising, the Japanese had used it as an excuse to post up to 15,000 soldiers to the region.

---

[2] Barnhart, *Japan Prepares for Total War*, p. 95.
[3] Barnhart, *Japan Prepares for Total War*, p. 75.
[4] Butow, *Tōjō and the Coming of the War*, p. 91.

The Marco Polo Bridge Incident derives its name from the medieval stone bridge, described in the *Travels* of Marco Polo, to be found to the southwest of Beijing. These days, it is within the ambit of the subway system, but in 1937 it was some way outside the city limits. Japanese soldiers on an "exercise" at ten in the evening claimed to have been fired upon by Chinese soldiers in the nearby fort of Wanping, and to be missing a soldier. Refused permission to search Wanping for the missing man, they opened fire, leading to a skirmish that went on for two days, until the missing man magically turned up, and a truce was declared.

However, instead of leaving, the Japanese recommenced firing on Wanping, calling in reinforcements amounting to 20,000 men from the Kwantung Army, and over a hundred planes as aerial support. Events soon escalated into a general Japanese assault on north China, led, co-incidentally, by one of Tōjō's former colleagues from his days in Switzerland. Fighting also broke out in Shanghai, from which Japanese "reinforcements" began making sorties so far outside the contested areas that they also attacked Nanjing, 300 km up the Yangtze River.

"We'll send huge forces," Army Minister Sugiyama assured the Lord Keeper of the Privy Seal, "smash them in a hurry, and get the whole thing over with quickly."[5]

By the end of the month, the fighting had received an imperial backing, with the Shōwa Emperor decreeing that his forces hoped to "urge grave self-reflection on China and to establish peace in the Far East without delay."[6]

However, China fought back. Although the Japanese had expected a fast Chinese capitulation, Chiang Kai-shek retaliated, while not all of Japan's Chinese allies turned out to be as loyal as had been hoped. In July 1937, the Japanese media printed shocked reports of a mutiny and massacre in Tongzhou, Hebei province, where Chinese soldiers of from a puppet regime killed many of the local Japanese garrison, as well as two hundred Japanese subjects.

Japanese reprisals launched from multiple points. Bombers out of

---

[5] Ienaga, *Japan's Last War*, p. 85.

[6] Butow, *Tōjō and the Coming of the War*, p. 99. The Marco Polo Bridge, it is worth noting, is not simply "on the outskirts" of Beijing. It overlooks one of the main arterial routes out of the city and into the center of China. In modern times, it is within a stone's throw of the start of the G4 Jinggang'ao expressway, which stretches for 1,400 kilometers all the way to Macao.

Taiwan attacked airfields around the mouth of the Yangtze on August 14, facing strong resistance from Chinese squadrons. In our time, August 14 is "Chinese Air Force Day," in celebration of its first air-to-air engagement. Throughout August, there were repeated engagements between Japanese and Chinese aircraft over Zhejiang and Anhui. Some of the pilots, however, were not necessarily Chinese. John Wong and Arthur Chin, two Americans of Chinese descent, were among the local flyers. In the same month, Chiang Kai-shek signed a Sino-Soviet pact, in which Moscow agreed to provide new aircraft to bolster the antiquated Chinese airplanes, as well as "volunteers" to fly them. Similarly, Claire Lee Chennault, an ex-U.S. Army instructor, in China as a consultant since that June, was promoted at the outbreak of the air war to be Chiang Kai-shek's "adviser." In other words, both the Soviet Union and the United States were already providing tacit aid to the Chinese war effort.

Japan was also losing the propaganda war. In September 1937, a Japanese Navy aircraft machine-gunned a car on the road from Nanjing to Shanghai, seriously wounding the British diplomat Hughe Knatch-bull-Hugessen—widely regarded as an unwarranted attack on a civilian (as if civilians had not been caught in Japanese cross-fires since at least 1894). The bombing of Nanjing on September 19 similarly did Japan no favors in the international community, nor did the indiscriminate manner in which Japanese soldiers, ordered to snatch vehicles and supplies locally, looted the houses of British, German and American residents, even stealing a car belonging to the American consulate.

It was plain that Japan was ignoring all semblance of cooperating with the Open Door policy, and the behavior of the Japanese Army was setting an ominous precedent. The Chinese were under attack, but the foreign community—that is to say, the *white* community in Shanghai and upriver—was no longer safe. The machine-gunning of Knatch-bull-Hugessen was only the first incident.

On the home front, Prime Minister Konoe started an initiative to unite the Japanese people behind the Army's China adventure. In October 1937, Konoe formed a new organization, intended to unite all contending parties and factions into a single-minded state body. His National Spiritual Mobilization Committee (*Kokumin Seishin Sōdō-in Chūō Renmei*) produced a 156-page *Cardinal Principles* briefing on acceptable beliefs, behavior and culture, forming the basis for sweeping changes in Japanese society and the school curriculum. In public life, opposition

The Pacific War (1937–45)

1000 km

Soviet Union

Lake Baikal

Mongolia

Manchukuo

• Nomonhan

Changchun •

Mukden •

Korea

Japan

China

Tibet

Nanjing •

Shanghai •

Chongqing •

Okinawa

Iwo

Nepal Buthan
Brit. India

Guangzhou •

Taiwan

Burma

Fr.
Indochina

Thailand

Philippines
(U.S.A.)

Guam
(U.S.A

North Borneo
(Brit.)

Palau

Brit. Malaya

Singapore •

Sarawak
(Brit.)

Manado •

Dutch East Indies

Papu
(Austr

Darwin •

Australia

Japan (1936)

China (Dec. 1941 Jap.)
Fr. Indochina (Jul. 1940 Jap.)

Thailand (Dec. 1941 Jap. ally)

Philip., Brit. Malaya (Dec. 1941 Jap.)
Pacific Islands, N. New Guinea,
D.E. Indies, Burma (Mar. 1942 Jap.)

Allies

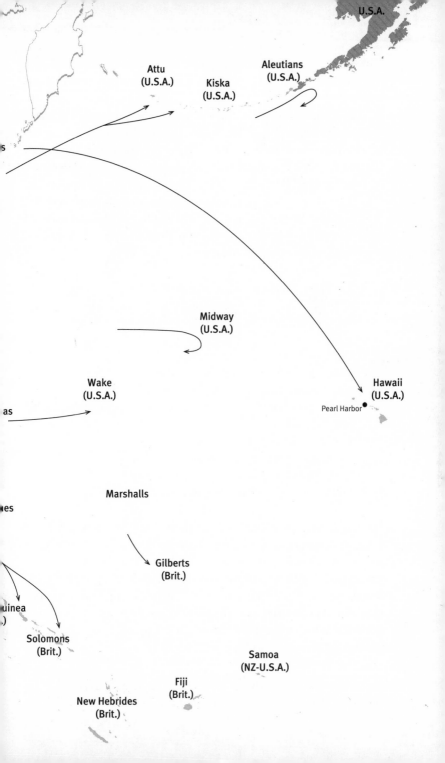

to the military becomes a crime against the Emperor, shutting down all political dissent. It began its activities with a song competition, intended to give the Japanese nation something to sing together.

The winning entry, "Soldiers Advance" (*Shingun no Uta*) turned out to only have impressed the judges, failing to become a widespread hit with the general public. It had, it was later thought, misjudged the mood of the time by concentrating solely on the mindset of soldiers at the front. Instead, it was the B-side, "The Bivouac Song" (*Roei no Uta*) that caught the popular imagination. On the surface, it seems very similar—a soldier's reverie on his duty. Crucially, however, it alluded to the support he received from his family, which took the form of an acknowledgement that he would probably die.

> I gallantly left my home, pledging victory
> How can I die without rendering distinguished service?
> Every time I hear the bugle call, the fluttering of banners.
>
> Pushing through the endless plains
> Where ground, grass and trees are in flames
> Steel helmets and the Rising Sun flag as we march
> Stroking my horse's mane, who knows what tomorrow will bring?
>
> Bullets, tanks and planes, all sleep tonight in the bivouac
> My father, appearing in a dream, urged me:
> "Come home in death."
> I wake up, and glare at the enemy's sky.[7]

The broad plains of China, once celebrated as virgin territory by the South Manchuria Railway, were now depicted as a fiery hell. Later verses recall comrades dying, bloodied, in the day's action, and the narrator's assumption that he will die overseas, for the glory of Japan. But it's his father's words, "Come home in death" (*shinde kaere*) that the scholar Sato Hiroaki identifies as truly catching the popular imagination, a recognition that neither the Chinese nor Japanese forces in the conflict were taking prisoners alive.[8]

---

[7] Osada, *Sensō ga Nokoshita Uta*, pp. 500–1; Mitsui, *Popular Music in Japan*, loc. 240.
[8] Sato, "Gyokusai," p. 7.

In 1937, the Japanese Cabinet Information Bureau for Unified National Patriotism announced the winner of a competition to find a song that would bring the entire Japanese empire together—"a national song for people to sing forever." The resultant "Patriotic March" (*Aikoku Kōshinkyoku*), first performed on Christmas Eve, would be released that year by six different record companies and sell over a million copies, partly out of enthusiasm, but also because it became a mandatory inclusion at school ceremonies and public events.

> See the eastern dawning sky, the shining morning sun
> Hope and vivacity shine in both Heaven and Earth
> Among the Eight Provinces, in the midst of bright morning clouds
> Mount Fuji stands perfect and glorious, the pride of our Japan.[9]

Considering that the song was intended to bring together the various subject peoples outside the Japanese home islands, its dogged concentration on the "eight provinces" and Mount Fuji seemed counterproductively parochial—the lyrics are substantially more general in its official English translation. Later verses half-heartedly alluded to the "people of the Four Seas, blooming like flowers amid a just peace." The fact that this was publicly selected as the song of the moment was a matter of some surprise even among the Japanese. Prime Minister Konoe Fumimaro's younger brother Hidemaro, a prominent conductor, felt that musical integrity was being compromised by an overly populist approach. "There is no way," he wrote in a Tokyo newspaper, "that these judges and that method of selection could possibly produce a 'Patriotic March' that would successfully marry lyrics to melody, and for the people of this country to sing forever."

The science fiction author Unno Jūza satirized the government's media obsessions in a novella published in *Modern Nippon* magazine. *The Music Bath at 1800 Hours* (*Jūhachi-ji no Ongaku-yoku*) imagined a future dystopia where citizens are expected to give their all for the state, where both smoking and alcohol have been outlawed, and where even having free time is regarded as a subversive act. In order to spur citizens onto ever greater heights of productivity, they are made to endure a half-hour broadcast of stirring, inspirational songs every evening at

---

[9] Osada, *Sensō ga Nokoshita Uta*, p. 497.

6pm. In it, the president of an authoritarian state brags of the power of his musical propaganda.

> Thanks to the tremendous power of [the] music bath, the nation is under my complete control. At the end of each bath, it is as if each and every one of my citizens has been reborn. Each and every person burns with the same ideals of this nation and is ready to apply themselves full to their duties with an equal passion. They do my bidding without exception—just like androids. [10]

Despite such misgivings, there were further attempts to whip up the Japanese population into supporting a unified war effort. A national campaign to encourage women to have more children was given the unambiguously militaristic title of the Precious Children Battalion (*kodakara butai*), as if women themselves were now industrial machines, cranking out new soldiers for the future.[11] One song, "Mother of a Military Nation" (*Gunkoku no Haha*, 1937) purported to summarize the feelings of the women of Japan, cheerily waving off their sons.

> Die honorably without worry
> For the sake of your country.
> Encouraging, without tears,
> I see my son off at the station in the morning.
>
> Fall, cherry blossom of a young tree
> Be born as a man on the battlefield
> Raising gun and sword for the Emperor
> The long-cherished ambition of a Japanese man.
>
> I doubt you'll return alive.
> When I receive a plain wood coffin
> I shall praise you.
> Well done, my son, you make your mother proud.

---

[10] Unna, *Eighteen O'Clock Music Bath*, loc. 115. For more on Unna, see Clements, "Unno Jūza." The story was published in April, drawing upon an ongoing obsession with ever more fanatical propaganda, even ahead of the China Incident.

[11] Otsubo, "Feminist Maternal Eugenics," p. 57.

Strongly and bravely, on guard behind the guns [i.e. on the home front]
We mothers are women for whom
The words devotion and loyalty hold value.[12]

The song was rushed into production, although even its lyricist regarded it as ludicrous and its sentiments pathological. "After the war in China broke out," wrote Koga Masao, "I was ordered to write a militaristic popular song. I thought nobody would ever want to sing something like that, but I did not have a choice."

In China, the Japanese Army demanded the surrender of Nanjing by December 10, under threat of reprisals with "no mercy." In the subsequent assault on the city, indiscriminate bombing of shipping on the Yangtze caused Japanese Navy planes to "accidentally" sink the gunboat U.S.S. *Panay* on the river outside Nanjing, claiming not to have seen the Stars and Stripes painted on its roof, or indeed to have realized that it was then functioning as an impromptu consular office for U.S. diplomats.[13]

Late in 1937, Japanese newspapers carried several admiring pieces about two Japanese soldiers who had entered into a high-spirited "killing contest," to see who could be the first to kill a hundred Chinese.[14] The newspapers, however, were conspicuously silent about the widespread atrocities committed in the city after it fell to the Japanese Army—some six weeks of murder, rape and looting. Estimates regarding the numbers of dead in Nanjing remain a contentious issue, since many of the bodies were burned, but run as high as 200,000.

There has been some confusion over the looting in Nanjing, since Japanese sources claimed that it was a necessary commandeering of resources due to a swifter than expected advance. John M. Allison, the U.S. consul, regarded it as ludicrous that the Japanese soldiers had outdistanced their own supply trucks, but reports from elsewhere to corroborate the Army's story—that poor logistics support had forced many of them to requisition supplies.[15] In many cases, this served as an excuse,

---

[12] Osada, *Sensō ga Nokoshita Uta*, pp. 321–2.

[13] Allison, *Ambassador from the Prairie*, p. 33. It was only a matter of time—Hotta, *Japan 1941*, p. 197, notes that Japan narrowly missed sinking the gunboat U.S.S. *Tutuila*, during a July raid on Chongqing.

[14] Matsumura, "Combating Indiscipline," p. 92.

[15] Allison, *Ambassador from the Prairie*, pp. 42–3.

or at least a gateway, towards more blatant looting.

This does not explain why the soldiers also murdered so many thousands of civilians. It has been suggested, by Japanese defendants themselves in the war crimes trials after 1945, that they chose to "act with such barbarity that the Chinese people's will to fight on and defend their homes and their country would be broken."[16] The Nanjing Incident, better known as the Rape of Nanjing, was hence excused as a deliberate exercise in punitive terror, possibly as a desperate attempt to speed up the rest of the campaign, already taking far longer than promised. Despite overwhelming evidence that such tactics only propelled the Chinese on to ever greater resistance, the policy of active terror would stretch on throughout the many years that followed.

Itagaki Seishirō, architect of the Mukden Incident, would insist for years to come that it would form a psychological warfare strategy to bring the Chinese to their knees:

> What we expect of offensive operations in the interior is the mental terror they will create among the enemy forces and civilians rather than the material damage inflicted directly on upon enemy personnel and equipment. We will wait and see them falling into nervous prostration in an excess of terror and madly starting anti-Chiang [Kai-shek] pacifist movements.[17]

However, the promises that the "China Incident" would be over by the end of the year turned out to be unfounded. Facing an ever-escalating commitment of troops and resources, the Japanese government enacted extreme controls on the economy that it had been rehearsing ever since the Osaka industrial exercise of 1929. The focus on military activity led to laws that impacted every area of everyday life. Only a few months into 1938, with Nanjing secured but Chiang Kai-shek still fighting on, the Army General Staff was obliged to consider a more realistic commitment of resources—2.5 billion yen, and twenty more divisions, which would have to be created, trained and equipped. It was difficult to see where the money would come from: there were already supply issues affecting soldiers in the field, and while it was theoretically possible to

---

[16] Russell, *The Knights of Bushidō*, p. 43.
[17] Russell, *The Knights of Bushidō*, p. 44.

invoke the 1918 Munitions Mobilization Law to increase productivity for the war effort, doing so would require the government to admit that it was indeed a *war*, and not a mere "incident."

Konoe's government, meeting in emergency sessions that summer, forced through legislation designed to make the Army's life easier, including the creation of a nationalized body to control production and distribution of synthetic oil, increased control over gold, steel, and iron. New government controls over imports and exports now prioritized military materials ahead of anything else. By the end of the summer, and despite strong opposition from some politicians, the Diet authorized the invocation of the Munitions Mobilization Law despite the fact that war was still not officially declared.

Konoe finally pushed through a National Mobilization Law (*Kokka Sodōin-hō*) in March 1938, placing all vital industries, including the media, under direct government control, and authorizing unlimited budgets for war production. Provisions in the new law, echoing the assurances of the Osaka exercise, promised to compensate business owners in full for any expenses incurred in the switch-over to wartime production. Prices were fixed, free speech was curtailed, and a national "service draft ordinance" allowed the authorities not only to co-opt all able-bodied adults into working in strategic industries, but in keeping them there—it was no longer possible to quit a job in any industry deemed vital to the war effort; to do so would be tantamount to deserting a military post. Songs like "Mother of a Military Nation" were co-opted into what was now an official National Mobilization genre, in which even music was drafted into the war effort.

Record companies took the National Mobilization Law to heart, searching for new themes that would emphasise the whole nation pulling together behind the military. The most conspicuous result of this was a song celebrating the resolve of Japanese women to support the troops. "Thousand-stitch belt" (*Sennin-bari*), about the old custom once condemned as superstition during the Russo-Japanese War, became a broadcast hit on NHK radio, and appeared in three different editions, owing to a singer, lyricist and composer from separate record companies. It emphasized a nation of women, united in a sewing ritual to bring luck to their men overseas.

At the foot of the bridge, in the corner of the town,
By the trees of the avenue, at the station,
So many folks bring a thousand stitches.
They sew away with love.

The newspaper extra issues fly out, the bells sound
Excited and tense
Please, one for your brother,
Your beloved, your uncle.

We are all different, but our hearts are one.
All for one, for the nation.
The Moon watches even in daylight,
Wishing she could add a stitch herself.[18]

The image it presented was romantic and demure—a far cry from the continued brutalities that Japanese soldiers were inflicting on the Chinese. Hayao Torao, a military psychologist, wrote a damning report in April 1938 that accused Japanese soldiers in Shanghai and Nanjing of betraying the expectations of the people back home. Far from even being an exercise in systematic terror, as would be claimed by the Army Minister Itagaki, Hayao just saw them as uncouth and undisciplined:

> …they carouse and act indecently with low-class prostitutes, brandish their swords for no reason and injure people, discharge their pistols, eat and drink without paying [in restaurants], and act in ways so regrettably contrary to the expectations of those back home in Japan. In truth, Shanghai has become the Japanese army's city of crime and Nanjing can hardly be any better. Truly, this only speaks of the decline of the Japanese army.[19]

Nor was the Army unaware of the incident. Regardless of Itagaki's claims that it was all part of the plan to terrorize the Chinese, in the aftermath

---

[18] Mitsui, *Popular Music in Japan*, loc. 1459; Osada, *Sensō ga Nokoshita Uta*, pp. 568–9. Some commentators have suggested that the custom existed in some form in the Sino-Japanese War, or possibly even earlier, but it only became a *national* phenomenon when Japan had a mass media to spread it.

[19] Matsumura, "Combating Indiscipline," p. 92.

of the "Nanjing Incident" the top brass approved a vast expansion of the use of military brothels, in an attempt to keep the soldiers occupied. Such "comfort stations" (*ianjo*) would need to be staffed, leading to an all-new issue all over the Japanese empire as girls were rounded up to be "comfort women" (*ianfu*). Over the next six years, up to 400,000 women were recruited, often under false pretenses, to work as military sex-slaves. Many were Korean or Chinese, others were Japanese criminals sentenced to military service, or the daughters of Japanese men who had been convicted of assaulting Japanese military police.

Hayao, however, regarded the comfort stations as a colossal failure, noting that many soldiers saw no reason to pay the 2-yen admission fee for thirty minutes with a prostitute, when they could take what they wanted for free outside.[20]

This is not the impression one gets from Japanese songs of the day, which saw an explosion in Chinese whimsy as if the Army was advancing towards an oriental paradise, with titles including "Suzhou Nights," "The Dancing Girl of Shanghai," and the "Canton Blues." One of the big hits of June 1938 was "Qing Lai" (*Qing Lai Bushi*), tens of thousands of copies of which were purchased by the Army and distributed by the crateful in China. "Qing Lai" derived its name from the invitation of a street magician, encouraging passers-by in broken Japanese to come closer and watch his show:

> We doing magic, everyone come!
> If we do well, be kind to us.
> Girls they pretty, too.
> *Qing lai, qing lai* [please come]
> *Qing lai, qing lai, qing lai.*

> Swords *bu yao bu yao* [no want, no want].
> Fighting bad. You should sow wheat instead!
> China such a wide, wide place.
> *Qing lai, qing lai*
> *Qing lai, qing lai, qing lai.*

---

[20] Matsumura, "Combating Indiscipline," p. 97.

We good at magic. You watch closely!
Girls they pretty. Take a look!
If they do well, buy them earrings!
Qing lai, qing lai
Qing lai, qing lai, qing lai.[21]

Six months after the Rape of Nanjing, this was the Army's effort in cultural outreach. Back in Japan, "Qing Lai" presented the newly occupied areas as a happy idyll, all trinkets, entertainments and the prospect of female companionship, its people blissfully implying that there was plenty of space to go around, and that newcomers were welcome. The song became a favorite among the Army personnel in China. It is hard to believe that the Chinese were taken in by it, not the least because the language in the song is a clueless foreigner's idea of Mandarin, which ham-fistedly uses the pejorative term *Shina* for China, not the natives' own word for their country.

The "Continental Melodies" (*tairiku melody*), celebrating the diversity and excitement to be found in all corners of the Japanese empire, which had first arisen in 1931, reached a fever pitch in the years from 1938–41, and would go on to include celebrations of the mango sellers of Java, the girls of Thailand, and the island ladies of Palau, romanticizing an Asian "Other," there for the taking. Even Korea's "Arirang" protest song was caught up in this performance of cosmopolitanism, in multiple variants, many of which drifted in Japanese away from the song's original, doleful tone to more prosaic tales of star-crossed lovers.

Manchukuo became a powerhouse of the Japanese supply chain— national industrial policies that had failed to pass the Diet in Japan were easier to force through in Manchukuo, which was now under the sway of a cabal of Japanese officials, many of them destined for high political office. Ayakawa Yoshisuke, founder of the Nissan corporation, was the head of the Development Corporation for Heavy Industries. Matsuoka Yōsuke, he of the crucifixion speech and a future Foreign Minister, was now the president of the South Manchuria Railway. Kishi Nobusuke, a future Munitions Minister (and post-war Prime Minister) was

---

[21] Osada, *Sensō ga Nokoshita Uta*, pp. 357–8. The magician's Japanese is shorn of grammar-modifying particles and peppered with what the writers much have assumed to be Chinese words. My translation is hence carefully racist, in keeping with the original.

Manchukuo's Vice Minister of Industrial Development. The three men, all related by marriage, were joined in their schemes by Tōjō Hideki, then the head of the Manchukuo military police, and Tōjō's old Switzerland classmate Hoshino Naoki, vice Minister of Financial Affairs. It was through their collusion that Manchukuo's pre-existing drugs problems escalated, turning Manchukuo into the world's leading source of heroin, morphine and opium. The narcotics monopoly in Manchukuo, formerly in the hands of warlords, was folded into national policy. Tōjō's police were in charge of shutting down the opium trade; instead, their "inspectors" openly controlled it, while Hoshino's agricultural policies zoned huge areas of land for opium poppies. Drugs were a fundamental cornerstone of the Manchukuo economy, and the native population a primary source of revenue. Rumors persisted that Japanese Golden Bat Export cigarettes (*Kinshi*), sold exclusively in China and Manchukuo, were laced with opium, creating thousands of new addicts. Opium, tobacco, saké, beer and other alcohols leeched money from the population of Manchukuo, generating up to 300 million dollars a year for Japan to reinvest in planning for war.[22]

In July 1937, as part of Japan's China mobilization, Prince Demchugdongrub had secured the area around Suiyuan, and renamed his new personal fiefdom "The Mongol Frontier" (*Mengjiang*). It would become yet another Japanese puppet regime, its coal and iron mines shipping directly to Japan, and to its south by 1938 there was a "Provisional Government of China," also bolstered by Japan. From 1938, south of the Yellow River, ruled from Nanjing, there was also the "Reformed Government of China," both of which would eventually be rebranded as the "Reorganized Government of the Republic of China"—a puppet regime, ruled by the collaborator Wang Jingwei in Nanjing, openly opposing the legitimacy of Chiang Kai-shek's Republic of China.

Japan had been making a mockery of the U.S. "Open Door" policy for years, but cordoning off entire sectors of the country to serve as factories for another country's war effort was sure to be regarded as a step too far by the Americans. From a business point of view, the United States was supplying both sides in the undeclared war—ethical considerations seemed less of an issue to the U.S. than the degree to which either

---

[22] Hotta, *Pan-Asianism and Japan's War*, p. 122; Hoyt, *Warlord*, p. 12; Smith, *Intoxicating Manchuria*, p. 40ff.

client would be in a position to keep paying their bills. By August 1938, a U.S. analyst was advising the Treasury Department that Japan would soon need to be acquiring all of its U.S. imports on credit that could only be redeemed if Japan won against Chiang Kai-shek's China.[23]

The signs of such financial disaster were visible in Japan's shopping areas. A 1938 Department Store Law restricted frivolous advertising. An austere Living Reform Act in 1939 banned the traditional mid-year and new-year gift-giving rituals; since the Japanese government had thereby effectively cancelled Christmas, or at least its local equivalent, newspapers and magazines were forbidden from carrying any advertising that promoted this forbidden custom. Instead, new slogans began to permeate public life, promoting austerity to help the war effort: "We don't desire until we win" and "Luxury is our enemy." When families all over Japan inevitably decided to sneak treats and gifts to each other at the end of the year, it was cause for a statistical report from the Post Office, and exposés in the national press.[24]

The ultimate invocation of the austerity measures was introduced in 1939, when the Army Ministry decreed that the 7th day of every month was a designated "flag" day, where citizens were invited to remember the contribution made to the nation by soldiers at the front. Citizens were urged to eat *hinomaru bentō*—a packed lunch so thrifty that it resembled the Japanese national flag—a bed of plain rice, with a single red pickled plum in the middle. The truly patriotic could buy their lunch from the military instead of making it themselves, thereby also contributing seven *sen* to the war effort.[25]

After the passing of a 1939 Film Law, the authorities had an even more invasive degree of control over the media. No film could go into production without licenses for both the cast and crew, and ideologically speaking, all films had to follow an approved message. They had to display upstanding morals, promote an austere lifestyle, and never waver from support of Japan's war effort. Whereas Yosano Akiko had once freely expressed her sadness and concern over the stationing of her brother overseas, portrayals of family farewells in the media were now encouraged to be relentlessly confident and bold—film-makers, like poets, novelists and journalists, were obliged to introduce a note of ambiguity.

[23] Barnhart, *Japan Prepares for Total War*, p. 106.
[24] Minowa and Belk, "Gifts and Nationalism in Wartime Japan," pp. 298–9.
[25] Harries and Harries, *Soldiers of the Rising Sun*, p. 445.

Amid the songs of the day, one stands out not for its musical or lyrical achievement, but for its tone. "Mother at the Nine Steps" (*Kudan no Haha*, 1939) was written for the spring ceremony at the Yasukuni Shrine, where the newest war dead would be ceremonially accepted into its halls. The song tells the story of a lady from the provinces, coming to the Nine-stepped Hill (*Kudanzaka*) that leads to the shrine's gate.

> From Ueno Station to the Nine Steps
> Frustrated by unfamiliar places
> Taking a whole day and relying on my walking stick
> I've come to see you, Son.
>
> A large gate that can reach the sky
> What an honor to be enshrined
> In such a magnificent place as a god.
> Your mother is shedding tears of joy.
>
> I put my hands together kneeling
> I find myself chanting a prayer to the Buddha.
> I am taken aback and flustered.
> Sorry, Son, I'm such a yokel.
>
> Just like a kite giving birth to a hawk
> I appreciate how fortunate I am.
> Just to show you your Order of the Golden Kite
> I've come all the way to Kudanzaka.[26]

It seems oddly ungracious to ridicule a bereaved mother for being a "yokel" in the big city, like she hasn't suffered enough. But for music historian Osada Gyōji, that is part of the song's subversive appeal. We have gone, in the space of two years, from the unlikely sight of mothers waving off their sons "without tears," to this broken old woman in the big city shedding tears that are plainly not "of joy" at all, but continuing to put a brave face on her personal desolation.

Not long after that year's spring celebrations of the war dead at the Yasukuni Shrine, the long-awaited battle with the Soviet Union broke

---

[26] Osada, *Sensō ga Nokoshita Uta*, p. 396.

out. The flashpoint was the river of Kalkhin Gol, which the Japanese regarded as the border between Mongolia and Manchukuo. However, the Mongols and Soviets believed that the border was actually sixteen kilometers further to the east, near the village of Nomonhan, which was what led several dozen Mongol cavalrymen to allow their horses to graze on the disputed land on May 11, 1939. They were shooed away by a scouting regiment of the Kwantung Army, but soon returned on the 13th in greater numbers.

The Kwantung men stationed on the Mongol border were relatively untrained and inexperienced, and lacked high-quality weapons. In the ensuing skirmishes, with the Mongols soon reinforced by Soviet troops, the Japanese lost over a hundred men.

By June, both sides had committed thousands more men to the area, with the Kwantung Army fielding 30,000 troops, and the Soviets sending tanks and armored vehicles under the command of General Georgii Zhukov. In a tactic that will, by now, be familiar, the Kwantung Army failed to seek approval from Tokyo before ordering planes from the Japanese Army Air Force to proceed over the Mongol border and to bomb three Soviet bases.

In July, a large Japanese force crossed the Kalkhin Gol, but was fought to a stalemate with the Soviets, who counter-attacked in August with a combined air and armor assault. The conflict at Khalkhin Gol was notable in military history for its extensive use of planes as both fighters and bombers, and for the commitment of large numbers of tanks to the field.

The Army Minister Itagaki Seishirō requested an audience with the Emperor, in order to discuss the fighting. The Emperor refused the request, on the grounds that it was pointless, but eventually allowed Itagaki into his presence. If Itagaki were hoping for some sort of imperial assent, he instead got a severe tongue-lashing. The Emperor listed a series of previous incidents in which the Army had disobeyed its orders, dwelling for some time on the Manchurian Incident of 1931, for which Itagaki had been one of the instigators. He was done with insubordinate soldiers, and regarded Itagaki as a man who had behaved just as irresponsibly and disobediently in 1931, only to be rewarded with a promotion and a ministerial post.

That same month, the Emperor directly commented that he disapproved of suggestions among his ministers that Japan court some sort of alliance with Germany. He also openly questioned Itagaki's competence, suggesting that he seemed unable to follow orders as either a soldier or a minister.[27]

However, just as the battle seemed about to escalate even further, with Soviet forces having the upper hand, Moscow and Tokyo agreed a ceasefire. The Soviet leader, Josef Stalin, had agreed a deal with Nazi Germany, and offered a similar neutrality pact with Japan. With a deal in place that the Soviet Union would not start a war with Japan, Stalin was free to turn his attentions to Europe, attacking Finland and Poland in 1939, and ultimately annexing the Baltic States. His promise to Japan would also shut down the lifeline supplying the Soviet Volunteer Group, airmen and planes that had been fighting on behalf of the Chinese. This, in turn, would lead Chiang Kai-shek to lean more heavily on support from Chinese-American financiers, and ultimately from the United States itself.

The pro-German faction within the Japanese government was wrong-footed in August 1939 by the announcement of the German-Soviet Non-Aggression Pact. It allowed, very briefly, for the Emperor to nudge his preferred candidate into the role of Army Minister, and to confide in a new Prime Minister that he had a deep distrust for the Army. Meanwhile, on the Chinese mainland, emissaries from Japan were deep in negotiations with representatives both of Chiang Kai-shek's regime and the pro-Japanese puppet regime set up in Nanjing.

The events at Kalkhin Gol seem to have taken the Japanese Army by surprise, and not merely because the ceasefire allowed the top brass to draw a careful veil over the fact that the Japanese Army had been put onto the defensive, and suffered heavy losses. In effect, the battle had been declared over before the Japanese had the chance to really lose. In hindsight, the battle demonstrated deep flaws in the Army's management of artillery, tanks and logistics, but the cease-fire encouraged the authorities to chalk up Khalkin Gol as a "victory," and not an indicator of serious issues that should be addressed.[28]

Having plotted for decades for a conflict with the Soviet Union, expected to range as far as Lake Baikal, Army strategists were now informed that the Soviet border was a neutralized threat. The "Strike

[27] Mauch, "The Shōwa Political Crisis," pp. 8–9.
[28] Tohmatsu, "Nomonhan/Kalkhin Gol," pp. 283–4.

North" doctrine, which had formed some part of Army thinking for over forty years, was suddenly declared over. Manchukuo was secure, at least from the Soviets, leaving the Army free to concentrate its efforts on China. The "Strike South" doctrine, favored by the Navy, and involving the seizure of South-East Asia, particularly Indochina and the Dutch East Indies, was now the big plan for the future. The Kwantung Army had reached the peak of its achievements, and henceforth would be eroded, its various divisions gradually reposted elsewhere in the empire, the threat of Soviet invasion now presumed nullified.

It seemed possible that some sort of peace in China might be hammered out, freeing the Japanese to deal with issues further afield. Advancing into South-East Asia made strategic sense, particularly for the Navy, which was keen to push its southern advance policy in opposition to the Army's obsession with Manchuria and the Soviet border. But it also made tactical sense for the war in China, since a Japanese presence in Singapore and Burma would cut off Chiang Kai-shek from the Allied supply lines that were sustaining his war effort in Chongqing.

All of this needed to be considered in terms of the outbreak of war in Europe—a completely different boardgame, but with game pieces that might easily shift to East Asia if the game were suddenly declared over. If the Netherlands were occupied by the Nazis (as they would be by summer 1940), there would be a chance that Germany would become more enmeshed in East Asian politics through its de facto ownership of the Dutch East Indies (the colony that would later become Indonesia).

However, while the battles of Kalkhin Gol were still raging, a far quieter, but arguably even more destructive blow was struck against Japan in New York, where the new wonder-fiber nylon was unveiled at the World's Fair. Nylon would soon be offering a cheap alternative to silk stockings, which, in the decades since women's dresses began to use less material and ruffles, had become the main use for Japanese silk. The arrival of nylon spelled disaster for Japan's own industrial calculations, suggesting that the silk-stocking industry, Japan's last big source of export revenue, was about to take a tumble. Without the $100 million per year that Japan earned from silk exports to the United States, the nation would have to rely solely on its dwindling gold reserves, and whatever revenue it could scrape from the drugs levies of Manchukuo.[29]

---

[29] Miller, *Bankrupting the Enemy*, loc.. 797, 3184–3192.

How much longer could Japan afford to fight? U.S. analysts believed that Japan might still have enough gold reserves to push on for another two years. After that, it was confidently predicted, Japan would be out of money, and out of time.

CHAPTER 8

Into the Tiger's Den

On February 2, 1940, a frail old man rose to his feet in the Japanese Diet and commenced a ninety-minute speech. Saitō Takao was seventy-one years old, an obscure politician who only occasionally spoke out on controversial issues, leading to one cartoonist to call him "the Lord of the Mice." But today, he could reasonably be said to have had enough. Saitō was no pacifist—he was a conservative, broadly supportive of Japan's expansion into Korea and Manchuria. The problem was, he began, that the stated aim of securing Japan's resources and materials had been accomplished. He simply couldn't see the point of the latest adventures in China, which were a costly and endless money pit.

Saitō's problem was with a revolving-door of governments that seemed to think that their responsibilities were discharged by resigning at the first sign of trouble. A million Japanese men had been sent overseas; a million more faced the same fate. A hundred thousand Japanese had died, and all for what? Saitō took apart the government's directives and policies, pointing out that they were riddled with contradictions. How could they claim to support China, while also trying to undermine it with rival regimes? Were they going to save China by destroying it? Is this what they meant by the "New Order in Asia," some misguided rip-off of what Hitler was doing to Europe? How could the Prime Minister embark on a costly war in Asia, while also promising that he would demand no indemnity from the Chinese if they surrendered—*who was going to pay for all this*?[1]

> If we ignore this reality, or camouflage it with the words "holy war," pointlessly neglecting the people's sacrifices for an array of elusive pretexts such as "international justice" or a "moral foreign

---

[1] Fouraker, "Saitō Takao," p. 16.

policy," or "co-existence and co-prosperity" or "world peace," and thereby lose a rare opportunity and thereby end up ruining the great state plan of the century... today's politicians will commit a crime that we cannot compensate for with our deaths.[2]

Saitō had witnessed the Army coming to his own district near Kobe, and ripping up the local railway tracks, taking them away for some unspecified industrial venture in South-East Asia. *How was this helping the Japanese? In what possible situation could the Japanese be compensated for the sacrifices they had already been called upon to make?*[3]

He conceded that there were exceptions: not all Japanese were being crushed by austerity. There were "boom firms" that were making a killing supplying the war effort, gobbling up military contracts.

"I do not understand the cause of this war," he said. "I do not understand why we are at war. I do not know. Do you gentlemen know? If you have it figured out, then explain it to me."

Saitō was heckled throughout by his fellow politicians, and much of the latter part of his speech was cut from the official record at the instigation of the Army's observer in the council chamber.[4] Politicians and the press derided him as a blasphemer against Japan's "holy war," and he received death threats and hate mail. He resigned from his party and was ejected from the Diet—his speech marked the moment when any further criticism of Japanese militarism was purged from the government.

And yet, there were still glimmerings of hope. Among the letters calling for him to do Japan a favor and kill himself, accusing him of being anti-war or anti-military, or even of being a British or American stooge, there were letters of support, thanking him for standing up for the common Japanese people. Despite a smear campaign in the media, he would later win re-election as an independent, although the Diet he re-entered was little more than an echo chamber for propaganda by that point.

At one point in his speech, Saitō referred to his belief that the China Incident was the largest war that Japan had fought with China in 2,600

---

[2] Fouraker, "Saitō Takao," p. 18. The ellipsis in the quote marks the point where Saitō was interrupted, as he frequently was, by shouts and cat-calls from the other politicians. The full text of his speech, with the two censored thirds restored, was not widely available in Japan until the publication of his memoirs in 1972.

[3] Kinmonth, "The Mouse that Roared," p. 335. See also Yoshimi, *Grassroots Fascism*, p. 59.

[4] Barnhart, *Japan Prepares for Total War*, p. 139.

years. His choice of numbering was quite deliberate, since the year 1940 in the Christian calendar had been determined by the Japanese government to mark a momentous occasion—the 2,600th anniversary of the legendary coronation of Japan's first-ever ruler, the Emperor Jinmu. Jinmu's very existence was a matter of unsubstantiated myth, while the dating of his enthronement to 660 BCE was the vague pronunciation of a medieval chronicle, but ever since 1873, his achievements had been celebrated in National Foundation Day, which fell on February 11. This, in turn, might sound at first like harmless legend, except it had already been used as a further argument for the superiority of the Japanese race. Ōkawa Shūmei (1886–1957), a former South Manchuria Railway employee, now a university professor, only released in 1939 after serving time in prison for his involvement in some of the attempted coups of the 1930s, had written a much-reprinted book arguing that since Japan was the oldest state in the world, it was its destiny to rule it.[5]

1940 was hence a year of grand ceremonial importance to Japan's state Shintō religion. On New Year's Day, the people not only of Japan, but also of Japan's empire overseas, had been ordered to bow, at precisely 9am, in the direction of the imperial palace in Tokyo, and to shout: "Long Live His Majesty the Emperor." There was no possible way that anyone could claim not to know their duty—the directive was printed in newspapers and broadcast on the radio. It was also written into neighborhood round-robin newsletters, which could not be passed on between households until the head of each family had affixed his seal. This was merely the first of a dozen timed mass rituals that would unite the Japanese in 1940, including moments of silence to mark Army Day, Navy Day and the anniversary of the Marco Polo Bridge Incident, and the twice-annual days when the Emperor conducted ceremonies for the war dead at the Yasukuni Shrine.[6]

The state broadcasting corporation, NHK, held a competition to come up with a "national song" to mark the occasion. Masuda Yoshio beat 18,000 contenders with his stirring lyrics for "The Year 2600" (*Kigen Nisen Roppyaku-nen*), which were set to music by Mori Yoshihachirō, and began with a reference to the Golden Kite of Japanese legend, which blinded the enemies of the Japanese, and settled on the bow of the

---

[5] Russell, *The Knights of Bushidō*, p. 15.
[6] Ruoff, *Imperial Japan at its Zenith*, pp. 57–8.

legendary Emperor Jinmu.

> Our bodies receive the divine light of the glory of Japan
> Shining from the Golden Kite
> We pray at the dawn of the Year 2600
> A hundred million breasts swell with pride.

> Standing firm on the jubilant earth
> We await the imperial decree in the Year 2600
> The clouds clear after the founding of our nation
> Growing up in a fractious world
> Our gratitude burns with a clean flame, in the Year 2600.[7]

The conflict in China, however, had been limping along for almost a decade, leading several satirists to come up with parody versions. Some of the most enduring refashioned Masuda's lyrics so that instead of declaring the divine providence of the Japanese Empire, they complained about the rising prices of cigarettes—not the free Onshino packs handed out to military men, but the everyday brands on sale to the general public. These included the super-cheap Golden Bat (*Kinshi*) brand produced by Mitsui, renamed Golden Kite in 1940 to reflect rising patriotic fervor. At the former price of 4 *sen* a packet, smokers had previously been able to buy 500 cigarettes for just one yen.

> [A pack of] Golden Kites is 15 *sen*
> It's 30 for a pack of Glorys.
> These days, prices are going up
> In the year 2600
> 100 million people weep.[8]

The rising price of cigarettes was part of a much wider-ranging series of shortages that had begun to bite. The 1-*sen* coin itself was discontinued in 1940, since Japan needed the copper to make ammunition casings. At the beginning of the year, a government report forecast a massive shortfall in Japan's food supply—five million *koku*, or roughly

---

[7] Osada, *Sensō ga Nokoshita Uta*, p. 80.
[8] Osada, *Sensō ga Nokoshita Uta*, p. 83.

900 million liters of rice. Bad weather had led to a deficit in hydroelectric power, forcing more power generators to burn coal.[9] Blackouts had already been in effect since 1939, but a 1940 Electric Power Adjustment Law placed a further limit on power usage. As the supply of shoes ran out, wooden clogs became a more common sight in the streets. The default fashions on the streets were now military uniforms or *monpe*—drab workplace overalls. Clothes were patched; department stores began selling salvaged second-hand furniture; staples such as sugar and rice were mixed and diluted with other products. Rationing, barter and the black market began to fill in the gaps left by the need to supply the ongoing war. Gift-giving was widely frowned upon, although some leeway was allowed in the media for advertising products that might be suitable for a care-package to be sent to a frontline soldier.[10]

Even the *hinomaru bentō*, the plain rice lunch that had once itself been a symbol of austerity, was now regarded as over-consumption—there are stories from 1940 onwards of children with a *hinomaru bentō* on flag day being bullied for being wasteful.

The Army Ministry nudged the *Yomiuri Shinbun* to run a competition of its own celebrating martial achievements. The winning song, a big enough hit in late 1940 to be released by four separate record companies, was "Sora no Yūshi" [Hero of the Sky], celebrating the Army airmen who had fought at Nomonhan in 1939, and gently avoiding any suggestion that their "victory" was a result of Soviet priorities elsewhere. The narrative of the song was as told by a grim pilot, smoking one of the Onshino cigarettes donated to military units by the Imperial household. The song identifies him as an *arawashi* (wild eagle), the term used in the Japanese air corps for an ace, but also mixes its metaphors, suggesting that the plane is firing "arrows."

> I'll have an Onshino cigarette
> On the eve of the death I have chosen
> Even the wind that blows across the plain reeks of blood
> I glare at the enemy sky
> Stars shine in twos and threes

---

[9] Barnhart, *Japan Prepares for Total War*, p. 127.
[10] Minowa and Belk, "Gifts and Nationalism in Wartime Japan," p. 300.

Now go! The order is given to the wild eagle
What impudent sparrows
Scattered by my prowess
The enemy flames out and drops

I turn my plane above the clouds
Signaling to the ground unit
To check on the prey I have brought down
Amid cries of triumph, [on] a stretcher in pain

Enemy tanks ahead!
I wait and let fly my arrow
Leaving behind a smoking mass of flames
As I head back to the base at ease
To a commander smiling through tears.

To the wild eagles of the land [army]
I fly the flag of the Rising Sun again today
Invincible wings forever
May Asia prosper, protected.[11]

In July 1940, the Army-Navy tensions within the government reached their peak, with Army representatives determined to make Lt General Tōjō Hideki the new Army Minister. Here, they noted, was a man with a reputation for getting things done, unheeding of people's feelings. The Emperor, however, still had feelings of his own, and insisted on his own recommendation for Army Minister.

Tōjō himself was reluctant to take the post—having served previously as a junior underling in the Army Ministry, he voiced his lack of interest in diplomacy, which he likened to being more like a barmaid than a military man. However, he agreed to take the position, allowing the Army's Chief of Staff to order the incumbent Army Minister resign. When the Army refused to offer up a replacement Army Minister to the sitting Cabinet, the government was brought down, and Tōjō was a mandatory hiring for whoever took over.

The Emperor was unimpressed, not only with the political mach-

---

[11] Osada, *Sensō ga Nokoshita Uta*, pp. 536–7.

inations of the Army, but with its over-riding of protocols by pushing for Tōjō as a successor. Nor was he thrilled about the news that Tōjō's replacement as Inspector-General of Army Aviation would be a general who had been instrumental in the 1936 attempted coup.[12]

The outgoing Prime Minister, a former admiral, was replaced with a man who seemed to be the only workable choice as Prime Minister, Konoe Fumimaro. The go-getting Tōjō endured a stressful audience with the Emperor, in which Hirohito vented his frustrations about the Army's disgraceful behavior and insubordinate activities which had, he said, "sullied Our nation's history." Hirohito openly called the Army Ministry "evil," and expressed his somewhat futile hope that Tōjō, his new Army Minister, would be a broom of sweeping change.[13]

Tōjō, however, had become Army Minister in a Cabinet whose leading ministers were all in broad agreement about the necessity of extending Japan's war effort even further. With Germany at the height of its power in Europe, there was a perceived need to managed the situation regarding Germany's likely occupation of former Dutch and French colonies in South-East Asia. In order to head Germany off, it was suggested by Matsuoka Yōsuke, now Konoe's Foreign Minister, that Japan openly extend its stated sphere of interest beyond China, Korea and certain Pacific islands. Just as Japan in the First World War had taken German possessions on behalf of the Allies, perhaps Japan could ally with Germany, and then take the Dutch East Indies to save Germany the bother?[14]

In suggesting open collaboration with the Axis Powers (Germany and Italy) the right-wing Matsuoka was wiping out his predecessors' more careful "middle road" strategy, of careful cordiality with the Germans, without antagonizing the Anglo-American powers. In April 1940, as the German *blitzkrieg* made Nazi domination of Europe seem like a likely prospect, an internal Japanese government memo warned that a victorious Germany, inheriting Dutch and French colonies, was likely to lose its "sympathy for our New World Order in East Asia."[15]

Among the big schemes inspired by Axis ideology, a National

---

[12] Mauch, "The Shōwa Political Crisis," pp. 12–13.

[13] Mauch, "The Shōwa Political Crisis," p. 14.

[14] Yellen, "Into the Tiger's Den," p. 557. Lu, *Agony of Choice*, p. 140, even has Matsuoka suggesting that Japan should go all-in and be prepared to "commit a love-suicide with Germany."

[15] Yellen, "Into the Tiger's Den," p. 559; Lu, *Agony of Choice*, p. 108.

Eugenics Law (*Kokumin Yūsei Hō*) crystallized much of the previous decade's arguments for creating a healthy workforce—it allowed for the sterilization of the severely disabled, while other drives in 1940 Japan called for discouragement of marriages between Korean men and Japanese women, and for subjects of the empire to favor marriage with "intelligent and superior" specimens. Unexpectedly, this turned out to be an insult to the ultra-nationalists, who were heard to complain that far from preserving the divine nature of the Japanese people, such policies reduced them to breeders little better than stud animals. The journal Yūsei (*Eugenics*) began encouraging Japanese womenfolk to consider marrying maimed veterans, on the understanding that while their bodies were mangled, their genes were still good, and indicative of true fighting spirit.[16]

The idea that Japan faced a vital, momentary window of opportunity became ingrained in popular parlance with the oddest of sound bites. The innocuous sentence "Don't miss the bus!" (*Basu ni noriokureru na*) became an oft-repeated catchphrase, both in Japanese government circles and among the general population.[17] The idea derived from two comments made by Neville Chamberlain (1869–1940), the British Prime Minister, who had observed that Adolf Hitler had two opportunities to strike a deathly blow against Britain and France in September 1938 and September 1939, but that on both occasions he had "missed the bus."

The Army could have talked the Foreign Ministry out of it, since as late as June 1940, General Koiso Kuniaki had communiqués from the German ambassador, assuring him that the Third Reich had no interest in the Dutch East Indies. This information, however, either never made it to the Cabinet, or was never solicited by them. Prime Minister Konoe needed little persuading. He agreed with the Foreign Minister and the Ministers for the Army and the Navy that Japan's "living space" (*seikatsuken*—a direct translation, it seems, of the German *lebensraum*) would ultimately extend as far south as New Zealand and as far west as India, and that policy decisions needed to plan for that goal.[18]

---

[16] Otsubo, "Feminist Maternal Eugenics," p. 47.

[17] Yellen, "Into the Tiger's Den," p. 561.

[18] Yellen, "Into the Tiger's Den," p. 564. Collingham, *The Taste of War*, loc. 1204 places this desire for *lebensraum* within the context of farming reforms in Japan. In order to achieve maximum efficiency on farmland in Japan, 31% of the agricultural population needed to be moved overseas in order to allow for larger individual plots.

A Japanese policy document, drawn up in June 1940, was the first to use the term "Greater East Asia"—implying that the "East Asia" of Japan, China and Manchukuo, now formed part of a larger sphere of interest, which also incorporated the "South Seas" (*Nanyō*), and the "Southern Areas" (*Nanpō*), which included India and South-East Asia.

Tōjō, meanwhile, had been radically reforming the Army Ministry, pushing out any staffers who did not agree with his plans, which, in a variant on the "missing the bus" rhetoric, were known as a "lightning strike" policy awaiting the ideal opportunity. Tōjō, however, insisted on being the one to insist what that opportunity might be. In September 1940, a Japanese battalion in south China "accidentally" crossed the border into French Indochina. Instead of wringing his hands and making excuses, Tōjō ordered the battalion leader to be court-martialed. For a moment, the Emperor might have almost believed that Tōjō was the man to bring the Army into line, and defuse the ever-escalating military situation.

Over the summer of 1940, the Navy conducted an elaborate, secret war-game to plot out the likely course of a southern strike. An attack on the Dutch East Indies, officers determined, could be successfully carried out, allowing Japan to secure some vital supplies, such as nickel from Borneo. But the act of seizing the islands would provoke the U.S. and Britain, which would be sure to retaliate from bases in Hawaii and Singapore, and also shut down all trade. The Navy would be put onto a war footing, consuming more fuel and resources, while simultaneously losing access to much of the vital imports. The United States, as friend or foe, was a critical component of any southward advance—Japan needed to either somehow keep trading with the U.S. for the next two years, or knock out its naval capabilities in the Pacific before seizing the Dutch East Indies.[19] The Navy, however, faced a ticking clock, since its chances of superiority in the Pacific were soon to be diminished. New U.S. plans for shipbuilding and naval expansion, put before Congress in June 1940, allowed for the possibility that by 1943, Japan's ratio of capital ships to the U.S. Navy's would be 50%, and a mere 30% by 1944. In the race behind the scenes to put enough ships in the water, Japan would reach its peak ratio versus the U.S., about 75%, in April 1941. After that point, the

---

[19] Barnhart, *Japan Prepares for Total War*, p. 147. Tōjō himself acknowledged a two-year fuel supply in a speech on November 5, 1941—see Collingham, *The Taste of War*, loc. 5181.

odds would begin to climb in American's favor, particularly if it began reassigning ships from the Atlantic to the Pacific.[20]

The Planning Bureau, which to add to its problems, had suffered a literal lightning strike in June 1940 that led to the loss of much of its records in a fire, pleaded with the armed forces not to provoke the United States—to do so would render all such ratios meaningless, since America's own industrial capacity, retooled for war, would outstrip Japan's even faster. The arch provocateur, however, was already ramping up the rhetoric—Foreign Minister Matsuoka Yōsuke, the former Manchukuo power-broker and a passionate advocate of saber-rattling at the Americans, continued to mock and belittle the United States in his addresses, and to push a wider colonial agenda. In August 1940, Matsuoka delivered a radio broadcast that put an end to talk of a New World Order, and introduced a new concept:

> The essence of our country's foreign policy must focus on the establishment of a Greater East Asian Co-Prosperity Sphere (*Dai Tōa Kyōeiken*) that centers on Japan, Manchukuo and China... It goes without saying that the South Seas are also included....[21]

Hoping that Germany was listening, Matsuoka added that Japan was willing to cooperate with any other nation that was ready to accept this "new state of affairs in East Asia." An alliance was on offer, as long as Germany recognized Japan's interest in Dutch and French colonies.

Germany *was* listening, but didn't quite get the message that Matsuoka was sending. Over tea that evening, the German ambassador, Eugene Ott, asked Matsuoka what precisely he meant by "the South Seas," leading Matsuoka to offer vague sentiments that it probably meant somewhere as far away as Thailand, or possibly a bit further. Ott took away the message that Japan *wasn't* interested in the Dutch East Indies after all, which he found odd, as to him it would have made more sense.

Matsuoka faced opposition within the Cabinet over his willingness to sign a treaty with Germany. He was warned that forming an alliance with Germany effectively placed Japan on a path towards entering the

---

[20] Asada, *From Mahan to Pearl Harbor*, loc. 5254 and 5307. As ever, the Japanese Navy was obsessed with warships. Japan would have fared better by making more of an effort to protect merchant shipping.

[21] Yellen, "Into the Tiger's Den," pp. 565–6.

war, and that Japan should not sign such a deal without considering that as a likely eventuality.

Matsuoka, however, remained bullish.

"One cannot capture a tiger's cub," he wrote dismissively in the margins of a policy draft, "without entering the tiger's den."[22]

Germany's general lack of interest, palpable through the spring of 1940, took a sudden change in the summer. Whereas the year had begun with many in the Axis Powers assuming that Britain would be neutralized, the air campaign known as the Battle of Britain had failed to reduce the Royal Air Force or impose sufficient economic harm to coerce it into an armistice. Britain's refusal to capitulate increased the risk that the U.S.A. would join the war on the British side. With Hitler increasingly distracted by the Soviet Union's activity in the Baltic and the Nazi invasion of Britain starting to look unlikely, the German authorities were led to reconsider their lukewarm conversations with the Japanese. Perhaps Germany would benefit after all from an ally in the Far East, shouldering some of the workload while it concentrated on pacifying Europe. An alliance with Japan now made sense, as it would surely spook the U.S.A. into staying out of the European war, for fear of starting one in the Pacific.

Konoe and his closest ministers were now convinced that, by the time the conflict was over, the world would be divided into four broad power blocs—the U.S.A., the Soviet Union, a German-dominated Europe, and a Japanese-dominated East Asia. Forming an alliance with Germany and Italy was hence regarded as the ideal way to keep at least two of those blocs at arm's length.

Foreign Minister Matsuoka saw Japan's options as limited. If it threw in its lot with the Anglo-American powers, they would "give up on our dreams for a New Order in East Asia, and spend at least half a century bowing our heads to Britain and America." An alliance with Germany at least gave Japan the prospect of securing its Co-Prosperity Sphere. There was, he suggested, no alternative. "Half the American people were of German descent," he lied, "so if Japan forms an alliance with Germany, the German-Americans will oppose any war."[23] And furthermore, he argued, if Japan allied with Germany, it was sure to greatly reduce the

---

[22] Yellen, "Into the Tiger's Den," p. 568. Butow, *Tōjō and the Coming of the War*, p. 309, has Hirohito quoting the same aphorism in October 1941.

[23] Terasaki, *Shōwa Tennō Dokuhaku-roku*, p. 61.

chances of war with America in the Pacific.

Even then, there were dissenters. The Navy Minister, Yoshida Zengo, was apoplectic with rage at the prospect of creating new enemies out of Britain and America, the world's other two greatest naval powers. He was so angry, in fact, that on September 5, he suffered a nervous breakdown, allowing for the appointment of a more cooperative replacement.

Ishii Kikujirō, who had himself been a Foreign Minister during the First World War, warned Matsuoka that Hitler was an unreliable ally who openly spoke of treaties as temporary measures. German policy since Otto von Bismarck, cautioned Ishii, was one of international agreements between a horse and a donkey, in which Germany was invariably "the horse."

However, Matsuoka remained aggressive towards the United States, openly proclaiming in a newspaper interview: "If she in her contentment is going to blindly and stubbornly stick to the same status quo in the Pacific," he said, "then we will fight America. For it would be better to perish than to maintain the status quo." He swiftly retracted his remarks after a U.S. backlash.[24]

The Tripartite Pact, between Japan, Germany and Italy, was signed on September 27, 1940, shortly after U.S. Treasury officials uncovered a vast fraud case in New York in which Japanese banks had been found to be misreporting foreign currency reserves. It was now considered that U.S. estimates of Japan's reserves were, at best, inaccurate, and likely to be a gross underestimation. Japan would not be on its knees by summer 1941 as Roosevelt and his advisers had previously predicted.[25]

Admiral Yamamoto Isoroku, however, still argued that Japan did not have enough. In November 1940, he staged a tabletop war-game to demonstrate that, in spite of rumbles from the junior officers that the time was right to strike the Dutch East Indies, Japan lacked the resources. Instead, he predicted, a Japanese attack on South-East Asia would only escalate into a war that would drag in both the U.S. and Britain.[26]

In January 1941, soldiers in the Japanese Army were issued with a new code of conduct, the *Field Service Code* (*Senjinkun*). Written at Tōjō's instruction, and also available in a gramophone form, with Tōjō reading it out himself, it was designed as a supplement to the antiquated

---

[24] Lu, *Agony of Choice*, p. 215.
[25] Miller, *Bankrupting the Enemy*, loc. 2143.
[26] Asada, *From Mahan to Pearl Harbor*, loc. 5323.

Imperial Rescript to Soldiers and Sailors, in the words of one of its authors, intended to put an end to a spate of incidents among the soldiers in China: "violence against superior officers, desertions, rape, arson, pillage" that had apparently "not been seen" on the battlefields of the 1890s and 1900s. According to the scholar Sato Hiroaki:

> What came to be known as the Nanjing Massacre was just one heinous manifestation of the loss of military discipline and order. So, most of the *Senjinkun* was devoted to reminding the soldiers, in much greater detail than the rescript, of the importance of upholding the honor of imperial soldiers.[27]

Amid its exhortations to honor the Emperor and not get drunk, it included a relatively benign section on avoiding capture—there is something similar in many other country's military manuals. But being captured, according to *The Field Service Code*, would bring shame on the Imperial Japanese Army.

"Never accept alive the shame of capture," it reads. "Die so as not to leave the disgrace of such an offense."[28]

Sato Hiroaki claims that the terminology is ambiguous, and that he does not believe—despite the claims of many contemporary officers and later historians—that it literally instructs soldiers that it is better to die than be captured.[29] But regardless of what the phrase may have meant, it came to be interpreted by the Japanese soldier as a maxim that rated death above capture. *The Field Service Code* became a major contribution to the attitude of the Japanese military, particularly towards enemy prisoners of war, who were deemed to have abrogated their rights to be treated as human beings.[30] It would also have a lethal effect on life expectancies within the Japanese military—rescue missions for downed Japanese pilots at sea were negligible, for example, and likely to have contributed to high casualty rates.[31]

America and Japan were in an odd position—5% of U.S. exports to

---

[27] Sato, "Gyokusai," p. 5.

[28] Victoria, *Zen War Stories*, p. 106; Hotta, *Japan 1941*, p. 124.

[29] Sato, "Gyokusai," p. 6.

[30] Victoria, *Zen War Stories*, p. 146.

[31] Bergerud, *Fire in the Sky*, p. 433. Bergerud observes that the category of "missing in action" seems to be non-existent in Japanese dispatches.

Japan comprised airplanes and airplane parts, some of which were presumed to be used in aerial attacks on Nanjing and Guangzhou.[32] American scrap metal was being sent to Japan, where it was used to make weapons that were then shot at America's Chinese allies. One anti-war campaign in the U.S. specifically pointed out the grim rumors that New York's Third Avenue elevated railway, dismantled and sold as scrap to Japan, had been repurposed as shrapnel and was now being removed by American missionary doctors from the bodies of grievously wounded Chinese.[33] But the U.S. was also heavily reliant on the Japanese for certain commodities—silk, for example, was not simply a luxury item, but also a crucial component in the manufacture of American parachutes. With China in a state of crisis, the best sources for it were Japan and Manchukuo![34] Fortunately for the U.S., there was enough raw silk stockpiled in the U.S. already to adequately equip 200,000 parachutists, although there were still concerns that the U.S. might run short of the coarse spun silk required in munitions' igniter cloth and lacing for artillery. Already in 1940, the supply of waste silk from Japan had become suspiciously thin—it was believed that the Japanese were stockpiling their own silk. The most crucial of the U.S. needs for silk was for use in naval cartridge cloth—the material used in powder bags for large-caliber ships' guns. This need was met by massive purchases from China, often of the offcuts from Japanese-owned mills.[35]

Japan was also affected by events in the European theater. The alliance with Nazi Germany kept Japan readily supplied with vital commodities such as potash, mercury and specialty alloys, all of which reached the industrial heartland of Manchuria by coming down the Trans-Siberian Railway. The outbreak of war between Germany and Russia in June 1941 shut down that lifeline, but also released Japan from the prospect of an immediate Russian attack on Manchukuo. Army divisions could be re-assigned to a prospective strike at South-East Asia.[36]

In April 1941, U.S. officials commenced a series of vulnerability studies, listing the degree to which Japan might suffer shortages in fifty

---

[32] Miller, *Bankrupting the Enemy*, loc. 1689.

[33] Miller, *Bankrupting the Enemy*, loc. 1967.

[34] Barnhart, *Japan Prepares for Total War*, pp. 166 and 205.

[35] Miller, *Bankrupting the Enemy*, loc. 3169–3176.

[36] Barnhart, *Japan Prepares for Total War*, p. 216; Miller, *Bankrupting the Enemy*, loc. 3569.

crucial resources. It was a consultation on "economic warfare," including not only discussion of sanctions and embargos on Japan, but on indirectly shutting off its supply by using U.S. funds to buy up supplies in certain materials from third parties, thereby shutting Japan out of the markets even in neutral countries.[37]

Japan was relying on American imports for half of its annual copper supply, more than 60% of its machine tools, and 80% of its oil, although American financial analysts had been secretly predicting the imminent bankruptcy of Japan. Treasury briefings had already assessed Japan's gold reserves as likely to run out in September 1939, or June 1940, or by "the middle of 1941."[38] Nor had the U.S. failed to notice Japan's stockpiling of materials—since the introduction of the Greater East Asia plans in summer 1940, Japan had been buying "extraordinary amounts" of U.S. oil at the maximum permissible octane level of 87. This, it was believed, was being brought to Japan in order to be distilled into military-grade 92 octane aviation gasoline. There were reports in 1941 of Japanese buyers in the U.S. acquiring cocktails of higher quality oils mixed with crude oil or gasoline, so that the quality on export was lower than the maximum, but could be separated into their components on arrival in Japan. Japanese buyers were also caught acquiring as many second-hand oil tanks as they could find, for shipping to Japan for use in stockpile storage. The Japanese grab for oil in early 1941 was so desperate that former whaling ships were being refitted as tankers to get it all across the Pacific.[39]

The April 1941 U.S. vulnerability study on Japan's oil made it plain—regardless of how Japan had squirrelled away its currency assets, a global embargo of oil exports to Japan would leave it with an estimated two-year stockpile of fuel. The only way to augment that would be through the acquisition of the oil fields of the Dutch East Indies. Japan, too, was aware of this—the same month saw a name assigned to a Navy plan to knock out U.S. facilities in Pearl Harbor, in order to buy time for the great push towards the Dutch East Indies. Evoking the Navy's finest hour in 1905, it was called Operation Z, after Admiral Tōgō's Nelson-inspired

---

[37] Miller, *Bankrupting the Enemy*, loc. 2576. See also Collingham, *The Taste of War*, loc. 4366 for details of the shortages on the Japanese food supply, particularly fish, already apparent in 1941.

[38] Miller, *Bankrupting the Enemy*, loc. 1235.

[39] Miller, *Bankrupting the Enemy*, loc. 3308–3331, 3422.

Z-signal: "The rise or fall of the empire depends on this battle."[40] Determined to exploit any available avenue to get the upper hand, Army Minister Tōjō also ordered the setting up of a committee to investigate the possibility of creating atomic weapons.[41]

In July 1941, the U.S. hit Japan with a blow "designed to bring it to its senses, not its knees" over the China conflict. President Roosevelt's Treasury advisers had found a handy loophole in an obscure law dating from the height of the First World War, the Trading with the Enemy Act (1917), which allowed for the freezing of dollar transactions not only with enemies, but "with any foreign country, whether enemy, ally of enemy or otherwise."[42] The dangerously vague wording allowed the U.S.

---

[40] Toland, *The Rising Sun*, p. 275.

[41] Dahl, *Heavy water and the wartime race for nuclear energy*, pp. 279–85. There is substantially more written on this topic in Japanese, although much of it is anecdotal evidence that leads back to a single multi-authored 1968 history of the Shōwa era, Yomiuri Shinbun-sha's *Shōwa Tennō 4*. Post-war censorship and destruction of materials, by both the U.S. and Japan, have occluded the story of Japan's atomic program, in which the ever-competitive Army and Navy both developed their own separate research projects. Depending on whom one believes, Japan either gave up on the prospect as being too long a developmental process to aid the war effort, continued research but with a focus on its use primarily as a heat source or power source, or was actively pursuing the development of an atomic bomb in 1945. A German U-boat, *U-234*, surrendered in 1945 en route to deliver uranium oxide to Japan, but since the cargo disappeared, it is impossible to tell whether it was "weapons-grade," and hence intended for a bomb project, or a lesser variant that would have been more likely to be used in synthesizing fuel. RIKEN, the Institute of Physical and Chemical Research, was certainly enough of a concern to the U.S. for it to be specifically marked on a Tokyo bombing map. I mention all of this, and include it in a footnote instead of the main text, because of a story that keeps resurfacing in the Chinese, Korean and Russian media in the 21st century suggesting that the Japanese program was *indeed* successful, and that the Japanese detonated a tactical atomic weapon in what is now North Korea in August 1945, just off the coast of Hamhung. The Koreans and Chinese have exploited this rumor as further proof of Japanese perfidy; the Russians as the *real* reason that the Soviet Union entered the war in its final days. And if you believe that, then you will also believe that the U.S. suppressed the story in order to gain Japan's research materials, and Japan kept it quiet in order to hang onto the moral high-ground post-Hiroshima. But there are already an awful lot of ifs in this paragraph, causing the diligent historian to file it as an intriguing fiction. My own assessment of Japan's atomics program is that military overconfidence in the early days of the war led to it being marginalized and overlooked, and that by the time anyone was taking the prospect of atomic weaponry seriously, it was already out of money and time. For a more in-depth survey, see the chapter in Dower, *Japan in War and Peace*, pp. 55–100.

[42] Miller, *Bankrupting the Enemy*, loc. 251 and 267. This was not the first time that Roosevelt had used the Trading with the Enemy Act—in 1933, for example, he had

to shut down Japan's use of foreign currency in trading; coupled with parallel actions by Britain and the Netherlands, it effectively locked Japan out of international commerce, only able to make trades in yen, a currency solely used within the Japanese Empire itself.

Japan seemed to have little choice—there was an agreement in the highest levels of government in July 1941, that war with the U.S. was now inevitable.[43] There was, in theory, the option of returning to the Americans, cap in hand, and offering some sort of diplomatic deal, but that would be political suicide for the incumbent government, writing off an entire decade's investment and sacrifice on the Asian mainland. Nor did it offer any future prospect beyond continued reliance on the United States, a power which had already shut down the lifeline to Japan to get its own way in both 1918 and 1941.[44]

The other option, itself a matter of some risk, was to paralyze American power in the Pacific with a surprise strike at the naval base at Pearl Harbor, seize the resource-rich islands of Dutch East Indies and British Malaya, and trust that the new territories acquired could be brought back online before a counter-attack arrived—it was assumed that the British and Dutch would sabotage their oil refineries if attacked.[45] Pearl Harbor was the key, since it was believed to be the only installation preventing a Japanese success. Evoking old-time rhetoric from four decades earlier, resurrected in a time of new technologies and longer ranges, Admiral Yamamoto Isoroku had referred to the fleet at Pearl Harbor as "a dagger pointed at Japan's heart," just as Korea had once been for his predecessors.[46]

Konoe asked Yamamoto, the commander of Japan's Combined Fleet, how he assessed the situation. Yamamoto replied, with incisive prediction, that such an attack would buy him six months to "run wild" (*zuibun abarete*), but that thereafter, the overwhelming power of American industry would be directed at a counter-attack.[47]

---

used it to pull huge amounts of gold out of public hands and into government vaults.

[43] Asada, *From Mahan to Pearl Harbor*, loc. 5526.

[44] Barnhart, *Japan Prepares for Total War*, pp. 239 and 242.

[45] Konoe, *Memoir*, p. 35.

[46] Asada, *From Mahan to Pearl Harbor*, loc. 5132.

[47] Prange, *At Dawn We Slept*, p. 11. See also Asada, *From Mahan to Pearl Harbor*, loc. 6038, in which Yamamoto's comments are assessed as being not quite clear enough about the likely danger. As Admiral Inoue Shigeyoshi argued after the war, a non-military man like Konoe should have been given a much clearer indication

The U.S. dollar was even crucial to Japan's alliance with Nazi Germany, since German clients did not want payments in yen, and refused to take the British pound. American banks hence became vital repositories for the funds that Japan needed to pay for material from its Germany ally. Sure that a freeze of assets was imminent, Japanese liquid assets in the U.S. were migrating to Brazil and other South American countries, where they were being used to buy up copper, oil and animal hides.[48]

In Japan, the Planning Bureau assessed the damage. Oil was the chief issue, and without vital German processing technology and thousands of miners, Manchukuo shale oil was never going to take up the shortfall. An imperial conference saw the government divided between those advocating war, and the outnumbered Konoe, armed with Admiral Yamamoto's predictions, who favored agreeing to American demands.

However, Yamamoto was already being misquoted. He had replied to a letter from an ultranationalist agitator, attempting to explain that just as China had turned into a quagmire for the Japanese Army, a Navy attack on the United States would only oblige it to commit an impossibly exponential number of non-existent forces to an ever-escalating conflict. "Should hostilities once break out between Japan and the United States," he wrote, "it would not be enough that we take Guam and the Philippines, nor even Hawaii and San Francisco. To make victory certain, we would have to march into Washington and dictate the terms of peace in the White House. I wonder if our politicians, among whom armchair arguments about war are being glibly bandied about in the name of state politics, have confidence as to the final outcome and are prepared to make the necessary sacrifices."[49]

His comment, shorn of its qualifying final sentence, spread through the Japanese media, as if he were in favor of an all-out attack on the United States.

On September 5, the eve of the conference, the leaders of the Army and Navy were summoned to a meeting with the Emperor, marked by pregnant pauses that sometimes stretched on for minutes at a time. Prime Minister Konoe was also present, and his account of the event is of a disbelieving and increasingly hostile Hirohito, openly doubting the

---

of the foolhardiness of the plan, not a comment that could have been interpreted as vaguely supportive of it.

[48] Miller, *Bankrupting the Enemy*, loc. 3464.

[49] Prange, *At Dawn We Slept*, p. 11.

promises of his generals.

Hirohito asked: if the Army got its wish and was ordered to take the Dutch East Indies, how long would it take?

Sugiyama Gen, Army Chief of Staff, replied that he was confident it would all be over in three months.

The Emperor turned on Sugiyama, reminding him that he had been the Army Minister in 1937, four years earlier, when he had just as confidently predicted that China would be pacified "within a month or so."

Sugiyama stammered that China was quite big, only for the Emperor to point out that the Pacific Ocean was even bigger.

After a long, embarrassed silence, the Navy Chief of staff stepped in, suggesting the analogy that U.S.-Japanese relations were currently like a gravely ill patient, and that only the riskiest of operations stood a chance of saving him. Without this "operation," the patient was fated to slowly waste away. With it, he stood a thin chance of survival.[50]

Joseph Grew, the U.S. ambassador to Japan, warned his masters in Washington that their trade freeze would not have the desired effect. The Japanese, he argued, were not like other nations. If denied a market economy, they were ready to make supreme sacrifices, turning their entire state into an engine of war. In Tokyo, the Navy Minister told Konoe that the Navy would prefer a diplomatic solution, but the Army refused to budge on the issue of its troops stationed in China. With so much manpower, resources and investment already committed to China, the Army was not prepared to give it up as part of negotiations with the U.S.—to do so would be a catastrophic loss of face and finances. The final decision on whether or not to go to war needed to rest with the Prime Minister.

Konoe resigned in October, to be replaced as leader by General Tōjō Hideki, who was already the Army Minister, his cabinet crammed with cronies from his Manchukuo days.

In November 1941, the last embers of U.S.-Japan trade faded away. The freeze on Japanese assets was complete, shipping was shut down, barter deals had been refused, and there were but a few lingering cargoes, offloaded in the last hours of legal trade, that had to have their

---

[50] Konoe, *Memoir*, p. 93. Konoe's account, possibly in an error of hasty recollection, redacts the story, in which Nagano Osami actually compared Japan to a gravely ill *child* with appendicitis and a 30% chance of surviving the operation. See Asada, *From Mahan to Pearl Harbor*, loc. 5829; Hotta, *Japan 1941*, p. 220.

details finalized and stamped. The very last Japanese imports into America were logged in the customs ledgers: some Christmas ornaments, a consignment of Kikkōman soy sauce, thirty bucks' worth of fishing tackle, and a crate of ceramic squirrels, valued at $11.32.[51]

Before the end of the month, six Japanese aircraft carriers had sailed in secret to the Kurile Islands, before turning south. American bases in the Pacific, including Pearl Harbor, were warned by U.S. military intelligence on December 1 that the carriers' destination was unknown.

---

[51] Miller, *Bankrupting the Enemy*, loc. 4432.

CHAPTER 9

Running Wild

The concept of a Japanese attack on Pearl Harbor had been considered by both sides for at least two decades. The Japanese Navy had first held a tabletop war-game exercise of a Pearl Harbor attack as early as 1927. It had even been the subject of American military exercises since the 1920s, including drills in 1932 and 1938 that specifically addressed the new threat posed by an aerial assault.[1]

It was air power that made the real difference, as the British had demonstrated in November 1940, with an aerial assault that disabled three battleships in Taranto harbor, striking a severe blow against the Italian Navy. Admiral Yamamoto Isoroku (1884–1943), often cited as the architect of the attack on Pearl Harbor, might be better described as the leading advocate of *an* attack on Pearl Harbor that used aircraft to disable the U.S. Pacific Fleet. His reasoning was uncommon in the Japanese Navy, where most of the top brass continued to cling to the idea of a single, dramatic "decisive battle" that would crush the enemy like the famous 1905 victory at Tsūshima. Yamamoto was far more tactical in his thinking, suggesting that an aerial attack on Pearl Harbor would not only have a drastic effect on enemy morale, but also clutter the docks and repair facilities. Yamamoto was loyal to the Navy's desire for a southern strike to seize the Dutch East Indies, and regarded the knocking out of Pearl Harbor purely as a delaying tactic in order to make such an action easier.

However, Yamamoto was strongly opposed to war with the United States at all. Having studied at Harvard from 1919 to 1921—where he learned to play poker and used his winnings to fund a grand tour of America—and participated in Japan's most crucial naval conferences of the previous decades, he was ridiculed and treated with suspicion

---

[1] Evans and Peattie, *Kaigun*, pp. 472–3.

for what was seen as his pandering stance toward the Anglo-American adversaries. It was Yamamoto who had apologized to the U.S. ambassador for the bombing of the U.S.S *Panay* in 1937, and Yamamoto who spearheaded admiralty resistance to the Tripartite Pact with Germany and Italy, both acts which led to him receiving death threats from ultra-nationalists. This has made him, famously, the "reluctant admiral"—the mastermind of the attack on Pearl Harbor, despite his own reservations about its efficacy.[2]

Yamamoto's master plan was put in the hands of Admiral Nagumo Chūichi (1887–1944), who commenced his attack in the morning of December 7, local time (December 8 already in Tokyo) with the call-sign "Climb Mount Niitaka."[3] 353 planes, including fighters, dive bombers and torpedo bombers, launched from six Japanese carriers, hitting Pearl Harbor shortly before eight o'clock on a Sunday morning, and inflicting immense damage. U.S. planes, clustered close together on the ground as defense against saboteurs, presented easy targets from the air, as did the battleships in port—the attacking Japanese sank four of the eight at the docks, as well as seven smaller ships. The Japanese fleet transmitted two repeating Japanese syllables in Morse code: *TO*, meaning "attack commenced," and *RA*, meaning "surprise achieved." To any eavesdropper, it would have sounded as if the radio operators were constantly tapping out the word for "tiger": *Tora! Tora! Tora!*

Not wishing to place his ships in undue danger, Nagumo then retreated, leaving 2,280 American dead. The only under-performing element of the Navy attack was the five two-man mini-submarines, each carrying two torpedoes, that had been instructed to sneak into the harbor and await the commencement of the air attack before striking at the ships from the water. It is unclear whether any of them successfully

---

[2] Asada, *From Mahan to Pearl Harbor*, loc. 6062. Hotta, *Japan 1941*, pp. 128–30, shrewdly observes that high-stakes gambles and outrageous bluffs were a common feature in Yamamoto's life, from the moment he wagered his career on recovering from an infected wound at Tsūshima, right up to his all-or-nothing assault on Pearl Harbor. "Yamamoto," she writes, "was a gifted bluffer, used to deftly concealing his greatest weaknesses."

[3] The phrase was deliberately arbitrary, but referred to a mountain in Taiwan known in Chinese as *Yu Shan*, "Jade Mountain." Hence, the command to initiate Japan's war on the United States also inadvertently contained a reference to the "jewel" of samurai tradition. For more on short-wave codes in both military and public transmissions, see Robbins, *Tokyo Calling*, pp. 77–9.

launched their torpedoes, and likely that only two even made it into the harbor. However, the crews of the submarines would ultimately be celebrated for making the ultimate sacrifice, with nine out of the ten feted back home as "war gods"—the tenth, having been ignominiously captured, was not mentioned.

Coordinated attacks on the same day also took locals by surprise in the Philippines, Hong Kong, Guam, Wake Island, Malaya and Singapore. Before long, both the U.S. and Britain would declare war on Japan in response. Germany and Italy would declare war on the U.S. in solidarity with Japan, linking the several conflicts already underway in the 1940s into a truly global war.

Back in Japan, the radio played non-stop military hits all morning, Navy and Army marches, and militarist classics dating back to the Meiji Restoration. It was twenty minutes to midday before the Emperor's official declaration was read out to the nation.

> The situation being such as it is, Our Empire for its existence and self-defense has now other recourse but to appeal to arms and crush every obstacle in its path.[4]

The reading was followed by a brief address by Tōjō himself, advising the nation that a "firm belief in the certainty of victory" would provide the key to success. "To annihilate this enemy," he announced, "and to establish a stable new order in East Asia, the nation must necessarily anticipate a long war."[5]

After Tōjō's announcement, the radio played the song "If We Go to Sea" (*Umi Yukaba*), which had become a ubiquitous musical accompaniment to solemn government broadcasts.

> If we go to sea, water will cover our corpses
> If we go to the mountains, grass will grow on the dead
> We shall die by the side of our lord
> We shall never look back.[6]

The song had been around since late 1937, when it had been knocked

---

[4] Butow, *Tōjō and the Coming of the War*, p. 409.
[5] Butow, *Tōjō and the Coming of the War*, p. 410.
[6] Osada, *Sensō ga Nokoshita Uta*, pp. 78–9. Cranston, *A Waka Anthology*, p. 155.

up as the tune-of-the-week on an Osaka music show. The lyrics derived from an eighth-century poem, which gained greater resonance as the war dragged on. Within three months of the bombing of Pearl Harbor, "If We Go to Sea" was increasingly heard on Japanese radios, and came to be associated with the deaths of soldiers. Its modern-day lyricist, who had essentially just copied out the 1,200-year-old original, had initially intended it to be sung briskly and strongly, but "If We Go to Sea" grew ever more funereal, particularly after it came to be associated with the return of remains from battlefields. It, and songs like it, grew to dominate the airwaves, as purges of unsuitable material left nothing fit for broadcast except military songs, traditional folk songs and a small number of popular songs that still remained "appropriate" to the emergency situation.[7]

Bed-ridden after a stroke, the ailing Yosano Akiko still found the time to contribute several poems to celebratory collections of the outbreak of the Great East Asia War. Some, admittedly, expressed her sorrows at the thought of further conflict, but the bulk of her output was performatively patriotic.

> How strong! They fear not heaven / nor shame on earth
> Our brave soldiers in battle.[8]

There was, however, a faint echo of her famous anti-war poem "Do Not Lay Down Your Life," to be discerned in the verses she wrote about her son.

> Though I await news from the battleship / with my son aboard / it does not come.
> Ah, may the fortunes of war be with him. [...]

> Becoming a navy lieutenant / my fourth son / goes now to the sacred war
> Fight bravely!

Some reactions were counter-intuitive. In China, Generalissimo Chiang Kai-shek danced for joy, sure that help would soon be coming in his own fight against the Japanese. After hearing the news that a Japanese

---

[7] Atkins, *Blue Nippon*, p. 129.
[8] Rabson, "Yosano Akiko at War," p. 62.

sneak attack on Hawaii had killed more than two thousand people, the British Prime Minister Winston Churchill reported that he went to bed and "slept the sleep of the saved and thankful."[9]

Not everybody was so positive. Matsuoka Yōsuke, who had assured his colleagues that the alliance with Germany and Italy would keep America *out* of war with Japan, belatedly recognized his role in creating the exact situation he had been intent on avoiding. Sick in bed at his home, the ousted politician began to weep.

"I am now painfully aware that the signing of the Tripartite Pact was the biggest mistake of my lifetime," he said. "When I think of this, it will bother me even after I die."[10]

"What on earth!" said Konoe Fumimaro to his son-in-law. "I really feel a miserable defeat coming."[11]

The attack on Pearl Harbor merely marked the first and most surprising of a series of Japanese victories. On December 8, Japanese troops under General Yamashita Tomoyuki made an amphibious landing in Malaya, and Japanese bombers, now in range from south Indochina, attacked Singapore. With support from Malay fifth columnists, and unexpectedly mobile thanks to the use of bicycle-infantry on jungle paths, the Japanese advanced along the coast. The British ships *Repulse* and *Prince of Wales* were sunk by Japanese air assault on December 10, marking a major score for Japan, and soon celebrated in songs, poems and films.

In January 1942 Japan deployed paratroopers in battle for the first time during the Battle of Manado. Horiuchi Toyoaki, a flamboyant, bearded officer nicknamed "The Octopus" for his love of and promotion of gymnastics in the Navy, led a strike force of 507 parachutists, dropping behind enemy lines to seize the Dutch forces' airfield and seaplane base. In a tactic that would have surely attracted more notice had it not been overshadowed by the parachute achievement, 22 soldiers landed a sea-plane on an inland lake, allowing an anti-tank unit to penetrate deep into enemy territory.

The idea of Japanese soldiers bodily hurling themselves out of a

---

[9] Hotta, *Japan 1941*, p. 26.

[10] Yellen, "Into the Tiger's Den," p. 576; Lu, *Agony of Choice*, pp. 247–8, observes that Matsuoka had significantly changed his tune within the space of a few hours. He spent the morning cheering Tōjō on, only to become substantially more circumspect as the implications began to dawn.

[11] Hotta, *Japan 1941*, p. 28.

flying machine into the middle of enemy territory had an electric effect on the Japanese public. The *Yomiuri Shinbun* dubbed them the "Divine Sky Warriors" (*Sora no Shinpei*), prompting a journalist at the rival *Mainichi Shinbun* to write a poem about the romance of their achievement. Before long, "Divine Sky Warriors" had been set to music, broadcast on the radio and released as a gramophone record, becoming a nationwide hit.

> In the great sky, bluer than blue
> It is as if, suddenly a hundred thousand white roses bloom
> Behold! Parachutes descend from the sky.
> Behold! Parachutes conquering the sky.
>
> The parachute is the most glorious flower in the world.
> On its purest white, our soldiers regret not the spilling of red blood.[12]

The divine soldiers, so young that they still look like children, are repeatedly likened to blossoms fluttering in the sky, descending from the heavens, to magically reclaim territory held in enemy hands.

In something of a low blow, the Army fought back by rushing out a propaganda movie, *Divine Sky Warriors* (1942, *Sora no Shinpei*) a documentary about the training of an Army paratrooper unit that not only presented close-up imagery of technology and procedures that the Navy still proclaimed to be classified, but blatantly used "Divine Sky Warriors" as its theme tune, as if to imply that the achievement on Manado had been an Army operation. The Ministry of Education, keen to distract the population from increasing Japanese losses in the war at sea, gave the film a cultural award, and decreed that it should be compulsorily screened in every cinema in the country.[13]

The national enthusiasm over the Navy paratroopers' success obscured the terrible losses that they had suffered. Twelve of them died

---

[12] Osada, *Sensō ga Nokoshita Uta*, pp. 690–93.

[13] Since one might only expect children to fall for such sleight of hand, the film was screened on a double bill for schools with a Chinese cartoon, *Princess Iron Fan* (1943). In response to the insult, the Navy would retaliate with cartoons of its own, *Momotarō's Sea Eagles* (1943, *Momotarō no Umiwashi*), celebrating the contribution of Navy pilots to the victory at Pearl Harbor, and Japan's first ever feature-length animation, *Momotarō's Divine Sea Warriors* (1945, *Momotarō, Umi no Shinpei*), a.k.a. *Momotarō, Sacred Sailors*.

before even reaching the landing zone, when their plane was shot down by a Navy fighter that had mistaken them for the enemy. In reprisal for the heavy casualties they had suffered in taking the airfield, Japanese officers carried out dozens of battlefield executions of their prisoners.[14]

This, however, was nothing compared to the deathly purges underway in newly occupied territories. In Singapore, for example, three days after its defenders surrendered on February 15, the Japanese Army conducted an extensive and brutal round-up of all adult Chinese males for the "great inspection" (*daikenshō*). They singled out journalists, former employees of the British authorities, men with tattoos (regarded as having likely crime affiliations), people from Hainan (suspected of being Communist supporters) and those known to have made charitable donations to support the Chinese war effort on the mainland. Depending on which source one believes, between 5,000 and 70,000 Chinese died, by firing squad or bayonet, in a three-week massacre known today in Singapore as the *Sook Ching* ("cleansing purge").

The Japanese military was already pushing further to the west, demanding a secure rear echelon unsusceptible to fifth-column activities and sabotage. In February 1942, Admiral Nagumo launched a carrier-based air assault against Darwin, Australia, severely compromising its water and fuel supply, and disabling the freight route supplying much of the defense of the Dutch East Indies. This was the first of more than a hundred air-raids on Australia over the next year.

Australia, however, was a side-show. The Japanese media continued to rejoice in the achievement at Pearl Harbor as the Navy's finest hour. With lyrics by the aging poet Kitahara Hakushū, who died not long after the song's release, "The Great Sea Battle of Hawaii" (*Hawaii Daikaisen*) began with an appeal to Confucian rectitude—that there cannot be two suns in the sky, nor two supreme powers ruling at the same time.

> Two suns cannot shine in the sky.
> But we may put to shame the Stars and Stripes
> The moment the Imperial edict is decreed
> "This is the battle," they push forward.
> Like a whirlwind, ten thousand leagues across the Pacific Ocean
> Objective: Hawaii, Pearl Harbor.

---

[14] Salecker, *Blossoming Silk Against the Rising Sun*, p. 7.

None could have foreseen, that dawn's
Dream, surprised by bombs.
Cutting through the clouds
See, the roaring attack
The sea eagles' deadly thunder
And the relentless submarines.

Are they gods or men? They sacrifice themselves
Those souls shall be passed on to eternity.
Why should we wail?
Oh, loyal wrathful spirits, pillars of flame.
Piercing the Earth's axis, along with the ship!
Crushing the enemy's primary force.

Now, U.S. Fleet, you learn of your divine punishment.
The resolution of the century is already decided.
The victory song is sung on this eighth day
Ten thousand leagues across the Pacific Ocean
We bear witness to Greater East Asia.[15]

Kitahara singles out the "relentless submarines" that actually achieved very little—five midget submarines, all of which were lost in the attack. As the war dragged on, a story surfaced regarding one of the doomed skippers, Petty Officer Katayama Heizō, who had repurposed an old song at his farewell party the day before the launch. In what would slowly become an underground hit with other military personnel, Katayama added new lyrics to a 1934 elegy to Korea's Mount Baekdu, pre-emptively inviting mourners to visit him at Kudanzaka, the hill that leads to the Yasukuni Shrine.

> "Don't cry, don't grieve, I shall return.
> Oh, wearing brocade in a paulownia box,
> Come to see me at Kudanzaka."[16]

---

[15] Osada, *Sensō ga Nokoshita Uta*, p. 679. "Confucius said: 'There are not two suns in the sky, nor two sovereigns over the people.'" *Mencius*, V:4.

[16] Osada, *Sensō ga Nokoshita Uta*, pp. 291–2.

In the United States, as Admiral Yamamoto had predicted, the entire nation had reacted with shock to the attack on Pearl Harbor—a date, as Roosevelt solemnly announced, that would "live in infamy." However, not even Yamamoto had foreseen the sheer energy of the American response, which capitalized not only on the incident itself, but decades of anti-Japanese policies and attitudes on the West coast of America.

Paranoia about the 127,000 Japanese Americans, the majority of which resided on the U.S. West coast, became a significant feature of the months following the attack on Pearl Harbor. Japanese immigration to the U.S. had not been permitted since the controversial Immigration Law of 1924, but some *issei* (first generation) immigrants predating that legislation still resided in the U.S., as did their children (*nisei*—2nd generation), and grandchildren (*sansei*—3rd generation), most of whom were U.S. citizens by birth.

In the aftermath of the attack on Pearl Harbor, much was made in the U.S. media of Japan's alleged spy network, which was supposed to have made Pearl Harbor and the fall of Singapore a foregone conclusion. There was, however, little evidence for this. There were, true enough, substantiated stories about Japanese subjects overseas buying machine tools and materials to ship home to Japan in contravention of the U.S. trade sanctions, but this was hardly "espionage." There *was* ample evidence of Japanese espionage operations worldwide, not only in the years leading up to Pearl Harbor, but in the decades previously—particularly in East Asia, where the Black Dragons and the "continental adventurers" had infiltrated many aspects of Chinese and Manchurian society, and where Pan-Asian rhetoric was fuelling a growing anti-colonial mood. However, there is remarkably *little* evidence of Japanese spy networks making good use of Japanese-Americans, who were mistrusted by "true" Japanese, who vastly preferred white or black recruits.

Figures such as Captain Patrick Heenan, for example, a New Zealander believed to have been recruited by a female Japanese agent in 1938, and caught reporting aircraft recognition codes by radio in December 1941. Heenan had survived in prison in Singapore until shortly before the fall of the colony, when he was executed by a military police sergeant.[17]

Such stories should have made it plain that nations could recruit their spies from anywhere, but nationalism had played such a huge part

---

[17] Matthews, *Shadows Dancing*, p. 52.

Itō Hirobumi (1841–1909), who in his youth was one of the Chōshū Five that sneaked out of Japan to study abroad, was the first Prime Minister of Japan and first Japanese Resident-General of the Colony of Korea. A controversial memorial in Harbin commemorates not him, but the Korean assassin who killed him. *Photo: Public Domain.*

The Taishō Emperor. Yoshihito (1879–1926) succeeded his father in 1912, marking the start of an era in which the Meiji Restorationists began to lose their grip. The Taishō period is remembered in Japan as a time of rising democratic dissent, but also of increasingly severe clampdowns on it. Suffering from neurological problems, he was kept out of the public eye. His son Hirohito became his regent in 1919, as soon as he reached the age of majority. *Photo: Imperial Household Agency.*

The Sounding of the Bugle. Woodblock print depicting the brave bugler who refused to retreat at the Ansong forts in 1895. At the time, he was misidentified as Shirakami Genjirō, who was later found to have already died in an earlier battle. *Photo: The Gene and Susan Roberts Collection.*

Gun Battery at Qingdao (Tsingtao). Japanese artillerymen fighting alongside the British at the Siege of Qingdao, China, in 1914, the largest action fought by the Japanese in the First World War. *Photo: National Army Museum, London.*

The Siberian Intervention. "Our army attacks from sky, water and shore." What appears at first to be an image of Japanese aircraft over Khabarovsk, Siberia in 1919 is revealed on closer inspection to show Army ground troops, cavalry and Navy ships also in action. *Photo: U.S. Library of Congress.*

The Shōwa Emperor. Hirohito (1901–1989), presided over the rise and fall of the Japanese empire throughout the 1920s and 1930s. With Japan's surrender in 1945, he became a controversial symbol of an enduring establishment—either a militarist Japan, or the Japan that had been overrun by the militarists. *Photo: Public Domain.*

The Little Black Dress. The introduction of Coco Chanel's "little black dress" in 1926 revolutionized fashion and crippled the earning power of the silk industry, on which Japan relied for much of its foreign trade. In the 1930s, silk exports to the U.S. plummeted to less than an eighth of their former level. *Photo: American Vogue.*

The Promised Land. A 1930s Japanese government poster urges imperial subjects to migrate to Manchuria, a "province fit for expansion," neglecting to mention it is actually a Chinese province. *Photo: Public Domain.*

The Asia Express. The train known as the Asia Express was the pride of the South Manchuria Railway and of the state of Manchukuo. Linking Dalian in the south with Harbin in the north, the train had a top speed of 135 km per hour. *Photo: Carpkazu.*

Korea Included. A stamp depicting "Japan" in the 1930s includes Korea within its borders, as the two states were regarded by the government as a unified whole. *Photo: Sandman Collection.*

Wearing Manchuria. A kimono from the 1930s is decorated with imagery of Japan's military presence in Manchukuo. *Photo: Melikian Collection.*

The Three Bomb Heroes. Propaganda poster commemorating the three men whose fatal mission became a famous incident in the fighting over Shanghai in 1932. Memorialized in poetry, films, songs and statues, their action was widely reported as heroic sacrifice, although it may easily have been an awful military blunder. *Photo: Ehagaki.*

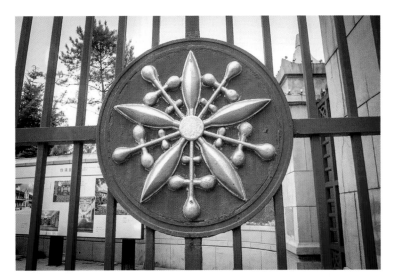

The Seal of Manchukuo. Although it has largely been scrubbed from history, the seal of the state of Manchukuo can still be found on the gates of its former center of power in today's Changchun, China, where it is now known as the "Palace of the False Emperor." *Photo: Kati Clements.*

Austerity Dining. As shortages began to bite, the Japanese authorities promoted the hinomaru bento as the ultimate patriotic meal—a single pickled plum on a bed of plain rice, evoking the image of the Japanese flag. *Photo: Tobosha.*

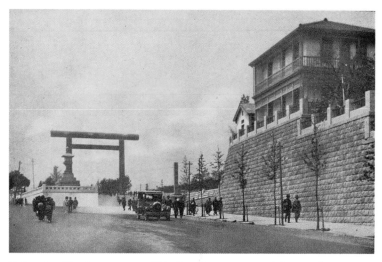

Kudanzaka. The "nine-stepped" hill to the entrance of the Yasukuni Shrine, celebrated in several wartime songs as a place of pilgrimage for the relatives of Japan's war dead. *Photo: Benichan.*

皇紀
2600
一月元旦

A Very Good Year. A Japanese New Year postcard from 1940 celebrates "2600 years" since the time of the first legendary Emperor Jinmu. The occasion was celebrated in a series of rituals coordinated by radio broadcasts. *Photo: Kinouya.*

Prince Konoe. A 1938 ceremonial portrait of Konoe Fumimaro (1891–1945), the aristocrat who presided as Prime Minister over the outbreak of the war in China and the military build-up preceding Pearl Harbor. Opposed to war with America, he predicted Japan's defeat by spring 1942. He would commit suicide in 1945, leaving a diary that was used as evidence to defend Hirohito. *Photo: Emiya1980.*

General Tōjō. Tōjō Hideki (1884–1948) was a key figure in the machinations of Japan's "Dark Valley" politics and in the corrupt actions of Manchukuo state. Back in Japan, he became the hawkish Prime Minister and leader of the armed forces throughout the Pacific War. He was executed as a war criminal on December 23, 1948. *Photo: Renokkusu.*

The Co-Prosperity Sphere. A Japanese 10-sen stamp from 1942 blithely depicts the full extent of Japan's possessions in East and Southeast Asia. *Photo: Carpkazu.*

The Cartoon Conflict. As the mass media were co-opted into the war effort, Japan's first feature-length cartoon was *Momotarō's Divine Sea Warriors* (1945), a propaganda retelling of the fall of Singapore using cartoon animals. *Photo: Anime Limited.*

The Battle of Okinawa. The USS *Bunker Hill* burns after being struck by two kamikaze aircraft during the Battle of Okinawa on May 11, 1945. *Photo: National Archives and Records Administration.*

Bigger Game. An advertisement for the Western Cartridge Company capitalizes on the U.S. victory at Guadalcanal in 1943 to suggest that hunting Japanese soldiers is not all that different from hunting wild animals. *Photo: Jon Mallard.*

Baka Bomb. A captured Ōka suicide plane at Yontan airfield on Okinawa. The Ōka plane's only purpose was to be used as a kamikaze. Fewer than a hundred were used at Okinawa and none damaged a major ship. Because of its ineffectiveness, U.S. personnel called the plane the Baka Bomb, "baka" being a Japanese word that means "foolish" or "stupid." *Photo: Vitalie Ciubotaru.*

Expendable Youth. A group of kamikaze pilots pose for a photograph at Chōshi airfield, 1944. Only one of the 18 men would survive the war. *Photo: Unknown source.*

Fat Man. The U.S. B-29 bomber Necessary Evil followed behind the Enola Gay in order to photograph the Hiroshima bomb. Cameraman George R. Caron took this photo of the mushroom cloud above the target. *Photo: National Archives and Records Administration.*

The Jewel Voice Broadcast. Shocked Japanese citizens listening to the Emperor's "Jewel Voice Broadcast," in which he commanded his subjects to "endure the unendurable" and accept surrender. Even though Japan was on the brink of starvation, military officers tried to seize the recording on the eve of its broadcast. *Photo: Raul654.*

Hirohito and MacArthur.
The Shōwa Emperor,
now referred to by his
first name, Hirohito,
seems dwarfed by the
towering figure of
Douglas MacArthur,
the Supreme Com-
mander of the Allied
Powers in Japan, Sep-
tember 27, 1945.
Photo: Gaetano Faillace.

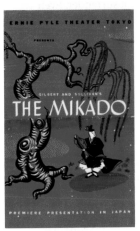

The Mikado **Returns.** As a test of the freedom to lampoon the Japanese establishment, the Allies put on a performance
of *The Mikado* at the "Ernie Pyle" Theater in Tokyo. The musical had been
banned in Japan for several decades,
and contained a snatch of a military
song, "Miya-san Miya-san," that was
technically illegal under Occupation
rules. *Photo: Worthopedia.*

OPPOSITE LEFT: **The Surrender.** Foreign minister Shigemitsu Mamoru signs
the instrument of Japan's surrender on the deck of the USS *Missouri* in
Tokyo Bay, September 2, 1945. *Photo: Naval Historical Center.*

Yasukuni Today. The Yasukuni Shrine as it appears today, complete with monuments to kamikaze pilots, fallen horses and Judge Pal, as well as a pavilion commemorating the rise and fall of the Japanese empire. *Photo: Wiiii.*

Judge Pal. The monument to Judge Radhabinod Pal (1886 –1967) at the Yasukuni Shrine, which selectively quotes from his incendiary dissenting judgment at the International Military Tribunal for the Far East. *Photo: Kakidai.*

The Fallen Gate. In Taichung, in what is now Taiwan, Republic of China, a fallen gate from a Japanese Shintō shrine is now used as a park bench by the local people. *Photo: Shitamichi Motoyuki.*

in the rhetoric of the Axis powers, that it now formed an element of the Allied response. Amid calls for those of German, Italian or Japanese descent to be interned, or at the very least, vetted, the Japanese came out particularly badly.

Alleged Japanese subterfuge also proved to be a useful excuse for covering up Allied incompetence. Nobody, it seems, bothered to ask why the "surprise" attack on Pearl Harbor had not been foreseen by policy-makers familiar with Japan's similar pre-emptive strikes in 1894 and 1904. In the long-term, the easy explanation of a Japanese spy network, infiltrating every aspect of American society, would play into the hands of the internment lobby.[18]

One incident in the immediate aftermath of Pearl Harbor had stoked the concerns of the anti-Japanese lobby in the U.S. government. During the December 7 attack, Nagumo's fleet had arranged an emergency pick-up operation for planes that were too damaged to make it back to the carriers. Pilots with damaged planes were ordered to make it to the western island of Niihau, which the Japanese Navy had incorrectly assumed to be uninhabited, to await a submarine pick-up.

In fact, Niihau was a private plantation, manned chiefly by Hawaiian laborers. Airman Nishikaichi Shigenori crash-landed his Zero in a field on the island, where he was taken in by Hawaiians initially unaware of the attack underway 228 kilometers away on Oahu. However, Nishikaichi somehow inveigled three Japanese plantation workers to help him escape, in a scuffle that ended with a Hawaiian husband and wife killing Nishikaichi with a rock and a knife, and one of his would-be helpers committing suicide with a shotgun.

One of the smallest-scale skirmishes of the Pacific War, the "battle" of Niihau would have explosive repercussions, providing the anti-immigrant lobby with further ammunition that Japan's militarist rhetoric— decades of proud boasts about the unity of the Japanese people, and their devotion to their cause—also applied to ethnic Japanese overseas.

On February 19, 1942, President Roosevelt signed Executive Order 9066, authorizing the creation of military exclusion zones, from which it would be legal to remove persons of suspicion. These zones included much of California, leading within a month to the first of many mass evictions of Japanese Americans from their homes, and their relocation

---

[18] Everest-Phillips, "The Pre-War Fear of Japanese Espionage," p. 249.

to internment camps further to the east. Internment of Japanese overseas also occurred to a lesser wide-ranging degree in Canada, Australia, Brazil and Mexico. The entire affair is notable not merely for the credence it invests in Japan's militarist boasts, but in racist suspicions—even in 1942, for example, there was commentary in the press about the convenient opportunity it offered white farmers in California to rid themselves of Japanese competition.

"We're charged with wanting to get rid of the Japs for selfish reasons. We do," commented Austin Anson of the Salinas Vegetable Grower-Shipper Association:

> It's a question of whether the white man lives on the Pacific Coast or the brown men. They came into this valley to work, and they stayed to take over. [...] They undersell the white man in the markets. [...] They work their women and children while the white farmer has to pay wages for his help. If all the Japs were removed tomorrow, we'd never miss them in two weeks, because the white farmers can take over and produce everything the Jap grows. And we don't want them back when the war ends, either.[19]

This remains an emotive issue beyond the scope of this book. However, it is worth mentioning that Argentina did not intern its Japanese ethnic minority, and did not suffer a surge of espionage or sabotage. Meanwhile, in Hawaii, it was impossible to intern the island's huge ethnic Japanese population, leading to the U.S. state with the largest Japanese minority only rounding up 1,200 alleged undesirables out of 158,000 in Hawaii, as opposed to the 112,000 out of 127,000 shipped off to camps on the mainland.

As Admiral Yamamoto had predicted, the six months after Pearl Harbor saw the high-point of Japanese military gains, an achievement made to look even more impressive by several daring raids that made Japan's ambitions seem substantially larger than they actually were. In March 1942, there was an attempt to bomb Pearl Harbor a second time, using two sea planes that refuelled from a Japanese submarine at French

---

[19] *Saturday Evening Post*, May 9, 1942, p. 66. I do not wish to downplay the threat of home-front espionage or sabotage, but the scandal of the internment incident, then as now, was that law-abiding American citizens were persecuted for no other reason than their ethnic origin.

Frigate Shoals, 900 kilometers from Oahu. However, bad weather on the day, made it impossible for the Japanese pilots to adequately assess repairs or to carry out their secondary mission of bombing one of the main docks before it could be fully fixed. Potential refueling sites were subsequently mined by the U.S. Navy, shutting down further missions.

A far more effective scare tactic was employed in April 1942 against the British, when carrier-based aircraft, again commanded by Admiral Nagumo, attacked Colombo, Ceylon, the main base of the British Navy in the Indian Ocean. Two days later, they raided naval facilities at nearby Trincomalee. In the combined action, losses to Japan amounted to a handful of aircraft (one of which was observed, seemingly deliberately, crash-diving into the Trincomalee fuel-storage depot). Losses to British and Commonwealth forces, however, were far greater, including two ships and an aircraft carrier, and many lives lost on the ground, and a genuine fear that the Japanese were on the verge of seizing the upper hand in the Indian Ocean.

A flotilla of Japanese submarines attacked Sydney, Australia, in May 1942, deploying three midget submarines, one of which sank a barracks ship, killing 21 sailors. The mother-ships then dispersed on a series of nuisance missions over the following month, attacking merchant shipping and briefly shelling Newcastle in New South Wales. All such operations were aimed at tying up as much as the Allied fleet as possible, in order to make it possible for the Japanese Navy to win a decisive action elsewhere. Tōjō continued to speak of invading Australia in his broadcasts, but this was an idle threat. His generals had already told him that Japan had nothing like the necessary manpower, so all talk of an Australian invasion was designed to buoy up the Japanese and scare the Allies.[20]

In May 1942, Allied and Japanese forces clashed in the Battle of the Coral Sea, off the coast of New Guinea, the first battle in which aircraft carriers faced aircraft carriers. Both sides would proclaim it as a victory—the Japanese having caused more damage, but the Allies having stopped, for the first time, a Japanese advance. In June 1942, in another

---

[20] Stanley, *Invading Australia*, p. 178 stresses that the Japanese attacked Sydney in order to sink the U.S.S. *Chicago*, but that Australian popular culture has continued to frame the event as an attack on, or even "invasion of" Australia. Tōjō had referred to the possibility of invading Australia in a meeting in March 1942, but merely as a vaguely defined "positive measure" to be undertaken after Britain and the United States had been defeated. See Butow, *Tōjō and the Coming of the War*, p. 421.

high-water mark, soldiers of the Japanese Army occupied the Aleutian islands of Attu and Kiska—remote and low on the list of priorities for a counter-attack, but nevertheless spun in the Japanese media as the "first" occupation of American territory by Japanese forces.

Such incidents remained an indication of the Japanese freedom to "run wild" while their enemies regrouped. In a Japan ignorant of Admiral Yamamoto's caveat, that six months would be all they had before reprisals followed, Konoe Fumimaro's government was returned to power by a high-spirited nation. Konoe's National Spiritual Mobilization Committee had been superseded by the Imperial Rule Assistance Association (*Taiseiyoku Sankai*) in 1940. In 1942, it subsumed several other organizations, including the Greater Japan Women's Association, for which membership was compulsory for all females over 20, and the Greater Japan Imperial Assistance Youth Corps (*Yokusan Sonendan*). In the same year's general election, the Imperial Rule Assistance Association, now an umbrella group "uniting" (at least officially) almost all the remaining political parties in Japan, carried 381 out of 466 seats in the Japanese Diet. There were no left-wing candidates, as such ideology had been illegal since 1940. The only party in opposition, winning seven seats, was the Tōhō-kai, a breakaway fascist organization that openly admired Saigō Takamori and the Satsuma rebels of 1877, and whose members thought Tōjō ought to act *more* like Hitler. The remaining seats went to independents like Saitō Takao, defiantly returned by his constituents despite having been ejected from the Diet in 1940. Otherwise, it was a landslide of support for the Japanese military, with many Army-endorsed candidates standing unopposed, and the council chamber effectively turned into a one-party body.

With the Great East Asia War now underway, Japan's government was obliged to manage expectations on a wider level, not only with continued support of the troops in the field, but to make it clear to the population that there were many sacrifices still ahead. One of the musical hits to arise out of the period dwelt on the melancholy of fallen soldiers, but also introduced a somewhat controversial notion—some had believed that the fall of Singapore would see the end of the fighting, but "Clutching the Relics of Fallen Comrades" (*Senyū no Ikotsu o Daite*) treated it merely as the opening act in a long series of battles to come.

He said "I'll go first"

Now, clutching the box that contains the remains of my fallen
comrade
On this morning in Singapore town
I'm a man, so why should I weep?
Biting my lip, I hold it back.
But when I hear the cry of "Banzai" from the mountain
A tear unbidden runs down my cheek.
I pick up the national flag he left me as a relic
We shall leave at the summit, their names on rain-drenched cloth
My friend, see the Southern Cross
In the calm sky above Malacca
Day turned to night as we made our assault
And together, you and I gazed upon those stars
Even though Singapore has fallen
There will be more battles to come
I'll go on, holding your relics
Comrade, watch over me.[21]

The lyrics were written by Tsujihara Minoru, a paymaster sergeant who
had been among the soldiers as they marched into Singapore, many of
them carrying bundles that contained the ashes of their fallen fellow soldiers. Printed in verse form in the soldiers' mimeographed newsletter,
it was set to music by a naval officer in answer to a forces competition
and first performed in Singapore to a military audience. The melancholy
song was well-received by almost all present, except the commanding
officer of the Southern Expeditionary Army, Count Terauchi, who declared it to be too sad, and unsuitable for the military repertoire. It did,
however, make its way to Japan, where it was released as gramophone
records with two different tunes.[22]

In Korea, there was an abortive attempt to get the natives to sing a
new, improved version of the "Arirang" folk song, now infused with the
proper martial spirit:

Arirang, Arirang, Arariyo
Know that it is a time of Emergency

---

[21] Osada, *Sensō ga Nokoshita Uta*, p. 687.
[22] Osada, *Sensō ga Nokoshita Uta*, p. 688.

When at the crossroads of peace and its opposite
The spirit of the Sun illumines the world
Fly the flag of peace![23]

It did not catch on.

The sheer speed of the gains in the early days of the war seems to
have caught the Japanese Army by surprise. Of all the Allied soldiers
captured during the war, 83% were apprehended in the first six months,
leaving the Japanese Army ill-prepared for processing and monitoring
290,000 prisoners. Particularly in Singapore and the Philippines, the
Japanese were overwhelmed by the number of captives, having not expected so many to surrender in such short order. Food supplies were
disrupted, camps were hastily constructed or requisitioned, and a severe
manpower shortage led to the hiring of Taiwanese or Korean prison
guards, who would later be the subject of many complaints over brutality and ill-treatment.[24]

In the Philippines, the surrender of Bataan in April 1942 left the
Japanese commander, Homma Masaharu with over 60,000 Allied prisoners of war, many of them sick, wounded or enfeebled by their long
siege with diminishing supplies. The Japanese also acquired another
38,000 civilian non-combatants, all of whom needed to be fed, watered,
and sheltered. Prisoners were stripped of their possessions, and anyone
holding Japanese artifacts was shot, on the grounds that they had probably looted them from Japanese bodies. The prisoners were then forced to
march a hundred kilometers under the hot sun, with no food for the first
five days, and with what little water they could scavenge from roadside
ditches and wells. This, in turn, gave many of them dysentery, although
if they fell behind, they were bayoneted.[25] It was subsequently believed
that the "Bataan Death March" was deliberately conceived by Homma's
underling, Tsuji Masanobu, the architect of the earlier *Sook Ching* atrocity in Singapore, in order to diminish the drain on resources caused by
the high number of prisoners. Prisoners were beaten and tortured, some
had their gold teeth smashed out as souvenirs.

Details of this, and other death marches (involving Dutch, Chinese, and Filipinos, as well as Americans and subjects of Britain and its

---

[23] Atkins, "The Dual Career of 'Arirang,'" p. 669.
[24] Sturma, "Japanese Treatment of Allied Prisoners," p. 525.
[25] Russell, *The Knights of Bushidō*, p. 117.

Commonwealth), soon reached foreign governments, but Tōjō ignored protests made under the terms of the Geneva Convention. Japan had agreed to the Convention of 1929, which outlawed corporal punishment, forbade collective punitive measures for individual crimes, and insisted upon provision of food, water and shelter. However, Japan had never actually ratified it, following opposition from the Army Ministry in 1934, on the grounds that agreement to the terms of the Convention would place prisoners of war in the bizarre position of having the right to better treatment than Japanese soldiers in their own Army, a "revision which was undesirable in the interests of discipline."[26]

It was another fatal conjunction of practices—the Army's own historical brutality towards its own soldiers, used to both refuse prisoners' rights, and to excuse the indignities visited by Japanese soldiers on those prisoners. Nor was the *Field Service Code* of any value, since it already established that a soldier should prefer death over capture. "Punishments," for offences real and imagined, came to incorporate, everything from slaps and beatings, to being made to walk barefoot on broken glass. The mistreatment of prisoners of war, and inhabitants of occupied areas would become a growing feature of the Japanese Army's public profile, both for the remainder of the war and for posterity. Most such incidents remained Army matters, partly because the Navy was in less of a position to take prisoners, and hence to deal with them in any large amount. There would, however, also be accusations against the Navy, or the mistreatment of prisoners during marine transport, such as prisoners aboard the *Nitta Maru*, en route from Wake to Yokoyama in early 1942, where the death penalty was threatened for even minor infractions such as talking without permission or walking around without authorization.[27]

In spite of such behavior towards its prisoners, the Japanese Navy was keen on celebrating its achievements with the Japanese public, in order to keep its profile high. The Navy had been using the same march, "Warships" (*Gunkan*) since 1893, a stirring tune with lyrics that referred to the "black iron that defends us" and the "floating fortresses of Japan." But after fifty years, it was regarded as a little outmoded, while also neglecting to celebrate any of the Navy's achievements throughout its

---

[26] Russell, *The Knights of Bushidō*, p. 57.
[27] Russell, *The Knights of Bushidō*, p. 102.

modern existence. The Navy Ministry asked the *Asahi Shinbun* newspaper to provide a new song—previous requests had led to national competitions, but in this case was met with lyrics written by Kawanishi Shintarō, who usually served as judge of the *Asahi's* lyrics competitions. Set to music by, Hashimoto Kuniaki, a professor at the Tokyo College of Music, "The Navy Song of the Great East Asia War" (*Dai Tō-A Sensō Kaigun no Uta*) made up for lost time with a grand medley of all the Navy's greatest successes, briskly alluding to Tōgō's Z signal at the Battle of Tsūshima, Pearl Harbor, Hirose the "war god" and his block ship at Port Arthur, the lost midget submarines at Pearl Harbor (again), the sinking of the *Prince of Wales* and the *Repulse*, the Battle of the Coral Sea, a little bit more about Pearl Harbor *and* the Battle of Ceylon, not to mention allusions to both cherry blossoms *and* the lyrics of "If We Go to Sea" and finishing with the Southern Cross constellation, a novel sight in the night sky for Japanese personnel in South-East Asia, and hence an icon of the southward advance.

> Look, the Z flag of our memory
> Flutters high on the masthead.
> The time has come, under the order
> Oh, the morning of the 8th December
> Stars and Stripes was the first to be torn
> Leviathans ripped and sunk.
>
> Inheriting the blood of our ancestors
> Who gave their lives to block Port Arthur.
> They dived at Pearl Harbor
> Oh, all the hundred million people wept.
> The lost five subs became
> The shattered jewels of nine war gods.
>
> From the frozen sea to equator to the south
> Miles and miles of waves
> Warship flags compete to rule the waves
> Oh, traditional people of the sea
> Off Malay and Java, the Coral Sea
> The British and Dutch are no longer there.

Young cherry blossoms become honorable
When they fall gallantly to become water-soaked corpses.
Look, they fly in sky and dive through the clouds.
Oh, brave sea eagles
Hurling themselves while holding a bomb
Crushing enemy ships to smithereens.

Advancing as far as the Indian Ocean
The praise of generations, minds clear
The Southern Cross smiles down upon them.
Oh, Great East Asia, a shaft of light
Proud and invincible iron
Hear the wind in the warships' flags.[28]

It is, in fact, something of an irony that the song's release, in July 1942, marked not only the high point of the Navy's achievement, but the high probability that there would be no need for any more verses. It made no mention of the fact that U.S. bombers had already attacked Tokyo, or that the Japanese had suffered cataclysmic losses at the Battle of Midway a month earlier—a fact from which the Japanese public had also been shielded. The signs were already there that Japan's six months of "running wild," as predicted by Admiral Yamamoto, were over.

---

[28] Osada, *Sensō ga Nokoshita Uta*, pp. 694–5. "War gods" here is pronounced *ikusa-ga-mi*, using the *kun* reading, not *gunshin*, the more common *on* reading. The Southern Cross is also a prominent feature on the Australian flag, but its use in imagery of the 1940s seems to derive from the fact that it was a visible and easily recognisable indicator that travellers were in a new realm far away from home.

The Allied Counter-Attack (1942–45)

1000 km

Soviet Union

Lake Baikal

Mongolia

Nomonhan

Manchukuo

Changchun

Mukden

Korea

China

Japan

Hiroshima

Tokyo

Nanjing

Nagasaki

Chongqing

Shanghai

Tibet

Okinawa

Iwo

Nepal Buthan
Brit. India

Guangzhou

Taiwan

Burma

Thailand

Fr.
Indochina

Philippines
(U.S.A.)

Guan
(U.S.A

Leyte Gulf

North Borneo
(Brit.)

Palau

Brit. Malaya

Sarawak
(Brit.)

Manado

Singapore

Biak

Dutch East Indies

Papua
(Austr

Darwin

Australia

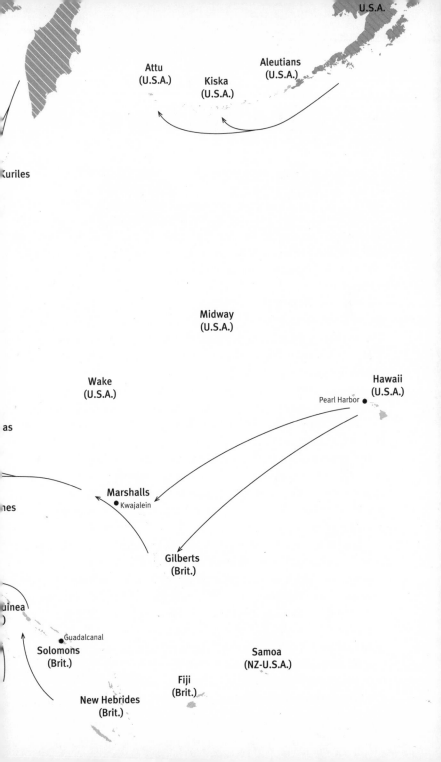

CHAPTER 10

The Iron Storm

This chronicle of Japan's defeats must necessarily overlap a little with the previous chapter's accounts of Japan's successes, as the first signs of the end of the six months "running wild" were downplayed or only acknowledged in hindsight, sometimes by the Japanese, and sometimes by the Allies.

The first American counter-attack took the Japanese by surprise, and was deliberately intended to rattle the military leaders and shake the common people. At noon on April 18, 1942, a squadron of sixteen U.S. planes appeared in the sky above Japan, dropping bombs on Tokyo, Osaka, Yokohama and Kobe. The harm they caused was relatively minimal—an aircraft carrier damaged at the docks, hits on fuel dumps, factories, schools and a hospital, but the psychological impact was immense.

The surprise value of what would become known as the Doolittle Raid, after its commanding officer James H. Doolittle, was that the bombers seemed to have come out of nowhere. President Roosevelt, who had been keen for a morale-building retaliation on the Japanese as soon as possible, even stirred speculation by claiming that they had launched out of "Shangri-La," naming a fictional Asian city from the novel *Lost Horizon*.

The full story of the Doolittle Raid was not released to the U.S. public for a further year. The bombers had launched from an aircraft carrier that had sneaked as close as possible to Japan. They had been stripped of all superfluous fittings in order to save fuel, and fitted with massive extra fuel tanks to allow them to reach their targets. Lacking the means to return to their place of origin, they planned to over-fly Japan and head for bases in China, to refuel and continue their journey. Forced to take off earlier than planned, none had the required fuel—one diverted to Vladivostok, where it and its crew were impounded by the Soviets. The rest crash-landed in China, where some crewmen were captured.

Sugiyama, the Army Chief of Staff, demanded that eight captured airmen be executed for committing a war crime. Eventually, owing to Tōjō's intervention, only three were killed, on the grounds that they had murdered children by hitting a school. Years later, at Tōjō's own trial, he put his case to his accusers:

> You probably won't be able to understand this unless you understand something about Japanese feelings at the time. This was the first time Japan had been bombed, and it was a great shock. Public feeling ran very high.[1]

The response was most grave in China itself, where Tōjō had already been wary of the risk posed to Japan by attacks from airbases in the Zhejiang and Jiangxi areas. A pre-existing plan to attack Chinese airbases was accelerated after it became plain that the Doolittle airmen had not only sought friendly landings in the area, but had been aided and abetted by local Chinese after they abandoned their planes.

From May to September 1942, a Japanese retaliatory campaign in Zhejiang and Jiangxi claimed a catastrophic number of casualties, with an estimated 250,000 Chinese dead. Even after the Japanese retreated, the damage continued, thanks to the bacteriological warfare Unit 731, which seeded the food and water supply with paratyphoid and anthrax. It was a high price to pay for Roosevelt's morale boost.

In June 1942, even as Hashimoto Kuniaki was setting "The Navy Song of the Great East Asia War" to music, the Japanese Navy finally got its wide-scale decisive battle, although not in the manner it had expected. The Doolittle Raid, along with frequent carrier-based assaults on Japanese bases, made it plain that U.S. carriers remained a threat, and one best neutralized. Admiral Yamamoto's preferred remedy would be a second attack on Pearl Harbor to lure the entire Pacific Fleet out for a final showdown, but without the element of surprise, a repeat of the previous year's success seemed unlikely. Instead, he hoped to lure U.S. carriers to the Midway atoll, an obscure dot of land conveniently beyond the range of any fighters operating out of Pearl Harbor. Any U.S. forces in

---

[1] Butow, *Tōjō and the Coming of the War*, p. 516. Admiral Yamamoto had also predicted this, saying to Konoe in the summer of 1941: "Even if we destroy their fleet and give a toast aboard our ship, enemy aircraft may attack Tokyo...". See Asada, *From Mahan to Pearl Harbor*, loc. 6136.

the area would hence have to rely on whatever they had with them, and what limited support was present on the atoll at the time of the attack.

Yamamoto's plan involved dispersing his fleet so widely that the Allies would not see the trap. The U.S. carriers, he hoped, would rush to engage Admiral Nagumo's own carrier force, not realizing that Yamamoto's battleships were already on their way to reinforce the carriers.

However, Yamamoto's luck had run out. The complex negotiations between the Japanese Army and Navy, required to authorize the plan, forced him to agree to the Army's plan to attack the Aleutian Islands. Reported in the previous chapter as a Japanese success, the June 1942 occupation of Attu and Kiska might also be parsed as a futile waste of time and resources, drawing some of Yamamoto's ships away from his surprise plan, to deliver soldiers to two icy rocks in Alaskan waters. Moreover, the variant speeds of Yamamoto's different groups made it difficult for one to keep up with the other—a factor that would lead to many of his most powerful warships failing to actually reach the subsequent Battle of Midway in time to open fire.

Worst of all, Yamamoto did not realize that U.S. intelligence had managed to decipher 85% of one of his most-used codes. Suspecting that Midway was the target for Yamamoto's scheme, the U.S. Navy transmitted a fake report of a breakdown of the island base's water desalination equipment. They were rewarded with a Japanese coded message ordering extra desalination equipment for an operation planned in early June. Midway would still be a surprise attack, but for the Japanese.

In the ensuing battle, Japan lost four carriers and more than three thousand men, including 40% of the Navy's best aircrews and flight technicians. The details of the battle were kept from all but the Emperor and the highest-ranking military officers, and Admiral Nagumo's own report was economic with the truth in several areas—he maintained that the enemy had been "surprised" at 5am, and was not lying in wait for him, and also neglected to mention that the three U.S. prisoners taken by the Japanese Navy were murdered in cold blood—two thrown overboard to drown, and another dispatched with a fire axe. Midway was reported in Japan as an overwhelming Japanese victory, with much emphasis on the loss of the carrier U.S.S. *Yorktown*, only recently repaired after suffering heavy damage at the Battle of the Coral Sea. The truth about the battle was carefully kept away from the Japanese public. It was not until 1953, and the Japanese release of the Gary Cooper film *Task Force* (1949) that many realized quite how much they had been lied to.[2]

Conversely, reporting in the U.S. was a little *too* open. Stanley Johnston, a reporter in Honolulu who, due to an administrative oversight, was not obliged to submit his text for censor approval, filed a story on the mainland that strongly implied that the Allies had broken the Japanese cipher. Published on June 7, 1942 in the *Chicago Tribune* and its sister newspapers, Johnston's story revealed to Tokyo what Nagumo had dared not confess. The Japanese code was changed three days later, although Allied code-breakers had already made substantial in-roads into deciphering its replacement.

Midway also cleared the way for the first mass Allied offensive of the Pacific War, on August 7, 1942 at Guadalcanal, dismissed at first by the Japanese merely as a raid, not as the tip of an invasion.[3]

When Japanese reinforcements landed two weeks later in a belated effort to remove the attackers, they were all but wiped out by the U.S. Marines, and their commanding officer committed suicide in atonement. Fighting wore on throughout the summer, between two relatively evenly matched forces, although the Japanese were cut off from significant resupply, while the Allies were not—in this, as in subsequent reporting of the Pacific War, I continue to write of "Allied" forces, since although the story is often told as a primarily American narrative, the U.S. majority were accompanied by personnel from, among others, Britain, Canada, Australia, New Zealand and the British Commonwealth.

The starving remnants of the Japanese defenders on Guadalcanal evacuated on New Year's Eve, over which time Tōjō had come to realize that his Navy colleagues had failed to appreciate the enormity of the American assault, and his Army colleagues had not informed him of their disadvantages until it was too late to provide adequate reinforcements. Remnants of the Japanese forces were evacuated, with face-saving claims that they were merely "a strategic withdrawal"—the first of many strategic withdrawals that the smarter reader of the Japanese press would start to understand were happening ever closer to the home islands. One surviving officer wrote of his experience, describing a war that was anything but the military glory promised to Army recruits. Instead, his war was one of endless hiding in the jungle, of a starvation diet of roots and

---

[2] Wilson, "Film and Soldier," p. 540.
[3] Hoyt, *Warlord*, p. 123.

grass, of dozens of cuts and scrapes from weeks in hiding, flies on his scabs, and thoughts of suicide.[4]

Some, however, mounted what the Allies called "banzai charges"—foolhardy, often hopeless advances, relying on surprise and shock. The name derived from the phrase reported by survivors of the assaults, the recurring battle-cry of *Tennō Heika Banzai* ("Ten Thousand Years to His Majesty the Emperor"). It was the Allies' first encounter with the kind of battlefield fanaticism that had been nurtured by a generation of propaganda and State Shintō—soldiers willingly charging to their deaths, in the vain hope of taking just a few enemies with them.

It was often cited not as an example of outrageous resolve, as it had been in earlier wars in which the Allies had not been the enemy, but as yet another example of the outrageous, inhuman savagery of the Japanese. Reporting back in the U.S. capitalized on decades of anti-Asian racism, now given a new impetus by dehumanizing propaganda. Guadalcanal, noted one article, was a "hunter's paradise... teeming with monkey men." In an effort to downplay the huge losses of life in the Pacific theater, U.S. reporters likened it to a hunting trip—"like many of their comrades they were hunting for Japs, just as they used to go after small game in the woods back home," commented a cover story in *Life* magazine. Advertising also cashed in, with one ammunition company juxtaposing a picture from Guadalcanal with an image of a hunter taking aim at a mountain sheep: "Now Your Ammunition is Getting *Bigger* Game." Such rhetoric even worked its way into military recruitment, with one U.S. Marine poster offering "Jap Hunting Licenses."[5]

In an era when one in four American males could be described as sports hunters, Guadalcanal was the first documented occasion in the Pacific War in which U.S. soldiers were observed taking "trophies" from the battlefield. Reports of such incidents began to show up in the American press, and in concerned memos within the armed forces, including accounts of an intra-force trade in skulls and teeth (both human and more valuable gold replacements), or of skulls, rib bones and ears sent home to loved ones.[6]

In May 1943, U.S. and Canadian forces retook the remote island of Attu, Alaska. Attu had been the high-water mark of Japan's "conquest" of

---

[4] Ienaga, *Japan's Last War*, p. 144.
[5] Dower, *War Without Mercy*, pp. 89–90; Harrison, "Skull trophies," p. 821.
[6] Harrison, "Skull trophies," pp. 823–4.

the United States. It was, surely, clear to all that if the Attu toehold had been lost, the Japanese were on the retreat. But reporting of the defeat carefully avoided such an idea. Territorial gains were not the only reason for fighting—Tōjō's plan remained one of dragging the Allies to a stand-still, and gaining some sort of conditional armistice that allowed Japan to retain much of its imperial gains. This, in turn, meant that even a defeat could be a win if it helped wear down the enemy's resolve, and made the Allies fear approaching too close to the Japanese home islands. And so, the loss of Attu, in which only 28 Japanese soldiers were taken alive from over 2,000 stationed on the island, was announced as some sort of spir-itual triumph. The media did not run the risk of reporting a "strategic withdrawal" like that from Guadalcanal; now, even the loss of territory was a victory of some sorts, because of the way that Japan had lost it.

Attu was announced on-air as a moving exemplar of Japanese cour-age, and the radio played "If We Go to Sea," as if to suggest that this was all part of Tōjō's plan. He answered the news of the fall of Attu with a huge increase in factory output of Japanese fighter planes, although he does not seem to have considered if, post-Midway, Japan would be able to train enough pilots to fly them. While the Japanese ships and carri-ers lost at Midway could be, and would be replaced, the loss of trained air and ground personnel would have a palpable effect on Japanese air power within the year.

There was also a notable change in the tone of Tōjō's rhetoric. Pre-vious speeches had frequently mentioned that Japanese victories were sure to carry them all the way to Australia—an idle boast from the start. Now, Tōjō subtly shifted to a new strategy, not of wild expansion, but of careful curation of what Japan could conceivably hold onto. The grand plan, it seemed, was now to cling to the Greater East Asia; doing so would require fighting the Allies to a stalemate.[7]

---

[7] Hoyt, *The Kamikazes*, p. 24; Keene, *So Lovely a Country*, p. 37. Stanley's *Invading Australia*, p. 224, offers a book-length account of shifting perceptions regarding Japan's intentions with regard to Australia, but quotes from Tōjō's own war crimes testimony, and an interview conducted shortly before Tōjō's execution, in which he admits that Japanese strategy, lacking the manpower to ever realistically mount an invasion, never extended beyond raids. Stephan's *Hawaii Under the Rising Sun*, p. 167, reports a similar drop-off in rhetoric, in which a "torrent of [Japanese] books on Hawaii in 1942," proposing it as the future westernmost edge of Japan's empire, "dwindled to a trickle in 1943 and virtually dried up in 1944."

A Japanese reporter in Buenos Aires, able to read both the official Japanese account of Attu, and the American version, issued a prediction that both sides would have accepted: "Attu will probably be the model for the Japanese army in future warfare."[8]

Following the Attu defeat, the Emperor's Aide-de-Camp, Jō Eiichirō, observed that "In recent times, 'moving stories' from the frontline, in many cases appear [intended] to make up for operational deficiencies."[9] The media spun the Attu defeat as a "tremendous stimulant to the fighting spirit of our nation."[10] Little mention was made of the evacuation of nearby Kiska, from which Japanese troops slipped away in heavy fog without the need to mount a suicidal attack, or that the wounded Japanese soldiers who "committed suicide" on Attu were often the victims of grenades tossed into their hospital tents by their own comrades. Instead, the newspapers seized on the romantic poetry of Japanese soldiers giving their lives. The *Asahi Shinbun's* competition winner was the "National Award Song for the Bloody Battle Heroes of Attu Island" (*Attu-tō Kessen Yūshi Kenshō Kokumin Uta*), which praised the brave efforts of one Colonel Yamasaki Yasuyo, as he and his men face the onslaught of "20,000 enemies," attacking not only from land, sea, and air, but also from north and south. Multiplying actual casualties by a factor of ten, the song claims that the Japanese managed to kill 6,000 enemies, knowing that help will never reach them across the cold ocean.

> There is no other plan
> But to leave the military name unsullied
> The wounded take their own lives,
> And fight on with their souls and spirits.
>
> Some one hundred brave soldiers yet remain
> And bow in prayer towards the Imperial palace
> Then, screaming a war-cry in unison
> They **shatter as jewels** (*gyokusai su*) upon the enemy force
>
> For the glory of the Emperor's army
> So that such virtue may endure forever

[8] Keene, *So Lovely a Country*, p. 34.
[9] Sato, "Gyokusai," p. 9.
[10] Toland, *Rising Sun*, p. 770.

Let us follow [the example of] such loyal spirits
And crush the hideous enemy.[11]

Gyokusai, the shattered jewel of suicidal loyalty and virtue, had now turned into a verb. It had also become an official military designation, first appearing in official documentation in the account of Attu, a marker to be appended to a particular kind of glorious defeat, to be spun as a spiritual victory, to inspire the Japanese and terrify their enemies in equal measure.

The Japanese media became ever more martial in tone. Playing music with no military relevance on the radio was now frowned upon, while clampdowns increased on seditious foreign songs. Although Anglo-American music had been banned since the attack on Pearl Harbor, many popular tunes endured on the radio and at public gatherings. Sometimes this was because many Japanese genuinely did not know that certain golden oldies were of foreign origin; in other cases, a matter of personal preference. But as the war became gravely serious, there was a renewed drive to rid Japan of American and British songs, on the grounds that they were "a disclosure of nationalities characterized by frivolity, materialism and paying high regard to sensuality." Menaces to society such as "Home on the Range," "Alexander's Ragtime Band" and the works of Stephen Foster were purged from the airwaves, both in Japan and around the empire.[12] Similarly, in Korea, there had been complaints from the Governor-General that too many Korean songs were melancholy and dispiriting, and that menfolk should be discouraged from listening to things like "Arirang," and allow themselves to be stirred into action by more martial songs. Perhaps finally acting on the fact that many of the "Arirangs" being performed in Korea were in fact coded anti-Japanese protests, even Korean folk songs were now ordered to be sung compulsorily in the "national language," (i.e. Japanese).[13]

The degree to which "enemy music" (*tekisei ongaku*) had infiltrated Japanese culture eluded many levels of society. Prime Minister Tōjō himself was visibly surprised when he was told that "Auld Lang Syne," a common school song since 1881, the traditional final evening number at many a Tokyo dance hall, and even a standard performance at Navy

---

[11] Osada, *Sensō ga Nokoshita Uta*, pp. 710–12.
[12] Mitsui, *Popular Music in Japan*, loc. 1471.
[13] Atkins, "The Dual Career of 'Arirang,'" p. 667.

graduation ceremonies, was a foreign tune.[14]

Tōjō's switch from an offensive to a defensive war became an official policy in September 1943. He agreed with the Emperor that the Japanese empire would have an Absolute Defense Line, which it would hold against all Allied attacks, and which could not be breached. Islands in the Pacific outside the line would be held simply as a delaying action.

Island defense, which had previously been a primarily Naval matter, was now left in the hands of the Army—an institution ill-prepared for holding tiny parcels of land, surrounded by sea. Forty battalions, mainly of conscripts with relatively little or no battle experience, were pulled out of barracks all over the empire, from Manchukuo to the Philippines, and scattered among Japan's island holdings in the Carolines and the Marshalls, in units of 2,000 men. At least one literally comprised raw recruits, the newly minted 52nd Division, only just formed in Kanazawa and shipped straight off to Truk.[15]

The next battle to be reported in Japan as a *gyokusai* event came that November, where a U.S. force, including seventeen aircraft carriers, commenced amphibious landings at the Tarawa atoll in the Gilbert Islands. Japanese soldiers dug themselves into dozens of concrete pillboxes along the shore, backed by four aging eight-inch artillery pieces—leftovers from a British arms deal made at the time of the Russo-Japanese War.[16]

After four days of fighting, which had been preceded by three thousand shells fired into the beach by U.S. cruisers and battleships, the remaining Japanese units began mounting "banzai charges" against the U.S. soldiers. At the end of the 76 hours of fighting, only 17 of the 3,636 defenders of Tarawa were left alive.

In December 1943, the Ministry of Education and the Imperial Rule Assistance Association (the replacement for Konoe Fumimaro's National Spiritual Mobilization Committee) adopted the miserable, deathly dirge "If We Go to Sea" as an unofficial "second national anthem," insisting that it be sung at every assembly and gathering to raise the morale of the Japanese people—it seems however, to have been intended less to

---

[14] Atkins, *Blue Nippon*, p. 151. The Japanese know the song as "The Fireflies' Light" (*Hotaru no Hikari*).

[15] Peattie, *Nan'yō*, p. 263.

[16] For a long while, the guns were controversially believed to have been captured from the British at Singapore. It was not until 1977 that the writer William H. Bartsch tracked down the serial numbers and confirmed with the Vickers arms manufacturer that the guns were from a legitimate trade in 1905.

raise morale than to manage expectations of further disasters to come.

At Kwajalein in February 1944, another "shattered jewel" event failed to keep the U.S. Marines from the shore. Hailed again as a triumph by Japanese military reports, only 51 survivors were left from a garrison of 3,500. A U.S. carrier-based air assault two weeks later on Truk, the largest Japanese naval facility in the Pacific, did not merely cost the Japanese a dozen military vessels, but an even greater number of transports, oilers and tenders, along with 200,000 tons of precious fuel.

Truk represented a breach in Tōjō's ultimate defensive line, putting the islands of Saipan and Tinian on the hitlist for the U.S. Navy. If *they* fell, the Allies would have access to runways, putting subsequent targets in the Marianas, Philippines and Taiwan in range of B-17 bombers. Moreover, the new B-29 Superfortress bombers, with twice the range of the B-17, would be in striking range of the Japanese homeland—the islands had previously been described by the Japanese as "unsinkable carriers" (*fuchin kūbo*), but could just as easily perform that function for the enemy.[17]

Tōjō answered the threat with predictable over-confidence, transferring the Army Minister Sugiyama to a lesser role, and taking on his post himself, along with that of Prime Minister. Sugiyama wrote to the Emperor in protest, pointing out that if Tōjō were the Army Minister, the Prime Minister, the Munitions Minister (in charge of the nationalized planning bureau) *and* the Chief of Staff reporting directly to Hirohito, then Tōjō was effectively a new Shōgun, with dictatorial control of Japan in the Emperor's name.

With the Navy having failed to keep out the enemy, Tōjō turned instead to the Army, proposing a ridiculously ambitious push through China into India. This, he hoped, would secure the victory on the Asian mainland that Japan had failed to secure in the previous thirteen years, magically freeing two million soldiers to be pulled away to the Pacific front. The plan, however, called not merely for doubling of efforts, but for super-human achievements that were physically impossible. Even the logistics documents prepared for the India assault made it clear that the soldiers would not have enough food for the journey, unless they were somehow able to move, on foot, three times faster than mechanized

---

[17] Hoyt, *Warlord*, p. 178. In 1983, the Japanese Prime Minister Nakasone Yasuhiro would use the same term to describe Japan itself as a U.S. ally in the Cold War.

infantry. Their guidebooks unhelpfully suggested that they eat the oxen that were supposed to carry their heavy equipment, or failing that, as they then lugged their heavy equipment themselves, they might have to eat grass. An officer who openly called the plan stupid (*bakamono*) was punitively transferred.[18]

Answering such a call to arms would require the Japanese to double yet again their already severe austerity measures and dedication to the war effort, leading Tōjō to make an emergency broadcast in February 1944, calling on the people of Japan to answer their nation's call with "100 million shattered jewels." As in previous broadcasts since the day of Pearl Harbor, his choice of number added 30 million subjects of the Japanese empire to the 70 million inhabitants of the home islands.[19]

A second Allied group was closing in further to the west. General Douglas MacArthur, fulfilling a promise to return to the theater of war when the time was right, was heading through the Dutch East Indies. In the course of a prolonged battle, stretching from May to August 1944 of MacArthur's combined U.S.-Australian force finally snatched the island of Biak, ideally suited for airfields that could help support the efforts of the U.S. elsewhere in the region.

Lieutenant General Numata Takuzō, chief of staff in the Japanese 2nd Area Army, had been unlucky enough to have been on Biak when the assault began. Realizing that the defenders' cause was ultimately hopeless, he arranged for a float plane to pick him up—he would live on to surrender to the British Army in Rangoon several months later. Numata left behind the local commander, Colonel Kuzume Naoyuki, who fought on for two more days, before burning his regimental colors to indicate to his men that none of them would get off the island alive. Kuzume committed suicide, by *seppuku*, on the June 28, leaving his men to fight on without him for several more weeks. This, too, was classified as a *gyokusai* event by an increasingly *gyokusai*-hungry headquarters, although nothing was mentioned of Numata's decision to fight another day.

Fighting on Biak was still underway as the U.S. advanced on Saipan, regarded by the Japanese as the last line of defense before fighting edged over the line from imperial possessions into Japanese home territory.

---

[18] Hoyt, *Warlord*, p. 185.
[19] Sato, "Gyokusai," p. 2.

Defenders on the island lacked serious Navy support, with most of Japan's nearby naval strength assigned to a futile attempt to retake Biak. By the time sea-borne support made it north again, the U.S. fleet was waiting, in what would become known as the "Great Marianas Turkey Shoot," in which the U.S. Navy shot down all but a hundred out of 430 Japanese planes, and sank three aircraft carriers. By this point, the Japanese were being defeated not merely by the enemy, but often by failures in their own logistics—in many cases, untrained pilots, supported by rookie ground crews, launching planes built in under-supplied factories by inexperienced workers and inadequate quality control. Nor were they well served by their own admirals, whose inability to coordinate attacks from separate carriers reduced the effectiveness of their overall military force.

The fight cut off the Japanese on Saipan from resupply, but the fighting continued from cave to cave, often with indiscriminate attention paid to whether a bolt hole contained civilians or combatants until after a flamethrower or grenade had been applied.

As victory approached, the Allied soldiers witnessed a new and terrible phenomenon, of hundreds of civilians leaping to their deaths from the shoreline features later named Suicide Cliff and Banzai Cliff. Military survivors of the deaths at Saipan later admitted that they had all been subjected to lectures on *The Field Service Code*, with its insistence that death was better than capture.[20] One such casualty was Admiral Nagumo Chūichi, the commander of the fleet that had attacked Pearl Harbor, who shot himself on Saipan to avoid capture. The civilians, however, had also been repeatedly told of the dire fates that awaited them if they were captured by the enemy, by a propaganda machine that not only promised rapes and tortures, but supplied evidence from American media to back it up, excerpting texts and images from some of the U.S. reporting on trophy-taking that had been a phenomenon since Guadalcanal. Notably, two days before the landings commenced on Saipan, even President Roosevelt had been dragged into the trophy-taking controversy, after he was presented with a letter-opener carved from the arm bone of a Japanese soldier. Caught up in the media backlash about trophy-taking, Roosevelt subsequently returned the gift with a note that it should be given a proper burial.[21]

[20] Victoria, *Zen War Stories*, p. 140; Harries and Harries, *Soldiers of the Sun*, pp. 432–3.
[21] Harrison, "Skull trophies," pp. 825–7.

Saipan spelled the end of Tōjō's career. He came within a hair's breadth of being assassinated by self-righteous military men not unlike his younger self, when senior officers inadvisably revealed to the Emperor's brother, Prince Mikasa, that they were planning to throw a bomb at his car in the third week of July. The prince immediately reported the conspirators, who were arrested and imprisoned.[22]

Tōjō was losing his posts, but hoped to reshuffle his cabinet. He was headed off by his long-time colleague, the Munitions Minister Kishi Nobusuke, who suddenly announced that there were sure to be air-raids in future, and that they would make it impossible for him to carry on his responsibilities for maintaining the manufacturing economy. In theory, unable to carry out his job, Kishi should have resigned, but he refused to do, on the grounds that this was not a situation of his own making, and that the whole cabinet would have to resign with him. Kishi's remarks carried with them a prophetic portent—that Saipan would undoubtedly mean air-raids, and air-raids would ultimately mean defeat, and there was no way that Tōjō's policy could continue, regardless of who took over.

On July 18, Tōjō dissolved his cabinet, claiming that he had only held onto his posts for so long in order to keep the government from falling into the hands of officials proposing an unconditional surrender. His enemies, he thought, were the *jushin* ("great counselors"), a group of imperial advisers largely comprising former prime ministers, which had served a similar unconstitutional, undefined role as the *genrō* of earlier generations. Former prime ministers, of course, included earnest advocates for not attacking the United States in the first place.[23]

Tōjō had failed as a guarantor of the militarist dream. His three years in power as the de facto dictator of Japan had not delivered on any of his promises. The war in China was still raging; his push towards Burma had failed; *gyokusai* "victories" in the Pacific were occurring ominously closer and closer to the home islands. His successor as Prime Minister, General Koiso Kuniaki, was the same officer whose report in 1915 on national mobilization had helped create many of the conditions that Japan now found itself in. Factories were operating seven days a week, now staffed increasingly with teenage boys and girls conscripted into the war

[22] Toland, *Rising Sun*, p. 906.
[23] Butow, *Tōjō and the Coming of the War*, p. 433.

effort. Extreme austerity measures bit into the food supply; newspapers now only came out in single, daily, much-reduced editions. Trains were so crowded and unreliable that there were increasing reports of vandalism as passengers took out their anger on the railways. Tōjō's own wife, herself something of a minor radio celebrity during his tenure, had started to receive multiple anonymous phone calls demanding that her husband set a date for his suicide.

Tōjō's successors, however, had inherited the same mess. Regardless of whether Tōjō the war-monger had been ushered into retirement, they still faced the oncoming Allies, and sat in notional control of a feuding Army and Navy, neither of which was prepared to back down on its hard-won colonial possessions.

"Optimistic war policies can no longer be implemented," admitted a confidential report from the War Guidance Group. "All that remains is to await the enemy's abandonment of fighting spirit due to 100 million shattering jewels."[24]

The implications were soon clear, as U.S. bombers appeared in the skies, at first over Kyūshū, and then other population centers. The 1944 song "Enemy Fires" (*Teki no Honoʼo*) attempted to turn it into a rallying call for further efforts.

> Hateful wings defile the blue sky of my homeland.
> Fury boils up in my heart, I clench my fist.
> See their insolent silhouettes!
> I shall break all the wings of our enemy
> Soon, to take revenge. […]
>
> Should my house be blown away and turned into a field
> My firm resolve shall not fade. My blood is boiling.
> Listen, American devils
> It's your turn. We're on our way.
> Soon, to take revenge.
>
> I woke up with a start, what am I praying?
> My desires and those of my brother are the same.
> Fly to their towns!

---

[24] Handō, *Seidan*, p. 269.

Drop the bombs! Let us all shout!
Never forget, to take revenge.[25]

There was little means of "taking revenge," since the Allies were now closing in. Conscripted into the Army and assigned to a military hospital in 1944, the psychologist Asai Toshio filed a report into some of the patients, observing that many previous diagnoses that inmates were "mentally deficient" were over-simplistic. Asai did not find the patients merely stupid—he thought that many of them were actually psychopaths, demonstrating a tendency to commit crimes within six months of conscription. But as with earlier psychological evaluations of Japanese soldiery, the assessment exonerated the Army itself—Asai's advice, echoing his predecessors, was better screening of conscripts *before* they joined the Army, not more careful treatment of them once in it.[26]

By 1944, however, the Army could ill afford to turn away any able-bodied man. Despite such advice, internal memos suggested that in the interests of keeping up troop levels, only the very worst psychopaths should be kept out of military service. "Mild" psychopaths, whatever that meant, were allowed into the ranks in the hopes that they could be "trained and guided."[27]

Such phrasing indicated a morose acceptance within the military that manpower itself was falling, that new soldiers were being recruited from a diminishing pool of candidates, rushed through slip-shod training regimes, and then sent out to fight with inadequate equipment. General Yamashita Tomoyuki, now overseeing the doomed defense of the Philippines, admitted as much to his men by calling upon them to become "human pillars" (*hitobashira*), sacrificial victims whose sole duty was to delay the enemy advance to buy time for Japan.[28] At Peleliu, in November 1944, the leaders of the crumbling Japanese forces committed suicide after transmitting the code signal for their lost base: "Sakura, Sakura."

As the defense of Japan turned steadily more desperate, the idea of "human bullets" was resurrected. Reports drifted in of soldiers with explosive charges strapped to their bodies, throwing themselves under tanks and personnel carriers. But a more fearsome form of suicide

---

[25] Osada, *Sensō ga Nokoshita Uta*, p. 708.
[26] Matsumura, "Combating Indiscipline," p. 86.
[27] Matsumura, "Combating Indiscipline," p. 94.
[28] Sato, "Gyokusai," p. 3.

squad was undergoing training at numerous sites around the empire, as the both Army and Navy flight schools turned to ever more desperate measures. It was difficult enough reaching the war's requirements for planes and ammunition, but pilots, too, were in short supply. The casualty rate had reached such a volume that it was proving hard to train replacements. New training regimes rushed cadets through flight school, but produced graduates who could barely get a plane into the air, lacking the usual training in aerobatics, combat or navigation, and with fuel shortages reducing their flight experience. Even the fuel was not what it had been, with corners cut on aviation fuel from 92 to 87 octane, reducing the efficiency and longevity of the engines. For the Navy, a pilot was supposed to have four hundred hours in the air to be trusted to take off and land from an aircraft carrier; eight hundred hours to be effective once airborne. The Navy's latest crop of new flyers had each had barely two hundred flying hours before graduation. There were attempts to put them to work on carriers, but the first attempts saw a huge increase in the number of training accidents. With grim humor, the doomed rookies came to be known as the black-edged cherry blossoms (*kurobuchi no sakura*), a reference to a variety of the flower that was thought to fall too early.[29]

This was not how their performance was reported in the Japanese media. On October 16, 1944, the Japanese news media reported an outstanding victory in the seas off Taiwan and Okinawa, in which the Navy had sunk ten U.S. aircraft carriers in a single battle, along with two battleships, three cruisers and a destroyer. Such a victory was a clear indicator that Japan was holding the line, and inflicting crippling damage on the enemy. The writer Itō Sei wrote triumphantly in his diary that the Navy had finally delivered on its "decisive battle" (*kantai kassen*) strategy, and that American power in the Pacific would take years to recover. All the suicidal sacrifices, it seemed, had been worth it.

> The decisive battle was fought in an unbelievably short time. I would like to tell our men who committed *gyokusai*, not only on Saipan, Tinian and Guam but on Attu, the Gilbert Islands, Kwajalein, Ruot and other places what has happened.[30]

[29] Hoyt, *The Kamikazes*, pp. 20–21. As a point of comparison, the average USAAF pilot at this time would have clocked 430 hours.
[30] Keene, *So Lovely a Country*, pp. 53–4. There was a battle in the area on around the

It was, however, entirely untrue—a fictional victory in a phantom battle, misreported even to the Emperor, who congratulated his admirals for a job well done. By the time Navy reconnaissance flyers reported that the American fleet was still very much intact, the news was too widespread to retract. Celebrations persisted in Japan, where the people presumed that the war was almost over, while their leaders desperately sought new solutions.

Serious discussions in Navy circles turned to tactics mirroring the Army's "shattered jewel" actions, including one that involved a carrier assault on the U.S. fleet in which the carriers would only have enough fuel for a one-way mission, and the pilots were expected to crash their planes into enemy ships.

Now outclassed by Allied aerobatic tactics and more powerful air-craft, the Zero fighters (and others) could still be remodeled as flying bombs, fixed with a modest-sized 250-kilogram explosive, and flown low across the water, before a sudden climb, and a gravity-assisted dive could theoretically smash it into an Allied target—even the explosives were cut-rate, since Allied dive-bombers were regularly equipped with 1,000-kilo loads. There were several reports of suicidal ramming in October 1944, but these incidents appear to have been independent actions by individual pilots. The first actual sortie by the Divine Wind Special Attack Units (*Shinpū Tokubetsu Kōgekitai*) was on October 25, 1944 at the Battle of Leyte Gulf, in which one of five planes successfully dodged anti-aircraft fire and ploughed into the flight deck of the escort carrier *U.S.S. St. Lo*. The resultant explosion of fuel and ammunition sunk the carrier. Over the next twenty-four hours, 55 more suicide planes fell out of the sky on the Allied fleet—47 struck targets with some degree of success, sinking five ships and seriously damaging 23 others.

With such results, the Special Attack scheme was rapidly expanded, not only with the training of further units, but with new options such as rocket-powered planes specifically designed to deliver an explosive payload—the Japanese called them "cherry blossoms," the Allies called them "*baka* bombs."

A six-year-old song about cherry blossoms had slowly evolved within multiple military academies, to become a hit. "Cherry Blossoms

---

date mentioned, but U.S. losses amounted merely to two cruisers damaged, versus 312 downed Japanese fighter-bombers.

of the Same Era" (*Dōki no Sakura*), now made oblique reference to the Special Attack Units.

> You and I are cherry blossoms of the same era
> Blossoming on the grounds of the same military school
> The flower that blooms is fated to fall
> Glorious to do so in for the sake of our nation [...]
> In a perfect dawn of a southern sky
> The first plane does not return. [...]
> Parted, parted we are, but
> In the treetops in the glorious capital,
> At the Yasukuni Shrine we shall bloom again.[31]

In Tokyo, a different Special Attack Unit was formed, expressly intended to bring down American bombers, and celebrated in the radio hit of January 1945. As the skies above Tokyo increasingly filled with B-29 bombers out of Saipan, shrugging off Japanese anti-aircraft fire, and raining bombs upon the city, there was little left for the Japanese media to do but speculate hopefully about the possibility of being saved by suicide attacks, as revealed in "Song of the Divine Wind" (*Kamikaze Bushi*).

> Blow, blow American storm
> It is but a drifting cloud, a blustering wind
> The Japanese islands are resolute
> A divine wind (*kamikaze*) will blow
> And consume the enemy
> Aye, aye, aye
>
> Ring, howl
> Firecrackers.
> They are only missed bullets, ricochets.
> A mole pops its head out
> Scowling up.
> Is it raining?
> Are those stars?
> Aye, aye, aye

---

[31] Osada, *Sensō ga Nokoshita Uta*, pp. 274–5.

The enemy's proud
Spineless dragonflies.
Swat them down in pieces.
Our three generations' desire
Shall strip off and crush
The masks of demons.
Aye, aye, aye

Our focus does not waver
Not even for an inch.
Oh, this is nothing, this morning storm.
Look and wonder at our daring.
Look at and hail the rising sun.
Aye, aye, aye.[32]

The characters *Shinpū* could also be read as *Kamikaze*, and indeed, one was a more poetic form of the other. Allied military interpreters and vernacular usage even in Japan tended to use the term *Kamikaze*, as it was more immediately evocative of the "Divine Wind" of the same name that had famously shielded Japan from a medieval invasion attempt.

The Tokyo Special Attack Unit, however, failed to reach its goals. Even stripped down to increase their range, the B-29s had superb aerial defenses, such that only a truly skilled pilot could even get close—by definition, the suicide pilots had not had enough training to be "skilled." According to U.S. reports, there were seventeen successful ramming attacks on B-29s in the skies over Tokyo, of which four damaged their target enough to bring it down.[33]

This low rate of success, and the failure of Tokyo's anti-aircraft batteries, left the B-29s free to drop incendiary bombs—calculated to cause the maximum damage in a city primarily comprising wooden buildings. Over 100,000 people died, but another million were left homeless—these

---

[32] Osada, *Sensō ga Nokoshita Uta*, pp. 492–4. The song definitely uses the term *Kamikaze* and not *Shinpū*—it has to, otherwise the lyrics don't scan.

[33] USAF, *Japanese Aircraft Industry in WW2*, pp. 33–6. Of the 18 Japanese airmen involved (one attacker was a two-seater), 11 died and 7 either parachuted to safety or were able to land after the collision. U.S. casualties amounted to 40 airmen. It is perhaps worth noting that both the Nazis and the Soviets also utilized ramming attacks mid-air—a lucky, glancing blow on the propellers or an aileron could bring a plane down just as well as a head-on collision.

remain contested figures, liable to have derived from Japanese attempts to *downplay* the extent of the damage, which did not merely cause an immense loss of life, but annihilated thousands of small cottage industries that supplied parts and piece-work for the war effort.[34]

The capture of Iwo Jima in March 1945 shut down one the main bases used by Japanese fighters in harassing the B-29s.[35] With a closer bolt hole to flee to in case of damage, they could now mount more effective raids on Japanese cities, although their next effective target was elsewhere. In an effort to disrupt Japanese shipping, B-29 raids in April 1945 seeded the waters off the Japanese coast with mines, shutting down three quarters of vital shipping routes, and crippling troop movements, and delivery of critical supplies. Operation Starvation, as it was termed, was designed to shut off the fuel, food and supplies that made Japan's fight even possible, driving the Japanese even further towards a *gyokusai* mindset in which suicidal attack was presented as the last remaining option. The author Yamada Fūtarō wrote of the Japanese desire for vengeance upon the bombers:

> Probably they do not recognize that the creatures living in the world below them are also members of the human race. No doubt they think of us as swarms of little yellow monkeys. […] That being the case, it is of course more than proper for us to wish to slaughter hundreds of thousands of Americans. […] It won't be enough to drag down to hell an American for each Japanese who dies. We will kill three of them for each one of us.[36]

Not all the Japanese were willing. The writer Watanabe Kazuo confessed that if he were handed a bamboo spear and told to charge invading Americans, he would prefer to simply surrender. He blamed the leaders of Japan for dragging the country into the mess it was in, and sardonically wrote punning new definitions of popular military slogans. *Gyokusai*, he suggested, was better rendered as "death out of despair."[37]

---

[34] Selden, "A Forgotten Holocaust." For facts and figures regarding the incendiaries and their use, see Harries and Harries, *Soldiers of the Sun*, p. 445.

[35] It had been hoped that Iwo Jima would also serve as a suitable base for fighters to escort bombers closer to Tokyo, but the distance proved too taxing on solo pilots.

[36] Keene, *So Lovely a Country*, p. 65.

[37] Keene, *So Lovely a Country*, p. 75.

War songs were repurposed to reflect the leadership's new, fanatical will for self-destruction. Inspired by the example of the doomed Petty Officer Katayama on the eve of Pearl Harbor, military singers came up with new words to the tune of "Song of Mount Baekdu" (*Hakutō-san bushi*), a 1934 elegy about the Korean border. In the light of the fate of so many young pilots, it was reimagined as the "Song of the Special Attack Units" (*Tokkō-tai bushi*).

> Weeping, I load
> Fuel enough for one way.
> Destination: Ryūkyū. A journey to the death
> A journey to the death.
>
> Once leaving the ground
> It means farewell to this world.
> I remember my mother's face
> My mother's face.
>
> Come rain
> At least you come down
> How painful for the ground crew.
> How painful.[38]

Conspicuously, the song refers to the Ryūkyū as the pilot's destination. Japan was no longer fighting in its imperial possessions, but on the outer edges of the home islands. Okinawa, the largest of the Ryūkyū Islands, was Japan's final chance to hold off an invasion of the home islands. It had also been regarded as such for over a year, so whereas Saipan's defenses were not complete when it was over-run by the enemy, Okinawa was a maze of concrete pillboxes, entrenchments and bastions.

It was hence an Armageddon for both sides—a commitment of the very last remaining resources of the Japanese Army and Navy, but also of the largest naval contingent assembled by the Allies in the Pacific War. The super-battleship *Yamato*, set out with only enough fuel for a one-way mission, while the aerial battle saw over a thousand Kamikaze planes in the air, sinking thirty-six British and U.S. ships. It was not

---

[38] Osada, *Sensō ga Nokoshita Uta*, pp. 291–2.

enough, however, to save the pride of the Japanese fleet.

By the time the island was in Allied hands, with photographs taken of the Stars and Stripes flying over Shuri castle, and dropped as leaflets over the disbelieving residents of Japanese cities, the defense of the island had cost 107,000 Japanese lives and the lives of more than 19,000 Allies, in what the Japanese referred to as the "Iron Storm" (*tetsu no bōfū*).[39]

Okinawa was also the last defeat of *The Field Service Code*, adherence to which had actually placed the defenders at a tactical disadvantage. It would have made sense, conceded the defeated Colonel Yahara Hiromichi, for him to have sent units to dig in further up the mountains, but he had rejected the idea because it would have involved ordering them to survive the battle in which any true soldier should have been eager to die.[40]

Worst of all, Okinawa spelled the culmination of Japan's militarist rhetoric. There was, in the Army's eyes, no civilian population to defend. Everybody on the island was expected to die in an agonizing war of attrition, in the vain hope that they might buy more time for defenders on the Japanese mainland. These included boys as young as thirteen in the Blood and Iron Imperial Corps (*Tekketsu Kinnōtai*)—illegally conscripted by the army as soldiers and suicide bombers, on the spurious grounds that they had all "volunteered." The Okinawan people regarded themselves, then and now, as caught between the dual indifference of the Japanese and Allied military, drafted as suicide soldiers, or shot at in their homes on the suspicion of being belligerents. As in Saipan, some of the Japanese casualties were civilian suicides and homicides, including parents killing their own children in preference to capture.

The casualty cost was so high that it caused a revision of U.S. expectations about the likely price of attempting landings on Japan. If three months on Okinawa were any indication, then the Allies were fated to lose *hundreds* of thousands of men in landings on Kyūshū or Honshū, in fighting that would only proceed inch-by-inch, against men, women and children. But it was only two weeks after Okinawa that the Potsdam Conference in Europe set out the Allies' specific terms for an end to the war in Japan in a joint statement from China's Chiang Kai-shek, Britain's Winston Churchill, and the new U.S. president Harry S. Truman

---

[39] Willbanks, "Okinawa," p. 291.
[40] Victoria, *Zen War Stories*, 141.

(Roosevelt having died in April). These included a return to the borders held by Japan before its imperial expansion from 1894, and the elimination "for all time of those who have deceived and misled the people of Japan into embarking on a world conquest." The Potsdam Declaration made it clear that the instigators of Japan's total war would be tried as criminals, and their influence dismantled, perhaps permanently. It ended by calling for the Japanese military's "unconditional surrender" as soon as possible, in order to prevent further bloodshed on both sides.[41]

The Potsdam Declaration alluded to the consequences of a Japanese refusal with a threat of "prompt and utter destruction." This was a reference to something else that happened two weeks after Okinawa—the Trinity atomic bomb test in New Mexico on July 16, 1945. A coded message regarding its success was sent to Truman in Potsdam.

> Doctor has just returned most enthusiastic and confident that the little boy is as husky as his big brother. The light in his eyes discernible from here to High Hold and I could have heard his screams from here to my farm.[42]

[41] Allen and Polmar, *Codename Downfall*, p. 119.

[42] Jones, *Manhattan*, p. 517.

CHAPTER 11

Merely Human

The prospect of atomic weaponry had been considered by both the Allies and the Axis powers. Japan's own researches had petered out in 1943, after a Navy-commissioned committee had determined that they were feasible, but that it was unlikely that either Japan or the Allies would develop them in time to use them in the war. Consequently, the Navy switched much of its development funding into radar, as a technology with more immediate application.[1]

Radar had its uses. Before dawn on August 6, 1945, for example, radar sites were able to notify the authorities that there were large groups of U.S. bombers inbound for five southern Japanese cities, leading to air-raid warnings early enough to get as many of the people on the ground into shelters. The all-clear was sounded in Hiroshima early in the morning, since there was only a single enemy plane in the sky.

The plane was the *Straight Flush*, one of three B-29s sent to assess weather conditions over the cities of Hiroshima, Kokura and Nagasaki. It transmitted a message to another inbound B-29, the *Enola Gay*, to the effect that cloud cover was minimal. "Advice: bomb primary."

At 08:15, Hiroshima's radio station abruptly ceased transmission. Phone calls could not get through, and telegraph lines went dead several miles outside the city.

Ten miles away from the sudden bright flash and the roaring explosion it had caused, the *Enola Gay* was buffeted in the air as if suffering

---

[1] Radar was not the only item. In March 1943, the politician Kamei Kanichirō founded the Holy War Technology Association (*Seisen Gijutsu Kyōkai*), a think-tank intended to apply high-tech solutions to pressing issues. One of its proposals, rejected as implausible, was from the science fiction author Kizu Tora, who suggested firing large quantities of tin foil into the air to confuse enemy radar. Allied technicians reached this conclusion independently, and would first employ it in July 1943 in raids on Hamburg, Germany, as Codename Window.

near misses from anti-aircraft fire. On the ground, 80,000 people were dead, or soon would be in the ensuing firestorm.

The men who had served on Japan's own abortive super-weapons project were flown to Hiroshima the following day to confirm U.S. claims—that the *Enola Gay* had dropped an atomic bomb. Top brass in Tokyo, however, remained defiant—the Navy Chief of Staff suggested that the Allies probably only had one or two more similar bombs, and that no single weapon should reverse the planned course for defending Japan.

The former Foreign Minister, Matsuoka Yōsuke, had spent much of the Pacific War years convalescing in bed from an illness. The man who compared Japan to Jesus crucified, who had run the Manchurian railways and brokered the alliance with Nazi Germany, had selected as his favorite bedside reading a life of Saigō Takamori, that same rebel who had once proclaimed it better to be a shattered jewel.

Shortly after Hiroshima, Matsuoka was summoned to a meeting with Army leaders, who were planning a guerrilla resistance. One group of suicide troops was to be stationed in Kyūshū to deliver a devastating blow to the first Allied landings. But the top brass would retreat into the mountains of Matsushiro, to a network of underground bunkers, constructed by Chinese and Korean slave laborers, intended to shield six thousand lucky aristocrats and businessmen from the coming apocalypse. As the time of the expected Allied landings approached, the elites fled to the bunker complex, while issuing orders to the rest of the Japanese in the region to defend the coastline "with rocks and swords."[2]

They would take the Emperor with them, to remove him from the influence of the peace-faction in Tokyo, while Matsuoka would be placed in charge of a new cabinet, committed to continuing the war. If the Emperor would not cooperate, he could be kidnapped, forced to abdicate and replaced with his brother, or his ten-year-old son Akihito.[3]

The Emperor, however, had been asking his ministers to sue for peace since June. He had given up all trust in claims of Japan's chances for victory, particularly after hearing that his subjects had resorted to making shovels out of American bomb shrapnel to dig their families out of ruined buildings. He faced repeated equivocations, prevarications and excuses from his war council, over the degree to which peace

---

[2] Driscoll, *Absolute Erotic, Absolute Grotesque*, p. 231.
[3] Lu, *Agony of Choice*, pp. 250–2. For his Saigō obsession, p. 254.

was possible, defeat would spell the end of the imperial institution, or the degree to which the Japanese people could be trusted not to rise up against their own rulers.

The Army Minister, Anami Korechika spent much of the first week of August claiming that the Allies only had one bomb, and that while Japan had certainly lost *militarily*, it was not possible to agree to the terms of the Potsdam Declaration, but was necessary to fight on in order to gain concessions. Even though the Emperor had suggested a cessation of hostilities, he had done so on the understanding that the *kokutai*—that nebulous national identity—would be preserved. This was, unfortunately, ambiguous enough for die-hard officers to argue that the Emperor was misinformed and needed to be saved from his own wrongful decision.

"Inasmuch as Japan was the one who started the war," noted Anami, "and inasmuch as American and British politicians feel that Japan's *kokutai* was the root cause of that act, they may insist on its complete elimination as a means of maintaining world peace."[4]

But it wasn't about the *kokutai*. It was about the wording of the Potsdam Declaration that specified the prosecution and dismantling of *those that had led Japan into war* in the first place. Under the terms of Potsdam, the end of the war would spell the destruction not necessarily of Japan, but certainly of the Imperial Japanese Army and the Imperial Japanese Navy. Japanese militarism itself was in a fight to the death.

The dropping of a second atomic bomb, on Nagasaki on August 9, made it clear that the U.S. had not been bluffing, at least about a *second* bomb. Japanese leaders suspected, rightly, that enemy supplies of atomic weapons were limited, and that itself was enough for the worst war-mongers to claim they were still prepared to tough it out. Of a far more immediate concern was the sudden entry of the Soviet Union into the war, with a surprise advance in Manchukuo on the same day. The official Soviet declaration of war came a few hours later, Pearl Harbor-style.

Manchukuo had been a military backwater since the signing of the Soviet-Japanese Neutrality Pact in 1941, while those soldiers of the Kwantung Army that had yet to be reassigned to the Pacific conflict had over-confidently believed that any attacker would cling to the

---

[4] Lu, *Agony of Choice*, p. 252. I have restored the original *kokutai* from Lu's translation of "national polity."

all-important railways. The Soviets, however, confounded Japanese expectations by sending the bulk of their forces along unexpected routes, the speed of their advance in some places limited only by their fuel. Paratroopers seized airfields and towns behind Japanese lines, in the hope of securing more supplies for the advancing divisions. Before long, Manchukuo was over-run and Korea was in their sights—an agreement had already been made with the U.S. to stop the Soviet advance at the 38th parallel, destined to be the initial border between the post-war North and South Koreas. Russian landings on Sakhalin Island made a crucial difference to Japanese plans for resistance. It had been believed that the Japanese would have weeks, or even months to prepare to resist an Allied invasion, expected to begin in Kyūshū. But now this new addition to the "Allies" had men on Sakhalin with orders to commence landings on Hokkaidō within ten days.

In the early hours of the morning of August 10, presented with the findings of a deadlocked cabinet, the Emperor remarked that he had no trust in the military's commitment to a "shattered jewel" suicidal defense.

"The experiences of the past… show that there has always been a discrepancy," he noted archly, "between plans and performance." With that in mind, despite the implications for the *kokutai*, he was ready to surrender.[5]

Plans went ahead to record the Emperor's address to the nation, the "Jewel Voice broadcast" (*gyokuon hōsō*) at the Imperial Palace. On August 14, his first attempt was deemed too soft-spoken, and it was his second take, high-pitched, clipped and so nervous as to skip over several words from the transcript, that was etched onto two phonograph records ready for the next day.

The Emperor's will was now, quite literally, a matter of record, but it would not be known to the people until its planned broadcast time at noon the following day. Unsurprisingly, junior officers of the Imperial Japanese Army attempted to seize control of the palace and halt the broadcast. They were, in effect, claiming to come to the defense of the *kokutai*—that dangerously undefined term that had been part of militarist rhetoric since it first appeared in the *Imperial Rescript on Education* in 1890.

---

[5] Frank, *Downfall*, pp. 295–6.

At 21:30 on the night of the 14th, Major Hatanaka Kenji and his men attempted to occupy the Imperial Palace, place the emperor under house arrest, and call for other soldiers loyal to the *kokutai* to participate in his coup. He lied to several accomplices that he had the support of Anami, the Army Minister (who was, in fact, committing suicide that evening somewhere on the other side of town), and killed the on-site commander who refused to authorize a forged order. With the phone lines cut, an anti-air-raid blackout in force and the outside world still oblivious, Hatanaka and his men conducted a frantic search for the all-important recording. At one point, they threatened the life of the palace chamberlain, Tokugawa Yoshihiro, a descendant of that same Shōgunal clan that had been deposed in 1868 by the men of Satsuma and Chōshū. Tokugawa however, refused to give in, and lied that he had no idea where the recording was.

As dawn neared, Hatanaka had still failed to find the recording, which was hidden with the Lord of the Privy Seal in a panic-room bunker beneath the palace. Facing increased resistance from soldiers on-site, who were starting to realize that he was not acting with the approval of the Army staff or minister, he fled into the night. He showed up at the NHK radio headquarters at five in the morning, brandishing a pistol and demanding to be allowed ten minutes on air to explain his actions to the Japanese people. When this, too, was refused, he raced through the street on a motorcycle, scattering flyers outlining his beliefs. His coup attempt was effectively over by eight in the morning, but Hatanaka remained at large for a few more hours. An hour before noon—the appointed time of the Jewel Voice Broadcast—he shot himself.[6]

At midday, radios all over Japan began playing the national anthem, "Kimigayo," not the "If We Go to Sea" that had accompanied so many military announcements during the Pacific War. The Emperor's voice announced an "extraordinary measure" to be taken to save the life of his subjects, the acceptance of the terms of the Potsdam Declaration, in the wake of the enemy's use of "a new and most cruel bomb."

His terminology was editorially inconsistent—he referred to a war that had lasted "four years," not the more obvious fifteen. But he was as

---

[6] He did so in the plaza in front of the Imperial Palace, which I take to mean that he did so in sight of the statue of Kusunoki Masashige, the samurai emblem of unswerving loyalty, and an icon of the Kamikaze pilots. For more on the meaning of Kusunoki, see Saaler, *Men in Metal*, pp. 166–7.

clear as he could be, that the *kokutai*, whatever it was, was safe as long
as the Japanese obeyed, and "paved the way for grand peace for generations to come by enduring the unendurable."

Millions were dead, and millions more in a strange limbo—5.4 million Japanese soldiers still alive, half of them scattered across territory
that was just about to no longer be part of the empire. These men would
now have to come home, to a country in ruins, as would 1.7 million
Japanese colonists, no longer welcome in Korea, Manchuria, Taiwan or
elsewhere.

The war was not immediately over for everyone. In some scattered
outposts, there were attempts to hide evidence and pre-empt reprisals.
There are stories of comfort women herded into caves and executed,
and attempts to wipe out prisoners of war in some camps. In Hokkaidō,
to this day, there are periodic media campaigns that call for the recognition that hundreds of Japanese subjects also died *after* the surrender:
Sakhalin refugees sunk by the Soviets, or locals killed in air-raids. The
Soviets, in fact, continued to fight on Japanese soil for another month,
until the Kurile Islands were secure in Russian hands. Two days after
Japan's surrender was announced, there were arson attacks on the homes
of two former Prime Ministers. Four days after Japan's surrender was
announced, a group of U.S. B-32s were attacked by planes from the Japanese Navy, the pilots of which were acting, in time-honored tradition,
without the authorization of their superiors, or with pointless belliger-
ence regarding the fact that the surrender was not yet *officially* signed.

On September 2, aboard the aircraft carrier U.S.S. *Missouri*, representatives of the Japanese government and armed forces put their sig-
natures on Japan's instrument of surrender. In a move that has seemed
increasingly insensitive with the passing of the years, they were made to
do so beneath the Stars and Stripes flag that Commodore Matthew Perry
had hoisted in Tokyo Bay in 1853, as if this were somehow the long-
term fulfillment of Perry's gunboat diplomacy, with extreme prejudice.[7]

The round-up of Japan's military leaders, however, did not begin
immediately. Possibly the Supreme Commander of the Allied Powers
(SCAP), General Douglas MacArthur, had other calls on his time. Or
possibly, as some in the foreign press speculated, he was giving the architects of Japan's war, "those who have deceived and misled the people of

---

[7] Dower, *Embracing Defeat*, p. 41.

Japan into embarking on world conquest" in the words of the Potsdam Declaration, time to commit suicide.[8]

Not all of them obliged. At his home awaiting arrest as a war criminal, General Tōjō entertained a series of foreign journalists, telling them that he was solely responsible for the Pacific War, but that did not make him a war criminal. As to whose fault it was, he was more circumspect: "You are the victors and you are able to name him now. But historians 500 or 1,000 years from now may judge differently."[9] He also complained that Allied bombing had destroyed his three best pine trees.

On September 11, when U.S. troops arrived to officially arrest him, he attempted to shoot himself in the heart, but with a certain historical irony much remarked upon at the time by both the Japanese and Allies, somehow missed.

On November 30, 1945, MacArthur signed an order that dissolved the Imperial Japanese Army and the Imperial Japanese Navy. The organizations that had come into being in 1868, and had grown like tumors in the Japanese state, seizing all of its resources and steering its political direction into disaster, were no more.[10] Tōjō was just one of the many men rounded up and transported to prison, for preliminary interrogations towards their upcoming trials. Konoe Fumimaro, however, his predecessor as Prime Minister, was not one of them. Having been ordered to report to Sugamo Prison on an appointed day in December, Konoe held one last party for his friends, and then drank a fatal poison.

Konoe left behind a sensational memoir—an account of his wartime frustrations that laid much of the blame for the war at the feet of those two old Manchuria colleagues, Tōjō Hideki and Matsuoka Yōsuke. It amounted to an earnest defense of the Shōwa Emperor as a man deeply troubled by his military's actions, trapped in a constitutional position that was modeled on that of the British monarch, but invested with crucially and fatally nuanced duty to act and yet *not*-act. The entire document, which runs to 112 pages in its English translation, was serialized in the *Asahi Shinbun* in the ten days before the end of the year, and amounted to a long and absent testimony by the late Prime Minister, sure to be a major factor in the upcoming war trials.[11]

---

[8] Butow, *Tōjō and the Coming of the War*, p. 445.

[9] Butow, *Tōjō and the Coming of the War*, p. 448.

[10] Harries and Harries, *Soldiers of the Sun*, p. vii.

[11] Lu, *Agony of Choice*, p. 255.

The fanaticism instilled in Japanese soldiery, and the ongoing influence of the *Field Service Code*, left some of them reluctant to surrender. Ōba Sakae, at large in the jungle of Saipan for over a year, finally gave up on December 1, 1945. He was only persuaded that his mission was over when Major-General Umehachi Amō, who had been the commander of the Saipan forces during the original battle, ventured into the jungle and began singing "A Footsoldier's Duty" (*Hohei no Honryō*), an infantry anthem since 1911.

> Weeping cherry is the color of the collar
> The flowers in Yoshino blown in the storm
> Born as a Japanese man
> Be a fallen petal in a skirmish battle.

Ōba and his 46 men slowly emerged from the jungle, whereupon Umehachi showed them their orders from the now-decommissioned Imperial headquarters. As they marched down the mountainside to surrender, they continued to sing, incongruously, of "old history and white snow," and of a mindset that was now discredited and discouraged:

> This is the footsoldier's duty.
> Oh, our brave infantry arm
> Congenial spirits,
> Let's carry out our duties together.

In January 1946, the Shōwa Emperor issued another public decree, *the Imperial Rescript on the Construction of a New Japan*. It was framed as his New Year greeting, and as such was front-page news on all Japanese newspapers. In it, he called attention to the policies and laws of his grandfather, the Meiji Emperor, in such a way as to suggest that modern Japan had started off as a democracy in the making, but had been dragged away from this path, and that its current condition was the result of "a protracted war ending in defeat." Japan, he said, should pursue civilization through peaceful means. Then, he made an announcement designed to dismantle much of the rhetoric of the last few militarist decades:

> The ties between Us and Our people have always stood upon mutual trust and affection. They do not depend on mere legends

and myths. They are not predicated on the false conception that the Emperor is divine, and that the Japanese people are superior to other races and fated to rule the world.[12]

In other words, the Shōwa Emperor was not a godly, unapproachable being whose thoughts needed to be guessed at. He was merely human. He was just a man called Hirohito. And he was the most crucial part of the *kokutai* to preserve—a symbol of continuity, not with the last three awful decades, but with the glory days of his father and grandfather. He would become a pawn for the Occupation forces, who presented a new, and often welcome argument to the Japanese, that they had been swindled and gaslit by a militarist machine. The Allies were here to save the *kokutai*, as they now defined it, by stripping from it the last vestiges of the military-industrial complex.

During the period of the Allied Occupation from 1945–52, Japan's old empire was dismantled. The Chinese took over in Taiwan, the Americans in South Korea, the Soviets in North Korea and what had been Manchukuo. British and Commonwealth officers set about breaking up Japan's domestic war industries. Chiefly, however, it was the U.S. forces in Tokyo under Douglas MacArthur, the Supreme Commander for the Allied Powers, that set about the most sweeping changes—which would ultimately result in a rewritten constitution that introduced women's suffrage, education reform, trade unions and labor standards.

Military songs, once a staple of the classroom and ubiquitous on the radio in the first half of the 1940s, were now forbidden, along with the national anthem itself—censored from the airwaves and public events. Instead, the soundscape was crammed with happy pop songs, the long-banned sound of Anglophone music, and the foreign lyrics of the new hit program, the language-learning series *Come, Come, English*.[13]

One of the entertainments reserved for the Occupation personnel themselves was to be found in the Ernie Pyle Theater, the renamed Takarazuka Theater. In August 1946, SCAP authorized a production of Gilbert and Sullivan's operetta *The Mikado*, featuring over a hundred cast members, a chorus line that was almost wholly Japanese, and many Japanese backstage personnel. In an unexpected move, the organizers

---

[12] http://www.chukai.ne.jp/~masago/ningen.html
[13] Dower, *Embracing Defeat*, p. 174; for the national anthem, p. 208.

invited a number of Japanese critics and opinion-formers to a dress re-hearsal on the August 11—the production itself, like other Pyle perfor-mances, was out-of-bounds to normal Japanese. It was widely believed that this was a deliberate experiment on the part of Douglas MacArthur, to test the degree to which SCAP's Occupation reforms had taken hold with the Japanese in the previous year.

The Mikado had never been openly performed in Japan before.[14] By staging a production in Tokyo, the Allies not only flouted previous Japanese reluctance to stage a performance that might be said to dis-respect the Emperor, but also contravened their own Occupation laws. Singing of military anthems was forbidden, but The Mikado contained an identifiable section of Japan's first ever modern militarist song, "Mi-ya-san, Miya-san," much garbled in transmission over the previous 80 years. Nonsense lyrics to most of the Americans, but an evocation of a forgotten world for the Japanese:

> Miya sama, Miya sama,
> On n'm-ma no mayé ni
> Pira Pira suru no wa
> Nan gia na
> Toko tonyaré tonyaré na?

If the theater critic Eguchi Hiroshi worked out that his willingness to see the Emperor being satirized was being put to the test, he did not show it. The depiction of the Emperor in The Mikado was of less interest to him than the jaw-dropping, fantastical carnivalization of the world around him—outside, Tokyo lay in blackened ruins; in the theater, a lavish fan-tasy world of singing Japanese aristocrats, as imagined by foreigners, a vision of the abundance and energy available to the Allied victors, but also perhaps of the degree to which so many of them had no hope of ever comprehending Japan.[15]

---

[14] Cortazzi, *Japan in Late Victorian London*, p. 69, observes that a production called *Three Little Maids from School* was staged in Yokohama as early as 1887. It was *The Mikado*, albeit with a name-change designed to deflect censure.

[15] Rodman, "A More Humane Mikado," p. 293.

The psychologist Murayama Masao suggested that the mindset of the Japanese Army had locked into a vicious cycle of self-directed aggression, that could only be mitigated by committing atrocities against others. In the words of Janice Matsumura:

> Maruyama contended that an environment of brutality within the military had promoted a "transfer of oppression," whereby soldiers, constrained in taking revenge against abusive superiors, experienced psychological compensation in tormenting those under their control.[16]

Regardless of who might ultimately be to blame—the officers, or the System or the "alien game" that had invited the sons of the samurai onto the world stage and then made them fight to be accepted there, there would be a reckoning in court. Along with half a dozen sister tribunals across the former Japanese empire, Tokyo's International Military Tribunal of the Far East, which commenced in 1946, would spend many weeks deliberating what a "soldier's duty" was, as well as the nature of war crimes, crimes against humanity, and a new, controversial concept—*crimes against peace.*

Many of the architects of Japan's total war faced trial, along with the bit players in the slaughter that went along with it. The two men who competed with one another to be the first to execute 100 Chinese in Nanjing were both shot as war criminals. So, too, was Homma Masaharu, convicted in the Philippines for failing to prevent atrocities on the Bataan Death March, and Yamashita Tomoyuki, who, despite overwhelming evidence, ceaselessly maintained that he had known nothing of the multiple orders to torture and massacre Malays, Chinese and prisoners of war, but went to the gallows on the eighth anniversary of Pearl Harbor.[17] Horiuchi "the Octopus" Toyoaki, who had presided over battlefield executions by his paratroopers at Manado, would also be executed, claiming not to have known of the bloodbath initiated by his own junior officers.

Wartime definitions, however, also provided a cloak that covered some other statistics. Many of the most brutal camp guards had been

---

[16] Matsumura, "Combating Indiscipline," p. 80.
[17] People's Court Daily, *Trials of Justice,* p. 430.

Koreans, brutalized by their own Japanese superiors, and taking it out on their foreign captives. This, too, was a consequence of militarism, as was the zeal to hit work targets of the civilian engineers on the Thai-Burma railway, believed to have been a major cause of many Allied deaths.

The narrative of vicious prison-camp guards also concealed a number of nuances in the causes of deaths among Allied POWs. A forced march, or work on the Thai-Burma railway were two of the main causes of death among prisoners, but it was believed that many of those lives could have been saved if the prisoners had not been refused access to their Red Cross food parcels. In the aftermath of the war, one doctor claimed to have uncovered enough undelivered parcels of food and medicine to have equipped a hospital for three years—a significant element of the war crimes trials in Singapore revolved around the degree to which many deaths from "malnutrition and disease" had been caused by criminal neglect through theft or seizure of Red Cross parcels by the Japanese.[18]

If a man had *allowed* a war crime to happen, then he was a Class-C criminal under the definitions of the military tribunals. If he had *committed* the war crime himself, he was a Class-B criminal. Some 5,700 people would stand trial in those two categories. Twenty-eight higher-ranking individuals were prosecuted as "Class-A" war criminals, on the charge that they had deliberately led the Japanese nation into a war of aggression. Many of these Class-A accused have been mentioned in this book. Itagaki Seishirō, who defended atrocities in China as a necessary terror tactic, was hanged, as was Tōjō Hideki, executed after a long trial in which he was repeatedly chastised for trying to smuggle arguments for the continuation of Japan's militaristic policies into what were supposed to be statements for his personal defense. In the process, he sufficiently made a case for his own guilt, quite possibly as a deliberate act to draw culpability away from the Shōwa Emperor. Koiso Kuniaki, whose 1915 report had become the playbook for total war planning, died

---

[18] Sturma, "Japanese Treatment of Allied Prisoners," p. 533. Less well known, however, are the number of Allied prisoners of war killed through "friendly fire." Conservative estimates suggest that over 10,000 Allied prisoners died when the ships they were on were sunk by Allied attacks, such as the 1,500 Allied prisoners killed when *HMS Tradewind* sunk a Japanese transport ship in September 1944. However, it is more complicated than that—Sturma goes on to note cases such as the sinking of the *Rakuyo Maru*, also in September 1944, in which many of the Allied captives survived, but were left to die in the water by the Japanese rescue ships. This, too, would count as "ill-treatment by their captors." Ibid., pp. 516–7.

in prison in 1950. Former Army Minister Araki Sadao was sentenced to life imprisonment, but would be released on health grounds in 1955.

Matsuoka Yōsuke died before his trial, but not without issuing a stern rebuke to his interrogators, to the effect that Japan had *liberated* multiple nations in East and South-East Asia.

> That is why I said historical facts contradict your judgment of Japan. [...] Japan doesn't annex the Hawaiian Islands by intrigue, or the [Panama] Canal Zone, or we don't start the Spanish-American War and take over the Philippines... and we don't take Texas or other places as you did.[19]

Others found their own ways to escape. Tsuji Masanobu, who not only provoked the Soviets into the Battles of Kalkhin Gol, but arranged the *Sook Ching* purge in Singapore and the worst of the Bataan Death March, fled to China, leaving his commanding officer Homma and two of his subordinates to face the death penalty for his schemes.[20]

Ōkawa Shūmei, implicated in several coup attempts of the 1930s, and author of a book that claimed it was Japan's destiny to rule the world, was the only civilian to stand trial as a Class-A war criminal—like his former colleague, Kita Ikki, he was accused of inciting the military to insubordinate and unsanctioned actions, particularly the establishment of Manchukuo. However, attempts by the prosecution to depict him as a Japanese propagandist were undermined by his own behavior in the court room, which included showing up in pajamas, forgetting his shoes, and even slapping the bald head of Tōjō while the former Prime Minister sat in the dock. Pronounced mentally unfit to stand trial, he was sent to an asylum, where he managed a miraculous recovery, sufficient to allow him to complete his ongoing translation of the entire Quran. He was released in 1948 and lived for another decade, apparently not mad any more.

However, the judges in the war-crimes trials were not unanimous. Radhabinod Pal (1886–1967), an Indian jurist from what is now Bangladesh, issued a scathing dissenting opinion which ran to some 1,235

---

[19] Lu, *Agony of Choice*, p. 257.
[20] He resurfaced in Japan some years later, when he successfully ran twice for political office. He was implicated, possibly without cause, in a planned 1952 coup attempt, and disappeared, whereabouts unknown, in Laos in 1961.

pages in its original typescript form. In it, he raised his objection to the very idea of "Class-A" war criminality, on the grounds that the Japanese were being held to account for an offense that had been invented after the fact. Inconveniently for the tribunal that was attempting to assign culpability away from the Emperor and people of Japan onto a small cabal of conspirators, Pal called for all the Class-A cases to be dismissed, on the grounds that:

> The constitution of the state remained fashioned as before in relation to the will of the society… These accused came into power constitutionally and only to work the machinery provided by the constitution… THESE PERSONS DID NOT USURP ANY POWER, AND CERTAINLY THEY WERE ONLY WORKING THE MACHINERY OF THE INTERNATIONALLY RECOGNIZED STATE OF JAPAN AS PARTS OF THE JAPANESE FORCE WHICH WAS AT WAR WITH THE ALLIED POWERS…[21]

War, he argued, in and of itself, was not a crime: "We cannot afford to be ignorant of the world in which disputes arise."[22] Certainly, Japanese military personnel had committed many documented atrocities, for which Pal hoped they would be held accountable, but these were easily covered within the remit of Classes B and C. He found no evidence that there was an agreed-upon government-level conspiracy to drag Japan into war, and even if there had been, states did not possess a legal right to police the activities of other states. The Allies had bombed civilian targets; the Allies had knowingly vaporized the cities and people of Hiroshima and Nagasaki; there was ample evidence, he believed, that the U.S. had *provoked* the Japanese into war in the first place. Ignoring this, but punishing the Japanese for similar acts, he argued, could never be called "justice." It was vital, argued Pal, for the future integrity of the Allies and the new world order they were creating, that justice *be seen to be done*, not left open to cavils, quibbles or accusations of bias.

---

[21] Pal, *Dissentient Judgement*, p. 698. Caps thus in the original.
[22] Pal, *Dissentient Judgement*, p. 107.

The so-called trial held according to the definition of crime *now* given by the victors obliterates the centuries of civilization which stretch between us and the summary slaying of the defeated in a war. A trial with law thus prescribed will only be a sham employment of legal process for the satisfaction of a thirst for revenge.[23]

Judge Pal was not wrong about the notion of victor's justice. The Allied narrative remained one of warriors fighting for a just cause, bringing down the enemies of righteousness not unlike the Meiji Restoration rebels who had removed the Shōgun. But some of the war-crime tribunals seemed oddly haphazard. Some suspects, like the Shōwa Emperor remained untried, of greater use in the establishment of the new order; others, like many prisoners of the Australians, were released after time served. Still others were suspiciously co-opted into the new order of the approaching Cold War—Kishi Nobusuke, for example, awaiting trial as a Class-A war criminal, was sprung by the Americans to lead a new political party to head off Communist factions; or Ishii Shirō of Unit 731, who had, at the end of the war, been planning to unleash a September 1945 plague attack on San Diego, but was offered immunity in exchange for his findings and expertise on bacteriological weapons.

The new Japanese Constitution, which came into effect in May 1947, introduced universal suffrage, freedom of religion and political belief, and women's rights. A new and enduringly controversial clause, Article 9, went much further than MacArthur's abolition of the old Army and Navy institutions:

> Aspiring sincerely to an international peace based on justice and order, the Japanese people forever renounce war as a sovereign right of the nation and the threat or use of force as means of settling international disputes.
>
> In order to accomplish the aim of the preceding paragraph, land, sea, and air forces, as well as other war potential, will never be maintained. The right of belligerency of the state will not be recognized.

---

[23] Pal, *Dissentient Judgement*, p. 21.

So much, then, for Japanese militarism, written out of existence... albeit by a caretaker government under the heavy influence of American policymakers—a situation not all that different from the treaty demands of Commodore Perry in 1853. Japan no longer had an Army or a Navy, at least on paper. Instead, it had a "Self-Defense Force" (SDF), deprived of long-range assault capacity, and an economy that would rely increasingly on state-guided investments and connections, soon masterminded by some of the economic planners that had run Manchukuo.

More than half a million Japanese in Manchukuo, mainly soldiers but also some civilians, were imprisoned by the Soviets and put to work in Siberian labor camps and as far away as Kazakhstan. Some 473,000 were eventually returned to Japan, with the Soviets denying Japanese claims that 100,000 further internees were unaccounted for and presumed dead.

Exploiting the fact that the military prisoners had maintained their wartime rank and attitudes inside the camps, Soviet recruiters focused on the brutalized lower-ranking men as potential recruits as Communists; professing a belief in Communism came to be the only way to secure return passage. In May 1949, a group of repatriated Japanese soldiers, disembarking from a ship back home in Japan, ignored their welcoming committee, linked arms and sang "The Internationale," proclaiming that the Emperor was their enemy, and that they were intent on saving Japan through socialist revolution.[24]

Such incidents only served to entrench the Occupation forces into clampdowns against the left, particularly as China's own internal conflicts resolved in 1949 with a Communist victory against Chiang Kai-shek's Nationalists. Whereas the Occupation of Japan had begun with proclamations of open democratic debate, increasing paranoia over the Soviet Union and the newly proclaimed People's Republic of China led to backlashes against labor unions and strike actions, and a new stigma for returnees from Communist countries—disrespected in Japan for being former militarists *and* possible Communists.[25]

With the outbreak of war in Korea in 1950, Japan was rebranded as

---

[24] Watt, *When Empire Comes Home*, pp. 126–9.

[25] Some 32,000 repatriates trickled home from China, including a thousand men who had been convicted in China of war crimes, and a group of Japanese soldiers who had briefly fought on behalf of Chiang Kai-shek's Nationalists in the civil war against the Communists. Watt, *When Empire Comes Home*, p. 136.

a new unsinkable aircraft carrier for a new war effort. Even as Japan's Constitution proclaimed the renunciation of war, its factories were put to work making materials for the Korean War; its territory continued to host vast air- and sea-bases for U.S. military personnel, now obliged to fight on Japan's behalf.

When the Korean War ground to a halt, the occupiers withdrew from most of Japan, although the controversial Article 9 led to large-scale military bases on Japanese soil, intended to protect the demilitarized nation during the newly proclaimed Cold War. With military songs purged from the airwaves, radios played foreign tunes, or studiously inoffensive Japanese popular music, although some of the hits of the Occupation and post-Occupation era contained coded references to the lost empire, often through the evocation of place names or travel—"A Platform at Night" (*Yoru no Platform*), "The Returning Ship" (*Kaeri no Fune*) and "A Mother on the Wharf" (*Ganpeki no Haha*) alluded, however obliquely, to the long journey homewards of repatriated Japanese subjects, while "The Bell of Nagasaki" (*Nagasaki no Kane*) played up the rich Christian past of Nagasaki, wiped out by an atomic bomb. "Siberia Elegy" and "Hills of a Foreign Land" (*Ikoku no Oka*) played like the Continental melodies of a generation past, but instead of evoking the rich potential of migration overseas, served to remind listeners of the many Japanese servicemen who remained prisoners in the Soviet Union.[26]

One song in particular would become a *cause celebré* in post-Occupation Japan, written by two convicted war criminals awaiting execution in the Philippines, lamenting the fate of the 74 men on death row at a prison in the Manila suburb of Muntinlupa. It was first sung at the prison on April 29, 1952, the day after the official end of the Allied Occupation of Japan, when the guards even looked the other way and allowed the inmates to sing "Kimigayo," the national anthem forbidden during the Occupation years. The inmates' self-penned song "Ah, the Nights Go On at Muntinlupa" (*Aa, Muntinlupa no Yo wa Fukete*) was sent by the prison chaplain to the singer Watanabe Hamako, who had herself formerly been detained as a prisoner of war in China, where she had been an entertainer for the troops. Watanabe was struck by the song's evocation of a mother separated from her son, and the son's

---

[26] Watt, *When Empire Comes Home*, pp. 146–7. Watt goes on to note, pp. 180–1, that many of the "repatriation" songs have become part of the fabric of Japanese tourist sites, literally inscribed in stone.

desire to return to Japan, as well as the constant anguish over whether the next day would be his last, which led her to badger the boss of the Victor record company into letting her record it with Utsumi Kiyoshi singing the two male stanzas.

> The night in Muntinlupa goes on
> My heart grows fonder and I am disconsolate
> Thinking of my faraway homeland
> In the shadow of the Moon clouded with tears
> I dream of my kind mother.

> The sparrows have come back again,
> But when will my beloved son return?
> A mother's heart flies straight to the southern sky
> Calling out, like melancholy birdsong.

> When morning comes to Muntinlupa
> I harbor the rising sun in my heart.
> I shall live strong, again, today
> I shall not fall
> Until I step on the soil of Japan.[27]

After some polishing by a professional lyricist and composer, the song was recorded at a tearful studio session in Tokyo attended not only by the prisoners' families, but relatives of the 17 fellow inmates who had already been executed by a firing squad. Released in Japan that September, the song became emblematic of what music historian Osada Gyōji has called, the "shadow tragedy" (*kage no higeki*) of the Occupation era—the fact that even though peace had been restored to Japan, so many of the men of Japan remained detained overseas. It went on to sell 200,000 copies.[28]

---

[27] Osada, *Sensō ga Nokoshita Uta*, pp. 747–8; see also Dower, *Embracing Defeat*, p. 515. I follow Dower's orthography here for space reasons, although Osada is more exacting—the original title was simply "The Song of Montinlupa" (*Montenrupa no Uta*). The title I use here, also used in Dower, is that of the record released in September 1952, after the attentions of professional amanuenses.

[28] Osada, *Sensō ga Nokoshita Uta*, p. 749. Osada gives the date of July 4, although the Philippines' independence day is actually on June 20—this is liable to have been a translation error over whose independence day was being celebrated.

Watanabe adopted the cause of the prisoners of Muntinlupa as her own, visiting the jail in person that October to give a concert of some of her old wartime hits, and finishing off with the prisoners' own song. Pointedly, the prison chaplain again allowed the singing of the Japanese national anthem. The following year, a Buddhist monk presented Elpidio Quirino, the president of the Philippines, with a gold-lacquered music box that played the song, taking the opportunity to explain the story behind it. In July 1953, Quirino sent the prisoners home, commuting their death sentences to life imprisonment, and allowing that the time be served in a Japanese prison. All were released before the end of the year, the fact that they had been convicted in Manila of capital offenses conveniently forgotten.[29] After being demobilized in 1953, the song's composer Itō Masayasu was even hired by the Ground Self-Defense Force, and continued to rise through the ranks, ending his career as head of the Camp Fuji military school.

Among many purges, the Occupation forces had also shut down Takushoku University in Hokkaidō, on the grounds that it was indelibly associated with the military regime and the training of the agents of Japanese imperialism. It was reconstituted under a different name, regaining the Takushoku name in 1952 after the Americans left, and today is renowned as a leading institution in security studies. According to its homepage, the alumni association still occasionally likes to join in a rendition of the "Horse Bandit Song."

How institutions of education, particularly for the young, handled Japan's recent past remains an ongoing topic of debate. Insofar as schoolchildren are expected to inculcate a sense of civic or social awareness through their studies, the Japanese school system was presented with the problem of discussing decades of militarism that led to disaster. Much has been written outside Japan about Japanese schoolbooks, and particularly the extent to which they acknowledge the past crimes of

---

[29] No Japanese source I have seen discussing the Montinlupa song and repatriations has bothered to reveal what it was the men were sentenced to death *for* in the first place. People's Court Press, *Trials of Justice*, pp. 434–8 observes that the Manila trials were the first of many Allied war-crimes tribunals, and "set up a model for the Tokyo trials." Representatives for the accused attempted to argue that prosecuting officers showed a lack of professionalism and admitted hearsay evidence, although Song Jianqiang, in his account of the trial instead notes that this was a convenient gloss over the fact there was so much evidence against the accused that prosecutors often stopped reading it all out.

imperial Japan. But as noted by historian Hashimoto Akiko, the story is substantially more nuanced than much foreign press coverage allows. There are, in fact, multiple high-school history textbooks in use in contemporary Japan, some of which use disingenuously soft language regarding the land-grabs and invasions of imperial expansion, although others openly blame a cabal of militarist conspirators for Japan's "war of aggression," while others emphasize a "war of necessity," to which Japan was driven by external political and economic pressures. None of them glorify Japan's activities in Asia, or attempt to valorize the "war-gods" of old; the Japanese people themselves are usually presented as both the villains and the victims.[30]

For younger students, a notable inclusion in the post-war high-school curriculum was Yosano Akiko's controversial 1904 poem "Do Not Lay Down Your Life." Despite her saber-rattling verses of the 1920s and 1930s, Yosano was now remembered by posterity for her youthful denunciation of war. For a new generation in Japan, educated to reject the nation's recent militaristic past, Yosano's early works became compulsory reading, whereas her later writings were carefully forgotten.

In a Japan seeking a new pathway towards peace and democracy, "Do Not Lay Down Your Life" was set to music and turned into a pacifist anthem, sung by students protesting in the streets about Kishi Nobusuke, the former Manchukuo mastermind and wartime minister, whose anti-left stance had spared him the war-crimes tribunal. Kishi became Japan's Prime Minister in 1957, igniting the protests by revealing that he was ready to renew the U.S.-Japan "Anpo" Security Treaty, which continued to allow the presence of U.S. bases on Japanese soil.[31]

The very last Japanese soldiers to come back from the war did not arrive for another generation. Sergeant Yokoi Shōichi (1915–1997) had been aware since 1952 that the war was over, but remained in hiding on Guam, ashamed the break the terms of the *Field Service Code* by giving himself up.

"It is with much embarrassment that I return," he announced to the press in Japan upon his 1972 homecoming.

Two years later, Onoda Hirō (1922–2014), a Japanese commando on Lubang island in the Philippines, gave himself up to the authorities.

---

[30] Hashimoto, *The Long Defeat*, pp. 105–6.
[31] Rabson, "Yosano Akiko on War," p. 46.

Onoda had followed the *Field Service Code* to the letter, refusing to believe pamphlets dropped over the jungle, announcing that the war was over, even when one of them contained a direct order to surrender from General Yamashita Tomoyuki. As with the Saipan holdouts a generation earlier, he only gave up when approached in person by his own former commanding officer.

Since he had murdered over 30 local farmers and police over the previous three decades, Onoda might have reasonably faced trial as a serial killer. But with remarkably diplomatic empathy, he was granted a pardon on the grounds that he had still *believed* the war was ongoing. Onoda returned to a Japan unimaginably different from the country he had left behind, and although feted as an icon of the old samurai spirit, would eventually leave for Brazil, where he became a cattle farmer.

In December 1974, Private Nakamura Teruo (1919–1979), a naked man living on Morotai in Indonesia, was apprehended by the local army, who lured him out of the forest by singing the national anthem, "Kimigayo," which they had spent some time practicing in Japanese. When the singers then switched to the "Patriotic March" (*Aikoku Kōshinkyoku*), the 1937 "national song for the people to sing forever," Nakamura realized that they were not native Japanese speakers, and opened fire with his well-maintained Arisaka rifle, before eventually being persuaded of their honorable intentions.

Nakamura's case turned out to be a particularly poignant ending to the story of the Imperial Japanese Army, tied up in several issues concerning the legacy of Japan's past. As a non-officer, he was not entitled to a backdated pension, and there was some debate over whether he was a legitimate holdout, loyal to the Imperial Japanese Army, or a deserter who had merely evaded capture for thirty years. But it was not even clear where Nakamura needed to be repatriated to. He was a Taiwanese aborigine, born as Attun Palalin in what had *then* been the prefecture of Taiwan. His attempt to return "home" was hence initially refused by a government which would have preferred to palm him off on the Japanese. Eventually, the Taiwanese authorities relented, and Nakamura returned home, having never once set foot in Japan itself.[32]

---

[32] His wife had since remarried, a fact not revealed to him until after their reunion. Mrs. Nakamura would subsequently divorce her second husband, although Nakamura himself declined back in Taiwan, suffering from alcoholism, tuberculosis and liver damage, and succumbing to cancer four years after his return home.

But even Nakamura was not the last. Rumors persisted into the 1990s that there were other Japanese holdouts in numerous locations around South-East Asia, but most are liable to have been tall tales invented to lure in the tourist trade. Two other Japanese soldiers did not hand themselves in until 1989, but these old, old men were *former* Japanese soldiers who had joined the Malaysian Communist insurgents.

In 1992, a farmer in Henan, China, was identified by his DNA as Ishida Tōshirō (1912–2009), an intelligence officer posing as a Buddhist priest, who had been declared dead in 1963. In fact, he had lost his hearing and memory to a bullet in the side of his head in the 1940s, and was briefly paralyzed by his injuries. Taken in by local villagers, he had learned how to walk again and toiled in the fields for fifty years, unsure of who he was.

Ishida, like an unknown number of other men missing in action, simply did not come home when the war ended. In the most recent case to date, one Uwano Ishinosuke (1922– ?) was declared legally dead in 2000, only to turn up in 2006 in Kiev, where he had been living with his Ukrainian wife, having left a Sakhalin labor camp sometime in the late fifties, and simply chosen not to return to the Japan that had sent him there in the first place as a teenage conscript.

It has been nearly eight decades since the end of the war—a timespan only a few years shy of the period 1868–1945 in which Japanese militarism rose and fell. But it is still possible to discern vestiges of Japan's militarist past, often in unexpected places. Most of the statues erected by the Japanese in their empire did not long outlast its fall, although a few can still be found, removed from their original pedestals, in local museums.[33]

The photographer Shitamichi Motoyuki has toured the former states of the Japanese empire cataloguing the ceremonial Japanese *torii* shrine-gates that can still be found in odd places, forming the pillars of new-built shanty towns, or strangely ornate entrances to cemeteries. His most compelling image comes from Taichung, Taiwan, where locals sit on a fallen *torii* as if it is a strange-shaped, three-sided park bench.

In Tokyo, the Yasukuni Shrine endures as a monument to the dead

---

[33] Saaler, *Men in Metal*, pp. 235–7.

from wars in service of the Japanese emperor. It continues to be a site of argument and revisionism, remembering and celebrating Japan's millions of war dead, but pushing an agenda that denies many well-documented atrocities, particularly in its affiliated private museum, the Yūshūkan. A large banner in the Yūshūkan's first room, the "Spirit of the Samurai" gallery, is presumed to show an ancient poem by the medieval official Ōtomo no Yakamochi:

> If we go to sea, water will cover our corpses
> If we go to the mountains, grass will grow on the dead
> We shall die by the side of our lord
> We shall never look back.[34]

Or does it? Surely those words would have been most familiar to all involved in Japan's Fifteen Years War from their use as the lyrics in "If We Go to Sea," the song that played after Tōjō's announcement that Japan was at war, and increasingly often as Japan faced incident after incident of "shattered jewels"—tactical defeats, but apparently spiritual victories?

Since 1978, the Yasukuni Shrine has also controversially housed the souls of many men who were convicted as Class-A war criminals, including Tōjō himself—thereby leading to the problematic translation issue of suggesting that they are "worshipped" at the shrine like the "war gods" of the past. In a gesture of defense and defiance, the Yasukuni Shrine also installed a memorial to Justice Pal, the accompanying Japanese text to which skirts around his clear condemnation of *actual* Japanese war crimes, to concentrate on his juristic unease with the idea of victor's justice. Its sole caption in English repeats Pal's own closing words from his dissenting opinion. With calculated provocation he, and the Yasukuni Shrine, chose to quote from Jefferson Davis, the defeated leader of the Confederates in the U.S. Civil War:

> When time shall have softened passion and prejudice, when Reason shall have stripped the mask from misrepresentation, then justice, holding evenly her scales, will require much of past censure and praise to change places.[35]

---

[34] Person, *Arbiters of Patriotism*, p. 28.
[35] Pal, *Dissentient Judgement*, p. 701.

The consequences of Japanese militarism continue to reverberate, both in their direct effects, and in the absences they have caused. Whatever the noble intentions of Pan-Asianism, Japan's twentieth-century actions left no other nation taking it seriously. As S.C.M. Paine observes:

> If Japanese prime ministers, generals and admirals of the mid-twentieth century could be returned to life, they would be horrified to realize that three generations later, their decisions have left Japan despised by many of its neighbors and its foreign policy hamstrung by their failure to consider the political implications of violence.[36]

One of the world's richest nations, Japan remains excluded from the permanent Security Council of the United Nations, a body set up by the victors in the Second World War. It still disputes sovereignty with Russia over four of the southernmost Kurile Islands, occupied by the Soviet Union in the closing days of the war, but regarded by the Japanese as possessions predating imperialist expansion, and therefore not included in the terms of the Potsdam Declaration.

The ghosts of the war still recur, in the oddest places. In Illinois in 2001, police were called after a human skull was found in Lake Springfield. It had belonged to a Japanese soldier, brought home by a Navy medic from Okinawa, and used for decades in the man's high school biology classes. After his death, it was found by his son, who had painted it gold, wrapped it in a bandana, and kept it in his bedroom. Eventually spooked by his own grisly trophy, the youth threw it in the lake, sparking a brief murder mystery, and prolonged negotiation with the Japanese authorities until it was eventually returned to Okinawa for burial in 2003.[37]

In 2007, Prime Minister Abe Shinzō conceded that Japan had essentially lost the war by 1943, and should have ended the war at that point, echoing the predictions of his own grandfather, Tōjō's Minister of Munitions, Kishi Nobusuke. A Japanese pressure group subsequently brought a court action against the government, claiming that the 105,000 lives lost in the 1945 fire-bombing of Tokyo had been a failure of the Japanese

---

[36] Paine, *The Wars for Asia*, loc. 101.
[37] Harrison, "Skull trophies," p. 828.

leadership. Their lawyers argued, in vain, that it had been incumbent on the Japanese authorities to realize that the war was already over by the end of 1944, and that had they surrendered then, the needless prolonging of the war for another year would have saved Tokyo, and many other cities, from destruction, and avoided the bombings of Hiroshima and Nagasaki.

In 2008, Tamogami Toshio, the Chief of Staff of the Japanese Air Self-Defense Force was made to resign after he suggested that Japan was provoked into attacking Pearl Harbor by an America already preparing for war. He did so, I suspect, as an act of calculated dog-whistle politics in the year he was due to retire anyway, courting controversy in order to ensure the public curtailment of his military career, and a large media splash for his subsequent run for political office.[38] The Japanese far-right, naturally, remains a last bastion of some of the rhetoric and beliefs of the militarist era. As a student in Kyōto, I once ran into a man standing on a van in front of a large billboard that called for the return of Sakhalin and Taiwan, bellowing into a loud-hailer about an infestation of unwelcome immigrants. I was the sole passer-by who stopped to listen, much to his embarrassment.

But such territorial outcries are not merely a matter for the far-right. In 2011, to mark the anniversary of the outbreak of the Pacific War, the Taiwanese death metal band Chthonic released *Takasago Army*, a concept album about Taiwanese conscripts in the Japanese military machine—the centerpiece was a song called "Broken Jade" (*Yusui*).[39] In 2012, the Japanese government provoked Chinese protests by buying the privately owned Senkaku islands off the coast of Taiwan. The

---

[38] Tamogami's essay, written for a deliberately provocative competition and anthology sponsored by a nationalist businessman, also argued that reports of military atrocities were fake news, that the Japanese occupation of China, Taiwan and Korea had led to economic prosperity there, and that Roosevelt had been pressed into provoking Japan by Communist agents. In other words, a bunch of things sure to excite the far right, which he would continue to do in retirement, with further published opinions on the need for Japan to reinstate corporal punishment and acquire nuclear weapons. In 2017, he was convicted in a Japanese court for financial irregularities arising during his campaign to become the mayor of Tokyo.

[39] "Cold comfort as I fall / Death coming for you all / Give my life for the Sun / In fire existence undone." Other modern appearances of the *yusui* term in Chinese, where the *yu* is still jade, not jewel, include Zhou Zhentian's Chinese novel *Broken Jade* (2004), and the 2006 TV series of the same name, which deal with intrigues over a priceless antique during the Japanese invasion of China.

uninhabited archipelago, known in Chinese as the Diaoyu islands since at least the 15th century, marks either the northernmost area of Taiwanese waters, or the southernmost extent of Okinawa Prefecture—the last, contemporary echo of an argument that first erupted in 1871.[40]

Protestors still gather every Wednesday outside the Japanese embassy in Seoul to mark the ongoing controversy over the drafting of "comfort women" into military brothels. The affair was marked even more enduringly in 2011 with the erection of a bronze statue outside the embassy—a girl sitting in a chair, staring impassively across the street, waiting for apology or remembrance. The embassy has repeatedly asked for the statue to be moved, but it was granted a protected status by the local council in 2017.

Understandably, the story of the rise of Japanese militarism, its beginnings, progress and even the way it was brought to an end, remains a political minefield, abrading family histories, national policies and even overseas political debate. In 2016, the U.S. vice president Joe Biden rebuked the presidential candidate Donald Trump for suggesting that Japan consider acquiring nuclear strike capabilities.[41]

"Does he not understand that we wrote Japan's constitution to say they could not be a nuclear power?" said Biden—words that ignited controversy back in Japan, where the extent to which the post-war Constitution was "written" by Americans remains a political hot potato, as does the degree to which the Japanese themselves were the architects,

---

[40] Anon. "Diaoyu Dao, an Inherent Territory of China," pp. 34–8. The PRC's case, that Japan has attempted to tack the Diaoyu islands onto the Ryūkyū islands, is persuasive. However, there is a whole additional level of drama, since even if diplomats agree that is the case, the islands would surely be reattached to the "province of Taiwan," which is to say, the Republic of China, not the People's Republic. Beijing has hence waded into a border dispute on behalf of its own "rebel" island.

[41] Moritsugu, "Biden's remark." The issue in Japan was not merely with the assumption (which, between you and me, is rather justified) that Americans "wrote" much of Japan's current Constitution, but with the fact that there was actually no mention of nuclear weapons in the Constitution. As noted above in this book, Japan's Constitution renounces *war of aggression*, but a suitably silver-tongued lawyer might have been able to argue that atomic weapons might be necessary for *defense*. It was Kishi Nobusuke's brother, Prime Minister Satō Eisaku, who in 1967 implemented the Three Non-Nuclear Principles on the basis of that Constitution, writing into Japanese law a non-nuclear policy that would win him the Nobel Peace Prize in 1974. Biden's words, off-the-cuff and said in haste, hence dismissed Satō's accomplishment in Japanese eyes.

prosecutors and ultimately victims of their own militarism, and agents of their own recovery from it.

Many years after the war, the composer Tamura Shigeru encountered an old soldier who gave him an object lesson in the enduring terror that Japanese officers struck into their subordinates. The man began singing a song to him: "Qing Lai"—that same propaganda ditty that had been mass-purchased by the Imperial Japanese Army in 1938 and strewn all over occupied China as a misguided effort in cultural outreach. The old soldier, however, was getting the tune wrong and would accept no corrections.

"I shouted at him: 'I wrote that song!'" recalled Tamura, "You should at least sing it properly in front of the composer!"

"I learned this song from a superior officer," the man replied. "There is no way it is wrong. You are the one who is wrong, sir."[42]

[42] Osada, *Sensō ga Nokoshita Uta*, p. 358.

Timeline

This timeline contains several events and scandals not mentioned in my main text, but still of likely interest to any reader seeking to contextualize historical events in Japan. As noted in the Introduction, events described as "incidents" in English can be either jiken or jihen in Japanese. The former is a mere "affair," the latter is a crisis of wider political or military implications, at the very brink of an act of war. In the interests of visualizing the way these moments are discussed in Japanese historiography, jihen are marked with an asterisk. In order to make clear the long-term influences of the factions who participated in the Meiji Restoration, I have marked figures born before 1868 with their place of origin if they came from Satsuma, Chōshū, Tosa or Hizen.

1853	Arriving on the Black Ships, Commodore Matthew Perry demands negotiations with Japan.
1860	With the purchase of Alaska, the westernmost edge of the United States is now within 700 miles of the north-easternmost edge of Japan.
1862	Charles Lennox Richardson is killed by Satsuma samurai for disrespecting their entourage (**Namamugi Incident**).
1863	British bombardment of Kagoshima (**Anglo-Satsuma War**).
1867	The shipwrecked crew of the *Rover* are murdered on the coast of Taiwan. Sudden death of the Kōmei Emperor, leaving a 14-year-old heir.
1868	The Meiji Restoration overthrows the old order in Japan. Edo is renamed Tōkyō.

1869   Establishment of the Shrine to Summon the Souls (*Shōkonsha*) to honor those who died in the Emperor's name.

Ezo is renamed Hokkaidō. Foundation of the Hokkaidō Development Commission.

1870   Assault by Tokushima samurai on the Inada family fort. Last legally ordered *seppuku* in Japanese history. (**Kōgo Incident***)

Foundation of the Mitsubishi corporation.

1871   Shipwrecked sailors from the Ryūkyū Islands are massacred by Paiwan tribesmen on the east coast of Taiwan.

Abolition of feudal domains—disruption of old samurai power.

Legalization of Christianity.

The Iwakura Mission sets sail around the world.

After Navy recruitment becomes based on merit, Satsuma men fail to dominate subsequent academy graduating classes.

1872   Charles Le Gendre begins advising the Japanese government.

Creation of a national conscript army.

Creation of Army Ministry and Navy Ministry—effective separation of the two services.

Establishment of national school curriculum.

Soldiers' Code establishes the seven virtues of military service.

1873   An annual national holiday is declared on the anniversary of the coronation of the legendary Emperor Jinmu.

A Japanese imperial envoy is turned away from Korea for using terminology reserved for the Chinese Emperor.

The Iwakura Mission returns from its world tour.

1874   Attempted assassination of Iwakura Tomomi by supporters of the Korean invasion plan (**Kuichigai Incident**).

Punitive exhibition to Taiwan. First overseas deployment of the Imperial Japanese Army and Imperial Japanese Navy.

1875   Japan gives Russia the southern part of Sakhalin in return for the Kurile Islands (**Treaty of St Petersburg**)

The Ryūkyū Islands cease all diplomatic interactions with China.

Japanese gunboat *Un'yō* trespasses in Korean territorial waters (**Ganghwa Incident**)

Charles Le Gendre becomes an adviser to Ōkuma Shigenobu.

1876   Ban on swords. Conversion of samurai stipends to government bonds.
        Japan forces the Ganghwa Treaty on Korea.

1877   Satsuma Rebellion. (**War of the Southwest**)

1878   Assassination of Ōkubo Toshimichi (**Kioizaka Incident**)
        Revolt among the Imperial Guard over lack of rewards for their service in the Satsuma Rebellion (**Takebashi Incident**).
        Adoption of a more Prussian-influenced General Staff.

1879   The Shōkonsha is renamed the Shrine to Quiet the State (*Yasukuni Jinja*).
        Establishment of Okinawa Prefecture in what was once the Ryūkyū Islands.

1880   French military advisers sent home.
        Manufacture of the Type-13 Murata rifle—first generation of locally made Japanese small-arms.

1881   Ōkuma Shigenobu calls for a national assembly. One is promised by 1890 although Itō Hirobumi protests that the Japanese people are not yet ready.
        Japanese military advisers arrive in Korea to train the Special Skills Force (*byeolgigun*).

1882   Riots in Korea over growing Japanese influence (**Imo Incident/Jingo Incident***).
        Imperial Rescript to Soldiers and Sailors establishes a code of conduct for the military, and cites them as the hands and feet of the Emperor.
        Japan produces first locally made breech-loading field gun.

1884   Navy acquires its first torpedoes, from Germany.

1885   Formation of first Cabinet, with Itō Hirobumi as Prime Minister.
        Treaty of Tianjin establishes rights of Japan and China to send evenly-matched troops to Korea in the event of a crisis.
        Chinese Immigration Act establishes a head tax on all Chinese entering Canada.

Fragments of the anti-Shōgun battle song, "Miya-san Miya-san" (1868) show up in Gilbert & Sullivan's *The Mikado*.

1886   Japan signs the Geneva Convention (1864).
        Chinese sailors fight with the Japanese police in Nagasaki (**Nagasaki Incident**).

1887   Peace Preservation Ordinance outlaws all secret societies and assemblies.

1888   Garrison system changes to deployable divisions—shift in the nature of the Army from defensive to offensive.

1889   Promulgation of the Meiji Constitution.
        Gen'yōsha terrorist attack seriously wounds Ōkuma Shigenobu.

1890   First meeting of the Diet (Japanese parliament).
        Charles Le Gendre leaves Japan to become vice-president of the Korean Home Office, and later that same year, adviser to King Gojong of Korea.

c.1890 U.S. overtakes France as Japan's main export market (silk).

1891   Assassination attempt on Crown Prince Nicholas (the future Tsar Nicholas II) (**Ōtsu Incident**).

1892   Russian naval base established at Vladivostok.

1894-5 Sino-Japanese War.

1894   Assassination of Kim Ok-kyun in Shanghai.
        Great Britain and Japan agree to strike extraterritoriality from their treaties.
        Opening of the Imperial General Headquarters.
        Safety Preservation Law (*hoan jōrei*) suppresses dissent against the Meiji oligarchs.
        Port Arthur Massacre Incident.
        Yamagata Aritomo offers to buy the Philippines from Spain for $40 million.

1895   Attempted assassination of Li Hongzhang in Shimonoseki.

Triple Intervention by Russia, Germany and France prevents Japan holding on to the Liaodong Peninsula.

Murder of Queen Min in Korea by Japanese soldiers (**Itsubi Incident***)

Annexation of Taiwan.

1896   Mahan's *The Influence of Sea Power on History* is translated into Japanese.

1897   Russian author Jacques Novikow coins the term "Yellow Peril" (*le péril jaune*).

King Gojong of Korea proclaims himself Emperor of Korea. End of Korean tributary status towards China.

Attempted ban on Japanese immigration to Hawaii. Japan sends the British-built warship *Naniwa* as a show of force.

1898   Hawaii is annexed as an American territory. Huge influx of migrant Japanese workers from Hawaii to the mainland United States.

Japan considers selling Taiwan to France.

United States acquires Guam and the Philippines as spoils in the Spanish-American War.

1899   U.S. Secretary of State John Hay issues the *Open Door Notes* affirming freedom of trade in China for all countries, in an effort to prevent the country being broken up into multiple colonies.

Nunobiki Maru, a Japanese ship carrying Japanese-made arms to the Philippines, sinks off the coast of Taiwan.

Britain gives up extraterritoriality in Japan. Beginning of the end of the Unequal Treaties.

Mahan's *The Interest of America in Sea Power, Past, Present and Future* is translated into Japanese as *On Sea Power in the Pacific*.

1900   *Bushidō: The Soul of Japan* by Nitobe Inazō defines Japan's martial nature, perhaps misleadingly, for readers in both East and West.

Boxer Uprising in China (**Hokushin Incident***)

Japanese plot to invade Fujian is covered up (**Amoy Incident**)

Public Order and Police Law prevents labor movements and strikes.

Taiwan Association School is established in Hokkaidō to train personnel for the administration and development of Taiwan.

1901   Australia introduces dictation tests for would-be Japanese immi-
        grants—a drastic curb on non-English speaking arrivals.
        Japan produces workable wireless radio telegraphy in imitation of
        the Marconi devices used elsewhere. Range: 70 miles.
        U.S. Congress approves plans for construction of a Naval Station at
        Pearl Harbor, Hawaii.

1902   199 soldiers freeze to death on a training exercise in north Japan
        (**Hakkōda Mountains Incident**).
        Anglo-Japanese Alliance—lasts until 1920—secures strategic coop-
        eration but also vital access to superior British coal.

1903   Japanese Army prepares an operational plan for war against Russia
        (December).

1904-5 Russo-Japanese War.

1904   Mori Ōgai coins the term "White Peril" (*hakka*).

1905   Hibiya Riots in protest at the settlement with Russia (**Hibiya Incen-
        diary Incident**—Japan's first modern mass protest)
        Sun Yat-sen suggests offering the Japanese Manchuria in exchange
        for their assistance in a Chinese revolution.
        Anglo-Japanese Alliance revised to mandate immediate assistance
        in the event of attack by a single third-party.

1906   San Francisco School Board orders all ethnic Japanese pupils to at-
        tend "Oriental" schools along with Chinese and Koreans.
        First draft of *War Plan Orange*, the U.S. strategy document outlining
        optimal responses in case of a state of conflict with Japan.
        The "Kwantung Garrison" is established to protect Japanese interests
        in Manchuria.

1907   Anti-Asian riot in Vancouver.
        Tanaka Giichi assigns two platoons from his unit to assist at a meet-
        ing of the Tokyo Patriotic Women's Society.

1908   Protestors in Tokyo are arrested for singing Communist anthems
        and calling for revolution (**Red Flag Incident**).
        The planned 1912 International Exposition in Japan is cancelled in
        order to help pay for ongoing debts of the Russo-Japanese War.

Revised handbook for barracks life intensifies the separation of soldiers from civilian life.

Establishment of the U.S. Naval Dockyard at Pearl Harbor.

1909   Alien Land Bill is first proposed in California to restrict Japanese
ownership of real estate.

Itō Hirobumi is killed by a Korean gunman in Harbin.

The South Manchuria Railway geology bureau discovers massive
iron-ore deposits at Anshan.

1910   Democrats in California campaign for election with the slogan
"Keep California White."

Kōtoku Shusui and other anarchists are arrested for plotting to assassinate the Meiji Emperor (**High Treason Incident**)

1911   Xinhai Revolution in China.

U.S.-Japan Navigation and Trade Treaty restores tariff autonomy to
Japan.

Anglo-Japanese Commercial Treaty.

1912   Death of the Meiji Emperor.

Collapse of the Saionji cabinet due to Army pressure.

Sun Yat-sen again offers Manchuria to Japan in exchange for loans.

1913   Alien Land Law signed into the California statue books, limiting
Japanese land ownership to three years.

Ministry of Education adopts the Army's physical education drills
for use in boys' schools.

1914   Outbreak of First World War.

Opening of the Panama Canal.

Ministry of Education adds several military subjects to the new
songbook for schoolchildren.

1915   Japan issues the Twenty-One Demands to China.

British soldiers and Japanese marines put down an insurrection
among Indian troops in Singapore.

A controversial military appropriations bill is found to have gained
support through political bribes (**Ōura Incident**).

1917   Lansing-Ishii Agreement with the U.S. acknowledges that Japan's
        proximity to China gives it "special interests" there.

1918   Formation of Japan's first party cabinet.
        End of First World War.
        Siberian Intervention sees thousands of Japanese troops mobilized
        on Asian mainland.
        "Spanish" influenza pandemic.
        Rice Riots—Army and reservists used in crowd control.
        Heavy clampdown on press reporting (**White Rainbow Incident**).
        The Taiwan Association School is renamed Takushoku ("develop-
        ment and industrialization") University.
        Munitions Mobilization Law establishes possibility of nationalizing
        important industries in a time of war.

1919   Death of Korean Emperor Gojong.
        Paris Peace Conference controversially awards Japan control of the
        former German colony of Shandong.
        March First Protests in Korea.
        May Fourth Protests in China, after China refuses to sign the Treaty
        of Versailles.
        Kita Ikki writes *An Outline Plan for the Reconstruction of Japan*.

c.1920 Oil takes over from coal as primary power source in first-line war-
        ships.

1920   Japanese massacred at Nikolaievsk-on-Amur by Soviet partisans
        (**Nikolaievsk Incident**)

1921   Assassination of Prime Minister Hara Kei.

1922   Nine-Power Treaty (U.S., Belgium, Britain, China, France, Italy, Ja-
        pan, Netherlands and Portugal) effectively writes the Open Door
        policy into international law.
        Washington Naval Conference and return of Jiaozhou Bay (Qing-
        dao) from Japan to China.

1923   Great Kantō Earthquake devastates Tokyo region.
        Massacre of Koreans in the aftermath.
        Murder of anarchists by a Japanese officer (**Amakasu Incident**).

Chinese Immigration Act effectively shuts down Chinese immigration in Canada.

Attempted assassination of Prince Regent Hirohito (**Toranomon Incident**)

1924   U.S. Immigration Act shuts down immigration from Asia.

1925   First radio broadcasts in major Japanese cities.

Public Security Preservation Law prohibits associations contrary to the "national body" (*kokutai*) or private property, outlawing socialism and Communism.

General Election Law grants the vote to all men over twenty-five.

Anti-Japanese, -British and -French protests in Shanghai and other Chinese cities.

Kwantung Army intervenes in a rebellion in Manchuria on behalf of the warlord Zhang Zuolin.

1926   Three separate radio stations are merged to form the Japanese Broadcasting Corporation (*Nihon Hōsō Kyōkai*, or NHK).

Singing of military songs in schools, discretionary for over a decade, is now compulsory.

1927   British government asks Japanese Army to intervene against KMT soldiers in Shanghai (request refused by Foreign Minister Shidehara Kijūrō).

Japanese Navy tabletop war-game simulates an attack on Pearl Harbor.

1928   NHK introduces daily broadcast calisthenics (*radio taisō*).

Mass round-up of suspected Communists and left-wing sympathizers (**March 15th Incident**)

Officers of the Kwantung Army assassinate Zhang Zuolin, the warlord of Manchuria (**Huanggutun Incident**).

Clash between Chinese and Japanese soldiers in Shandong (**Jinan Incident**).

First election with universal male suffrage returns many left-wing politicians.

Ministry of Education sets up the Student Division to police university intellectuals.

Deification of several Japanese military heroes as "war gods" (*gunshin*) including General Nogi, Lieutenant Hirose and Major Tachibana.

1929   Onset of the Great Depression. Worldwide economic slump lasts for
        the next ten years. 10% pay cut for the Japanese military.

1930   London Naval Treaty, seen in Japan as a continuation of the humil-
        iations of Washington (1922) and Versailles (1919).

1931   Chinese soldiers kill a Japanese soldier on a suspicious mission in
        the Manchurian hinterland (**Nakamura Incident**).
        False-flag attack on the Manchurian Railway leads to the Japanese
        annexation of Manchuria (**Manchurian Incident/Mukden Inci-
        dent***)
        Korean workers fight with Chinese farmers in Manchuria over an
        illegal ditch-digging (**Wanbaoshan Incident**).
        Thwarting of planned Army coup (**Imperial Colors/October Inci-
        dent**).

1932   Anti-Japanese protests in Shanghai escalate to riots and armed con-
        flict (**January 28th/First Shanghai Incident**)
        Proclamation of the state of Manchukuo.
        Establishment of secret "Tōgō Unit" (later Unit 731) under the aus-
        pices of the Kwantung Army Epidemic Prevention Research Lab-
        oratory.
        U.S. military exercise simulates a Japanese aerial attack on Pearl
        Harbor.
        Assassination of the pro-American head of Mitsui Bank (**League of
        Blood Incident**)
        Assassination of Prime Minister Inukai Tsuyoshi (**May 15th Incident**)
        The Lytton Report publishes a damning account of Japanese subter-
        fuge in Manchuria.

1934   Government collapses over an insider-trading scandal involving the
        Teikoku Rayon company (**Teijin Incident**)
        Aisin Gioro Puyi, the former Emperor of China, is proclaimed as
        the Emperor of Manchukuo.
        Thwarting of planned Army coup (**Military Academy/November
        Incident**).
        Failed attempts to reform the Public Preservation Law to also con-
        tain right-wing nationalists.
        Under Army pressure, Japan refuses to ratify the Geneva Convention
        of 1929 on the grounds that prisoners would be better treated than
        Japanese soldiers.

1935   Assassination of Nagata Tetsuzan (**Aizawa Incident**).

U.S. Neutrality Act forbids exports of arms and ammunition to a nation at war.

1936   The Shōwa Emperor disbands an attempted coup in Tokyo by military officers (**February 26th Incident**).

First issue of the journal Yūsei (*Eugenics*).

Kwantung Army and Manchukuo support a failed invasion of Inner Mongolia by Prince Demchugdongrub (**Suiyuan Incident**).

The Japanese Navy staff college produces a report advocating a pre-emptive strike against Pearl Harbor in the event of conflict with the United States.

1937   Skirmish outside Beijing (**Marco Polo Bridge Incident/Lugou Bridge Incident**) escalates into Japanese invasion of China (**China Incident***).

Massacre of civilians in Nanjing (**Nanjing Incident**).

Precious Children Battalion (*Kodakara Butai*) campaign offers incentives to mothers who have multiple children.

Founding of the Manchukuo Film Association (*Man-Ei*).

Japanese planes attack the *U.S.S. Panay* outside Nanjing (**Panay Incident**).

Japanese government urges people to donate gold.

Konoe Fumimaro forms the National Spiritual Mobilization Committee (*Kokumin Seishin Sōdō-in Chūō Renmei*) to oversee education and ideology.

1938   In Nanjing, a Japanese soldier strikes the U.S. consul John Moore Allison in the face (**Allison Incident**).

National Mobilization Law (*Kokka Sodōin-hō*)

Cancellation of 1940 Tokyo Olympics.

Ministry of Health and Welfare includes a Research Group for Racial Hygiene (*Minzoku Eisei Kenkyū-kai*).

Second U.S. military exercise simulates a Japanese aerial assault on Pearl Harbor.

1939   Battles of Khalkhin Gol between Japan and the Soviet Union (**Nomonhan Incident***).

Outbreak of war in Europe.

Demchugdongrub forms the puppet state of Mengjiang ("The Mongol Frontier").

1940   National celebration in Japan of "2600 years" of imperial rule
       Japan enters the Tripartite Alliance with Germany and Italy.
       National Eugenics Law (*Kokumin Yūsei Hō*) restricts sterilization
          and encourages breeding by "intelligent or superior elements."
       National Spiritual Mobilization Committee is superseded by the
          Imperial Rule Assistance Association (*Taiseiyoku Sankai*).
       Vichy France allows Japanese forces to occupy the north of French
          Indochina.
       U.S. Treasury officials uncover a New York banking fraud that has
          caused a gross underestimation of Japan's foreign currency reserves.
       U.S. shuts down all scrap metal exports to Japan.
       Pearl Harbor is redesignated as the main base for the U.S. Navy in
          the Pacific.
       Death of Saionji Kinmochi, the last *genrō*.

1941   Japanese Army issues *The Field Service Code* (*Senjinkun*) a manual
          to discourage insubordination and war crimes.
       Army Minister Tōjō Hideki orders a committee to investigate the
          potential of atomic weapons.
       U.S. shuts down exports of machine tools to Japan.
       Japanese troops occupy southern French Indochina.
       A U.S., British and Dutch freeze on transactions effectively locks the
          Japanese within a "yen bloc" of Japanese imperial territories.
       Japan attacks Pearl Harbor. United States enters the war.
       Temporary Regulation of Speech, Publications, Assembly and Asso-
          ciation Law heavily restricts freedom of speech and association.

1942   Special Wartime Criminal Law requires all political organizations to
          have government permission.
       The Navy-commissioned Committee on Research in the Application
          of Nuclear Physics (*Kaku Butsuri Ōyō Kenkyū Iinkai*) has its first
          meeting (July).
       Japan deploys paratroopers at the Battle of Manado.
       "Sook Ching" purge in occupied Singapore (**Singapore Overseas
          Chinese Massacre Incident**).
       U.S. interns over 100,000 people of Japanese ethnicity.

1943   Tenth and final meeting of the Committee on Research in the Ap-
          plication of Nuclear Physics concludes that atomic weapons are
          feasible, but unlikely to be developed by the U.S. (March).
       Battle of Attu. First use of the term *gyokusai* in an official report.

Battle of Tarawa (*gyokusai*)

1944   Battle of Kwajalein (*gyokusai*)
Tōjō's Emergency Broadcast calls for "100 million shattered jewels"
Battle of Biak (*gyokusai*)
Battle of Saipan (*gyokusai*)
First *kamikaze* attacks

1945   Battle of Iwo Jima (*gyokusai*)
Battle of Okinawa (*gyokusai*)
Atomic bombings of Hiroshima and Nagasaki.
Attempted coup on the eve of the surrender (**Kyūjō Incident**).
Surrender of Japan.

1946   Occupation authorities ban all films with a military background
"unless militarism is shown to be evil."

1952   End of U.S. Occupation of Japan. Return of sovereignty to Japan
(except Okinawa).

1960   Widespread protests in Japan regarding the renewal of the U.S.-Japan
Security Treaty ("*Anpo*") which allows for U.S. bases on Japanese
soil (**May 19th Incident / Hagerty Incident / June 15th Incident**).

1965   Ienaga Saburō sues the Ministry of Education on the grounds that
government approval of school history textbooks is unconstitutional.

1968   Japanese Association of Bereaved Families begins collecting and
disposing of soldiers' bones in Micronesia.

1972   U.S. officially returns Okinawa to Japan, while retaining its base
there.

1974   Onoda Hirō and Nakamura Teru, holdouts on remote islands, are
officially the last soldiers of the Imperial Japanese Army to surrender.

1978   Fourteen Class-A war criminals are consecrated as "martyrs" at the
Yasukuni Shrine.

1982   The Neighboring Country Clause requires the process for certify-
        ing school textbooks to consider the likely feelings of nations that
        suffered under Japanese imperialism.

1985   Nakasone Yasuhiro becomes the first post-war Japanese Prime Min-
        ister to visit the Yasukuni Shrine in an official capacity.

1990   Attempted assassination of Motoshima Hitoshi, the mayor of Naga-
        saki, after he suggests that Emperor Hirohito was to blame for the
        war.

2006   "Patriotic education" is re-introduced to the Japanese school curric-
        ulum.

2007   Okinawa administrators complain that government history books
        downplay the Japanese Army's coercion of locals to kill themselves
        in 1945.

2008   Tamogami Toshio, Chief of Staff for Japan's Air Self-Defense Force,
        is made to resign after claiming that Japan was provoked by the
        U.S. and China into attacking Pearl Harbor.

2012   Provoking protests from China, the Japanese government purchases
        the privately owned Diaoyu/Senkaku islands off the coast of Tai-
        wan.

2016   Then-vice president Joe Biden rebukes then presidential candidate
        Donald Trump with the words: "Does he not understand that
        we wrote Japan's constitution to say they could not be a nuclear
        power?"

Notes on Names

I have done my best to keep names as simple as possible, clinging to the most relevant figures for this particular narrative, even at the expense of people who might be better known to posterity. Some readers may be surprised at the famous men reduced to a walk-on role (including Admiral Tōgō and Prince Saionji, on whom I have written entire books), or the minor actors thrust into prominence, but such shufflings are necessary to avoid burying everybody in a tidal wave of names and dates. I have even broken with tradition by not using the full terms Imperial Japanese Army (IJA) and Imperial Japanese Navy (IJN) throughout, in order to spare the reader unwieldy sentences and a surfeit of acronyms.

The Japanese have not helped by the flurry of modern renamings, not only of samurai-era cities and domains, but of people. Japanese often did not even have surnames, until one of the modernizing reforms of the 1870s imposed a family registration system that required them—hence the sudden flurry of households identifying themselves by the nearest geographical feature—Down-the-Mountain (*Yamashita*), or In-the-Fields (*Tanaka*) or Upper-Village (*Murakami*). Princes and emperors would rename themselves, sometimes on multiple occasions, with childhood nicknames, official public monikers, era-names, Buddhist names, and posthumous temple names, while fostering and the need for the continuation of family lines would see friends and relatives swapping children. I've done my best to pick the most relevant name someone uses in their lifetime, even if its use at particular times might technically be an anachronism. Similarly, I have usually used earlier place-name for those locations that exist in Japanese documents under a colonial title, so—Mukden, for the city known today as Shenyang and often in the 1920s as Fengtian, and Changchun for the city that was the "New Capital" of Manchukuo—in Chinese *Xinjing*, in Japanese, *Shinkyō*; the Korean name of the sacred mountain Baekdu, not the *Hakutō* by which it was known in Japanese, nor even the *Changbai* by which it is known in China. I've made an exception for Port Arthur, which the Chinese called Lushun, and for the archaic "Kwantung" Army, as both the Chinese *Guandong* and Japanese *Kantō* are both frustratingly confusing soundalikes for other places.

Of particular irritation, to both writer and reader in a book of this nature, is changing ranks and roles. It's difficult enough to assign a man the correct rank at particular moments in his career, and then deeply frustrating when a song written to commemorate him uses his posthumous rank, an honorary title that he did not hold at the time he died. Tachibana Shūta was a Major when he got himself killed at the Battle of Liaoyang. For the next forty years, the song written in his honor and sung by generations of schoolchildren, called him a Lieutenant-Colonel.

Further Reading

War attracts many an armchair general, and every single conflict this book comes with an overwhelming archive of reports, opinions, articles and analyses. A history specifically of Japanese militarism, however, is less interested in the minutiae of battles and more concerned with the history of two organizations whose existences spanned the years 1868 to 1945: the Imperial Japanese Army and the Imperial Japanese Navy. Each has its own historians and factions—respectively, I recommend the Harrieses' *Soldiers of the Sun* and Evans' and Peattie's *Kaigun* as the ideal places to start. I am a particular fan of the works of Sarah C. Paine, whose books on "the wars for Asia" perceive them not as isolated events, but as an evolving, runaway Great Game across multiple decades and players. Her books are a good investment for anyone seeking to go beyond this work's populist tone into more academic and richly cited areas.

When it comes to a history explicitly of *militarism*, I urge the reader not to make the common mistake of assuming that it's all about the war stories. The militarily uneventful 1920s, subject of my fourth chapter, was a crucial period in turning the Imperial Japanese Army into the sinister institution that would dominate the 1930s, and are best covered in Humphreys' *The Way of the Heavenly Sword*.

This book deliberately reflects modern concerns, not only over the evils of colonialism, but of the importance of metadata—it is truly illuminating to see the events of the twentieth century described in financial terms, as in Miller's *Bankrupting the Enemy*, or in terms of the trade logistics outlined in many of the essays included in Minohara et al.'s *The Decade of the Great War*. My jaw dropped on many occasions while researching this book, but never quite so much as when reading Michael Sturma's account of Allied prisoners of war, including its discussion of the thousands of deaths of POWs caused by "friendly fire."

Accordingly, I have done my best to retell this old and oft-told story with as fresh an insight as I can muster, dragging up lesser-known oddities and anecdotes, to illustrate certain points and fix certain personalities and biographies in the reader's memory. In this, I've enjoyed the focus of the works of Sven Saaler, who has been instrumental in game-changing accounts of both Pan-Asianism and military statuary, and of Stewart Lone, who consistently finds new ways to prod the history of Japanese militarism in unexpected places. In particular, in his focus on provincial anecdotes of the war, Lone is a rare voice of humanity and even comic relief, recounting the effects of the war in the most unexpected arenas, from brothel slang to playground games. He argues that such notes of levity are not mere distractions from the grim nature of war, but crucial indicators that Japan's home-front was anything but the single-minded pro-war state that it was claimed to be by its own propaganda. We have him to thank, for example, for a bizarre report in 1905 when a patriotic businessman, following government advice to write a letter of support to a random soldier and to sign it with a lady's name, found his correspondent inconveniently surviving the battlefield, and returning to Japan demanding a date.[1] Eri Hotta has a similar eye for unexpected humorous detail and historical irony, not the least in her *Japan 1941: Countdown to Infamy* when she records numerous sarcastic nicknames used about certain military figures behind their backs, including the Dozing Admiral, the White Elephant, and the Goldfish Minister.

I also recommend *Japan at War: An Oral History*, by Cook and Cook, for the kaleidoscopic view it presents not only of soldiers and sailors, but of almost every other sector of Japanese society during the Pacific War, from lathe operators to nurses.

I did not begin this project with the intention of chronicling the songs that the Japanese sung about themselves, but as I waded through the sources on popular culture from the 1860s onwards, I found a great number of references and call-backs in popular discourse to the music of the day, now in the public domain and lurking in obscure corners of the Internet. In essence, this book turned into the history of a particular militaristic meme. I have been inspired in this direction by Osada Gyōji's wonderful 800-page *Sensō ga Nokoshita Uta* [*Songs Left by the War*], which goes into great and granular detail about military poetry competitions, wartime record sales, and the increasingly sinister co-option of school assemblies and music classes into centers of indoctrination. My sources for the songs that bring the period to life, all of which can be found online, extend beyond printed matter to the music that I have listened to while writing this book, particularly the CD set *Nihon gunka senji kayō daizenshū* [*The Complete Collection of Japanese Military Wartime Popular Songs*, CRCN-45127-8] and *Manshū no Uta* [*Songs of Manchuria*, KICG-3241].

---

[1] Lone, *Provincial Life and the Military in Imperial Japan*, p.61.

Writing on Japan at war tends to polarize people, and not only into teams of aggrieved foreign POWs, vengeful Chinese, or defensive Japanese. Such factionalism, however, goes back long before the events of the Pacific War. Donald Calman's *The Origins and Nature of Japanese Imperialism* regards the entire foundations of English-language writings on Meiji Japan to be corrupted by a different "victors' story," as told by the Meiji revolutionaries and industrialists that had been backed by the British, and by hand-wringing excuses from anyone who could get away with it. Similarly, Eri Hotta notes in *Pan-Asianism and Japan's War* that the wartime narrative was under the control of the far right, but that when the story was re-told by educators and historians *after* 1945, the bias swung far to the left. Even referring to the conflict as the "Fifteen Years War" becomes a political act, assigning the blame for starting it to the activists of the Kwantung Army in 1931.

Herbert P. Bix's *Hirohito and the Making of Modern Japan* is determined to give the Shōwa Emperor the trial he never had in 1946, while recent Japanese publications are just as keen to exonerate him. I have even seen Romulus Hillsborough's work, meticulous in detail about the events of the Meiji Restoration, derided online as propaganda published by "a local vanity press that is, in all likelihood, a CIA front," which I am sure is a great surprise to my (and his) editors at Tuttle. Or *is it*...?

So, it is unlikely that anyone can write a book that will please everybody on a subject like this. I have tried to remain focused on a storyline and a narrative, but the choices I make will not be for everybody—I choose to spend a whole page on the Battle of Ueno, whereas the aforementioned Hillsborough, whose *Samurai Revolution* devotes 600 pages to the events of the first half of my first chapter, skates past it in just two lines.

Often, this has been a depressing book to write, particularly when it comes to documenting a narrative of atrocity. I remained mindful of the late Iris Chang, whose months of research into wartime and murder may have contributed to her own suicide. And there is so much to read—not merely the published accounts of the Tokyo war crimes cases, but many subsidiary accounts and anecdotes. For the reader in search of new perspectives I recommend the recent 1000-page anthology *Trials of Justice*, published by the *People's Court Daily*, which documents many obscure cases heard not only Tokyo, but also in Singapore, Indonesia, and in Nationalist and Communist China, the last of which continued proceedings until 1956.

Allan, James, *Under the Dragon Flag: My Experiences in the Chino-Japanese War*. New York: Frederick A. Stokes, 1898 [Dodo Press POD reprint, undated].

Allen, Thomas B. and Norman Polmar. *Codename Downfall: The Secret Plan to Invade Japan*. London, Headline, 1995.

Allison, John M. *Ambassador from the Prairie, or, Allison Wonderland*. Boston: Houghton Mifflin, 1973.

Anon. "Diaoyu Dao, an Inherent Territory of China" in Information Office of the State Council of the People's Republic of China, *White Papers of the Chinese Government 2012*. Beijing: Foreign Languages Press, 2013, pp. 27–44.

Asada Sadao. *From Mahan to Pearl Harbor: The Imperial Japanese Navy and the United States*. Annapolis, MD: Naval Institute Press, 2006.

Ashmead-Bartlett, Ellis. *Port Arthur: The Siege and Capitulation*. Edinburgh: William Blackwood & Sons, 1906.

Atkins, E. Taylor. *Blue Nippon: Authenticating Jazz in Japan*. Durham: Duke University Press, 2001.

_____. "The Dual Career of 'Arirang', the Korean Resistance Anthem That Became a Japanese Pop Hit" in *The Journal of Asian Studies*, Vol. 66, No.3 (August 2007), pp. 645–87.

Aydin, Cemil. "Taraknath Das: Pan-Asian Solidarity as a 'Realist' Grand Strategy, 1917–1918" in Saaler and Szpilman, op. cit., pp. I: 304–10.

Barclay, Paul. *Outcasts of Empire: Japan's Rule on Taiwan's "Savage Border" 1874–1945*. Berkeley: University of California Press, 2017.

Barnhart, Michael A. *Japan Prepares for Total War: The Search for Economic Security, 1919–1945*. Ithaca: Cornell University Press, 1987. [2013 Kindle edition consulted]

Beasley, W.G. *Japanese Imperialism 1894–1945*. Oxford: Clarendon Press, 1987.

Bennett, Terry. *Japan and the Illustrated London News—Complete Record of Reported Events 1853–1899*. Folkestone, UK: Global Oriental, 2006.

Berger, Gordon Mark. *Kenkenroku: A Diplomatic Record of the Sino-Japanese Wat, 1894–5*. Princeton, NJ: Princeton University Press, 1982.

Bergerud, Eric M. *Touched with Fire: The Land War in the South Pacific*. New York: Viking, 1996.

_____. *Fire in the Sky: The Air War in the South Pacific*. New York: Basic Books, 2001.

Best, Antony. *British Engagement with Japan, 1854–1922: The Origins and Course of an Unlikely Alliance*. London: Routledge, 2021.

Bisher, Jamie. *White Terror: Cossack warlords of the Trans-Siberian*. London: Routledge, 2005.

Bix, Herbert P. *Hirohito and the Making of Modern Japan*. Oxford: Duckworth, 2001.

Blacker, Carmen. *The Japanese Enlightenment: A Study of the Writings of Fukuzawa Yukichi*. Cambridge: Cambridge University Press, 1964.

Bulwer-Lytton, Victor et al. *League of Nations: Appeal by the Chinese Government—Report of the Commission of Enquiry* [i.e. the Lytton Report]. Geneva: League of Nations Publications, 1932.

Butow, Robert J.C. *Tojo and the Coming of the War*. Palo Alto, CA: Stanford University Press, 1961.

Calman, Donald. *The Nature and Origin of Japanese Imperialism: A reinterpretation of the Great Crisis of 1873*. London: Routledge, 1992.

Caruthers, Sandra T. "Anodyne for Expansion: Meiji Japan, the Mormons, and Charles LeGendre" in *Pacific Historical Review*, Vol. 38, No. 2 (1969), pp. 129–139.

_____. "Filibustering to Formosa: General Charles LeGendre and the Japanese" in *Pacific Historical Review*, Vol. 40, Nofriday 13. 4 (1971), pp. 442–456.

Cassel, Pär Kristoffer. *Grounds of Judgement: Extraterritoriality and Imperial Power in Nineteenth-Century China and Japan*. Oxford: Oxford University Press, 2012.

Cave, Peter. "Story, song and ceremony: shaping dispositions in Japanese elementary schools during Taishō and early Shōwa" in *Japan Forum*, Vol. 28, No. 1 (2016), pp. 9–31.

Chaen Yoshio. *Zusetsu Ni Niroku Jiken* [*The Illustrated February 26 Incident*]. Tokyo: Nihon Toshō, 2001.

Chaïkin, Nathan. *The Sino-Japanese War*. Martigny; Nathan Chaïkin, 1983.

Chiba Isao. "From Cooperation to Conflict: Japanese-Russian Relations from the Formation of the Russo-Japanese Entente to the Siberian Intervention" in Minohara et al., op. cit. (2014), pp. 130–48.

Chōnan Masayoshi. *Shin Shiryō ni yoru Nichi-Ro Sensō Rikusen-shi* [*A History of the Russo-Japanese Land War According to New Sources*]. Tokyo: Namiki Shobō, 2015.

Clements, Jonathan. *Admiral Tōgō: Nelson of the East*. London: Haus, 2010.

_____. "The Chance of a Millennium" in Alan Sharp (ed) 28 *June: Sarajevo 1914–Versailles 1919, the War and Peace that Made the Modern World*. London: Haus, 2014. pp. 146 –50.

_____. "Unno Jūza" in John Clute, David Langford et al. (eds) *The Encyclopedia of Science Fiction*. London: Gollancz, updated 12th August 2020. http://www.sf-encyclopedia.com/entry/unno_juza

Collingham, Lizzie. *The Taste of War: World War Two and the Battle for Food*. London: Penguin, 2011.

Connors, Lesley. *The Emperor's Adviser: Saionji Kinmochi and Pre-War Japanese Politics*. London: Croom Helm/Nissan Institute for Japanese Studies, 1987.

Cook, Haruko Taya and Theodore F. *Japan at War: An Oral History*. New York: The New Press, 1992.

Cortazzi, Hugh. *Japan in Late Victorian London: The Japanese Village in Knightsbridge and the Mikado, 1885*. Norwich: Sainsbury Institute, 2009.

Cranston, Edwin A. *A Waka Anthology—Volume One: The Gem-Glistening Cup*. Palo Alto, CA: Stanford University Press, 1993.

Crowley, James. "Japanese Army Factionalism in the 1930's" in *Journal of Asian Studies*, Vol. 21, No.3 (May 1962), pp. 309–26.

d'Anethan, Baroness Albert [Mary Haggard]. *Fourteen Years of Diplomatic Life in Japan*. London: Stanley Paul, 1912. [Kindle edition]

de Bary, William Theodore, Carol Gluck and Arthur E. Tiedemann (eds). *Sources of Japanese Tradition*, Second Edition, Vol.2. New York: Columbia University Press, 2000. [Kindle edition]

De Weyer, Geert. "Censorship in Belgian Comics" at *Europe Comics*, 26th February 2021. http://www.europecomics.com/censorship-belgian-comics-p-1/

Dorwart, Jeffery M. "James Creelman, the *New York World* and the Port Arthur Massacre" in *Journalism and Mass Communication Quarterly*, Vol. 50, No.4 (December 1973), pp. 697–701.

Dower, John. *War Without Mercy: Race and Power in the Pacific War*. London: Faber & Faber, 1986.

_____. *Japan in War and Peace: Selected Essays*. New York: New Press, 1993.

_____. *Embracing Defeat: Japan in the Aftermath of World War II*. London: Penguin Books, 2000.

Driscoll, Mark. *Absolute Erotic, Absolute Grotesque: The Living, Dead, and Undead in Japan's Imperialism, 1895–1945*. Durham, NC: Duke University Press, 2010.

Dunscomb, Paul E. *Japan's Siberian Intervention, 1918–1922: "A Great Disobedience Against the People."* Lanham, MD: Rowman & Littlefield, 2011.

Duus, Peter. *The Abacus and the Sword: The Japanese Penetration of Korea, 1895–1910*. Berkeley: University of California Press, 1995.

_____. "Nagai Ryūtarō: The White Peril, 1913" in Saaler and Szpilman, op. cit., pp. I: 160–67.

Esthus, Raymond. "The Taft-Katsura Agreement—Reality or Myth?" in *The Journal of Modern History*, Vol. 31, No. 1 (March 1959), pp. 46–51.

Everest-Phillips, Max. "The Pre-War Fear of Japanese Espionage: Its Impact and Legacy" in *Journal of Contemporary History*, Vol. 42, No. 2 (2007), pp. 243–65.

Exley, Charles. "Popular Musical Star Tokuko Takagi and Vaudeville Modernism in the Taishō Asakusa Opera" in *Japanese Language and Literature*, Vol. 51, No. 1 (April 2017), pp. 63–90.

Fenby, Jonathan. *The Siege of Tsingtao: The only battle of the First World War to be fought in East Asia*. Melbourne: Penguin Books, 2014.

Fouraker, Lawrence. "Saitō Takao and Parliamentary Politics in 1930s Japan" in *Sino-Japanese Studies*, Vol.12, No. 2 (April 2000), pp. 3–28.

Fraleigh, Matthew. "Songs of the Righteous Spirit: 'Men of High Purpose' and Their Chinese Poetry in Modern Japan" in *Harvard Journal of Asiatic Studies*, Vol. 69, No. 1 (June 2009), pp. 109–71.

Frank, Richard B. *Downfall: The End of the Imperial Japanese Empire*. New York: Penguin, 1999.

Gamsa, Mark. *Manchuria: A Concise History*. London: I.B. Tauris, 2020.

Gates, Rustin B. "Out with the New and in with the Old: Uchida Yasuya and the Great War as a Turning Point in Japanese Foreign Affairs" in Minohara et al., op. cit., pp. 64–82.

Goodman, Andrew. "The Fushimi Incident: theatre, censorship and *The Mikado*" in *Journal of Legal History*, Vol. 1, No. 3 (1980), pp. 297–302.

Goodwin, Mike and Richard Starkings. *Japanese Aero Engines 1910–1945*. Sandomierz: MMP Books, 2017.

Gordon, Leonard. "Japan's Abortive Colonial Venture in Taiwan, 1874" in *The Journal of Modern History*, Vol. 37, No. 2 (June 1965), pp. 171–185.

_____. "Taiwan and the Powers, 1840–1895" in Leonard Gordon (ed), *Taiwan: Studies in Chinese Local History*. New York: Columbia University Press, 1970. pp. 93–110.

Grunden, Walter E. "Kita Ikki" in Perez, op. cit., (2013) pp. 179–81.

Handō Kazutoshi. *Seidan: Shōwa Tennō to Suzuki Kantarō* [*Sacred Decision: The Shōwa Emperor and Suzuki Kantarō*]. Tokyo: PHP Kenkyūjo, 2006.

Harries, Meirion and Susie Harris. *Soldiers of the Sun: The Rise and Fall of the Imperial Japanese Army*. New York: Random House, 1991.

Harris, Sheldon H. *Factories of Death: Japanese Biological Warfare. 1932–1945, and the American cover-up*. Revised Edition. New York: Routledge, 2002.

Harrison, Simon. "Skull trophies of the Pacific War: transgressive objects of remembrance" in *Journal of the Royal Anthropological Institute*, Vol. 12 (2006), pp. 817–36.

Hashimoto Akiko. *The Long Defeat: Cultural Trauma, Memory and Identity in Japan*. Oxford: Oxford University Press, 2015.

"Hillsborough, Romulus" [Jeff Cohen] *Samurai Revolution: The Dawn of Modern Japan Seen Through the Eyes of the Shōgun's Last Samurai*. Rutland, VT: Tuttle, 2014.

Hotta, Eri. *Pan-Asianism and Japan's War 1931–1945*. New York: Palgrave Macmillan, 2007.

_____. "Konoe Fumimaro: 'A Call to Reject the Anglo-American Centred Peace', 1918" in Saaler and Szpilman, op. cit., pp. I: 310–17.

_____. *Japan 1941: Countdown to Infamy*. New York: Alfred Knopf, 2013.

Hoyt, Edwin P. *The Kamikazes*. London: Robert Hale, 1983.

_____. *Warlord: Tōjō Against the World*. New York: Cooper Square Press, 2001.

Huffman, James L. *Creating a Public: People and Press in Meiji Japan*. Honolulu: University of Hawaii Press, 1997.

_____. "High Treason Incident" in Perez, op. cit., (2013) pp. 117–8.

Humphreys, Leonard. "Crisis and Reaction: The Japanese Army in the 'Liberal' Twenties" in *Armed Forces and Society*, Vol. 5, No.1 (November 1978), pp. 73–92.

_____. *The Way of the Heavenly Sword: The Japanese Army in the 1920's*. Palo Alto, CA: Stanford University Press, 1995.

Ienaga Saburō. *Japan's Last War: World War II and the Japanese, 1931–1945*. Oxford: Blackwell, 1979.

Iguchi, Gerald. "Continental Adventurers" in Perez, op.cit., (2013) pp. 61–3.

_____. "Genyōsha Nationalism" in Perez, op.cit., (2013) pp. 91–2.

Iida Yumiko. "Fleeing the West, Making Asia Home: Transpositions of Otherness in Japanese Pan-Asianism, 1905–1930" in *Alternatives*, No. 22 (1997), pp. 409–32.

Itō Yukio. *Itō Hirobumi: Kindai Nihon o Tsukutta Otoko* [*Itō Hirobumi: The Man Who Created Modern Japan*]. Tokyo: Kōdansha, 2009.

Jansen, Marius B. "Opportunists in South China During the Boxer Rebellion" in *Pacific Historical Review*, Vol. 20, No. 3 (August 1951), pp. 241–50.

Jiang Niandong et al. *Wei Manzhouguo Shi* [*A History of the False Manchukuo*]. Changchun: Jilin Renmin Chuban, 1981.

Jones, Vincent. *Manhattan: The Army and the Atomic Bomb*. Washington, DC: United States Army Center of Military History, 1985.

Joos, Joël. "The Gen'yōsha (1881) and the Premodern Roots of Japanese Expansionism" in Saaler and Szpilman, op. cit., pp. I: 60–67.

Keene, Donald. *Emperor of Japan: Meiji and His World 1852–1912*. New York: Columbia University Press, 2002.

_____. *So Lovely a Country Will Never Perish: Wartime Diaries of Japanese Writers*. New York: Columbia University Press, 2010.

Kim Bongjin. "Sin Ch'ae-ho: 'A Critique of Easternism', 1909" in Saaler and Szpilman, op. cit., pp. I: 190–94.

Kim Jeong Ha, "Rethinking Colonialism: Korean Primary School Music Education during the Japanese Colonial Rule of Korea, 1910–1945" in *Journal of Historical Research in Music Education*, Vol. 36, No. 1 (October 2014), pp. 23–42.

Kim Kyu Hyun. "The Sino-Japanese War (1894–1895): Japanese National Integration and the Construction of the Korean 'Other'" in *International Journal of Korean History*, Vol. 17, No. 1 (February 2012), pp. 1–26.

_____. "Tarui Tōkichi's *Arguments on Behalf of the Union of the Great East, 1893*" in Saaler and Szpilman, op. cit., pp. I: 72–83.

Kimura Masato. "Securing the Maritime Trade: Triangular Frictions between the Merchant Marines of the U.S., UK and Japan" in Minohara, op. cit. (2014), pp. 107–29.

Kinmonth, Earl H. "The Mouse that Roared: Saitō Takao, Conservative Critic of Japan's 'Holy War' in China" in *Journal of Japanese Studies*, Vol. 25, No. 2 (1999), pp. 331–60.

Kitamura Jun. *The Causes of the Manchurian Incident: A Non-Marxist Interpretation*. Vancouver: University of British Columbia, 2002. [PhD Thesis].

_____. *A Forgotten Lesson of the Russo-Japanese War: Vladivostok Squadron's commerce-destroying operations, February–July 1904*. Tokyo: Center for Navalist Studies, 2020.

Konoe, Fumimaro. *Memoir by Prince Konoe: The Secret Negotiations Between Japan and the U.S. Before Pearl Harbor*. [Introduction and commentary by Jenny Chan and Barbara Halperin]. San Francisco: Pacific Atrocities Education, 2020.

Kuhn, Arthur K. "The Lytton Report on the Manchurian Crisis" in *American Journal of International Law*, Vol. 27, No. 1 (January 1933), pp. 86–100.

Kwong Chi Man. *War and Geopolitics in Interwar Manchuria: Zhang Zuolin and the Fengtian Clique during the Northern Expedition*. Leiden: Brill, 2017.

Lamley, Harry J. "Taiwan Under Japanese Rule, 1895–1945: The Vicissitudes of Japanese Colonialism" in Murry Rubinstein (ed) *Taiwan: A New History*. New York: M.E. Sharpe, 2007. pp. 201–60.

Lawrence, E.P. "The Banned Mikado: A Topsy-Turvy Incident" in *The Centennial Review*, Vol. 18, No. 2 (Spring 1974), pp. 151–69.

Le Gendre, Charles. *Notes of Travel in Formosa*. Tainan: National Museum of Taiwan History, 2012.

Lee Eun-jeung. "An Chung-gun: 'A Discourse on Peace in East Asia', 1910" in Saaler and Szpilman, op. cit., pp. I: 204–10.

Li Maojie and Lai Zhuo'an (eds) *Manzhouguo Jingcha Shi* [*A History of the Manchukuo Police*]. Jilin: Jilin-xian Gong-an Ding Gong-an Shi Yanjiu-suo, 1990.

Lindgren, Scott. "A station in transition: The China Squadron, Cyprian Bridge and the first-class cruiser, 1901–1904" in *The International Journal of Maritime History*, Vol. 27, No. 3 (2015), pp. 460–483.

Lone, Stewart. *Japan's First Modern War: Army and Society in the Conflict with China, 1894–95*. London: Macmillan, 1994.

_____. *Provincial Life and the Military in Imperial Japan: The Phantom Samurai*. London: Routledge, 2010.

Lu, David. *Agony of Choice: Matsuoka Yōsuke and the Rise and Fall of the Japanese Empire, 1880–1946*. Lanham, MD: Lexington Books, 2002.

Macri, Franco David. *Clash of Empires in South China: The Allied Nations' Proxy War with Japan, 1935–1941*. Lawrence, University Press of Kansas, 2012.

Mann, Michael. *States, War and Capitalism: Studies in Political Sociology*. Oxford: Oxford University Press, 1988.

Matsumura, Janice. "Combating Indiscipline in the Imperial Japanese Army: Hayao Torao and Psychiatric Studies of the Crimes of Soldiers" in *War in History*, Vol. 23, No. 1 (2016), pp. 79–99.

Matthews, Tony. *Shadows Dancing: Japanese Espionage Against the West 1939–1945*. London: Robert Hale, 1993.

Mauch, Peter. "The Shōwa Political Crisis: The Imperial Japanese Army Courts a Breach with its Sovereign, 1940" in *War in History*, 25th February 2019, pp. 1–19.

Mayo, Marlene J. "The Korean Crisis of 1873 and early Meiji foreign policy" in *Journal of Asian Studies*, Vol. 34, No. 4 (August 1972), pp. 793–819.

McCullagh, Francis. *With the Cossacks: Being the Story of an Irishman Who Rode with the Cossacks During the Russo-Japanese War*. London: Eveleigh Nash, 1906.

McWilliams, Wayne C. "East Meets East. The Soejima Mission to China, 1873" in *Monumenta Nipponica*, Vol. 30, No. 3 (Autumn 1975), pp. 237–75.

Meehan, John D. "From Alliance to Conference: The British Empire, Japan and Pacific Multilateralism, 1911–1921" in Minohara et al., op. cit. (2014), pp. 45–63.

Menning, Bruce W. "Misjudging One's Enemies: Russian Military Intelligence before the Russo-Japanese War" in *War in History*, Vol. 13, No.2 (2016), pp. 141–70.

Miller, Edward S. *War Plan Orange: The U.S. Strategy to Defeat Japan, 1897–1945*. Annapolis, MD: Naval Institute Press, 1991.

_____. *Bankrupting the Enemy: The U.S. Financial Siege of Japan before Pearl Harbor*. Annapolis, MD: Naval Institute Press, 2007.

Minohara, Tosh, Tze-ki Hon and Evan Dawley (eds). *The Decade of the Great War: Japan and the Wider World in the 1910s*. Leiden: Brill, 2014.

Minowa Yuko and Russell W. Belk. "Gifts and Nationalism in Wartime Japan" in *Journal of Macromarketing*, Vol. 38, No.3, pp. 298–314.

Mitsui Tōru. *Popular Music in Japan: Transformation Inspired by the West*. New York: Bloomsbury, 2020.

Mitter, Rana. *The Manchurian Myth: Nationalism, Resistance and Collaboration in Modern China*. Berkeley: University of California Press, 2000.

Moritsugu Ken. "Biden's remark on Japanese Constitution raises eyebrows" at *AP News*, 18th August 2016. https://apnews.com/article/af-44536131b34653a146b1b1807086d7

Myers, Ramon H. and Mark R. Peattie (eds) *The Japanese Colonial Empire 1895–1945*. Princeton, NJ: Princeton University Press, 1984.

Najita Tetsuo. *The Intellectual Foundations of Modern Japanese Politics*. Chicago: Chicago University Press, 1974.

Nakatani Tadashi. "The Changeover at Paris in 1919," in Minohara et al., op.cit., pp. 168–88.

Naraoka Sōchi. "A New Look at Japan's Twenty-One Demands: Reconsidering Katō Takaaki's Motives in 1915" in Minohara et al., op. cit., pp. 189–210.

Nish, Ian. "Japan's Indecision During the Boxer Disturbances" in *The Journal of Asian Studies*, Vol. 20, No. 4 (August 1961), pp. 449–61.

_____. (ed) *The Iwakura Mission to America and Europe: A Reassessment*. Richmond: Japan Library, 1998.

Nordlund, Alexander M. "A War of Others: British War Correspondents, Orientalist Discourse, and the Russo-Japanese War of 1904–1905" in *War in History*, Vol. 22, No. 1 (2015), pp. 28–46.

Norman, E. Herbert. "The Genyosha: A Study in the Origins of Japanese Imperialism" in *Pacific Affairs*, Vol.17, No.3 (September 1944), pp. 261–84.

O'Conroy, Taid. *The Menace of Japan*. London: Paternoster Library, 1937 (rep. of 1931 edition with afterword).

O'Dwyer, Emer. *Significant Soil: Settler Colonialism and Japan's Urban Empire in Manchuria*. Cambridge, MA: Harvard University Press, 2015.

Ōe Shinobu. *Chōhei-sei* [*The Conscription System*]. Tokyo: Iwanami Shoten, 1981.

Oka Yoshitake. *Five Political Leaders of Modern Japan: Itō Hirobumi, Ōkuma Shigenobu, Hara Takashi, Inukai Tsuyoshi and Saionji Kimmochi* [translated by Andrew Fraser and Patricia Murray]. Tokyo: University of Tokyo Press, 1986.

_____. *Konoe Fumimaro: A Political Biography* [translated by Shumpei Oka-moto and Patricia Murray]. Lanham, MD: Madison Books, 1992.

Osada Gyōji. *Sensō ga Nokoshita Uta: Uta ga Akasu Sensō no Haikei* [*Songs Left by the War: The Background to the War as Revealed by Songs*]. Tokyo: Zen-On Music Company, 2015.

Otsubo Sumiko. "Feminist Maternal Eugenics in Wartime Japan" in *U.S.-Japan Women's Journal* (English Supplement), No. 17 (1999), pp. 39–76.

_____. "Fighting on Two Fronts: Japan's Involvement in the Siberian Inter-vention and the Spanish Influenza Epidemic of 1918" in Minohara et al., op. cit. pp. 461–80.

Paine, S.C.M., *The Sino-Japanese War of 1894–5: Perceptions, Power and Pri-macy.* Cambridge, MA: Cambridge University Press, 2005.

_____. *The Wars for Asia, 1911–1949.* Cambridge University Press, 2012.

_____. *The Japanese Empire: Grand Strategy from the Meiji Restoration to the Pacific War.* Cambridge: Cambridge University Press, 2017.

Pal, Radhabinod. *International Military Tribunal for the Far East: Dissentient Judgement of Justice Pal.* Tokyo: Kokusho-Kankokai, 1999.

Peattie, Mark R. *Nan'yō: The Rise and Fall of the Japanese in Micronesia, 1885–1945.* Honolulu: University of Hawaii, 1988.

[*People's Court Daily*] *Trials of Justice: Commemoration of the 10th Anniver-sary of the Victory of the Chinese People's War of Resistance Against Japanese Aggression.* Beijing: People's Court Press, 2015.

Perez, Louis G. (ed.) *Japan at War: An Encyclopedia.* Santa Barbara: ABC-CLIO, 2013.

Person, John. *Arbiters of Patriotism: Right-wing Scholars in Imperial Japan.* Honolulu: University of Hawaii, 2020.

Porter, Patrick. *Military Orientalism: Eastern War Through Western Eyes.* Lon-don: Hurst & Company, 2009.

Prange, Gordon. *At Dawn We Slept: The Untold Story of Pearl Harbor*. New York: Penguin Books, 1982.

Rabson, Stephen. "Yosano Akiko on War: To Give One's Life or Not—A Question of Which War" in *The Journal of the Association of Teachers of Japanese*, Vol. 25, No.1 (1991), pp. 45 –74.

Ravina, Mark. *The Last Samurai: The Life and Battles of Saigō Takamori*. Hoboken, NJ: John Wiley, 2004.

Robbins, Jane M. J. *Tokyo Calling: Japanese Overseas Radio Broadcasting 1937–1945*. Sheffield, UK: University of Sheffield, 1997 [PhD thesis].

Rodman, Tara. "A More Humane Mikado: Re-envisioning the Nation through Occupation-Era Productions of the Mikado in Japan" in *Theatre Research International*, Vol. 40, No.3 (2015), pp. 288–302.

Russell, Edward ("Lord Russell of Liverpool") *The Knights of Bushidō: A Short History of Japanese War Crimes*. Bath: Chivers Press, 1989 (1958).

Rzadek, Wieslaw. "Field Manual of Valor—Meiji Woodblock Prints and the Creation of the Heroic Myth for the Meiji Armed Forces" in *Silva Iaponicarum*, Vol. 34–36 (2010), pp. 119–48.

Saaler, Sven. "The Kokuryūkai, 1901–1920" in Saaler and Szpilman, op. cit., pp. I: 120–31.

_____. "Pan-Asianism, the 'Yellow Peril,' and Suematsu Kenchō, 1905" in Saaler and Szpilman, op. cit., pp. I: 140–47.

_____. and Christopher W. Szpilman (eds) *Pan-Asianism: A Documentary History* [in two volumes]. Lanham, MD: Rowman & Littlefield, 2011.

_____. *Men in Metal: A Topography of Public Bronze Statuary in Modern Japan*. Leiden: Brill, 2020.

Safford, Jeffrey J. "Experiment in Containment: The United States Steel Embargo and Japan, 1917–1918" in *Pacific Historical Review* Vol. 39, No. 4 (1970), pp. 439–51.

Sakai Yu. "Survive to be critical: The *Wartime Graphic* as a 'masquerading media' in the Russo-Japanese War, 1904–1905" in *War in History*, 7th June 2020 [online original].

Sakurai Tadayoshi. *Human Bullets: A Soldier's Story of Port Arthur*. Boston: Houghton Mifflin, 1907.

Salecker, Gene Eric. *Blossoming Silk Against the Rising Sun: U.S. and Japanese Paratroopers at War in the Pacific in WWII*. Mechanicsburg, PA: Stackpole Books, 2010.

Sato Hiroaki. "Gyokusai or 'Shattering Like a Jewel': Reflections on the Pacific War" in *Asia-Pacific Journal*, Vol. 6, No. 2 (February 2008), 2662: 1–10.

Satow, Ernest. *A Diplomat in Japan*. San Francisco: Stone Bridge Press, 2006 [1921].

Schencking, J. Charles. *Making Waves: Politics, Propaganda and the Emergence of the Imperial Japanese Navy, 1868–1922*. Palo Alto, CA: Stanford University Press, 2005.

_____. "The Imperial Japanese Navy and the First World War: Unprecedented Opportunities and Harsh Realities" in Minohara et al., op. cit. (2014), pp. 83–106.

Selden, Mark. "A Forgotten Holocaust: U.S. Bombing Strategy, the Destruction of Japanese Cities, and the American Way of War from World War II to Iraq" in *Japan Focus*, Vol. 5, No. 5 (2007). https://apjjf.org/-Mark-Selden/2414/article.html

Seo Gijae. "*Shonen Kurabu* and the Japanese Attitude Towards War" in *Children's Literature in Education*, No. 52 (2021), pp. 49–67.

Smith, Norman. *Intoxicating Manchuria: Alcohol, Opium and Culture in China's Northeast*. Vancouver: UBC Press, 2012.

Stalker, Nancy. "Suicide, Boycotts and Embracing Tagore: The Japanese Popular Response to the 1924 U.S. Immigration Exclusion Law" in *Japanese Studies*, Vol. 26, No. 2 (September 2006), pp. 153–70.

Stanley, Peter. *Invading Australia: Japan and the Battle for Australia, 1942*.

Camberwell, Victoria: Viking, 2008.

Steele, M. William. "Edo in 1868: The View from Below" in *Monumenta Nipponica*, Vol. 45, No.2 (Summer 1990), pp. 127–55.

Stephan, John C. *Hawaii Under the Rising Sun: Japan's Plans for Conquest After Pearl Harbor*. Honolulu: University of Hawaii Press, 1984.

Storry, Richard. *Japan and the Decline of the West in Asia, 1894–1943*. New York: Macmillan, 1979.

Sturma, Michael. "Japanese Treatment of Allied Prisoners During the Second World War: Evaluating the Death Toll" in *Journal of Contemporary History*, Vol. 55, No. 3 (2020), pp. 514–34.

Sweeney, Michael S. "'Delays and Vexation': Jack London and the Russo-Japanese War" in *Journalism and Mass Communication Quarterly*, Vol. 75, No.3 (Autumn 1998), pp. 548–59.

Szpilman, Christopher W. A. "Miyazaki Tōten's Pan-Asianism, 1915–1919" in Saaler and Szpilman, op. cit., pp. I:132–40.

Taguchi Chikashi. "Tokoton yare bushi ni tsuite" [Concerning the 'Get-it-Done Song'] in *Waseda Daigaku Toshokan Kiyō*, Vol. 20, No.3 (1979), pp.126–35.

Takahara Shūsuke. "The Wilson Administration and the Mandate Question in the Pacific" in Minohara et al., op. cit., pp. 149–67.

"Tanin, O. and E. Yohan" [O. Tarkhanov]. *When Japan Goes to War*. London: Lawrence E. Wishart, 1937.

Tankha, Brij. "Okakura Tenshin: 'Asia is One', 1903" in Saaler and Szpilman, op. cit., pp. I: 93–100.

Terasaki Hidenari, *Shōwa Tennō Dokuhaku-roku* [*The Statement of the Shōwa Emperor*]. Tokyo: Bungei Shunjū, 1995.

Toland, John. *The Rising Sun: The Decline and Fall of the Japanese Empire, 1936–1945*. New York: Modern Library, 2003 (1970).

Tyler, William F. *Pulling Strings in China*. London: Constable, 1929.

Unno Jūza. *Science: Hopes & Fears—Juza Unno, the father of Japanese science fiction—Volume 2: Eighteen O'Clock Music Bath*. [no place of publication given]: J.D. Wisgo, 2018.

USAF. *Japanese Aircraft Industry in WW2: USAF Report of 1946*. Bromley, UK: Galago Publishing, 2006.

Usui Hiroyuki. "Prelego pri Esperanto por japanoj en Pekino" [Lecture on Esperanto for the Japanese in Beijing] at http://esperanto.china.org.cn/2013-01/29/content_27827049.htm

Wang Shaoyong. "Cuncun Heshan, Cuncun Jin: cong lishi ziliao kan dizhi zhanxian de Kangri Zhanzheng" [Shattered Mountain: Shattered Gold: The Anti-Japanese War on the Geological Front, Viewed from Historical Documents] Beijing: China Geological Survey, 2015. https://www.cgs.gov.cn/xwl/ddyw/201603/t20160309_303270.html

Watt, Lori. *When Empire Comes Home: Repatriation and Reintegration in Postwar Japan*. Cambridge, MA: Harvard University Press, 2009.

Wei Songmin. *Mantie Shi* [*A History of Mantetsu*]. Beijing: Zhonghua Shuju, 1990.

Willbanks, James H. "Okinawa, Invasion of" in Perez, op. cit., (2013) pp. 290–91.

Wilson, Sandra. "Film and Soldier: Japanese War Movies in the 1950s" in *Journal of Contemporary History*, Vol. 48, No. 3 (2013), pp. 537–55.

Yano, Christine. "Defining the Modern Nation in Japanese Popular Song, 1914–1932" in Stephen Vlastos (ed) *Japan's Competing Modernities*. Honolulu: University of Hawai'i Press, 1998, pp. 247–264.

Yellen, Jeremy A. "Into the Tiger's Den: Japan and the Tripartite Pact, 1940" in *Journal of Contemporary History*, Vol. 51, No. 3 (2016), pp. 555–76.

[Yomiuri Shinbun-sha] *Shōwa Tennō 4* [The Shōwa Emperor 4]. Tokyo: Yomiuri Shinbun-sha, 1968.

Yosano Akiko. *Travels in Manchuria and Mongolia: A Feminist Poet from Japan Encounters Prewar China* [trans. Joshua A. Fogel] New York: Columbia University Press, 2001.

Yoshimi Yoshiaki. *Grassroots Fascism: The War Experience of the Japanese People* [trans. Ethan Mark]. New York: Columbia University Press, 2015.

Young, Louise. *Japan's Total Empire: Manchuria and the Culture of Wartime Imperialism.* Berkeley: University of California Press, 1998.

Zachmann, Urs Mattias. "Konoe Atsumaro and the Idea of an Alliance of the Yellow Race, 1898" in Saaler and Szpilman, op. cit., pp. I: 84–92.

Acknowledgments

L ong, long ago, I saw a map of Japan on the wall of Kweku Ampiah's office at the University of Stirling. It was from 1915 or thereabouts, and hence included Korea, in the same color as the "rest" of Japan. The sight has haunted me for many years, as have my childhood memories of wandering Portobello Road with my father, in search of props for an amateur production of *Hamlet*, and inadvertently casting the skull of a Japanese soldier as Yorick. It was just sitting there, in a glass case, along with bead necklaces, ivory chess pieces and signet rings, just one more fragment of the past, and presumably brought back to Britain by a World War Two veteran.

It was Robert Goforth at Tuttle who requested a book that offered a new perspective on the rise of Japanese militarism. I did promise him something for the general reader like my earlier *Brief History of Japan*, specifically without footnotes, but it soon became apparent that the subject of this book was so contentious, and relied so heavily on the support and work of other scholars, that it would be counter-productive and, frankly, rude not to give credit where credit was due. My apologies to him for making him check five hundred page-numbers.

While writing this book, I have had many fruitful conversations with Lee Brimmicombe-Wood, not only about Japanese militarism, but also about what might be missing from existing accounts, and what needs to be clarified in a narrative for the general reader. So, his interest in popular culture as a reflection of militarism, and of the rise and fall of the "war gods," is at least partly to blame for the indignities inflicted upon his wife, my long-term research associate Tamamuro Motoko, as I began spamming her with translations of propaganda songs, fascist ballads and sundry other pop-culture horrors. I then persuaded Adam Newell to be my first reader, in the hope that I could smooth out some of the book's crazier moments. However, any mistakes or error or interpretation that remain are mine and mine alone.

Index

Published by Tuttle Publishing, an imprint of Periplus Editions (HK) Ltd.

www.tuttlepublishing.com

Copyright © 2022 by Jonathan Clements

Library of Congress Cataloging in Publication Data in process

ISBN 978-4-8053-1647-4

25 24 23 22
10 9 8 7 6 5 4 3 2 1   2201TO
Printed in Malaysia

TUTTLE PUBLISHING® is a registered trademark of Tuttle Publishing, a division of Periplus Editions (HK) Ltd.

Distributed by:

North America, Latin America & Europe
Tuttle Publishing
364 Innovation Drive, North Clarendon
VT 05759 9436, USA
Tel: 1(802) 773 8930
Fax: 1(802) 773 6993
info@tuttlepublishing.com
www.tuttlepublishing.com

Asia Pacific
Berkeley Books Pte Ltd
3 Kallang Sector #04-01
Singapore 349278
Tel: (65) 6741 2178
Fax: (65) 6741 2179
inquiries@periplus.com.sg
www.tuttlepublishing.com

Japan
Tuttle Publishing
Yaekari Building 3rd Floor
5-4-12 Osaki Shinagawa-ku
Tokyo 141 0032 Japan
Tel: 81 (3) 5437 0171
Fax: 81 (3) 5437 0755
sales@tuttle.co.jp
www.tuttle.co.jp